SOCIAL WORK PRACTICE WITH CHILDREN

Social Work Practice with Children and Families
Nancy Boyd Webb, Series Editor

SOCIAL WORK PRACTICE WITH CHILDREN
Nancy Boyd Webb

Forthcoming

Andrew Malekoff *on Group Work with Adolescents*
Douglas Davies *on Basics of Child Development*

SOCIAL WORK PRACTICE WITH CHILDREN

NANCY BOYD WEBB, D.S.W.
Fordham University
Graduate School of Social Service

Foreword by
Edward Zigler, Ph.D.
Yale University

THE GUILFORD PRESS
New York   London

© 1996 The Guilford Press
A Division of Guilford Publications, Inc.
72 Spring Street, New York, NY 10012

Printed in the United States of America

This book is printed on acid-free paper.

Last digit is print number: 9 8 7 6 5 4 3

Library of Congress Cataloging-in-Publication Data

Webb, Nancy Boyd
     Social work practice with children / Nancy Boyd Webb.
         p.   cm.—(Social work practice with children and families)
     Includes bibliographical references and index.
     ISBN 1-57230-149-X
     1. Social work with children.   I. Title.   II. Series.
HV713.W39   1996
362.7—dc20
                                                                              96-25483
                                                                              CIP

In loving memory of my parents,
ANGIE and EARL BOYD;

to my first grandchild,
KATHERINE MARGARET SCOTT (6-14-94);

and
to all children of the 21st century

Acknowledgments

This book reflects reverberating influences from a number of sources. At the risk of seeming sentimental, I wish to acknowledge my parents, Earl and Angie Boyd, who always supported my desire to read and learn. My father, a mathematics teacher with a daughter ill adept in math, set an example for a future play therapist about tuning in to a child's anxiety. On the other hand, when I begin to form a relationship with a child, I think about my mother's innate capacity to play and to communicate with children of all ages.

I cannot possibly name all the significant influences in my life who contributed indirectly to this book. However, I must indicate my intellectual debt to Erik Erikson and to Carel Germain, whose view of individual "problems" included a wide-ranging appreciation of the contributing factors in the social environment, as well as of the reciprocal influences of the individual, the family, and the society on one another. This ecological perspective permeates my own assessment and work with children and families.

For the most part, this book represents my work during the course of the past 10 years with children and families. All the case material has been disguised to protect client confidentiality, except in instances where this privilege was previously waived. Several cases reported here were treated by social work students, who agreed to their use. In most instances, clients (including children, whenever possible) gave their written permission. The profession owes a tremendous debt of gratitude to these parents and children, who permitted the use of their personal situations to benefit future social workers and other practitioners in their efforts to help children and families.

I am especially grateful to the filmmaker Kathryn Hunt, and to the staff of the First Place School in Seattle, Washington, for consultation and assistance in writing the chapters about the "Smith" family. Without the assistance of Deb Brinley-Koempel and Eugene Harris, it would have been impossible to have written Chapters 3, 4, and 5, which build upon the rich case material from Kathryn Hunt's documentary film. I sincerely hope that professionals working in shelters for homeless families around the United States will learn from the discussion of this case example. I also thank the "Smiths" for their willingness to share their lives, so that others may learn from their experience.

Mary Ann Quaranta, Dean of the Fordham University Graduate School of Social Service, deserves special recognition for supporting this book, both by endorsing its philosophy and by facilitating realistic work assignments to permit its completion. I am grateful for her friendship and her inspired leadership as a social work administrator.

Because this volume is the first in Guilford's series on Social Work Practice with Children and Families, I want to acknowledge the commitment made by this commercial publishing house to the issues confronting social work practice. I am especially grateful for Sharon Panulla's creative support, and for Seymour Weingarten's endorsement of a venture that connects The Guilford Press to cutting-edge issues in social work practice in the 21st century. Over the course of the book's production, I enjoyed working again with Judith Grauman, whose efforts as Editorial Supervisor always permit the best intent of my work to reveal itself.

The following social work educators and practitioners in diverse fields have offered consultation and/or read portions of the manuscript: Francesca Bowman; Christina Cartegna; Linda Conte and the BOCES social work staff, Yorktown Heights, New York; Christina Fewell; and Madeline Zevon. I am very grateful to them for their expertise and willingness to offer their ideas and experience.

My former students Suzanne Santana and Stephanie Senter also deserve grateful acknowledgment for contributing cases. In addition, Miriam Sivak, a social work doctoral student, diligently retrieved references as my research assistant, and also worked on several graphic designs. Recognition and thanks should also be given to Chris Campbell, reference librarian at Marymount College, and to Barbara Nussbaum of the State Education Department, The University of the State of New York, for their assistance with research questions. Green Chimneys, a residential treatment center in Brewster, New York, renowned for the use of farm animals as aids to treatment of children, enthusiastically permitted the use of the "Dorinda" case in Chapter 14.

Once again, my husband, Kempton, has provided concrete help and assistance, combined with steady optimism and respect for the value of my work. The birth of our first grandchild, Katherine Margaret Scott, during the writing of this book has further deepened my lifelong commitment to children and to their basic rights.

NANCY BOYD WEBB

Preface

This book has been written with great hope and conviction. As I complete almost 20 years as a social work educator and more than 30 years as a child and family social work practitioner, my mission is to draw attention to the special needs of children, and to the necessity for using helping methods that are appropriate for child clients. Well-meaning but ill-informed workers often treat children as miniature adults: Youngsters are expected to sit in adult chairs and verbalize their concerns to strangers who fail to present their role and the purpose of the interview in language the children can understand. It is time for us to stop giving children adult "hand-me-downs"; they deserve their own child-sized garments.

I have been increasingly dismayed by the lack of attention in social work education to the needs of young children as *individuals,* and to the training of students to employ methods of helping children that are appropriate to children's developmental age and understanding. Major texts on child welfare, for example, ignore or discuss only briefly the use of play therapy as the method of choice in working with children under 12 years of age. In addition, the recent emphasis on upholding the principle of family preservation, although based on a worthy goal, unfortunately serves to push the unique needs of the individual child in the family even further into the background. Children who have been abused and neglected, as many of those in the child welfare system have been, require attention over and beyond that devoted to helping their families resolve the various difficulties that resulted in the need for their placement. Helping young children, *while they are children,* serves an important preventive purpose that may avert many years of future problems for the individual children, for their families, and for society.

In the closing years of the 20th century, social work education has made a commitment to addressing the needs of people of color and of all sexual orientations, across the life cycle. This commendable goal implicitly includes children, but fails to spell out either the nature or the extent of course content essential to train students adequately for practice with children. The Council on Social Work Education permits each school of social work to carry out its own curriculum design, provided that a focus on these designated client populations is included.

This textbook contains content useful for courses at both the baccalaureate and master's levels; it is designed to provide both basic and advanced material. The first three sections of the text present a theoretical framework, use an extended case example to depict the overall process of helping children, and then describe different methods of helping. The fourth and longest section of the book deals with helping children in special circumstances. Case examples and the accompanying discussions in the chapters of this final section address such topics as working with AIDS orphans in residential settings and foster care; the challenge of helping children in the midst of custody disputes; and work with children who have Posttraumatic Stress Disorder and attachment difficulties as a result of witnessing family violence. Many of these cases illustrate cutting-edge issues for social workers trying to help children in desperate situations, such as those growing up in chemically dependent families, or those who have been orphaned by war. Because I focus on children in the most difficult of circumstances, social workers and other practitioners who are struggling in their daily work to find ways to help such children may find new approaches in this book.

Although I began the book intending it as a text for direct practice with children and families, larger-scale political and economic issues have consistently and inevitably presented themselves. Advocacy approaches are urgently needed in order to improve and resolve many children's problems that accompany the spiraling effects of chronic poverty. Nothing would satisfy me more than to have this book used to link "micro" and "macro" approaches to helping children. If we are to be truly helpful, this linkage must occur, and social workers can and should play a leadership role in this compelling effort.

NANCY BOYD WEBB

Foreword

It is difficult to imagine a more daunting period in history in which to undertake social work practice with children. Seemingly every era brings its cries of social alarm, yet the problems besieging young children and their families today seem so deep as to be almost fathomless, so vast in scope that they appear to threaten the growth and development of nearly every child, not only a disadvantaged few.

Families and children today face extraordinary levels of economic and social stress. Among the primary causes of such stress are increasing homelessness, teen pregnancy, child abuse, crime, poverty, lack of affordable child care, lack of health care, and the rise of substance abuse in many regions of the country. These factors are, not surprisingly, major contributors to family instability and grave emotional risk to children. An additional source of difficulty for children is the threat of losing a parent through divorce or even death. Increasing numbers of children must, at a very young age, learn to cope with the early death of family members due to violence, substance abuse, or illnesses like AIDS. In some disturbing cases, the child himself or herself may face death from AIDS, possibly having contracted the disease from a beloved family member.

Unfortunately, even as these many potential sources of physical and emotional harm continue to accumulate, the social infrastructure meant to support families and children has failed to grow and to change adequately to meet present service requirements. This is not purely an economic problem, although lack of funds certainly contributes to the challenge we face. The problem is also one of focus and of resource allocation. Part of the difficulty is a failure on the part of society to recognize the importance of building a solid mental health foundation in early life; such a foundation is one of the most effective ways to lessen the risk of psychological damage from environmental factors. Through an understanding of the important role of mental health in child development, we as a society are better equipped to devise effective means to help children make a satisfactory adjustment to the dislocations and risks of a rapidly changing world.

Decades of child development research have demonstrated that the most critical early influence in a child's life is the family, and that interventions that strengthen the family unit necessarily result in benefits for children. Clearly children do not grow in isolation but within a complex of interacting influences composed of family, the health system, school, child care, and other systems (Belsky, 1981; Bronfenbrenner, 1979). Although I myself have argued consistently for this ecological approach (e.g., Zigler & Berman, 1983; Zigler & Gilman, 1990), we must nevertheless, as Nancy Boyd Webb reminds us, take care not to lose sight of the importance of the child in our efforts to assist the family as a whole.

Despite the enormity of current risks to children's well-being, there remains a distressing lack of available assessment and treatment strategies that are tailored specifically to a child's needs. Paradoxically, the current model of intervention that takes the family as the unit of treatment and, in one recent mode of child welfare practice, seeks at all costs to preserve the family as a functioning system may have resulted in the unintentional neglect of abused and troubled children as individuals. In the present volume by Nancy Boyd Webb, this dearth of attention to children and expert guidance for the practitioners who work with them is admirably addressed. This is not to say that her work ignores family process and the other systems with which the child interacts; the difference here is that the work is *child-centered*.

Social Work Practice with Children is intended as a textbook for students of social work at the undergraduate and graduate levels, but it profitably could and should be read by any professional who works with children. Based on her broad experience as a seasoned clinician and social work educator, Nancy Boyd Webb utilizes an illustrative case study method to great advantage. By selecting examples of real children grappling with various issues including custody disputes, parental illness and death, substance abuse, child abuse, AIDS, Attention-Deficit/Hyperactivity Disorder, Posttraumatic Stress Disorder, and the problems specific to refugee children, she draws the reader into the experiential world of the child client. While family members and family dynamics are by no means neglected, the child's assessment and welfare remain the primary focus. Remarkable for its comprehensiveness and clarity of presentation, her book does not shrink from such thorny issues as confidentiality and divided loyalties when the child's and parents' wishes are in conflict. Full of practical advice, the book also shares with the reader a substantial library of useful assessment and therapeutic aids, such as how to use drawings, specialized board games, and life journals with children. The author provides considerable wisdom and guidance in conducting group work, play therapy, and cognitive-behavioral therapy. As an additional avenue to learning, discussion questions are appended to each chapter.

Although the book details the principles and techniques of helping children who are already in the throes of serious problems, this is a work that takes prevention as its goal. For Nancy Boyd Webb, the key to helping children to lead satisfying lives is to identify and treat the problems of childhood while the clients are still children. Unusual in the scope of her understanding and her breadth of knowledge, the author of this timely, gracefully written, and perceptive text urges her readers as clinicians and as members of society to do their best work for their young clients. For, she realizes, most of these children will one day find themselves, for good or for ill, in their own families, in the roles of parents, workers, citizens. The social work students who read and apply the wisdom in Nancy Boyd Webb's splendid text will be making a good start in preparing to help the next generation become well-integrated, mentally healthy, and whole people.

EDWARD ZIGLER, Ph.D.
Sterling Professor of Psychology
Director, Bush Center in Child
Development and Social Policy
Yale University

REFERENCES

Belsky, J. (1981). Early human experience: A family perspective. *Developmental Psychology, 17,* 3–23.

Bronfenbrenner, U. (1979). *The ecology of human development: Experiments by nature and by design.* Cambridge, MA: Harvard University Press.

Zigler, E., & Berman, W. (1983). Discerning the future of early childhood intervention. *American Psychologist, 38,* 894–906.

Zigler, E., & Gilman, E. (1990). An agenda for the 1990s: Supporting families. In D. Blackenhorn, S. Bayme, & J. B. Elshtain (Eds.), *Rebuilding the nest: A new commitment to the American family* (pp. 237–250). Milwaukee, WI: Family Service America.

List of Tables

List of Figures

List of Cases

Contents

APPENDICES

SOCIAL WORK PRACTICE WITH CHILDREN

PART I

An Ecological–Developmental Framework for Helping Children

❖ CHAPTER 1 ❖

Children's Problems and Needs

The birth of a child sets in motion a chain of inevitable responsibilities for the parents, the rest of the family, and society, all of whom at some future time will be expected to provide in varying ways for this dependent new life. When the parents cannot care for their child, relatives may do so, and when the extended family is unavailable, the state steps in. Society therefore maintains a vested interest in the adequacy with which families meet children's needs.

THE SOCIAL CONTEXT OF CHILDREN'S LIVES

Garbarino, Stott, and Associates (1989) list the basic needs of children as nurturance, responsiveness, predictability, support, and guidance. Meeting these needs may be impossible for unmarried mothers and others living below the poverty line.

The incidence of children under age 18 living in a one-parent family in 1990 was 25%, as compared with 10% in 1960. In addition, the number of children entering foster care doubled between 1987 and 1991, because of increased reports of abuse and neglect. Twenty-one percent of U.S. children under age 18 live in families below the poverty line. These statistics, reported in *The New York Times* (Chira, 1994), were compiled by the Carnegie Corporation of New York in a report warning about the threat to youngsters' intellectual and emotional development posed by the "bleak picture of disintegrating families, persistent poverty, high levels of child abuse, inadequate health care, and poor-quality child care" (Chira, 1994, p. A-1). Intervention to help the children in these families will require broad-based efforts that press for political and economic remedies for this serious social crisis.

A committee of the American Bar Association, using data from various national studies, has proposed specific recommendations for legal reform to assist U.S. children at risk (American Bar Association Working Group, 1993). This document addresses children's essential needs in the areas of income, housing, education, health, juvenile justice, and child welfare. Similarly, the Children's Defense Fund (1992) and the National Commission on Children (1991) have reported on the state of U.S. children and argued for political agendas targeting the well-being of children and families. As the public increasingly hears and responds to these voices, the necessary political pressure for action will increase. However, economic reality probably precludes rapid or extensive changes; improvement in the quality of life for families and children at risk will take time. Meanwhile, children are responding with self-destructive and antisocial behaviors that echo their inner frustrations and conflicts.

The present book focuses on methods for helping children with mental, emotional, and behavioral problems and their families. Because of the interplay of influences between children and their social environments, it is essential to consider *simultaneously* a troubled child's biological/temperamental/developmental status, the familial/cultural context, and the physical and social environment (see Figure 1.1). Although political advocacy may be essential for long-term improvement of the insidious effects of poverty, substance abuse/dependence, and violence, immediate supportive assistance must be offered to children and their families who live in the midst of these conditions. Children demonstrating troubled and troubling behaviors require prompt, direct services, even when these are provided in less than ideal social environments.

———————— ❖ ————————

THE CASE OF JACOB, AGE 10, AND DAMIEN, AGE 14

This information is taken from a front-page article in *The New York Times* (Wilkerson, 1994).

Presenting Problem

Damien, age 14, and Jacob, age 10, were arrested for armed robbery in the shooting death of a pregnant woman when she refused to hand over money she had withdrawn from an automated teller machine. Jacob gave the go-ahead signal for the robbery, and Damien, a drug dealer who was trying to obtain money to pay drug debts, carried out the shooting. Damien pleaded guilty to second-degree murder, and both boys received the maximum sentence for juveniles—remaining in state custody until the age of 21.

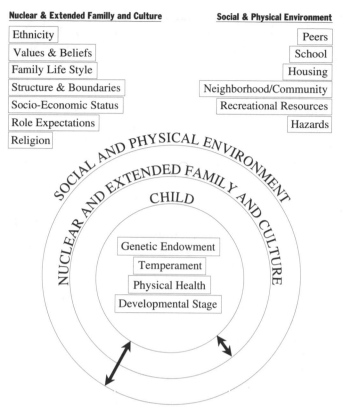

Nuclear & Extended Family and Culture

Ethnicity
Values & Beliefs
Family Life Style
Structure & Boundaries
Socio-Economic Status
Role Expectations
Religion

Social & Physical Environment

Peers
School
Housing
Neighborhood/Community
Recreational Resources
Hazards

SOCIAL AND PHYSICAL ENVIRONMENT
NUCLEAR AND EXTENDED FAMILY AND CULTURE
CHILD

Genetic Endowment
Temperament
Physical Health
Developmental Stage

FIGURE 1.1. Interactive influences of child, family, and environment.

Family Information

Both boys were born to mothers on welfare, each of whom had first given birth at age 14. Damien's father had abandoned his family, and Jacob's father was shot to death in a bar fight when the boy was 4 or 5 years old. Both boys grew up in an atmosphere of physical abuse; Jacob's father used to beat his mother, and Damien said that he ran away from home because his mother beat him. Both boys lived in crack houses, and Jacob's mother had a history of alcohol and crack dependence.

Jacob was the youngest of eight children, in a family in which he saw relatives and friends use guns to settle disputes. He saw his sister shot in the face when he was 4 or 5. Another sister introduced him to marijuana when he was 9. His mother did not appear for Jacob's first court hearing on the armed robbery charge, and when she subsequently came to testify, she was drunk and could not remember Jacob's birthday.

Damien dropped out of school after the seventh grade and went to live with an older teenage brother, who was a drug dealer and who initiated him into the drug trade. (Damien had earlier been a ward of the court after his mother was accused of beating one of his brothers. He apparently had no contact with his father.) Damien took the gun used in the robbery/murder from his brother's house; in preparation for the attack, in Jacob's presence, Damien sharpened the bullets.

Discussion

It is not difficult to identify the familial and social factors that coalesced in the behaviors resulting in this tragic murder. An overview of the information available in this case summary reveals the presence of the following negative influences in the lives of these boys:

> *Family disintegration*:
>   Female-headed households
>   Absent fathers (Jacob's was killed; Damien's abandoned the family)
>   Youthful runaway behavior (Damien)
> *Poverty* (both families were supported on welfare)
> *Exposure to violence*:
>   Witness to spouse abuse (between parents—Jacob)
>   Witness to child abuse (parental abuse of sibling—Damien)
>   Personal experience of child abuse (Damien)
>   Witness of gun fights within family (Jacob)
> *Exposure to substance abuse*:
>   Residence in crack houses
>   Parental alcohol and crack dependence (Jacob)
>   Sibling drug dealing (Damien)
>   Drug abuse/dependence in the neighborhood
>   Encouragement to use drugs

Jacob's lawyer summarized his young client's situation by stating that "Jake is the product of his environment. He comes from a dysfunctional family. The older neighborhood boys were his heroes. They sold drugs. They had guns. They were his role models. He wanted to be like them" (quoted in Wilkerson, 1994, p. A-14).

A lawyer and forensic psychologist, Charles Patrick Ewing, comments in his book *Kids Who Kill* (1990): "Juvenile killers are not born but made.

. . . Virtually all juvenile killers have been significantly influenced in their homicidal behavior by one or more of a handful of known factors: child abuse, poverty, substance abuse, and access to guns" (p. 157). Certainly these conditions do not *always* produce child killers, since many youngsters manage to survive the ravages of noxious familial and social environments without succumbing to antisocial acts. Some even achieve great success, against all odds (Anthony & Cohler, 1987). Nonetheless, when the cards are stacked so heavily against healthy development, as they were for both Jacob and Damien, the outcome in terms of antisocial behavior is understandable. Furthermore, in addition to Ewing's list of factors contributing to homicidal behavior, we should consider the possibility that Jacob may have been born with fetal alcohol syndrome and/or the effects of his mother's crack addiction, and that Damien may have suffered head injuries as a result of the serious and repeated beatings he received. We know nothing about either boy's academic performance—possible learning or hyperactivity problems, or individual areas of achievement.

This case illustrates how the cumulative influence of individual, familial, and social factors can culminate in juvenile criminal behaviors. Even when social and familial factors appear to predominate as causal, however, remediation will necessitate intensive work with such youths on an *individual* basis. It is likely that after years of abuse and neglect, youngsters such as Damien and Jacob internalize and then replicate the dysfunctional behavior they have witnessed and experienced during their formative years. Rehabilitation will require more than environmental change to significantly alter such youngsters' sense of personal identity, their sense of self-respect and competence, and their views about future goals for their lives.

INCREASED RATES OF EMOTIONAL
AND BEHAVIORAL PROBLEMS

There is a growing perception, both among the general public and in the professional literature, that children's problems are getting worse. LeCroy and Ryan (1993) state that "severe emotional disturbance in children and adolescents is a national problem requiring immediate action" (p. 318). Knitzer (1982) and Hewlett (1991) have documented the adverse effects of deteriorating social conditions on children's emotional and physical well-being.

In an attempt to answer the question "Are American children's problems getting worse?", Achenbach and Howell (1993) compared scores on the Child Behavior Checklist (CBCL) from three different years: 1976,

1981, and 1989. The CBCL (Achenbach & Edelbrock, 1983) is the most widely used measure of its kind in the world for documenting children's everyday problems, according to a report in *The New York Times* (Goleman, 1993). In each of the three years, a random sample of more than 2,000 children from 7 to 16 years of age was rated. Achenbach and Howell found that problem scores were somewhat higher on the 118 items describing behavioral and emotional problems, and that competence scores were lower, in 1989 than in the earlier assessments. Teachers' ratings agreed with those of parents in showing small increases in problem scores and decreases in competence scores. Therefore, Achenbach and Howell answered "Yes" to the question, although they could not determine why this was so. No significant differences to explain the findings could be attributed to age, gender, socioeconomic status, or black–white ethnicity.

Another important finding among Achenbach and Howell's 1989 sample was a significant rise in the proportion of children scoring in a range indicative of a need for clinical services (18.2%), despite the exclusion from this sample of 8.3% who had already received mental health services in the preceding year. "More untreated children would be considered to need help in the 1989 than in the 1976 sample," Achenbach and Howell concluded (1993, p. 1153).

Specific Problem Syndromes

The following groupings of problems derived from parent, teacher, and self-report forms of the CBCL as administered to the 1989 sample were presented in *The New York Times* (Goleman, 1993). Each specific item appears on the CBCL.

Withdrawn or social problems:
   Would rather be alone
   Is secretive
   Sulks a lot
   Lacks energy
   Is unhappy
   Is too dependent
   Prefers to play with younger kids
Attention or thought problems:
   Can't concentrate
   Can't sit still
   Acts without thinking

Is too nervous to concentrate
Does poorly on schoolwork
Can't get mind off certain thoughts
Delinquency or aggression:
Hangs around kids who get into trouble
Lies and cheats
Argues a lot
Is mean to other people
Demands attention
Destroys other people's things
Disobeys at home and at school
Is stubborn and moody
Talks too much
Teases a lot
Has hot temper
Anxiety and depression:
Is lonely
Has many fears and worries
Needs to be perfect
Feels unloved
Feels nervous
Feels sad and depressed

All of these behaviors worsened over the 13-year period from 1976 to 1989. Achenbach stated that "it's not the magnitude of the changes, but the consistency that is so significant" (quoted in Goleman, 1993, p. C-16). He went on to suggest that multiple factors probably contribute to such widespread increase in children's problems. Among these, he cited children's exposure to violence; reduced time with parents and reduced parental monitoring of children; more families with both parents working; more single-parent families; and fewer community mentors to help children learn adaptive social and emotional skills.

Implications for Social Workers

The fact that millions of children are suffering from serious mental health problems means that social workers, teachers, and others will encounter these children in schools, in child welfare institutions, in jails, in foster homes, and on the streets (LeCroy & Ashford, 1992). Their presence is by no means restricted to mental health clinics, since only about half of the children needing mental health services receive them, and many who do receive inappropriate services, according to Saxe, Cross, and Silverman (1988). Important decisions about what services to offer, and which family members to include and in what setting, depend on a careful bio-psychosocial assessment that takes careful account of cultural as well as other factors. This is discussed in Chapters 4 and 5. It is essential that those working with children have basic knowledge about child development, about cultural variations in child rearing, and about the various deviations from children's usual developmental course in order to evaluate a presenting problem in a manner that fully considers the inner world of the child, in addition to all relevant external factors.

AN ECOLOGICAL PERSPECTIVE ON ETIOLOGY

The Need to Consider Multiple Factors

Nothing in life is simple, as we quickly realize when we are attempting to ascribe causality to human behavior. "The task of unraveling causes and determinants of childhood mental disorders is formidable because of the complexity of interactions between biological, psychological, social, and environmental factors" (Institute of Medicine, 1989, paraphrased in Johnson & Friesen, 1993, p. 27). The current view of the etiologies of mental and emotional disorders in children and adolescents has been summarized as follows:

> Support for multifactorial or systems understanding of the etiology of mental disorders has been accruing rapidly during the past two decades. Systems views are replacing univariate and stage theory models in all mental health disciplines, including social work, psychiatry, special education, clinical psychology, and others. (Johnson & Friesen, 1993, p. 27)

Of course, social work has a long history of employing extensive psychosocial assessment, as pointed out by Lieberman (1987); the addition of "bio-" to "psychosocial" represents increased awareness of the importance of innate factors (whether genetic or acquired) that can impinge significantly on a problem.

The concept that a child himself or herself may be an active agent influencing the systems of family, school, and government was first proposed by Bronfenbrenner (1979). It has subsequently been elaborated in the works of Stern (1985) with regard to the infant–mother interaction, and in the publications of the Erikson Institute (Garbarino et al., 1989), which stress the mutual influences between children and their physical, social, and cultural contexts. The implications of this dynamic view lead to more complex understandings about social interactions, which are no longer viewed as unidirectional.

For example, when a highly active, intensely reactive, distractible child is adopted by a low-key, calm mother, she may believe that the child is "hyper" because of her inability to soothe and quiet the baby. However, temperamental differences between parents and children, whether the children are biological or adopted, attest to the notion of "match" or "goodness of fit" between parent and child as the appropriate unit of attention, rather than the maladaptation of the individual parent or child (Thomas, Chess, & Birch, 1968). Simplistic, single-cause explanations no longer suffice in a systems perspective that attempts to consider "the continual, mutually influencing forces of biology, culture, behaviors of significant others, organizational processes, economics, and politics" (Johnson 1993b, p. 86). If this wider view seems cumbersome and broad, it certainly avoids the previous overemphasis on parental pathology as *the* cause of children's problems. Germain and Gitterman (1987) state that "neither the people served, nor their environments, can be fully understood except in relationship to each other" (p. 493).

The Need to Consider Cultural Factors

It is also essential that social workers understand their own cultural biases and learn about the culturally based beliefs of their clients regarding role expectations, typical ways of expressing feelings, and patterns of social exchange. For example, a male child who has been taught both implicitly and explicitly that being "macho" means "Stand up for yourself and don't let anyone get away with insulting you or your family," cannot be criticized for initiating a fist fight with a bully who said he was a "wimp" and his sister was a "tramp." To label this child "aggressive" misses the child's compelling motivation to defend his family's honor in a culturally sanctioned manner. This situation challenges the school social worker, who may be brought in to devise a creative response that respects the child's cultural identity even as it discourages fighting on the school premises. Huang (1989) points out that children and adolescents in immigrant families are often in conflict between two competing sets of values and norms, which may require them to follow one set of behaviors in the family setting and another in the school and community. This situation will require concerted attention from school social workers and others dealing with increasing numbers of immigrant children.

CURRENT ISSUES IN SOCIAL WORK WITH CHILDREN

Historical Overview

A consideration of current issues will have more meaning when these are viewed in a historical perspective. The practice of social work with children has taken many forms—from its beginnings in court-affiliated clinics for juvenile delinquents in 1909, in which social workers studied cases and treated families, to agency and private practice in the 1990s, in which social workers may work with families, with children in groups, or with individual children (using play therapy and other methods appropriate for young clients). Parent counseling has always been an essential component of working with children, even when children reside with extended family members or live in foster homes. Intervention with a child's biological parent(s) remains central to the work with the child, because of social work's enduring belief about the importance of family identity to the child's sense of personal identity, and because of the profession's commitment to the concept of family preservation (to be discussed in the next chapter).

During the early decades of this century, social workers intervened with families according to their understanding of the problem, which took the form of a "diagnosis" of social factors contributing to the problem situation (Richmond, 1917). During the next phase of more specialized and regulated practice, many social workers worked under the guidance and direction of psychiatrists in child guidance clinics; the psychiatrists treated the children, while the social workers "guided" the parents, thus introducing the concept of "parent guidance." In situations when a family failed or was in danger of failing to meet the child's basic needs, the child welfare system assumed the role of parent surrogate, "doing for the deprived, disadvantaged, dependent child what the effective family does for the advantaged child" (Kadushin, 1987, p. 267). During the 1950s and 1960s, child welfare enjoyed special recognition and status as a specialty area within social work. More recently this elite status has diminished, as other professionals have become involved in child placement decisions, abuse investigations, and adoption procedures (Kadushin, 1987).

After the promulgation of family therapy in the 1970s and later, social workers tended to view a child's problems as symptomatic of a troubled marriage; therefore, intervention tended to focus on the marital dyad or on the family unit, rather than on individual members of the family. As a result, the child's presenting problem might be downplayed or ignored by family therapists, who considered it just the tip of the iceberg. An important goal in family therapy has been to remove the child from the role of the "identified patient" (Satir, 1983). More recently, there is growing recognition that symptomatic children may have internalized problems and therefore require individual help, regardless of whatever assistance is offered to the parents or to the family unit. Social workers increasingly utilize specialized methods such as play therapy in their work with young children.

Current Cutting-Edge Issues

Practice in the mid-1990s and in the century ahead must take major account of the social environment, which has a very heavy impact on many families and children, even as social workers continue to pay attention to children's biological and emotional condition. Methods of intervention must be grounded in a thorough understanding of *all* relevant contributing factors, and adapted to both the internal and external needs of children with problems.

The following list of cutting-edge issues, though by no means exhaustive, represents matters of concern to me, my students, and my colleagues in our mutual efforts to provide relevant and helpful service to children and families in the mid-1990s. The chapters that follow address these issues through case examples and literature reviews, as well as through my own experience of many years as a social work practitioner and educator.

1. *The impact on children of deteriorating social conditions, such as violence, poverty, and substance abuse/dependence.* Where and how can we intervene for the purpose of protecting children and enhancing the quality of their lives? Many children, especially in urban areas, report that they fear going to school because of possible outbreaks of violence involving guns and knives. The trip from home to school may be marked by episodes of gang warfare in which innocent bystanders are injured or killed. When children's basic safety is in jeopardy, how can they concentrate and learn in school, and complete their basic developmental tasks as well?

2. *Selecting intervention alternatives at multiple levels* (with the child, with the parent[s], with the extended family, with the community, and with government [political advocacy]). How can individual social workers be expected to intervene in *all* areas simultaneously, as might best serve the needs of a particular situation? In view of extensive individual, family, and social needs, should the profession focus on developing subspecialty areas of expertise? For example, should specially trained practitioners carry out lobbying/advocacy efforts, while family practitioners work with family units, and child specialists work with individual children? What would be some advantages and disadvantages of this ap-

proach? Whereas we might like to do it all, the maxim "jack of all trades, master of none" bears careful thought as demands for more specialized practice increase.

3. *Providing culturally sensitive practice.* How can social workers develop sufficient knowledge about numerous ethnic groups to practice effectively within their own communities? Is it desirable to work primarily with one's own ethnic group, or are there advantages to a team approach, in which members of different cultural backgrounds can provide diversity and opportunities for diffusion of knowledge about diverse cultures among practitioners?

4. *Helping children and families in the throes of the AIDS epidemic.* Statistics indicate the certainty of growing numbers of children orphaned by AIDS and infected by HIV. Child welfare agencies will be overwhelmed by the need to provide homes and other services for these children. What interventions are most appropriate, and how can these best be implemented to meet the needs of these vulnerable and bereaved children?

5. *Working with severely traumatized children with Posttraumatic Stress Disorder (PTSD).* Children are increasingly suffering the effects of exposure to traumatic events, such as war atrocities and gang, community, and family violence. The symptoms of PTSD represent dysfunctional, defensive coping responses to environmental assaults on an individual's level of anxiety tolerance. Will social workers who have special training in crisis intervention with children assume the leadership in helping these traumatized children? As a corollary, will social workers lead in efforts for *early* intervention with such children, to prevent the development of future problems (which often become more entrenched with the passage of time)?

CONCLUDING COMMENTS

Social work with children is a demanding, all-inclusive field of practice. No longer can a practitioner focus primarily on a child's inner world; nor will it suffice to intervene exclusively with the child's family or social environment. A multifaceted approach is essential to understanding, just as it is essential in planning and carrying out helping interventions.

Social workers must learn to scan a child's world and see the broad picture before determining where and how to initiate the helping process. The skills of listening, observing, and empathizing will assist practitioners, who must be able to see through a child's eyes in order to comprehend the child's situation with both head and heart.

DISCUSSION QUESTIONS

1. How can a social worker avoid becoming discouraged when faced with a child who has been victimized by physical and emotional abuse and neglect in a home where both parents use multiple substances?

2. What services would be appropriate to offer within a school setting to recent immigrant children and their families, for the purpose of assisting with their adjustment and integration into the community? What form of initial contact would make the children and families most comfortable?

3. Review and discuss the selected cutting-edge issues presented just above, giving pros and cons for your responses.

❖ CHAPTER 2 ❖

Necessary Background
for Helping Children

This chapter begins with an overview of the varying social work roles and functions related to helping children. It then reviews the value base, knowledge base, and practical skills that are essential for this work, and concludes with some guidelines for avoiding pitfalls that sometimes confront social workers in this field of practice. An annotated bibliography of texts on child development is appended to the chapter.

UNDERSTANDING THE MULTIFACETED ROLE
OF THE SOCIAL WORKER

A social worker attempting to help a child does not work in a vacuum. Many different adults often participate in the helping effort, and frequently the social worker serves as self-appointed case coordinator, to facilitate sharing of information and to promote collaboration in the child's best interests. Each setting has its own group of professional experts who have input regarding the child's problem. In addition, each situation dictates its own unique protocol for the involvement of special personnel to evaluate and treat a child with problems. For example, when an 8-year-old third-grader threatened to throw himself out of a window in school, the social worker at the emergency walk-in psychiatric clinic to which the child was brought consulted with the staff child psychiatrist, the school guidance counselor, and the child protective services (CPS) worker who was investigating allegations of child abuse in this family (Price, 1991). These contacts, some "in-house" and others collateral, were as essential for understanding the situation as were interviews with the child and his mother. Because the social worker had a broad view of the problem situation, she understood the importance of contacting other professionals for their input.

A team approach to helping often serves a child and family well, since each specialist's expertise can contribute to a fuller understanding of the child's situation. When the social worker subscribes to a multifactorial view regarding etiology, as discussed in Chapter 1, the participation of other professionals with different perspectives about the child's situation is welcomed and valued. Usually the social worker synthesizes all the relevant information obtained from various sources and organizes it into a biopsychosocial summary, which later will be discussed with the parent(s) and with the child (when feasible) as part of the treatment planning and contracting. This assessment process is reviewed in detail in Chapters 4 and 5.

The following case illustrates the different social work roles of clinician, case manager, consultant, and advocate.

---------- ❖ ----------

THE CASE OF JOSÉ, AGE 6½

Presenting Problem

José, a Hispanic 6½-year-old foster child, was referred for counseling by the committee on special education of his school because of his traumatic and chaotic background. José had both witnessed and been subjected to domestic violence, child neglect, abuse, and abandonment, prior to being placed in foster care at age 4½ with his two younger brothers. When the foster mother later found it too difficult to manage the care of the three active boys, José's brothers (ages 3 and 5) were moved from the home. At that time, José was enrolled in a special day school. He became very oppositional both at home and at school, and began having delusions of characters from horror movies telling him to kill himself and hurt others. When José proceeded to act on these violent commands, he was admitted to a psychiatric hospital.

Family Information

Both of José's parents were drug addicts, and all three of their sons had been exposed prenatally to drugs and alcohol. The father was incarcerated for stealing, and the mother for selling drugs. Before the mother's incarceration, when the boys resided with her, they were often left alone and neglected. Their initial placement in foster care occurred after the police found them wandering alone in the streets at midnight.

Case Overview

José spent 2 months in the psychiatric hospital, during which time the social worker from the special education school visited him weekly for counseling. She wanted to maintain continuity in their relationship, because she assumed that he would return to the same school program upon discharge. She also knew that José would be placed in the same foster home with his brothers following discharge, and that his mother was due to be released from prison 6 months later.

Discussion

Even the bare outline of this case permits us to appreciate the complex, multifaceted role of the school social worker who faced the challenge of gathering together the unraveling threads of this child's life. She wanted to create some sense of unified purpose among the various professionals involved with this child, in order to coordinate the planning and clarify future goals.

The following list identifies the array of personnel who were involved with José's life either directly or indirectly, and whom the school social worker attempted to involve in this planning:

- Foster care worker
- CPS worker
- Psychiatric hospital staff (psychiatrist, social worker, nurses, psychologist)
- Mother's prison caseworker and/or future probation officer
- José's special education teacher
- José's speech and hearing specialist
- José's pediatrician

An eco-map (see Figure 2.1) was used to diagram these different helpers; it also included the genogram and relevant family members. (See Hartman, 1978, for details about the construction of an eco-map and a discussion of its use.)

Different Roles

In her role as *case manager*, the school social worker obtained reports from the professionals involved with José, and convened a case conference to which all were invited. Learning more about the nature of José's psychiatric diagnosis and prognosis helped prepare the worker for her ongoing involvement with this child in her role as his *clinician*. The worker also more clearly understood José's untrusting manner of relating to her and others at the school when she heard details from the CPS worker about the mother's history of abandonment and abuse of her

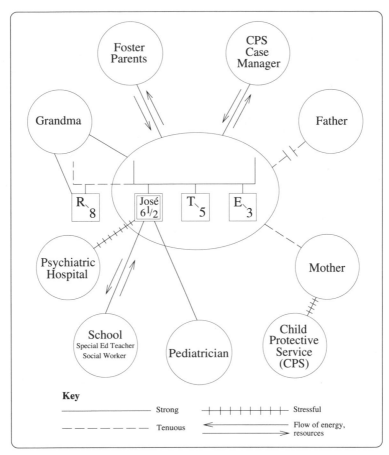

FIGURE 2.1. Eco-map of José.

children. By contrast, the worker served as *consultant* to the hospital staff
when she visited José during his stay: She provided information to the
personnel there about the boy's hearing loss in one ear and about his
hyperactivity and short attention span, which had become apparent to
his teacher.

Because of the worker's concern about José's mother's rehabilitation,
she took on an *advocacy* role in regard to the need for the mother to receive counseling and parenting education in prison, plus drug and alcohol treatment prior to her discharge. The worker also advocated for the
children to begin visiting their mother on a regular basis, to prepare them
for possible future reunification of the family.

Different Settings

In addition to working with many collaborators in a variety of roles and functions, the professional social worker involved with children must also demonstrate versatility in working with clients in a wide range of locations. The tenet of "meeting clients where they are" usually refers to tuning in to their psychological/emotional state. However, it can also refer to meeting the clients on their *physical* terrain. This means that social workers who deal with children's problems work in all locations where children live, learn, and play, and where they receive care and counseling when they are injured, neglected, abandoned, or otherwise troubled. Thus, social workers help children in hospitals, schools, foster homes, residential treatment centers, family agencies, mental health clinics, and shelters for the homeless. Although each setting has its particular focus and specific procedures for helping, certain basic principles and a core of knowledge about child and family behavior and needs must guide the practice of all social workers who help children, regardless of the setting in which they provide services.

COMMITMENT TO A CORE OF VALUES AND CODE OF ETHICS

The helping process, rooted in the emotion of compassion, flourishes into a beautiful hybrid in its goal of meeting human needs. Beginning with a compassionate "natural helper," professional education develops this individual into a practitioner who demonstrates disciplined "use of self," appropriately applying theoretical knowledge and practical skills. However, knowledge and skills, though necessary, are not sufficient for the task of helping. The situations in which social workers are engaged often require difficult decisions in which no single "right answer" applies. The workers must consider ethical principles and weigh the pros and cons of various possible outcomes in the effort to serve everyone concerned most effectively.

The Code of Ethics

Values serve as guides or criteria for selecting good and desirable behaviors. Most social workers agree about the basic values of client participation, self-determination, and confidentiality (Lowenberg & Dolgoff, 1992). However, the complexity of a client's situation can often make decisions very difficult. Ideally, clients participate in decisions affecting their own lives; however, when interests of family members conflict, and/or when abuse and neglect of a minor is a possibility, then the social worker may have to make a recommendation based on his or her judgment regarding the best interests of the child.

In 1979, the National Association of Social Workers (NASW) first adopted a code of ethics to "provide social workers with principles to help them resolve ethical dilemmas encountered in practice" (Reamer, 1987, p. 804). Containing principles derived from values, this code of professional ethics "identifies and describes the ethical behavior expected of professional practitioners" (Lowenberg & Dolgoff, 1992, p. 22). Among the principles emphasized are those of confidentiality, self-determination, and expectations pertaining to standards of professional behavior. The newly revised code of ethics (NASW, 1996) continues the general tone of the previous version, therefore requiring sensitive interpretation and case-by-case application in ambiguous and conflictual situations.

Although the code articulates the value base of the social work profession, it does so with a high level of abstraction that fails to provide specific guidelines for the resolution of ethical dilemmas. Thus, although students and practitioners are expected to subscribe to this code, its implementation may be unclear and subject to differing personal interpretations. The new code (NASW, 1996, p. 5) states this plainly:

> This code offers a set of values, principles, and standards to guide decision making and conduct when ethical issues arise. *It does not provide a set of rules that prescribe how social workers should act in all situations.* Specific applications of the code must take into account the context in which it is being considered and the possibility of the code's values, principles, and standards. *Ethical responsibilities flow from all human relationships, from the personal and familial to the social and professional.* . . . Ethical decision making is a process. There are many instances in social work where simple answers are not available to resolve complex ethical issues. (emphasis added)

Issues of Confidentiality/Consent in Work with Children

With regard to children, questions of ethics often become especially thorny. For one thing, neither society nor the helping professions have taken a stand regarding whether children have the same rights of privacy and confidentiality as do adults, especially with regard to parents' access to information about their children's counseling/therapy.

Actually, the federal Family Educational Rights and Privacy Act (P.L. 93-380, 1974) gives parents the right to inspect their children's medical and school records; therefore, social workers cannot legitimately promise confidentiality to children. Moreover, because social work with a child *always* involves work with a parent or guardian, the issue of confidentiality becomes entangled with the question "who is the client?" The parent or guardian has both a need and a right to know in a general way about the course of the child's progress and ongoing problems. In addition, the seasoned practitioner realizes that it is counterproductive and impossible to *promise* a child confidentiality. Ironically, this type of promise is the last thing many children would expect anyway, since they know that their parents or guardians "check up" on their work in school and other areas of involvement. Why should counseling/therapy be any different?

My own view about confidentiality as applied to children is that it is a concept more relevant to work with youngsters over 12 years of age, and even then it has the same limitations with regard to parents' legal right to access to the records of their children under the age of 18. I believe that it is far more useful to *encourage* the sharing of information between a child and parent, albeit in a sensitive and general manner that does not divulge details that would be embarrassing to the child. Sometimes the achievement of improved parent–child communication represents a major goal in the helping process.

Another ethical issue pertinent to working with children is whether a child has the "right" to refuse treatment, as an adult who is not a danger to self or others and who is not legally mandated to receive treatment does. Can a 5-year-old decide what is in his or her own best interests? At what age *can* a child decide?

Anyone who works with children knows that almost *all* children begin as involuntary clients. They may realize that they are unhappy with their lives, but in most cases they have no idea that there are people who can help them with their worries and troubles; furthermore, they are wary of adult strangers and uncomfortable trying to talk with them. It is the responsibility of the social worker to introduce a child to the notion of a "worry person" or "helper" who knows how to help children with their troubles. Once this message has been conveyed to the child, and repeated a few times, the child may be able to make a decision about participating in the helping effort. Even then, a child who has been repeatedly disappointed or betrayed by adults may find the offer to help impossible to believe. Gaining such a child's trust will take time.

For all of these reasons, my personal recommendation is that the social worker ask the responsible adults to continue to bring the child for appointments, even when the child seems unwilling. This initial "resistance" will almost always be converted into eager participation once the child experiences the reality of a relationship in which he or she is listened to and valued.

Ethnic/Cultural Sensitivity

When we meet someone for the first time, our initial impressions automatically register such personal characteristics as age, gender, and race, in addition to factors about the individual's personality and mood. When the person resembles ourselves, we may make certain assumptions about him or her, based on our own experiences regarding the shared characteristics. Of course, all middle-aged white women (for example) are not alike, but the likelihood of empathy increases with similarity of personal characteristics.

What does this mean, then, in view of the fact that "children of color are the most rapidly increasing group in the U.S. population, [that they] are the largest risk group for disabilities and developmental delay as a result of conditions associated with poverty[,] and that *most professionals who work with this population are from the dominant culture*" (Rounds, Weil, & Bishop, 1994, p. 12; emphasis added)? If, as predicted, by the year 2010 one of every four children in the United States will be a child of color, then social workers and other helping professionals must prepare themselves to work effectively with these children and their families. Lieberman (1990, p. 101) states that "right from birth, babies become reflections and products of their culture," and notes that child-rearing traditions and values about parent–child roles and attitudes are strongly shaped by cultural beliefs.

Since 1973, the Council on Social Work Education (CSWE) has "mandated that instruction concerning the lifestyles of diverse ethnic groups become an integral part of social work education" (Devore & Schlesinger, 1987, p. 513). Subsequent policy statements have reiterated and expanded on this position (CSWE, 1984, 1992a, 1992b), with the result that courses in the baccalaureate and master's curricula must reflect content regarding cultural diversity for groups distinguished by ethnicity and race, as well as by gender, age, religion, disablement, and sexual orientation (Carrillo, Holzhalb, & Thyer, 1993). The implementation of this mandate takes many forms; the work of Lieberman (1990) and Rounds et al. (1994) contributes helpful guidelines for practice with children of color and their families.

These and other writers emphasize the importance of self-awareness regarding one's *own* culture as a foundation for understanding the culture of others. The core technique of the "conscious use of self" requires workers "to be aware of and to take responsibility for their own emotions and attitudes as they affect professional function" (Devore & Schlesinger, 1987, p. 103). This, of course, includes the worker's cultural beliefs. Honest, critical self-examination should occur in conjunction with social work courses and in the field practicum, and should continue as the mark of professional behavior as long as a social worker engages in practice. Some specific tools and references that can assist students and practitioners in examining their own cultural beliefs include Ho's (1992) "Ethnic competence–skill" model, the exercises and self-assessment inventories reviewed in Randall-David (1989), and Cournoyer's (1991) overview of a variety of self-assessment measures related to cultural diversity.

The "culturagram" (Congress, 1994) provides the social worker with a tool for understanding the unique cultural background, beliefs, and circumstances of diverse families. Use of the culturagram encourages appreciation of the impact of the culture on a particular family, even as it discourages stereotyping of members of a particular cultural group. Because children in culturally diverse families often struggle to reconcile the values and beliefs taught at home with those they observe in the wider community, it is important for social workers to understand such families' backgrounds and the belief systems to which the children have been exposed. Congress (1994) presents construction and use of the culturagram as a method of developing greater empathy for ethnic/cultural differences.

Other steps toward improving ethnic/cultural sensitivity as summarized by Rounds et al. (1994) include acknowledging and valuing diversity, recognizing and understanding the dynamics of difference, and acquiring cultural knowledge. With regard to the recommendation that practitioners have an in-depth understanding of the cultural background of their clients, Lieberman (1990) reassures us that "it is impossible to be culturally sensitive as a general quality because this would demand an encyclopedic ethnographic and anthropological knowledge well beyond the reach of most of us" (p. 104). She suggests instead that we "think of cultural sensitivity as a form of *interpersonal sensitivity*, an *attunement* to the specific idiosyncracies of another person" (Lieberman, 1990, p. 104; first emphasis in original, second added). Insofar as social workers always try to imagine walking in the shoes of their clients, this attunement effort will result in practice that attempts to understand the clients' subjective world as it respects and honors the clients' attempts to carry out the cultural/ethnic traditions that they have inherited and that form the intrinsic core of their identity. As Erikson (1963) has stated, "the ego identity is anchored in the cultural identity" (p. 279).

THE ESSENTIAL KNOWLEDGE BASE
FOR WORK WITH CHILDREN

We have all been children ourselves, and many social workers also have firsthand experience with children in their role as parents. To assume, however, that personal life experience will prepare one for the type of complicated work described in the case of José is as foolhardy as suggesting that anyone who likes to eat can prepare a gourmet five-course meal! Liking food on the one hand, and memories of childhood on the other, can provide the motivation and even the foundation for success in either venture, but specialized training and study are necessary to move beyond the novice stage of either cooking or work with children.

A solid foundation of basic knowledge is essential for social workers and other practitioners whose work deals with young children and their families. This base of essential knowledge includes a grounding in the "normal" course of child development, as well as in deviations from this course (i.e., childhood mental and emotional disorders). The knowledge base also includes information about the ways family dynamics, developmental phases, and events affect children (and vice versa). With this foundation, for example, the practitioner will be in a position to evaluate the significance of severe nighttime fears when they occur in a 9-year-old child as opposed to a 3-year-old. The knowledgeable practitioner who understands the importance of attachment relationships, and appreciates the interplay between the child's temperament and stressful events, may discover through skillful questioning that the 9-year-old may have overheard arguments between the parents after she went to bed that led her to the conclusion that a parental divorce was imminent. This "discovery" of the source of the child's fear is not made by accident; it occurs because the social worker is well versed in normal child development milestones, which indicate that nighttime fears are atypical of a 9-year-old child in the absence of traumatic experience or upsetting family events. Nighttime fears, by contrast, are typical in 3-year-olds, and the knowledgeable social worker will counsel the parents of the 3-year-old about their common occurrence at this age, at the same time offering guidance about ways to comfort the child so as to keep the anxiety within tolerable limits.

Understanding of Child Development

Basic Information

Courses in social work with children usually do not teach the basics of child development, since instructors assume that students have acquired this knowledge in the required core courses in human behavior and the social environment. In the event that this content has not been adequately covered or mastered, an annotated list of references on child biological, psychological, and social development appears at the end of this chapter. In addition to these references in the professional literature, there are numerous works written for the general public that summarize basic information on child development. The list at the end of the chapter also includes a selection of these works.

Attachment and Bonding

The seminal writings of John Bowlby (1958, 1969, 1973, 1977, 1979, 1980, 1988) highlight the essential role of attachment and bonding "as a basic component of human nature" (1988, pp. 120–121). "Attachment" refers to an enduring, reciprocal bond of affection that focuses on a particular person or persons. The child's attachment figures are typically the parents or primary caretakers, who play a critical role in the nature and quality of the child's attachment relationships. For example, the child with a "secure" attachment relationship with his or her parents feels confident about leaving the safe proximity of this "secure base" to explore his or her environment, knowing that the parents will respond comfortingly when he or she returns and wants reassurance. However, in situations when parents are inconsistent and/or unreliable toward the child the resulting relationship may be characterized as an "anxious resistant attachment" (Bowlby, 1988); this results in the child's exhibiting separation anxiety, clinging behavior, and fear about exploring the world. Bowlby also identifies a third form of attachment, "anxious avoidant attachment," signifying that the child actually *expects* rejection from his or her self-involved caretakers or parents, who use threats of abandonment as a means of controlling him or her. This interaction understandably leads the child to become unable to trust others, because he or she expects or fears abandonment in future relationships with other adults.

Many of the children known to social workers show signs of attachment difficulties. Children who have experienced inconsistent care, and who demonstrate anxious, insecure attachment to their parents, resist engagement with social workers because of their inability to trust adult strangers (James, 1994). These children, with backgrounds devoid of consistent loving relationships, require extreme patience, sensitivity, and understanding. Remkus (1991, p. 144) quotes the leading attachment theorists in stating, "failure to establish a secure attachment relationship limits the emotional, cognitive, and social development of the child (Sroufe & Waters, 1977; Sroufe, 1979a, 1979b; Ainsworth, 1979; Ainsworth & Bell, 1971; Mahler, Pine, & Bergman, 1975)."

Parents, usually mothers, bear a major responsibility for the quality of children's attachment (A. Freud, 1970). However, when parents are overwhelmed with multiple stresses, they may be unable to respond lovingly and consistently to their needy children. Indeed a parent may not be able to bond to his or her own child because of the parent's *own* attachment-deprived history. Unfortunately, the parent–child relationship may become angry and abusive when the parent cannot focus on the child's needs. Chapter 14 discusses this sad circumstance, with case examples and implications for intervention.

The fourth edition of the *Diagnostic and Statistical Manual of Mental Disorders* (DSM-IV; American Psychiatric Association, 1994) describes the criteria for the diagnosis of Reactive Attachment Disorder of Infancy or Early Childhood, which occurs as a result of deficient care and leads to marked disturbance in the child's social relatedness. This condition, which begins before age 5, causes the child to react in two different ways: (1) to be excessively inhibited or contradictory in responses, or (2) to be indiscriminately sociable and apparently unable to attach selectively to attachment figures. James (1994) discusses some guidelines for working with these children. Students and practitioners who work with children with attachment and trauma disorders will benefit from studying the literature on trauma and its impact on development (Eth & Pynoos, 1985; Herman, 1992; van der Kolk 1987, 1989).

Mental and Emotional Disorders of Children

Social workers deal with children in a variety of circumstances (foster placement, underachievement in school, and a parent's terminal illness, to name only a few). Referrals may occur because of the circumstances of the situation (e.g.. foster placement), or because the child's extreme behavior alerts someone about the child's need for help.

Children express their anxieties in various ways, and the social worker or other practitioner to whom a symptomatic child may be referred must be knowledgeable about the different manifestations of childhood symptoms in order to make an assessment that will result in a helpful treatment plan. The worker's knowledge of normal child development serves as a baseline against which to evaluate the troublesome behaviors presented by the child. LeVine and Sallee (1992) state that "the more we understand about normal variations in development, the more we are able to determine which behaviors and reactions are indicative of problems in children" (p. 51).

In addition to understanding "normal" behavior, however, the practitioner needs to understand the deviations from the normal developmental course. The concept of "psychopathology" affixes a label to a set of behaviors; in the case of children, such labeling may ignore the reality of their rapid development. Nonetheless, practitioners must be familiar with the extremes of human behavior as manifested in children, so that they can recognize severely troubled children who require specialized interventions. An ability to apply the diagnostic categories of the DSM-IV does not preclude understanding the multifaceted etiology of a child's problem. However, refusal to recognize that children can exhibit serious behavioral disturbances may lead to neglect based on the ill-founded resistance to applying medical/psychiatric classifications to children. Wachtel (1994) states that "fear of pathologizing children has led to an excessive 'normalizing' of children who could really benefit from . . . psychotherapeutic work" (p. 8). Chapter 4 includes further discussion of the process and tools of child assessment.

Resilience and Coping in Children

Because human behavior is the end product of multiple influences, we note with relief that a noxious environment does not *always* bring disastrous results to the children. The concepts of "resilience" and "coping" attest to the ability of some children to thrive and do well despite factors that defeat many of their peers in seemingly similar circumstances. The work of E. James Anthony demonstrates that some children not only survive, but actually do well despite all odds to the contrary. Often, the influence of *one* adult makes enough impact to tip the balance of a negative environment in a child's life. Although these "invulnerable children" (Anthony & Cohler, 1987) are exceptional, their life experience argues for the positive impact of professional helpers on the lives of at-risk children who are "vulnerable."

Understanding of Family–Child Influences

Family Dynamics Affecting Children

The family's critical role in shaping a child is widely accepted by both professionals and the lay public. From the moment of birth, the mood and circumstances of the infant's mother and significant relatives provide the setting in which the child will feel safe and protected or insecure and threatened. The status of the family itself can influence the attitudes of various members about the infant's birth. For example, a first-born, planned child will experience a different reception than will a fifth-born, unplanned baby. However, birth order is merely one of many factors to be considered in evaluating the family's reactions to the infant. A first-born child of a 14-year-old unmarried mother may be resented because its birth was unwanted, whereas a fifth-born infant in some families may be highly valued for unique reasons having to do with the history of that family and the particular circumstances of the parents and the siblings at the time of birth. Every family is different, and the meanings of relationships cannot be assumed.

Developmental Stages of the Family

The family is an entity unto itself, with a course of development that has been charted by various theorists (Carter & McGoldrick, 1980; Duvall, 1977; Haley, 1973; Minuchin & Fishman, 1981; and Zilbach, 1989). These writers refer to "beginning," "middle," and "late" stages of family development, with family tasks at each stage, and significant family milestones occurring with the entry and departure of children. The importance of family developmental phases, and of family factors in general, in evaluating children cannot be overemphasized. Lidz (1963) describes the impact of the family on the child as follows: "The family forms the first imprint upon the still unformed child and the most pervasive and consistent influence that establishes patterns that later forces can modify but never alter completely" (p. 1).

The Reciprocity of Child and Family Effects

When a family is troubled (e.g., by marital conflict, health problems, or employment concerns), it passes along its tension to a child, who, in typical egocentric thinking, concludes that he or she created the difficulty. Sometimes the "problem" in a family *does* originate with the child; this may be true, for example, with a child who has Attention-Deficit/Hyperactivity Disorder and who presents management problems at home and at school. When the family is viewed as a system, however, a problem for one member brings problems to all. Therefore, the practitioner needs to think about this reciprocity in trying to understand all the ramifications of the presenting problem. Wachtel (1994, p. 71) comments as follows:

> In assessing the role of family dynamics we try to determine what events may have shifted some stable patterns in the family or what might be going on developmentally in the lives of the children that is affecting family interactions. Understanding the effect of developmental or other changes on the family system involves having a well-articulated sense of the predominant transactional pattern of the family.... Understanding how the psychodynamic issues of the child relate to those

of other family members is another important aspect of a systemic assessment.

In short, the family has an impact upon the child, and the child has an impact upon the family. We shall see various examples of both dynamics at work in the cases throughout this book. However, the facts that *all* families experiencing extreme stress do not generate problematic behaviors in *all* the children in their families, and, conversely, that families with problematic children do not *always* exhibit disturbed familial functioning, speak to the subtleties and vital importance of considering both individual and family strengths and resilience in evaluating the specific impact of events on different individuals and families.

The Effects of Family Crisis

Many children come to the attention of social workers and other practitioners at a time of family crisis, such as the divorce of their parents, the need for placement following an abusive experience, or their families' becoming homeless. It is essential that practitioners have an understanding of the impact of stress and trauma on children, and know the principles of crisis intervention so that they will be able to help in a timely way. Such help may reduce the likelihood of later development of the serious symptoms of Posttraumatic Stress Disorder. The use of "tripartite crisis assessment" (Webb, 1991) can assist the social worker in evaluating the resources in the social environment and in formulating appropriate long- and short-term goals.

NECESSARY COMPETENCIES IN WORK WITH CHILDREN

Accessing the Network of Children's Services

Practitioners who work with children must know how to make appropriate referrals to meet the special needs of the children in their care. Anyone who has contact with children in a professional role, for example, may become aware that a child in his or her office has signs of physical abuse; in addition, children sometimes disclose experiences of physical or sexual abuse to their social workers. Chapter 14 discusses the assessment of both physical and sexual abuse. It is mandatory for practitioners to report such evidence or disclosures. All social workers who have contact with children must be familiar with the laws in their states regarding their responsibility and the procedures flowing from a child's disclosure or suspicious evidence of physical or sexual abuse.

In addition, there may be times when referrals to crisis services, to CPS, or to hospital facilities will be necessary in order to meet the special needs of a child. Because of the unpredictable multiple needs of children, social workers must be familiar with referral policies of the relevant agencies in their locale, in order to make their clients' access to services as smooth as possible.

Blending Generalist and Specialized Practice

It is apparent that some of the tasks described in this chapter fall into the category of "basic skills," familiar to beginning-level social work students, whereas other skills require specialized knowledge, more typical of the training of the "advanced generalist" or "clinical" social worker. Unfortunately, many of those who work with children do not obtain specific levels of training, as apparent in the child welfare field, in which "it has been found that many Child Welfare workers lack the specialized knowledge and skills necessary to function in complex case situations" (Maluccio, 1985, p. 743). The requisite ecological perspective and multifaceted role expectations implicit in work with children mean that practitioners must make extra efforts to offer services to the best of their ability.

Ideally, work with children combines simultaneous attention to the impact of the person on the environment and that of the environment on the person, as characteristic of generalist practice (Sheafor & Landon, 1987). In addition, it must be grounded in knowledge of "normal" child and family development, and in familiarity with the deviations from the usual developmental course, as described above. Practitioners must be able to refer children for more specialized services when these are indicated, as well as to convene case conferences including professionals from different disciplines. Clearly, this work is demanding and challenging. The next two sections discuss methods for helping workers meet this multifaceted challenge.

AVOIDING POTENTIAL PITFALLS IN WORK WITH CHILDREN

Children's dependence, honesty, playfulness, and openness have a special appeal for many social workers, who decide to work with children because they genuinely like young people and want to help them. This admirable motivation for helping can sometimes obscure the snares implicit in this work, which must be recognized and avoided by all practitioners whose work focuses primarily on children.

The "Rescue Fantasy"

Probably most social workers who are engaged in work with children have at one time or another experienced a strong desire to "rescue" a child from a situation that appears to be clearly detrimental to the child's healthy development. Perhaps a 10-year-old girl is cast in the role of the "parentified child," taking care of several younger siblings after school, and trying to keep the peace when her alcoholic parents begin to argue at dinner. The social worker knows that the child should be more involved with after-school activities, peers, and schoolwork, and she resents the parents' obliviousness to their daughter's age-appropriate needs. The social worker knows that this child would love to be involved in cheerleading, and that she has already qualified for the squad. However, this involves rehearsals every day after school, which would conflict with the child's family responsibilities. The social worker writes the mother a note, stating that she has arranged transportation home for the girl after daily practice, and that she hopes the mother will support her child's special interest in this wholesome activity.

What is wrong with this scenario? Will it work? What did the social worker overlook in her eagerness to be helpful to the child client? At least two errors threaten the success of this well-intentioned plan: (1) The worker has moved too fast, and (2) the worker has "taken over," without involving the child's parents in the planning. In cases such as this one, when workers want to help and can see a clear-cut method to do so, it is hard for them to slow down, put on the glasses with wide-angle lenses, and include significant others in "their" treatment plan. Remembering that the child is part of a family system in which he or she carries out a designated role, a worker must consider the impact on the entire system when that role changes. Obviously, in the example given here, the ability of this child to be away from home every day depends on someone else's providing babysitting, and any plan that does not allow for this cannot succeed.

Competing and "Triangulating" with the Parents

Another typical pitfall in work with children demonstrated in this example is the danger of the worker's aligning with the child and either consciously or unconsciously becoming the "good" parent, in situations where the child's own parent appears to be deficient or even "bad." This attitude is always doomed to failure, since the parent will soon begin to resent the worker, and will find "reasons" to discontinue the child's counseling/therapy. Unfortunately, the worker is usually not aware of the impact of his or her actions until it is too late. Palombo (1985) states that "children may arouse intense infantile longings in the therapist [and] the therapist comes to be considered by [the child] as [a] substitute parent and induce in the therapist a parenting response rather than a purely therapeutic response" (p. 40). In my opinion, the more needy the child, the more likely it is the worker will respond to the impulses to become the "good" parent and rescue the child. In the absence of supervision and/or careful self-monitoring of practice, the countertherapeutic activity will proceed unchecked.

SUPERVISION AND SELF-MONITORING OF PRACTICE

Because the process of helping is interactive and involves the use of self in the helping relationship, and, furthermore, because it is difficult to be objective about one's own actions, supervision provides an opportunity for social workers to review their work and to learn about their own strengths and weaknesses in carrying out the helping process. As mentioned previously, the complexity of work with children makes supervision critically important, both for student social workers and for more seasoned practitioners. The two current registries of clinical social workers require a minimum of 2 years of post-master's-level supervision, and it is not uncommon for workers who wish to enhance their learning to arrange peer supervision groups or to make arrangements for private supervision, if their place of employment does not offer this opportunity.

When the worker/counselor/therapist becomes aware of a problem or impasse in the course of the helping process, it is the worker's responsibility to try to understand the reason for the breakdown. In a previous publication (Webb, 1989), I have reviewed some techniques that can be helpful in unlocking an impasse. Often such a difficulty stems from a similarity between the worker's own family background and that of the client he or she is trying to help. When these similarities are not recognized, the worker may unknowingly respond to the client (or to a member of the client's family) as if this person were a sibling or parent from the worker's own past. It must be emphasized that considerations of this type do not mean that supervision becomes therapy. "The *educational goal* of supervision argues against this occurrence and insists that the focus begin and end on the *work*" (Webb, 1983, p. 44; emphasis in original). Palombo (1985) challenges us to cast aside the past in our clients' best interests:

> We grow in our acceptance of our patients and we increasingly understand and accept ourselves. We grow also as with time and experience,

our knowledge is transformed into therapeutic wisdom, but over and above that, we grow as we accept the challenge to question the old, the tried and the true when it no longer works. (p. 47)

DISCUSSION QUESTIONS

1. How can the social worker best guide a parent whose child says that he or she does not want to go for "help"? How can the social worker try to engage this child, once the parent brings the child to the office?

2. If you have been assigned a new case involving a family from a culture about which you know nothing, what can you do in preparation for your first meeting with the clients? What can you do in the initial session with the clients to enhance your relationship with them?

3. Suppose that in the case conference about José, it becomes apparent that the foster care worker is vehemently opposed to the possibility of future family reunification following the mother's discharge from prison. The school social worker, knowing how much José misses his mother, favors a plan to reunite the family. How can the school social worker continue to collaborate with the foster care worker, in the face of this disagreement about goals?

4. How can a social worker best utilize supervision for his or her own learning? Please respond in terms of the "ideal" situation.

RECOMMENDED TEXTS ON CHILD BIOLOGICAL, PSYCHOLOGICAL, AND SOCIAL DEVELOPMENT

Brazelton, T. B. (1992). *Touchpoints: Your child's emotional and behavioral development.* Reading, MA: Addison-Wesley.—This book is the latest in more than 10 works for parents by a pediatrician who has both medical and psychoanalytic training; it includes information about child development from physical, cognitive, emotional, and behavioral points of view.

Erikson, E. H. (1993). *Childhood and society* (rev. ed.). New York: Norton.—Erikson's book outlines the eight stages of human development from birth to adulthood, emphasizing the developmental tasks at each stage. Erikson's conceptualization expands on Sigmund Freud's by viewing the individual in interaction with the social environment.

Freud, A. 1963). The concept of developmental lines. *Psychoanalytic Study of the Child, 18,* 245–265.—Anna Freud's view of child development emphasizes the push for growth that is intrinsic to human nature.

Freud, S. (1963). *The sexual enlightenment of children* (P. Rieff, Ed.) New York: Macmillan. (Original work published 1907)—Although many practitioners today consider Sigmund Freud's work culture-bound and sexist, he must be recognized as a pioneer who first gave attention to the concept that children can have sexual feelings, and who formulated a theory of childhood psychosexual development based on his retrospective work with adult patients.

Fraiberg, S. (1959). *The magic years.* New York: Scribner's.—This classic work, written by a social worker/child analyst, gracefully conveys solid knowledge about the preschool years in a readable style that belies its wealth of information.

Ilg, F. L., Ames, L. B., & Baker, S. M. (1981). *Child behavior* (rev. ed.). New York: Harper & Row.—This book is a classic guide and manual for parents, written by the cofounders of the Gesell Institute at Yale University.

Kagan, J. (1984). *The nature of the child.* New York: Basic Books.—An overview of child development is provided by a child development specialist.

Piaget, J., & Inhelder, B. (1969). *The psychology of the child.* New York: Basic Books.—This work establishes the framework of cognitive development of the child, pointing out basic differences in the thinking of children that affect their understanding of the world and their communications with adults. It is *essential* that practitioners working with young children understand and apply this conception of children's cognitive development in their work with children.

Thomas, A., Chess, S., & Birch, H. G. (1968). *Temperament and behavior disorders in children.* New York: New York University Press.—This landmark work documents the intrinsic childhood temperamental qualities that endure throughout life and resist modification by parents and other caretakers.

PART II

The Process of Helping Children: A Running Case Illustration of a Child in a Single-Parent Homeless Family

❖ CHAPTER 3 ❖

Building Relationships
with All Relevant Systems

Social workers often must reach out to needy children and families even when their attempts to help are ignored or refused. Families that are overwhelmed and burdened with survival concerns may prioritize their needs differently than do professional "helpers," who want to jump in and "rescue" dependent young children whose lives appear to be at risk because of adverse familial and/or environmental influences. The parents in such families may not agree with the professionals' views about the families' needs, thereby causing the helpers to struggle between conflicting ethical responsibilities to two sets of clients—that is, the children and the parents. A parent's right to self-determination and "the best interests of the child" are not always synonymous.

These dynamics ebbed and flowed in the case of Barbie Smith, who grew to the age of 10 in a family with a mother who was in prison for extended periods, a father who was physically abusive to her and her mother, and no positive role model who could instill hope for a better future. Barbie's life had always been unstable, with homelessness and lack of schooling her prevailing realities. The girl's situation demonstrates the challenge of helping children when their everyday environment victimizes rather than nurtures them. These are the unfortunate circumstances for many children for whom social workers attempt to provide services. Barbie's case is used to illustrate the gap between the ideal and the possible, as I describe, over the next three chapters, the process of helping children. This process begins with the challenge of establishing initial relationships with reluctant or resistant family members; it continues with formulating the biopsychosocial assessment of a child, and with planning and services to help in a manner that respects the family members' right to make choices in their own behalf.

---------------- ❖ ----------------

THE CASE OF BARBIE, AGE 10

> The ache for *home* lives in all of us, the safe place where we can go as we
> are and not be questioned. It impels mighty ambitions and dangerous
> capers. . . . [We hope] that . . . home will find us acceptable or, failing
> that, *that we will forget our awful yearning for it.* (Angelou, 1986/1991,
> p. 64; emphasis added)

Even a child who has had only *brief* periods of time in a "home" can
experience this feeling of longing. Barbie stated at the beginning of the
videotape *No Place like Home* (Hunt, 1992), "I'm afraid that we're never
going to get a home again of our own. It scares me." Barbie's life as depicted in this tape consisted of a series of moves from one motel or shelter to another, with no stability. Barbie's older brother, David, age 16, said,
"It's not that bad. Instead of renting a house, we rent our own motels."
Barbie, however, complained that she was getting tired of packing. A
photo of her hugging a doll as she buried her bowed head in the doll's
clothing (Figure 3.1) conveys the sadness and resignation that permeated
her life.

FIGURE 3.1. Barbie Smith, as she and her family were packing for yet another move.
Photograph by James E. Nicoloro. Reprinted by permission of the photographer and
the Smith family.

Background on the Case

At the beginning of the videotape, Barbie's mother confirmed that the family had moved seven times over a 6-month period, resulting in Barbie's attending *five different schools* during this time! When Barbie was eventually referred to a special school for homeless children, she came to the attention of a filmmaker, Kathryn Hunt, who obtained the mother's permission to tape the family and their various future moves over a period of time. I saw the resulting video at a professional meeting in connection with a presentation about the special school, First Place School in Seattle, Washington. Because I immediately recognized that Barbie's experience as a homeless child was like that of many disadvantaged children, and that it would be useful for teaching purposes, I decided to establish contact with Barbie's family, in order to obtain their permission to write about them in this book. Many months later, having finally obtained the signed releases and some of Barbie's school records, I now struggle with the task of presenting the family members' situation in all its complexity, while also trying to depict their lives with sensitivity and compassion. Their *prior* decision to be videotaped resulted in full disclosure of their identity and life circumstances. Nonetheless, I use only their first names and a fictitious last name, "Smith," in this discussion.

Family Information

Child client	Barbie, age 10, third grade; reading and writing below grade level. Physically abused in foster care at age 6.
Mother	Lori, age 34, unemployed, former bartender and drug abuser. Prison record for possession of drugs and firearms.
Father	Jim, age unknown, occupation unknown. Lived out of state; physically abused Lori and Barbie, according to Lori's and Barbie's statements on video. At time of referral, parents had been separated for 3 years and divorced for 1 year. Barbie had not seen her father since the divorce, although he maintained occasional telephone contact with her.
Brother	David, age 16, Lori's son by a previous partner (father's whereabouts unknown). School dropout; working on general equivalency diploma (GED).
Sister	Donna, age 18, Lori's daughter by another previous partner (father died of kidney disease). School dropout. At time of referral, living away from family, because mother disapproved of her boyfriend; later returned to live with family. Had kidney and heart problems.

The family was Caucasian; religious affiliation was unknown. Financial support came from Aid to Families with Dependent Children and food stamps.

Referral

The social worker at the shelter where the Smith family was then residing spoke to Mrs. Smith about a special school program for children like Barbie, who do not have permanent homes. Because this program provided transportation, Mrs. Smith agreed to take the bus with Barbie the next day in order to complete the necessary registration forms to enroll Barbie in the school. This school program was created to educate children who are "in transition" and to assist their families with counseling and other services. The application process, conducted by a social worker, includes a detailed history of the child and the family. Mrs. Smith cooperated fully with this process and openly shared information about her past incarceration and drug abuse, stating with pride that she had been "clean" since her release from prison 3 years earlier. She also revealed that Barbie and her siblings had each been physically abused in the separate foster homes in which they were placed while she was incarcerated.

IDENTIFICATION OF THE NEED FOR SERVICES

We can assume that homeless families have multiple problems and needs, including not only housing, but also concerns related to welfare and matters pertaining to schools, employment, and other agencies (Phillips, DeChillo, Kronenfeld, & Middleton-Jeter, 1988). In the case of Mrs. Smith, her reason for contacting the special school program for homeless children was to arrange for her daughter's education, which had been highly erratic during the previous 6 months. Every time the family had relocated, Mrs. Smith had enrolled Barbie in the nearest school. Mrs. Smith was not aware that the First Place program was different from the others, in that an array of services would now be available to her and her family.

Mrs. Smith as an "Involuntary" Client

Whereas a philosophy of support to *families* seems appropriate and necessary in order to help educate homeless children most effectively, Mrs. Smith came to First Place in connection with her youngest child's educational needs, rather than to obtain help for herself and her other children.

Her willingness to give family information to the intake worker reflected her belief that this was an expected part of the application procedure, rather than that she was applying for counseling or other forms of help. Indeed, the filmmaker (who later gained Mrs. Smith's trust over a period of time) clarified that because of the children's previous experiences of abuse in the foster care system when Mrs. Smith was in prison, she was wary and mistrustful of "the whole helping system." Thus it is understandable that she never attended any of the parent support group meetings that were held at First Place, even when transportation and babysitting were available. Another reason for her noninvolvement may have been her history as a former felon—a status that could have stigmatized and set her apart in the group, and prevented her sharing parenting and other life concerns with other single mothers. Perhaps these obstacles could have been anticipated and resolved on an individual basis if the social worker had prepared Mrs. Smith to enter the group.

Necessary Focus on Clients' Perceived Needs

Mrs. Smith's failure to avail herself of counseling services at the school highlights how important it is for social workers to understand the *clients'* point of view regarding their own needs for service. We cannot assume that *our* views about the clients' needs match the individuals' own assessments of the kinds of services they need or want. Mrs. Smith's top priority evidently was to find permanent housing for her family. She succeeded in this goal approximately 2 months after Barbie began at First Place; this resulted in Barbie's transfer to a neighborhood public school. In addition to housing, Mrs. Smith was concerned about obtaining medical care for Donna, who had kidney and heart ailments and who lived with the family sporadically. Also, Mrs. Smith was obligated to meet regularly with her parole officer and to have contact with the local department of social services in order to receive financial assistance. Dore (1993) notes that in work with poor families, "assistance in obtaining concrete resources is central, not adjunctive, to the helping process" (p. 552). Mrs. Smith proved able and willing to seek out the help she wanted for her family without assistance from professional helpers. She did not, however, identify a need for counseling for herself or for her children.

Figure 3.2 is an eco-map illustrating the various agencies with which Mrs. Smith had regular contact during the 2-month period that Barbie was enrolled at First Place School. None of these agencies, except the school, appeared to offer services related to helping with the emotional or interpersonal issues of individuals or the family unit. Because this fam-

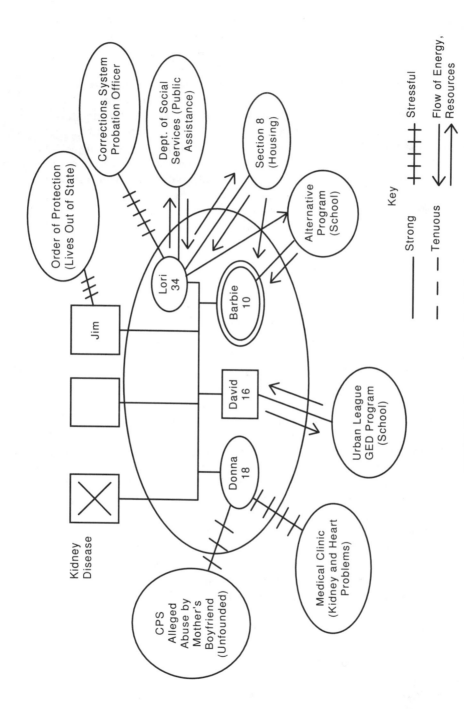

FIGURE 3.2. Eco-map of the Smith family.

ily had experienced numerous problems—spousal and father–child physical abuse; divorce and subsequent absence of the father; lengthy and stressful periods of maternal separation and child placement; conflict between the mother and a daughter (Donna); two children who dropped out of school (David and Donna); and the mother's drug abuse, imprisonment, and felony record—it seems obvious that some type of counseling in the form of family intervention and/or parent support would have been appropriate, to attempt to interrupt the intergenerational transmission of dysfunctional interaction patterns leading to violence, unhappiness, and dependence. Although provision of concrete services was essential, this brought only short-term relief, and did not address the prevention of future repetition of the same difficulties. The lack of *long-term* planning, goal setting, and counseling with the members of this family deprived them of the opportunity to extricate themselves from the cycle of homelessness and poverty that characterized their lives when they initially became known to First Place School.

How and by whom might counseling services have been offered and implemented in this situation? Certainly there was no lack of professional helpers involved in this case, as shown in the eco-map. Unfortunately, however, collaboration in *goal setting* among the helpers was not evident, with the result that Mrs. Smith probably felt scattered and unfocused in her efforts to help her family. The discussion that follows presents the "ideal" management of this case, in the hope that this retrospective analysis will lead to more effective interventions with others like the Smiths, who have multiple problems, multiple needs, and few resources with which to cope with the difficulties of their lives.

INTERAGENCY COLLABORATION ON BEHALF OF CHILDREN AND FAMILIES

The move away from the philosophy of "child rescue" to consideration of services as "family-supportive and family-strengthening" argues for delivery of services in a family's home or natural community environment (Whittaker, 1991). In addition, the recommendation to integrate and coordinate the mental health system with social welfare, juvenile justice, health, and special education to "form a more unified children's service system" (Lourie & Katz-Leavy, 1991, p. 277) suggests a new model of intervention that attempts to avoid fragmentation of services, while facilitating greater participation of parents in the care of their children. How might services have been better coordinated in this case? In order to put that question in context, we need first to consider Mrs. Smith's degree of openness to receiving help.

Work with the "Involuntary" Client

Mrs. Smith appears to have been uninterested in counseling services for herself and her family, although she did everything in her power to obtain financial, medical, and educational services on her family's behalf. Both of her daughters had received some form of counseling following their abuse in foster care 3 years earlier, and Mrs. Smith had participated in drug rehabilitation while she was in prison. She may have felt that these matters had been "taken care of."

Although the key to the family's well-being lay primarily in Mrs. Smith's hands, she did not currently perceive the need for counseling for herself. She may have associated this with being "weak" or "mentally ill" or "addicted." It was also possible that she was overwhelmed and even depressed, since we know that depression is more prevalent among persons at the lowest socioeconomic level (Dore, 1993). Moreover, Mrs. Smith's own childhood history of sexual assault (which she mentioned on the videotape) and her repeated experiences of victimization in her marriage could have resulted in learned helplessness (Hooker, 1976), feelings of hopelessness (Beck, Rush, Shaw, & Emery, 1979), and the inability to conceive of any improvement in her life (Browne, 1993). It certainly was sadly revealing when Mrs. Smith stated on the tape that she could not project what she wanted for Barbie's future, and Barbie, in turn, stated that she wanted to be just like her mom!

It was not clear whether Mrs. Smith's probation officer knew about her struggle to obtain housing, or whether anyone had ever made any efforts to help her obtain employment. She indicated on the school intake form that her difficulty in obtaining permanent housing was related to her "record." If this was indeed true, it would have contributed to feelings of discouragement and anger. This would have merited exploration with the probation department and the housing authority. One of the helpers involved in this case could have offered to make a phone call to clarify this matter.

Efforts to engage Mrs. Smith in counseling for herself would probably have failed unless these were tied directly to issues related to something of concern to *her*, such as Barbie's schooling. In presenting strategies for working with an "involuntary" client, Rooney (1988) suggests a "let's make a deal" proposal, in which something the client wants is paired with an issue considered essential by the worker. This permits the client to exercise some choice, thereby enhancing his or her autonomy and reducing possible resistance. An example of how this might have been presented to Mrs. Smith follows:

WORKER AT BARBIE'S SCHOOL: Mrs. Smith, we're concerned about Barbie's delayed skills in reading and writing. In addition, she does not have a very good sense of self-esteem, because her skills are not on the same level as other children her age. We're prepared to help her with the academics, but it will only work if you help her with her feelings about herself.

MRS. SMITH: How can I do that? I'll help in any way I can, but I don't really know what you mean.

WORKER: Maybe I can make a suggestion. I know how Barbie admires you; when we talk in school about what the children want to do when they get older, Barbie says that she wants to be just like you. That is a great compliment, since I know that your life has not been easy!

I wonder if we could help Barbie in a kind of roundabout way, by arranging some job training for *you*. A lot of the mothers of our students never had a chance to develop job-related skills, so we're going to have some special classes to help mothers just like you to figure out what kind of job training they want and then help them get it.

MRS. SMITH: I really don't like to go out at night and leave the kids alone in that place. It's full of pimps and addicts. Besides, I don't really see how doing this would help Barbie.

WORKER: Barbie needs to have more faith that girls can be successful in their lives. We don't want her to "give up" and think that she is "stupid" when she is only 10 years old and never had a chance to stay at one school long enough to learn.

We're going to have the job meetings in the morning. You can ride the bus with Barbie, and tell her that you're trying to figure out what you want to do with the rest of your life because you want a better life. You'll not only be helping yourself, but you'll be helping Barbie.

MRS. SMITH: OK. Just tell me when the first meeting is and I'll be there.

WORKER: It's day after tomorrow. We're going to start Barbie's special tutoring the same day. It's really important for you to tell Barbie that you and she are both going to try your best to improve your lives. If she knows that *you* are enthusiastic, it will help her feel optimistic. And I'm going to keep track of how you like your class. So I'll meet you after your class finishes day after tomorrow.

School-Based and Shelter-Based Service Models

As the preceding dialogue suggests, the issue of job training for single mothers is critical for homeless women if they are to overcome poverty and move beyond the extremely limited financial assistance provided by welfare. It seems logical for such employment counseling and training to take place in a school setting, since statistics indicate that two-thirds of homeless parents never graduated from high school (Nuñez, 1994). Another option for intergenerational education is the model of shelter-based education programs as implemented by the Homes for the Homeless project and study (Nuñez, 1994), which have demonstrated that both children and parents become more enthusiastic about school and education after as short a period as 8 weeks in family-based educational programs. The project's philosophy is that "it is education, rather than housing, that holds the greatest potential for ameliorating the deplorable crisis" (of homelessness; Nuñez, 1994, p. 29). Other authors (Dupper & Halter, 1994) have pointed out the lack of parents' involvement in their children's schooling as a key factor in the poor school attendance of many homeless children. Therefore, stimulating mothers' interest in furthering their *own* education brings positive benefits to their children.

The facts that Mrs. Smith's two older children had both dropped out of school, and that Barbie was absent for 15 out of 31 school days during the 2-month period when she was enrolled at First Place, suggested that Barbie was at risk of following in her siblings' footsteps. We do not have any information about Mrs. Smith's own schooling history. However, it seems clear that *all* of the Smiths would have benefited from educational counseling with regard to training for future employment. Shelter-based services as recommended by Nuñez unfortunately do not reach homeless families like the Smiths, who often resided in motels rather than shelters, and who moved frequently.

A school-based model of help, with the school social worker assuming an outreach role with homeless families in transitional housing, holds promise. However, it needs to be backed with transportation, career counseling, liaisons to welfare and probation counselors or officers, health services, and all social service providers with which homeless families have contact. It also requires that the social worker have a small enough caseload, as in the Homebuilders program (Kinney, Haapala, & Booth, 1991), to allow time to work intensively with each family for the period necessary to initiate some positive changes.

Commitment to Case Management and Collaboration

Homeless families headed by single women tend to have fewer and less stable support networks than those of families headed by poor women with housing (Bassuk, 1993). Because they may have exhausted the willingness or ability of their extended family members and friends to help them, these single mothers must rely upon social agencies to meet their basic needs. Unfortunately, many agencies fulfill the minimal requirements of client service without considering a wholistic approach to their clients' situations. Thus, in Mrs. Smith's case, her probation officer tended to focus primarily on whether she was drug-free, without attending to her housing or employment circumstances or to her children's needs. The coexistence of two unemployed teenagers in a shelter accommodation or a one-bedroom motel might be considered a disaster waiting to happen! However, when agencies shortsightedly address only the narrow concerns mandated by their specific purpose, preventive goals fall by the wayside.

The need for a case coordinator or case manager in this situation is evident, just as it was in the case of José (Chapter 2). Without this coordination, in fact, the helping efforts the Smiths did receive lacked the combined positive impact the family members would have experienced from a group of social service professionals organized to mount a united effort on their behalf (Schlosberg & Kagan, 1988).

There is no doubt that coordinating the various helpers in the Smiths' case would have taken time and effort. A single meeting, however, attended by the various personnel involved with this family, *together with the mother*, would have provided the opportunity to set realistic goals for each family member. The anticipated long-term benefits to the family of such collaboration would have made the effort worthwhile, and ultimately cost-effective. The lack of such planning and oversight deprived this family of the opportunity to benefit substantially from the separate helping efforts offered by the separate agencies involved with the family at the time of Barbie's referral to First Place School. (A follow-up regarding the circumstances of the family 2 years later appears at the end of Chapter 5. It compellingly portrays the chronicity of homelessness and its relentless intergenerational transmission, in the absence of counseling and long-term educational/employment intervention for all family members.)

ESTABLISHING PROFESSIONAL RELATIONSHIPS

The Smiths' case, like most, would have required that the social worker relate to many different individuals—both clients and other professionals—in the process of carrying out the social work role.

Relationships with Clients

Almost 20 years ago, Perlman (1979) identified the main features of professionals' relationships with clients as stemming from their purpose, their time-limited and client-centered nature, and the implicit expectation that the professional will exercise responsibility and self-control in carrying out his or her role. Beginning workers who relate easily and well in their *social* relationships soon learn that the worker–client relationship is quite different; it is essentially unbalanced, because of the primary focus on the client and on the purpose of the contact. The experience of personal validation through being the full center of another person's attention is a rare occurrence. The power of the professional relationship flows from its relative uniqueness in life, apart from infancy and the state of romantic love.

Perlman bases the attributes of relationship on Carl Rogers's client-centered approach to therapy (see Rogers, 1951), which emphasizes the special qualities of warmth, acceptance, empathy, caring/concern, and genuineness (Perlman, 1979, pp. 54–62). These attributes become evident in a helping relationship in which the worker listens carefully to the client's concerns, and communicates both verbally and nonverbally an attitude of acceptance. This positive relationship is the foundation for the worker–client alliance—a joining together for the purpose of working on some agreed-upon goals, once the client feels accepted by and "safe" with the worker.

Initiating Relationships by Telephone

Once a telephone appointment is made the worker–client relationship develops through face-to-face contact, since this offers the best opportunity for two people to meet and begin the process of getting to know one another. People communicate nonverbally through body language such as eye contact, posture, gestures, and dress. In conversations on the phone, these visual cues are absent, and the speakers must rely primarily on words and tone of voice. When clients make a telephone call to inquire about services, the worker obtains the necessary information about the referral in an abbreviated manner, knowing that the face-to-face interview will yield more extensive and possibly more reliable information.

When I decided to contact Mrs. Smith to obtain her permission to write about her family, I obtained her phone number from the filmmaker, Kathryn Hunt, with whom the family had a very positive relationship. Because my call occurred on the evening before the family was being evicted from the apartment they had lived in for almost a year, they were in the midst of packing and preparing to move (the same situation Ms. Hunt depicted in the video). I had to make several calls before I reached Mrs. Smith, and in the process I spoke briefly with David and with Barbie. Ms. Hunt had told Mrs. Smith that I would be calling, and what the purpose of my call was. Mrs. Smith had told Ms. Hunt that she would agree to my request, but I wanted to speak with her personally and ask her to sign release forms.

Because I had already seen all members of the Smith family in the videotape (Hunt 1992), I had their physical appearance in my mind as I was speaking to them. My initial comments to Barbie, to David, and to Mrs. Smith when I spoke to each of them referred to the video, and to my (telephone) relationship with Kathryn Hunt. My mention of Ms. Hunt's name was critical in the family's acceptance of me. I also identified myself as a professor of social work in New York, despite the risk that they might have negative feelings about social workers. This did not register as important in any way I could determine, because they (especially Barbie) were excited that I was calling from *New York*, and my association with Kathryn Hunt insured their willingness to speak with me.

My contact with Mrs. Smith surprised me in its intensity. When I said something to her about how impressed I was by her struggle to keep her family together, she began crying and spoke almost nonstop for at least 10 minutes. It was hard to understand everything she said because of her sobbing and her clipped, rapid speech; nonetheless, I sensed her strong need to vindicate herself and to reveal some of her own sad history. I shared with her my feelings of regret that I was so far away and therefore unable to offer any real assistance to the family. This did not seem to trouble Mrs. Smith, since her opening up to me seemed to serve the purpose of ventilation, rather than to indicate any expectation that I would help. Certainly I experienced Mrs. Smith as being very open to forming a helping relationship, and in no way would consider her as "resistant" or "involuntary" once I conveyed some genuine feelings to her.

Initiating Relationships with Child Clients

In beginning work with a child client, the worker needs to set the tone for a type of adult–child relationship that is different from others the child has experienced. The child has had limited life experience with different kinds of adults, and usually expects the worker to relate to him or her as a teacher or parent usually does, with corresponding expectations that the child "behave" in a proscribed manner. Because the nature of the helping relationship is so very different and unfamiliar to most children, it is the worker's responsibility to say something to the child, in language that the child can understand, about the nature of the helping process. A statement about who the worker is ("I'm a [lady, man, doctor] who helps children and parents with their troubles and worries") and about how the worker will help ("Sometimes we talk, and sometimes we play") gives the child the framework for this unique relationship, even though he or she may not comprehend it fully. It is also important to have some preliminary discussion with the child regarding the reason for the child's contact with the worker, since this is usually a source of conflict and anxiety for the child and the family. Children, like adults, deserve to be treated with honesty and respect as the basis for an effective helping relationship.

Using Toys to Engage and Work with Children

As will be apparent in many examples of intervention with children in this book, the preferred method for engaging and working with children involves the use of toys and play. Although children have limited verbal abilities, they communicate their worries and anxieties very graphically through play. Therefore, it is essential for social workers to have familiarity and a degree of comfort in using toys with children, in order to interact effectively with their young clients. I have conducted workshops across the United States and abroad for the purpose of helping social workers learn the rudiments of communicating with children through the symbolic language of play. Although mastery of the complexities of play therapy requires specialized knowledge and training, I believe that every social worker can and should have basic knowledge about working with children using play techniques. Given the likelihood of having to work with young children in family sessions, or in schools, foster care, residential settings, pediatric units of hospitals, mental health agencies, and family service agencies, social workers must be prepared to use both verbal and nonverbal communication in their interactions with child clients.

Figure 3.3 lists the basic play materials that should be available in every office to permit appropriate interactions with child clients, and the Appendices list a number of suppliers of these materials. Students who are beginning their careers and expect to work with children should begin to acquire play materials that they can carry with them in a tote bag, so that they will not be dependent upon the presence of supplies in the particular offices where they are doing their internships. In a previous publication (Webb, 1991), I have reviewed various play materials and their use in work with young clients. In the present book, examples of the use of drawings can be found in Chapters 4–8 and 10–14; an example of puppet play is given in Chapter 7; and examples of the use of family dolls are provided in Chapters 11, 12, and 15. A videotape demonstrating play techniques is also available (Webb, 1994b).

Trying to engage young children in a helping relationship without the use of toys and play materials would be as unthinkable as trying to communicate with a deaf person without the use of sign language. A young child may have a rudimentary understanding of verbal communication, and a hearing-impaired person may be able to communicate in writing or may have some knowledge of lip reading, but neither situation respects the basic principle of "starting where the client is." Children (and the physically challenged) have too often been overlooked and treated like inferior beings. Attention to the concept of "adultcentrism" (Petyr, 1992; Tyson, 1995) and its call for more equitable treatment of children demands that social workers accord children the rights that are

---

Drawing materials

File folders with variety of colored papers.
(Papers include special ethnically colored paper.)
Colored markers (washable; two sets, one "thin," one "fat"). (The fat markers are available in multicultural colors so children can realistically portray their ethnic identity.)

Cutting and pasting

Scissors, two sets with blunt ends. Glue.
Stapler for making "books." Scotch tape.

Dolls and puppets

Bendable family dolls (available in Hispanic, black, white, and Asian).
Most sets include mother, father, boy, girl, baby.
Optional varieties of hard plastic and wooden dolls include a variety of workers, the elderly, and the physically different.
Hand puppets available as family puppet figures.
Animal puppets (in selecting animals, choose two or three "aggressive" and two or three "neutral").

Miniature doll furniture

Kitchen (small table, chairs, refrigerator, stove, sink).
Bedrooms (double bed and single beds). (Other rooms available.)

Games

Card game: Feelings in Hand (Western Psychological Services, Los Angeles, CA).
Board game: Talking, Feeling, and Doing Game
(Creative Therapeutics, Cresskill, NJ).

Optional items

Play-Doh (four colors). Doctor kit. Tape recorder.
Toy telephones (2). Blocks, beginner set.

FIGURE 3.3. Equipping the "average" office for work with children.

due them, beginning with the use of communication methods that are "user-friendly" to child clients.

Relationships with Other Professionals

Any social worker involved with providing services to children will, of necessity, have reason to interact with other professionals. Depending on the circumstances of the particular case, it may be necessary and appropriate to collaborate with the following range of persons who may have contact with the child:

- The child's teacher
- The school psychologist
- The child's special education teacher
- The child's physician
- The child's caseworker/guardian *ad litem* (i.e., a lawyer or other individual assigned to protect the child's legal interests)

Necessary procedures must be followed prior to any discussion with other professionals. *A social worker must have signed releases from a child's parent(s) prior to engaging in any contact with others involved in the case.* In addition to obtaining these releases, it is a good idea to discuss with the parent(s) just how much information about the family they are comfortable about having the worker disclose (Wachtel, 1994). For example, parents may understand the importance of the worker's learning about test results (either medical or education), in connection with the agreed-upon purpose of helping their child with self-esteem issues. However, they may not see the utility of the worker's sharing information about his or her psychosocial assessment and intervention with school personnel. Wachtel (1994) points out how helpful it can be for the teacher to be able to reinforce certain goals with the child in the classroom, so that the teacher, parents, and worker are all emphasizing the same objectives. When this is presented to parents as in their child's best interests, the parents usually will permit the worker to use his or her professional judgment regarding what to share with others.

As a rule, a worker should exercise restraint about sharing family information that is not directly related to helping the child. Other professionals do not necessarily subscribe to the same code of confidentiality as that of the social work profession, and once personal matters move into the "public" domain, the clients' right to privacy can no longer be guaranteed. A continuing focus on the *purpose* of sharing information will help determine what and how much to share; the best interests of the clients should be the guiding ethical principle in each instance.

CONCLUDING COMMENTS

The quality of relationships between clients and a social worker, and among the various helpers in a specific case, often determines the success or failure of the helping contact. Positive relationships can inspire motivation and hope for change, whereas negative relationships can reinforce feelings of futility and even hostility. Because of the *purposive* focus of the helping relationship, a client can begin to believe that something different can happen, and that he or she will receive assistance in planning and creating a life change. Listening carefully to the client's vision of what he or she wants is the key to the worker's understanding and empathy. Weick and Pope (1988) point out that the client's views may be different from what the worker envisions, and that true client self-determination flows from the worker's appreciation and respect for the inner meaning of the client's reality.

This principle of respect for the client applies in work with children through the necessity for adults to communicate with children in *their* language of play, rather than expecting children to use words exclusively. A relationship between a social worker and a child client therefore makes special demands on the worker, who must join with the child on his or her developmental level, while simultaneously attempting to comprehend the meaning of the child's play so that the worker can respond helpfully within the play metaphor.

Similarly, the need to convey respect applies when working collaboratively with other professionals. There may be differences in language and viewpoints between a social worker and other professionals, such as teachers or physicians. The very attempt on the worker's part to understand how another professional views the client's situation conveys an attitude of appreciation for the contribution of the other individual. If terminology or language differences interfere with understanding, it is appropriate for the worker to ask for clarification.

Workers who use family and small-group modalities are familiar with the need to maintain a neutral stance and to listen and observe each member, without forming alliances with any one person. The same principle applies in work with the many individuals involved in most helping situations. The goal of objectivity does not imply coldness, but rather the ability to relate to many different people according to their own specific needs, and to keep the purpose of all relationships clearly in mind.

DISCUSSION QUESTIONS AND ROLE-PLAY EXERCISES

1. Imagine that you are the school social worker assigned to work with the Smith family. Consider where, how, and with which family member(s) you would structure the *first* meeting. Give reasons for your decision.

2. Role-play several alternative scenarios of the initial meeting with the Smith family, such as the following:

    a. With Mrs. Smith and the worker, at the school.
    b. With Mrs. Smith, Barbie, and the worker, at the school.
    c. With Barbie and the worker, at the school.
    d. With the entire family, at the shelter.

After the completion of all of these, discuss the different type of information obtained in each format, and the relative degree of pressure on the worker in each interview situation.

3. Again, imagine that you are the school social worker. What other professionals would you want to contact in connection with your work with Barbie and Mrs. Smith? How would you approach Mrs. Smith to gain her approval of these contacts? Role-play this exchange.

❖ C H A P T E R 4 ❖

The Biopsychosocial
Assessment of the Child

Most social workers rely on assessments and treatment plans to guide them in their work. The process of helping a child depends on understanding as fully as possible *all* the factors that have contributed to and that are maintaining a problematic situation, so that a worker can formulate, propose, and implement an appropriate remedy. Because "the problem" as presented by the parents, by the school, or by others often represents only the tip of the iceberg, and there is a great deal more material beneath the surface, it is essential to look up, down, and all around while trying to analyze the totality of the problem situation. For example, parents may refer a child because of his or her troublesome behavior when the "real" problem is their disturbed marriage, to which the child is reacting. In Barbie's situation (Chapter 3), Mrs. Smith identified Barbie's educational needs, but not the family's lack of stability and multiple problems.

Before embarking upon a course of action with a child and family, a social worker must have a clear sense of the strengths and weaknesses of the vessel in which all parties are traveling, as well as of the possible detours and obstacles that may be encountered in trying to reach the destination. It is also essential to know about the possible rescue resources available in the event of an emergency. The biopsychosocial assessment functions like a compass and a nautical chart: It assists the worker in navigating toward the goal desired by the child and the family.

WHAT IS AN ASSESSMENT?

Meyer (1993) describes assessment as "the thinking process that seeks out the meaning of case situations, puts the particulars of the case in some order, and leads to appropriate interventions" (p. 3). Although the assessment process is time-consuming, and often difficult because of its complexity, it may reveal exciting discoveries. The worker, like an explorer or a detective, uncovers as much as possible about the presenting problem in order to determine its history, magnitude, and ramifications.

Factors to Include in Assessments

Northen (1987, p. 172) stresses the *appraisal* component of assessment, in which the worker analyzes the interrelationship among biological, psychological, and sociocultural factors in the context of a client's positive motivations and capacities. Defining assessment as "the worker's professional opinion about the facts and their meaning" (p. 179), Northen maintains that "the content of assessment is essentially psychosocial in nature" (p. 175), because that focus conforms to the purpose of social work. However, social workers must also consider and include biological elements in their assessments. Recognition of the potential importance of biological factors (e.g., temperament and prenatal addiction) in children's problems may lead a social worker to identify the need for specialized medical, psychological, or educational evaluations and refer such children accordingly.

For example, in assessing the factors contributing to Barbie Smith's poor school performance (Chapter 3), the school social worker might have considered the possibility that her academic delays were perhaps related to fetal alcohol/addiction syndrome, because the mother had probably used substances during her pregnancy with Barbie. The fact that Barbie changed schools so frequently may have been only partially responsible for her academic difficulties. Had timely testing been completed, and specific disabilities been revealed, Barbie's educational planning could have targeted remediation of her specific learning deficits.

Important Points about Assessment

1. Collecting data during the initial phase of work does not mean that the client's pressing needs for immediate help are put on hold while the worker systematically and single-mindedly goes about formulating the biopsychosocial assessment. *Assessment and intervention typically occur simultaneously.*

2. The assessment process is not over when the biopsychosocial summary is written. *Assessment is an ongoing process*, and therefore subject to elaboration and revision throughout the contact with the clients.

3. Assessment of children is always tentative, because children's development is in flux. *Child evaluations, therefore, should be repeated periodically to allow for normal developmental changes.*

CONFLICTING (AND SOMETIMES CONFUSING) ISSUES IN ASSESSMENT

Before describing the components and process of making an assessment, I want to examine some myths and issues that have arisen because of changing views about social work practice and social workers' roles. Perceptions about the nature of client–worker interactions have evolved substantially since the publication of Mary Richmond's *Social Diagnosis* in 1917. The following three changes in role conceptualizations have become evident in regard to the assessment process:

1. The growing antimedical bias among social workers.
2. Shifting preferences about the nature of the social worker's role (i.e., a move away from the role of "expert" and toward one of egalitarian partnership with the client).
3. The perceived dichotomy between linear and systemic thinking.

The Antimedical Bias

There has been growing disapproval of terms such as "diagnosis" and "treatment," which reflect a "medical model" of practice. This model is derived from social work's association with physicians and psychiatrists in clinics and other health and mental health settings—an association that began in the 1920s and continues to the present day. As social work "came of age" as an independent profession, social workers began in the 1960s to use alternative terms: "assessment" instead of "diagnosis," "intervention" instead of "treatment," "client" instead of "patient," and so on. However, social workers who are employed in medical settings and in other settings (e.g., child guidance, mental health, and family service clinics) that require *Diagnostic and Statistical Manual of Mental Disorders* (DSM) diagnoses for insurance reimbursement purposes must understand and speak this medical language in order to communicate with their medical colleagues, and in order to prepare reports that enable their agencies to receive payment for services rendered. In addition, students who are placed in medical settings for their fieldwork training must also learn and adhere to these agencies' practices in regard to language. These students become confused and concerned about whether it is acceptable in class and in term papers to refer to their clients as "patients" when their professors express an antimedical bias.

In my view, this unfortunate and unnecessary state of affairs denigrates the medical and psychiatric subspecialties that constitute a legitimate segment of social work's heritage and current practice. As long as schools of social work continue to train students in medical/clinical settings, and social work graduates continue to accept employment in them, it seems to me to be counterproductive and disingenuous to criticize and renounce the operative language of these settings. Social workers, in fact, have influenced physicians to broaden *their* concept of assessment, as reflected in Axes IV and V of the DSM diagnostic profile (American Psychiatric Association, 1994). Axis IV lists psychosocial and environmental problems as these pertain to the individual's situation, and Axis V rates the individual's psychosocial, social, and occupational functioning.

Enthusiasm for social work's broader, more systemic approach to assessment, which includes environmental factors (see, e.g., the Person-in-Environment assessment system; Karls & Wandrei, 1994), must not cause workers to abandon recognition of individual clients' troubled and troublesome feelings and behavior when these constitute bonafide Axis I diagnoses of clinical disorders, according to designated criteria. Turner (1994) distinguishes between "assessment" and "diagnosis," and argues persuasively for retaining *both* terms in our professional vocabulary, because diagnosis "forces us to think concretely about our clients" and because it "describes the factual basis on which accountable actions are initiated" (p. 169). Turner also reminds us that "diagnosis is not the sole property of the *medical* profession" (p. 168, emphasis added). Thus, despite the Smith family's numerous and severe problems in social functioning, which would have been cited on Axes IV and V of Barbie's multiaxial DSM diagnosis, the child may also have merited one or more Axis I diagnoses labeling her serious educational deficits. The specifics of Barbie's DSM diagnoses are discussed later in this chapter.

The Shift from an "Expert" to an "Egalitarian" Role

The worthy goal of client empowerment (Meyer, 1993), combined with postmodern views emphasizing the importance of the client's subjective experience (Hartman, 1991), seems contrary to the notion of the social worker as an "expert." Instead, some social workers now cast themselves in an egalitarian role with clients, who are expected to set their own goals and methods for reaching them.

In the abstract, this philosophy of respect for the individual emphasizes the value of self-determination and is very appealing. However, in actual practice, this view seems insensitive to overwhelmed clients' genuine need and desire to rely on someone who offers understanding based on professional experience and education beyond their own. Certainly social workers must not encourage clients' long-term dependence. However, clients often benefit, *in the short term*, from the direction and structure provided by a social worker who understands that the clients are floundering in the face of multiple stressors, and who offers them a temporary respite from having to make all the decisions alone. Once such a respite has been provided, successful helping aims to involve clients in efforts on their own behalf as much and as soon as possible. Therefore, when a professional "expert" initially offers specific guidance, this is done with the clear understanding that this is temporary and that when a client is ready, he or she will assume increasing responsibility for self-direction. The "expert" encourages the client to consider alternatives and weigh the consequences of different decisions.

For example, the videotape *No Place like Home* (Hunt, 1992) concluded with the announcement that Barbie Smith's father had mailed her a one-way ticket to visit him out of state. It would have been beneficial, in my opinion, for the mother and child to have discussed with a professional the pros and cons of whether Barbie should go. Plans for Barbie's schooling were not clear when she left, nor was there an agreement in place regarding her return to her mother. A social worker could have assisted the family in thinking through these matters in a way that respected Barbie's wish to see her father, while also raising legitimate, reality-based concerns *before* Barbie's departure.

The goal of client empowerment (letting clients decide for themselves what is best for them) can backfire when the outcome is negative. In contrast, when a responsible professional "expert" helps a client anticipate obstacles, this actually contributes to stacking the deck favorably toward success, and results in the client's feeling confident and truly "empowered."

The Dichotomy between Linear and Systemic Thinking

The social work profession has benefited greatly from the wider perspective of systemic thinking (Hearn, 1958; Janchill, 1969; Hartman, 1970; Germain, 1968; Meyer, 1983; Nelsen, 1975), which encourages a broad view of all the complex interacting variables in any one case. Use of the eco-map (Hartman, 1978), the genogram (McGoldrick & Gerson, 1985), and the culturagram (Congress, 1994) can result in deeper and more comprehensive understanding of the different people and unique experiences that shape a given problem situation. Perlman (1979) pointed out that empathic feeling develops from greater understanding. There is no doubt that the more a worker knows about a case, the better able the worker is to empathize with the client and comprehend the case's many facets. However, the worker will probably never have *all* the fragments of the puzzle, and frequently he or she must try to see the larger picture despite the missing pieces.

A systems perspective employs a wide-angle lens. In work with children, however, the etiology of their problem behaviors can sometimes be "zoomed in on" rather clearly. For example, Anna's nightmares after her apartment building burned down in the middle of the night (Chapter 7), and Sabrina's problems in concentrating in school when her mother was about to be hospitalized for surgery (Chapter 12), both seemed to be reactive to a recent stressful experience. In each instance it was helpful to know about other family members and friends who could be available as sources of support, but it was not necessary to complete a genogram, eco-map, and culturagram to understand the derivation of the child's symptoms and to formulate a diagnosis. Therefore, in my work with children I embrace *both* linear and systemic thinking, and I do not consider this contradictory. Although I find it essential to think systemically in the process of treatment planning, a simpler, linear approach often suffices for determining the diagnosis, especially in situations involving a clear precipitating stressor of recent origin.

THE ASSESSMENT PROCESS

The purpose of conducting an assessment is to understand the multiplicity of factors that are contributing to the presenting problem, so that an agreement can be made about how to alleviate it. The following basic questions must be considered in planning the steps of the assessment:

1. Who/what is to be assessed? (Child? Parents? Entire family or subsets of the family? Peers? Neighborhood?)
2. What collateral information should be obtained? (School, medical, psychological, legal reports?)
3. In what order should the assessment be conducted? (Should parents, child, or whole family be seen first?) And what general guidelines should be followed in contacts with each party?
4. What assessment tools should be employed? (A few of the options for selection: Developmental history and family background; tripartite assessment forms; genograms, eco-maps, etc.; DSM-IV; psychological and educational testing.)

5. How should the relevant data be summarized?
6. How should the assessment be reviewed with parents and others?

I devote the remainder of this chapter to discussing these questions.

DETERMINING WHO/WHAT IS TO BE ASSESSED

Determining the "unit of attention" is a basic task in beginning work with any case situation. Most individuals live in families, and these families, in turn, are subject to both the favorable and the noxious influences of their surrounding environment. A systems viewpoint recognizes that every part is influenced by the whole to which it belongs, just as the whole, in turn, is affected by its individual members. Chapter 1 has discussed and diagrammed an ecological perspective on etiology, upon which this chapter expands. In two previous books (Webb, 1991, 1993), I have presented different versions of a tripartite conceptionalization of assessment, taking account of three groups of factors that interact and provide balancing effects in any assessment:

• Factors related to the individual
• Factors related to the problem situation
• Factors related to the support system

When a child comes to the attention of a social worker, it is imperative that the worker keep these three general categories of factors in mind as he or she tries to understand the complex dimensions of the problem situation. Like a juggler tossing balls into the air sequentially and keeping them aloft, the worker must possess the ability to divide his or her attention among the numerous people and events related to the particular case. Figure 4.1 diagrams the interactive components of a tripartite assessment.

I have developed three different forms to guide the worker in obtaining, organizing, and recording information preparatory to formulating a biopsychosocial assessment. These are presented and discussed in the section on assessment tools later in this chapter. The amount of information to be collected can seem overwhelming, especially to the beginning social worker, who may not immediately comprehend its relevance. It is important to stress that the purpose of data collection is to guide the worker in setting goals and planning intervention strategies. Therefore, while my assessment model is comprehensive, in order to apply to a wide range of problem situations, each separate assessment need not include information on *all* the items listed on the forms. *The worker's judgment about the relevant factors in each case situation guides the assessment process accordingly.*

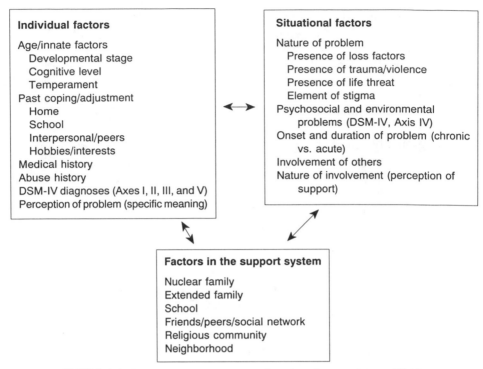

FIGURE 4.1. Interactive components of a tripartite assessment: Webb.

OBTAINING COLLATERAL INFORMATION

Information about a child and family usually comes from a number of sources, in addition to the personal observations and interviews of the social worker. These other sources of data include reports of the clients' past contacts with other agencies, in addition to summaries of past and current school, medical, and legal contacts. Except for existing past records in the same agency, *releases must be signed by the client (or the client's parents) before the worker can request collateral information.* Sometimes a client arranges to have reports sent directly to a worker, after signing necessary releases for the reporting agency. However, more typically, in the first meeting with a client or parent the intake worker determines the collateral information that is relevant, discusses this with the client/parent and obtains his or her signature prior to requesting the information.

In cases involving children, some agencies routinely ask parent(s) to sign releases to obtain the child's school and medical records. Occasionally a parent objects to having the school know that a child is receiving counseling, and if the problem is not school-related, there is no necessity to obtain school records. For example, a child with a sibling/family conflict may be doing well in the academic sphere, and this would make school and medical records superfluous. However, in cases when the worker believes that school records are essential, he or she may need to help parents with their negative feelings about the school as a helping resource for their children.

Sometimes a worker decides to speak with a child's teacher and make a school visit. Sometimes a home visit is appropriate in order to observe a child's interaction with a babysitter, or to assess the atmosphere in the home. Often a telephone conference with the child's pediatrician is helpful, especially if the child has somatic complaints. When the child's troublesome behavior is the focus of concern, the worker may ask the parents and the teacher to fill out a behavior checklist (see "Assessment Tools," below). Again, the decision about what information to obtain depends on the circumstances in each case and the worker's judgment about what information will lead to improved understanding.

ORDER AND GENERAL GUIDELINES FOR ASSESSMENT

The Usual Order of Assessment for a Child Client

It is a truism that first impressions may be lasting. Therefore, a social worker must consider carefully the impact of seeing one family member before another. The worker's observations and impressions weigh heavily in the assessment process, and when the worker interviews one family member prior to another, that individual enjoys the possible advantage of having his or her point of view heard *first*. Sometimes the worker inadvertently forms an alliance with the family member seen first, thereby putting members who are seen later at a disadvantage. Ideally, the worker remains neutral and objective, regardless of the order in which clients are seen.

The usual order of assessment, when the presenting client is a child, is as follows:

1. The worker meets with the parent(s). In situations of separation or divorce, contact with the noncustodial parent may involve a separate interview or a telephone conference.

2. The worker conducts two or three play evaluation sessions with the child.

3. The worker sees the entire family when the problem situation seems to have reverberations for other family members. (This step may be postponed until later or, in some cases, may never occur.)

4. (Optional) The worker contacts the child's teacher by telephone, and, depending on circumstances, makes a school visit and/or requests school records. (See "Obtaining Collateral Information," above.)

5. The worker refers the child for psychological or educational testing, if appropriate.

6. The worker obtains a report from the child's pediatrician. (See "Obtaining Collateral Information.")

General Guidelines for Contacts with the Parent(s)

There are several important reasons to see the parent(s) first when the child is under 10 years of age:

- To form an alliance with the parents (essential for ongoing work with the child)
- To obtain a developmental history of the child, including matters the parent(s) may not wish to discuss in the child's presence
- To prepare the parent(s) to prepare the child for the assessment sessions
- To obtain signed releases for all collateral contacts

General guidelines for pursuing the first three of these goals follow.

Forming an Alliance with the Parent(s)

Helping children requires that the worker include parents as essential partners in helping their children. When parents are not included, the worker walks the dangerous ground of ignoring the very roots of children's identity and being. Insofar as a child's identity consists of his or her dual inheritance from a male and a female parent, the child instinctively attributes the basis of his or her identity to those two people. Even when a parent is unknown, the child has fantasies about that parent, which may reflect the child's expectations about his or her own future life.

Most parents are imperfect, insofar as they are human, and some are so disabled by their own upbringing that they do not know how to parent effectively. Work with children is complicated by the fact that the counselor has to deal not only with appealing youngsters who may be "victimized," but also with parents who, out of ignorance or desperation, may have "caused" or substantially contributed to their children's problems. Blaming a parent, however, is *never* productive, and may ultimately result in a worker's inability to help a child. Even in the most compellingly incriminating situations of parent neglect, abuse, criminality, and/or abandonment, we must not minimize parents' ongoing influence on their children. A child who was unwanted, resented, and abused by a parent must constantly cope with the meaning of this rejection. Eventually the child must come to some understanding about the abuse related to the parent's own deficiencies, but this realization usually does not occur until adulthood. Parents are major influences in their children's lives, both in reality and as symbols. Workers, therefore, must put all judgments aside and find ways to include parents in the process of assessing and helping.

Obtaining the Child's Developmental History

The assessment of a child is difficult because of the many factors that may contribute to the child's presenting problem. Obtaining the developmental history serves two purposes: (1) It provides a template against which to measure the course of the child's emotional and physical growth; and (2) it gives a sense of the family environment into which the child was born and in which he or she has developed. The developmental history form presented later in this chapter is one of several assessment tools. The history should be obtained either from a parent or from someone else who has been intimately involved in the child's upbringing.

In addition to the specifics of the child's development, the worker learns a great deal from the *manner* in which the parent or other caretaker conveys the information. Does he or she seem to take pride in the child's development, or is the child pictured as troublesome and annoying? Sometimes a parent can remember very little about the child's early life, which suggests that the parent was or is not very tuned in to the child. Possibly a mother's difficulty recalling details results from postpartum depression or drug/alcohol abuse, and the worker may appropriately inquire about this.

For example, in the process of obtaining information from Mrs. Smith about Barbie's language and social development, a sensitive school social worker would have empathized with Mrs. Smith's life circumstances during Barbie's early childhood. The worker's caring attitude might have encouraged this mother of three children and victim of spousal abuse to openly acknowledge her use of drugs and alcohol as a means of dealing with her depression and frustration at this time. Had Barbie been present during the intake, Mrs. Smith might not have felt comfortable disclosing her own addictive behavior. Barbie was 10 years old at the time of the referral to the special school program for homeless children, and Mrs. Smith brought her daughter with her when she visited the school to enroll her. Under these circumstances, it is usually possible for the school social worker to arrange a private meeting with the mother to obtain the history and release forms, while the child visits the classroom.

Preparing the Parent to Prepare the Child for the Assessment

Although this was not what happened in Barbie's case, a parent often applies for services for a child and meets with an intake worker without the child's being present. An example is the case of Tammy, age 4 (Chapter 7), whose serious separation problem in nursery school prompted her teacher to suggest that the mother obtain some counseling to alleviate the child's unhappy, withdrawn behavior.

In situations like this, when a parent meets with the worker first, the worker then has the opportunity to help the parent think about how to prepare the child for subsequent meetings with the worker. Parents often want to avoid telling their child anything ahead of time, possibly because they themselves feel uncomfortable about "the problem" and because they do not know what to say to the child. I have found that parents are very relieved when I give them explicit suggestions. First, I propose that they tell their child that because they have been concerned about the fact that they can't seem to help him or her, they have found and spoken with somebody who "helps children and families with their troubles and worries." I further suggest that the parents tell the child that they will be bringing the child to see this person, who has toys and who helps children "sometimes by talking and sometimes by playing with them." I assure parents that, if necessary, they may remain with their child during part or all of the session, depending on the child's level of comfort. I also convey my experience that most children greatly *enjoy* the assessment sessions, so that the parents will approach their child with an optimistic spirit.

General Guidelines for Assessment Sessions with the Child

It is usually advisable to see children for two or three play evaluation sessions. The child's behavior with a stranger during the first session may not be typical, and, in any case, the worker will need to see repeated examples of the child's behavior before coming to any conclusions.

The First Session

The most important task of the worker in the first session is to establish a relationship with the child in which the child feels understood, listened to, and respected as a person. Initially the child will expect the worker to be like other adults, such as parents or teachers, so the worker must make a point during the first session of clarifying the helping role. The worker may ask the child something like this: "Did your mother explain to you who I am, and why she brought you here?" (Most children do not answer this question clearly.) As suggested in Chapter 3, the worker can then say something like the following: "I am a [doctor, lady, man] who helps children and their parents with their troubles and their worries. Do you know what 'worries' are? [Pause for child's response.] Sometimes we'll be talking, and sometimes we'll play."

Preparing the Office for Child Evaluation Sessions. Evaluation sessions differ from the less structured play therapy or helping sessions that may follow the assessment. Just as the social worker beginning with an adult client usually follows an interview guide in obtaining specific information during the intake, the play therapist or social worker who is meeting a child client for the first time needs to prepare in advance and have planned activities and appropriate materials on hand. The worker selects these to serve the dual purpose of (1) making the child client feel comfortable (by offering age-appropriate play material), and (2) providing the worker with information that will assist in understanding the nature and scope of the child's difficulties. Therefore, the office setup for an evaluation session with a 9-year old differs from that for a 4-year-old because of the types of play materials that the worker makes available to each child.

In evaluation/assessment sessions I have a limited number of toys in view, in order to avoid overstimulating the child and causing scattered play. Table 4.1 outlines suggested play materials for assessment sessions with children of different ages. This table is only a general guide, and should not be used rigidly. Work with children requires spontaneity, flexibility, and a tolerance for surprise; the overriding obligation is to respond to the uniqueness of each child.

Suggested Activities for the First Session. I provide drawing materials to children of all ages, and routinely ask them in the first session to make two specific drawings: (1) the Draw-A-Person, and (2) the Draw-A-Family. When a child spends a long time on the first drawing, and appears to have expended a great deal of effort on this task, I do not ask him or her to complete another drawing during that session. On the other hand, some children can readily complete both a Draw-A-Person and a Draw-A-Family, with energy and enthusiasm. I then invite these children to do a third drawing that can be anything they wish (optional drawing). My videotape *Techniques of Play Therapy* (Webb, 1994b) illustrates different responses of three children in initial sessions to my request that each child make some drawings. The youngest child, Trey, age 3½, refused to draw anything; 5-year-old Willie spent more than 10 minutes completing his Draw-A-Person (Figure 4.2); and the third child, Natalie, age 4½, completed a Draw-A-Person, a Draw-A-Family, and an optional drawing within a 5-minute interval (Figures 4.3–4.5).

TABLE 4.1. Suggested Play Materials for Assessment Sessions with Children of Different Ages

Materials	Ages 3–5	Ages 6–7	Ages 8–10
Colored paper	×	×	×
Colored markers	×	×	×
Scissors	×	×	×
Glue, Scotch tape	×	×	×
Play-Doh	×	×	
Clay		×	×
Small, bendable family dolls	×	×	
Dollhouse furniture (especially kitchen and bedroom)	×	×	
Blocks	×	×	
Animal puppets	×	×	×
Feelings in Hand card game (see Figure 3.3)		×	×
Talking, Feeling, and Doing Game (see Figure 3.3)		×	×

The worker must be attuned to the child's ability and level of energy, and should tailor requests for specific drawings to this. Future sessions will provide additional opportunities to obtain further drawings from the child. The worker should keep in mind that establishing a relationship with the child is the primary goal in the first session, and that the toys and activities are means to that important end.

After a child has completed one or more drawings, I usually suggest a change of activity. If the child is age 7 or younger, I introduce a set of small family dolls and doll furniture, and suggest that the child might like to make up a story about this family. Children over age 7, especially boys, may not want to play with dolls, so I typically offer puppets or "therapeutic" (i.e., special/structured) board or card games to older children.

Subsequent Sessions

During the second and third play assessment sessions, I follow a pattern similar to that of the first session. That is, I usually begin by asking the child whether he or she would like to draw, and then introduce other toys and activities. Of course, the child remembers the first session and often comes to subsequent meetings eager to resume a play activity he or she enjoyed in the first session. The worker should take special note of all such requests, since they may have particular significance in understanding the child's circumstances.

FIGURE 4.2. Willie's Draw-A-Person. From Webb (1994b). Copyright 1994 by The Guilford Press. Reprinted by permission.

What to Look For in Child Evaluation Sessions

During the evaluation, the social worker is trying to learn as much as possible about the child by observing the child's play and the manner in which he or she relates. After each play session, the worker should take some notes about the following aspects of the child's behavior:

1. *Developmental factors: Age-appropriateness of child's play.* What developmental tasks/issues and concerns are typical of the "average" child of the age under consideration? The worker should evaluate the child's play (including drawings) in terms of age-appropriateness.

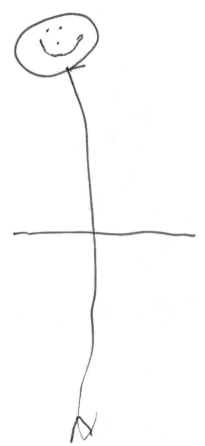

FIGURE 4.3. Natalie's Draw-A-Person. From Webb (1994b). Copyright 1994 by The Guilford Press. Reprinted by permission.

2. *Mood/quality of child's play.* How can this child's play be characterized with regard to the dimension of creativity–constrictiveness? Has this varied over the course of the session(s)? In instances where constriction is noted in the child's play, does this appear to be evidence of anxiety or of the child's temperament?

3. *Themes in child's play and possible areas of conflict.* What significant themes can be noted in the child's play? How often do those themes occur? And what factors in the child's life might they stem from? (This last question is merely speculative; however, *numerous* occurrences of aggressive or abandonment play themes [for example] should be noted for further exploration, as should other themes, such as nurturance.) Are

FIGURE 4.4. Natalie's Draw-A-Family. From Webb (1994b). Copyright 1994 by The Guilford Press. Reprinted by permission.

FIGURE 4.5. Natalie's optional drawing. From Webb (1994b). Copyright 1994 by The Guilford Press. Reprinted by permission.

there similarities or differences between the types of conflicts or problem situations presented by the child in play, and those noted in the
parent's or caretaker's earlier reports?

4. *Separation anxiety/ability to relate to worker*. What indications of
separation anxiety are noted in the child's actual separation from parent
or caretaker in the first session? Do themes in the child's play or inter-
ruptions in the play reflect separation concerns? How does the child relate to the social worker? Consider behavior of different points in time,
especially variations in the child's response within a particular session
and among successive sessions.

5. *Ability to concentrate in session*. How distractible is the child? Can
he or she focus on a task until completion? Does the child seem to be
attending to noises outside the room?

When the worker has completed the evaluation sessions with the
child and obtained all other necessary reports (see "Obtaining Collateral
Information," above), he or she meets again with the parents to give them
a verbal summary of the assessment and recommendations, and to involve
the parents in setting goals and formulating a treatment plan.

ASSESSMENT TOOLS

Many different tools are available to assist the worker in forming an
assessment of a child and family. Few workers (if any) will use all the
tools described below in any one case. The nature of the agency often
dictates the use of particular assessment methods, such as the DSM in a
mental health clinic, or a genogram in a child welfare or family services
agency. Although we may all agree that "the more information we have,
the better" about an individual child, time constraints often prevent the
completion of a comprehensive assessment. Reality dictates that the
worker choose the assessment tools that promise to produce the most
useful information for the purpose of a specific evaluation within a reasonable time frame.

Among the possible choices of assessment tools are the following:

- Developmental history form
- Tripartite assessment forms
- Genogram
- Eco-map
- Social network map
- Culturagram

- Person-in-Environment (PIE)
- Educational and psychological testing
- Specific drawing exercises
- Projective questions

Developmental History Form

The developmental history form I have created for my practice and teaching (Table 4.2) includes a sweeping view of the child's life from birth to the present, concluding with an appraisal of the child's ego strengths and weaknesses. The developmental history constitutes the core of the assessment, pointing to areas of developmental delay, difficulties in separation/individuation, the child's school history, and affective social development. Appraisal of the child's development depends on the worker's solid knowledge of typical developmental norms. As discussed in Chapter 2, this knowledge base is essential in work with children.

The experience of relating information about the child's life sometimes makes a parent very contemplative. The review can, in itself, help a parent understand significant pieces of the child's life in a manner that is meaningful to him or her. This occurred, for example, in the intake with Tammy's mother (see Chapter 7), who began to realize as I questioned her about Tammy's friends and babysitters that she had never permitted Tammy to be cared for by anyone other than herself or her own mother. The fact that Tammy's mother was currently having difficulty getting pregnant a second time seemed to cause the mother to cling to the child, even as the child was clinging to the mother.

In contrast to Tammy's insightful mother, who was able to make meaningful connections between her child's behavior and her own anxieties, other parents seem to have difficulty remaining focused on their child during the intake. This seemed true in my one lengthy telephone call with Mrs. Smith, when I asked her to tell me about what things were like for Barbie before she started school. Mrs. Smith began crying and talking about how unsupportive her family was, and how she eventually had decided to "pay back to others what they had done" to her, even though she knew now that it was wrong. I am still not sure about the meaning of this statement other than as a possible explanation for her drug-dealing activities, which had led to her imprisonment. I sensed during that phone conversation how very needy Mrs. Smith was; in retrospect, I recognize how difficult it would have been to obtain a developmental history of Barbie, because of her mother's preoccupation with her own numerous problems.

TABLE 4.2. Developmental History Outline

I. *Identification and description of child and family* (outline). Give age, birthdates, gender, and occupation of all family members. These may be separated into (1) relatives in the home, (2) relatives outside the home, and (3) nonrelated persons living in the home.

II. *Presenting problem* (one or two sentences, in the parents' own words). State the problem that brings the child to the agency, the referring source, and the source's statement of the problem.

III. *History of problem.* Include how problem got started (onset, duration, intensity) and circumstances under which the problem manifests itself.

IV. *Family background* (including three-generation genogram). Indicate ethnicity, religion, socioeconomic status, educational and occupational data, and some conceptualization of patterns of interaction within the family, especially with regard to the child.

V. *Specific developmental history*
   A. Family atmosphere into which the child was born
      1. Marital situation
      2. Financial situation
      3. Was pregnancy planned or unplanned?
      4. Parental attitudes toward children; maturity for parenting
      5. Physical living situation—space?
      6. What kind of community environment?
   B. Delivery
      1. Abnormalities, difficulties, unusual procedures
      2. Gender of child (parental/sibling reactions)
      3. Birth weight
   C. Infancy
      1. Physical development (feeding, toileting, activity level, motor development)
      2. Emotional responsiveness and sensitivity
      3. Quality of mothering (maternal availability for positive, fulfilling relationship); who was the primary caretaker?
      4. Parental perception of child's temperament (easy–difficult)
   D. Early childhood
      1. Language development
      2. Separation/individuation (18–36 months)
         a. Physical separation (any delays in development?)
         b. Maternal reactions to toddler's greater independence
         c. Outside factors affecting mother and child (medical, psychological, social)
      3. Other factors affecting child's early emotional development
         a. Sibling births
         b. Separations from parents
         c. Medical problems/health-related difficulties
         d. Unavailable or severely deprived parents
      4. Reactions to nursery school or other separation
      5. Discovery of anatomical sexual differences (reactions)
      6. Exposure to sexual activity or materials
      7. Exposure to traumatic events
      8. Affective/social development
      9. Fantasy life and play

(continued)

TABLE 4.2. (Continued)

VI. *School history*
  1. Separation reactions
  2. Ability to learn, concentration, cognitive development
  3. Superego formation (clear sense of "right" and "wrong")
  4. Any noted difficulties in behavior or learning
  5. External factors (teachers, moving, etc.)

VII. *Ego strengths and weaknesses*
  1. Friends
  2. Hobbies/special interests
  3. Frustration tolerance, ability to delay gratification
  4. Previous symptoms or difficulties

VIII. *Current functioning* (one or two sentences describing child's present adaptation).

Tripartite Assessment Forms

Following the completion of the developmental history, the worker begins to weigh the significance of the numerous events and experiences in the child's life. The three forms I have developed for use in tripartite assessment (Tables 4.3–4.5) help the worker organize the data into distinctive categories that further assist in identifying pivotal influences on the child's life.

Applying Developmental History/Tripartite Assessment Principles: The Case of Barbie

Before I continue with the description of various assessment tools, it may be instructive to consider how the tasks of obtaining a developmental history and conducting a tripartite assessment were carried out, and might have been carried out, in the case of Barbie Smith. First, I want to emphasize that in the case of a child as disadvantaged as Barbie, the most useful way of beginning an assessment may be to consider the child's strengths. On the *No Place like Home* videotape (Hunt, 1992), Barbie presented as an appealing youngster who had not yet been destroyed by the cruel circumstances of her life. She was open about her feelings, conveying resignation about her homeless circumstances and past beatings. Yet she demonstrated the ability to be playful and enjoy herself when she went roller skating and when the filmmaker allowed her to experiment with a camcorder. Barbie had not only "survived" her difficult childhood; she had matured into a preadolescent with appeal that caught the interest of a filmmaker and myself. She had learned to take basic care of her-

TABLE 4.3. Individual Factors in the Assessment of the Child: Webb

1. Age _____ years _____ months   Date of birth_____
                                      Date of assessment_____

   a. Developmental stage: b. Cognitive level:
      Freud_____   Piaget_____
      Erikson_____   c. Temperament:
                                    Thomas and Chess_____

2. Past coping/adjustment
   a. Home (as reported by parents): Good___Fair___Poor___
   b. School (as reported by teachers and parents): Good___Fair___Poor___
   c. Interpersonal/peers (as reported by parents and self): Good___Fair___Poor___
   d. Hobbies/interests (list)_____

3. Medical history (as reported by parents and pediatrician)— describe serious illnesses,
   operations, and injuries since birth, with dates and outcome _____
   _____
   _____

4. Abuse history
   a. Physical: No___ Yes___ Reported (Y or N)___ Child's age___
      Single episode___ Repeated___ Perpetrator_____
      Outcome (give details)_____
      _____

   b. Sexual: No___ Yes___ Reported (Y or N)___ Child's age___
      Single episode___ Repeated___ Perpetrator_____
      Outcome (give details)_____
      _____
      _____

5. Exposure to traumatic events (give details with dates and outcome)_____
   _____

6. DSM-IV diagnosis: Axis I_____Axis II_____Axis III_____

7. Child's personal perception of problem: What is the specific *meaning* of this difficulty
   to the child at this time?_____

Note. This form is one part of a three-part assessment of the child, which also includes an assessment of situational factors (Table 4.4) and an assessment of the child's support system (Table 4.5).

self, and the videotape showed her washing her own hair, cooking a simple meal, and even serving it to her mother. In many respects she seemed old for her years, especially when she applied eye makeup prior to going skating, as if she were preparing for a "date"—behavior that probably imitated her mother and sister.

Any social workers or other professional helpers entering Barbie's life would have done well to ask themselves whether and how this youngster could have a more fulfilling life than that of her mother, and how the helpers could insure that this child not be swept along the relentless

TABLE 4.4. Situational Factors in the Assessment of the Child: Webb

1. Nature of problem
   a. Presence of loss factors
      Separation from family members (list relationship and length of separation)_____

      _____
      Death of family members (list relationship and cause of death)_____

      _____
      Loss of familiar environment (describe)_____

      _____
      Loss of familiar role/status (describe; temporary or permanent?)_____

      _____
      Loss of body part or function (describe, with prognosis) _____

      _____
   b. Presence of trauma/violence
      Witnessed: Verbal___ Physical___
      Experienced: Verbal___ Physical___
   c. Presence of life threat
      Personal (describe)_____

      _____
      To family members (describe, identifying relationship) _____

      _____
      To others (describe)_____

      _____
   d. Presence of physical injury or pain (describe)_____

      _____
   e. Element of stigma/shame associated with problem (describe)_____

      _____
2. Psychosocial and environmental problems: DSM-IV, Axis IV (list problems)_____

   _____
3. Onset and duration of problem
   a. Chronic (give details, including child's age at onset, and frequency of occurrence)

      _____
      _____
   b. Acute (give child's age, and duration of problem)_____

      _____
4. Involvement of others
   a. Nature of involvement (describe)_____
   b. Perception of support: Sufficient___ Insufficient___

Note. This form is one part of a three-part assessment of the child, which also includes an assessment of individual factors (Table 4.3) and an assessment of the child's support system (Table 4.5).

TABLE 4.5. Assessment of the Child's Support System: Webb

---

1. Nuclear family members
   a. How responsive are they to the child's needs? Not at all ___ Somewhat ___ Very ___
   b. To what extent is the child included in discussions about "the problem situation"? Frequently ___ Never ___ Sometimes ___
   c. Do parents tend to show a judgmental attitude toward the child's behavior? Yes ___ No ___

2. Extended family members
   a. How frequently are they in contact with the child? Rarely ___ Monthly ___ Weekly ___ Daily ___
   b. Describe nature of the relationships, indicating who is the most supportive relative to the child _____
   c. To what extent do the views of the extended family differ or agree with those of the nuclear family on matters pertaining to the child? (give details)

   _____

3. School/peers/social network
   a. Child's grade in school ___
   b. Child's friendship network: How many friends does child have? Many ___ "A few" ___ None ___
   c. Would child like to have more friends than he or she has? Yes ___ No ___
   d. How many days after school, on the average, does the child play with another child? Most days ___ Once or twice ___ Never ___

4. Religious affiliation
   a. Does the child/family participate in religious services? Yes ___ (If yes, give name of religious group:) No ___
   b. If yes, indicate how frequently the child/family participates: Weekly ___ Major holiday observances ___ Rarely ___

5. Neighborhood/school activities
   a. Is the family involved with neighborhood/school activities? No___ Yes___
   b. If yes, describe _____

Note. This form is one part of a three-part assessment of the child, which also includes an assessment of individual factors (Table 4.3) and an assessment of situational factors (Table 4.4).

current of poverty, dependence, and a constricted belief in her future options as a woman.

Information Actually Obtained about Barbie at Time of Referral

The intake interview at the time of Barbie's entry to the special school program for homeless children required (or involved) numerous forms and releases. In addition to factual information about the family's current living situation, details were obtained about Barbie's health and educational history. The forms did not include information about the child's developmental history, but the social worker nonetheless obtained some information about Barbie's history of foster care while her mother was in prison for possession of firearms and possession/manufacture of methamphetamines.

According to the information given by Mrs. Smith at intake, she began using drugs when Barbie was about 3 years old, and she was imprisoned for 20 months when Barbie was between 5 and 6 years old. All three children were placed in separate foster homes at that time, where, according to Mrs. Smith, the girls were molested and beaten. These charges were investigated and later dropped by the district attorney. The girls received counseling for about 2 years, and Mrs. Smith stated that she herself had also been in treatment several times. She claimed during the intake that she had been drug-free since she was released from prison, when Barbie was about age 7; she was employed as a bartender for a while following her release.

The intake also revealed information about Barbie's father. Barbie's parents were married when she was 4 years old, having lived together for 2 years prior to her birth. They separated a year later, and were divorced when Barbie was 9. According to Mrs. Smith, her former husband had physically abused her and the children, and she had taken out many court orders of protection against him. He later moved out of state, and Barbie had not seen him since she was 9, although he maintained occasional telephone contact with his daughter.

Reconstruction of Significant Factors in Barbie's Developmental History

In this case, as in many presented to social workers, comprehensive information was (and still is) lacking, and a social worker would have had to make professional judgments despite many missing pieces. Because homeless children require prompt emergency services, it is understandable that the school did not get *detailed* facts about the child's history beyond the preceding 2 years. Actually, the information obtained by the intake worker exceeded the minimum required on the form.

In order to reconstruct the important events in Barbie's development, I devised a time line, listing pivotal events of each year of the child's life from her birth to the time of the Hunt videotape. There was virtually *no* information about the period from Barbie's infancy until she was 3 years old, when her mother stated that she began using drugs. We can speculate that this period may have been characterized by Mrs. Smith's alternating states of feeling overwhelmed by the care of three children, and trying to medicate herself with drugs or alcohol. If Mrs. Smith used amphetamines, these would have had a stimulating affect on her mood, and typically, according to Straussner (1993, p. 311), alcohol serves a sedating function for users of amphetamines. We do not have any information about Mrs. Smith's *alcohol* use, but a colleague of mine—a professor who teaches courses on alcohol and other substances—commented about the similarity between Barbie's facial features (as depicted in the publicity photo for *No Place like Home*) and those of children with fetal alcohol syndrome (U.S. Department of Health and Human Services, 1993, p. 203).

Whether or not Barbie's mother was using alcohol prior to her admitted substance abuse when Barbie was age 3, we can reasonably question the quality and consistency of Barbie's early parenting experiences. The marriage to Barbie's father lasted only a year, and Mrs. Smith's incarceration soon after, when Barbie was 5, suggests that the family circumstances were tumultuous and not conducive to a child's need for emotional calm and stability.

Pivotal factors in the assessment of individual factors in Barbie's development (see Table 4.3) included the following:

1. *Abuse history* (item 4 in Table 4.3). Details are lacking, but Mrs. Smith referred to *multiple* instances in which Barbie's father physically abused both her and the children. On the videotape, Barbie asked pointedly, "Just because he hit us, that doesn't mean he doesn't love us, does it?" In addition to physical abuse by her father, Mrs. Smith stated that Barbie was physically and emotionally abused in foster care. Details about this are unknown.

2. *Exposure to traumatic events* (item 5 in Table 4.3). Barbie's early life was characterized by the "loss" of both parents, as well as the loss of her familiar intact family. We do not know what Barbie was told at age 5 when she "lost" her mother to the prison system. She also "lost" her sister, brother, and father at the same time, and her father never returned to live with the family after her mother was released.

The assessment of the child's support system (see Table 4.5) was also revealing. There appeared to be very few supports available to the Smith family in the usual form of extended family members or religious or community affiliations. Mrs. Smith spoke on the tape about her poor relationships with her own family, and she conveyed an attitude of anger and resentment toward them. She had a friendly manner, however, and she appeared to have some male friends, who were shown on the tape helping the family move. In view of the frequency of the family's moves (seven times during a 6-month period), it was remarkable that this mother had the stamina to persevere in her determination to keep her family together. She verbalized this goal frequently, and this may have reassured Barbie about her own personal worth and value. Barbie admired her mother and wanted to be like her. The child seemed unaware of her mother's deficiencies and failures, choosing instead to identify with her strengths. The mother's strong love for Barbie had helped the child endure repeated experiences of abuse and loss. Given the severity of Barbie's early life experiences, it was truly remarkable that she related as well as she did to adults. No information was available about her relationships with peers, however, which certainly would have been compromised by the family's frequent moves. Homeless children typically demonstrate lowered self-esteem and difficulty in making friends (Timberlake & Sabatino, 1994).

❖

Genogram

I now continue with the discussion of assessment tools per se. The genogram, probably one of the most useful of assessment tools, enables the worker to diagram on one page all the members of both the nuclear and the extended family, together with identifying information about them (e.g., ages, occupations, marital status, dates and manner of deaths, and the quality of relationships among various family members). Students wanting instruction in the construction of genograms can consult McGoldrick and Gerson (1985) and Hartman (1978).

"Reading" a genogram can reveal the following helpful information about a child and family:

- The similarity or difference between the position of the child in his or her nuclear family, and the corresponding position of a parent in his or her family of origin
- Relative(s) the child was named for
- Repetition of problems across the generations (e.g., learning disabilities and alcohol dependence)
- Patterns of "cutoffs" when family conflict is not resolved
- Patterns of dependence and lack of separation linking family members, regardless of age or marital status

The worker usually constructs the genogram together with the parent(s). If the child is present, this process can provide important information regarding how much the child knows about extended family members. If the child is *not* present, it may be helpful to involve the child in constructing a separate genogram later; however, the worker should keep in mind that developmental considerations probably prevent a child under 6 years of age from being able to conceptualize family relationships on paper.

M. Seligman (personal communication, 1995) has devised a novel way of using the genogram with children: She invites a child to mark the genogram with colored stickers representing the child's feelings about different family members. The color key includes yellow stickers for happy relationships, blue for sad, red for angry, and green for worried. This could be a potentially revealing assessment tool to probe for the child's view of family relationships.

The school for homeless children where Barbie Smith was enrolled does not routinely construct genograms with the families of students. My attempt to produce a genogram of the Smith family is based on the scant information presented on the videotape and the intake forms. Because no information was available about members of Mrs. Smith's family of origin, the genogram consists of only two generations. Some of the data may be inaccurate; these would have had to be confirmed or corrected by Mrs. Smith, during the process of working with her.

Because the genogram of the Smith family is so sketchy, I have combined it with an eco-map to illustrate the various helping agencies with which the family was involved (see Chapter 3, Figure 3.2). In many homeless urban families like the Smiths, the helping system serves as an essential substitute for the extended family, whose members may be unable or unwilling to offer financial or other support.

Eco-Map

Together with the genogram, the eco-map (Hartman, 1978) offers a visual representation of the persons and potential resources that depicts the family's connections with their environment. As shown with regard to the Smith family, the genogram diagrams family relationships, whereas the eco-map illustrates contacts with social agencies and other community resources. The eco-map also usually contains an abbreviated genogram in its center, showing the members of the household in which the clients reside.

Social Network Map

The social network map (Tracy & Whittaker, 1993) gives information about the types of support available to a family, the gaps that exist in the available supports, and the potential resources that could fill the gaps. It highlights in a grid format the social support that is provided through *informal* helping networks, such as that provided by friends when the Smith family moved. The social network map comprehensively depicts both the structure and function of specific relationships, and therefore is more detailed than the eco-map.

A possible disadvantage of social support mapping is its somewhat complex nature. Few workers welcome another form to fill out during the intake process, especially one that may take from 15 minutes to an hour to complete. However, practitioners who learn to use this tool consider it quite helpful, according to Tracy and Whittaker (1993). Clearly, clients' perceptions of the people they can count on in their circle of acquaintances merit documentation, as does a listing of their unmet needs. Perhaps in the future, someone will devise a single diagrammatic tool that combines the genogram, the eco-map, and the social network map.

Culturagram

As a family assessment tool, the culturagram (Congress, 1994) offers social workers an important method for recognizing and individualizing the impact of ethnicity on culturally diverse families. The families with which social workers interact usually come from many different cultural backgrounds, and a tool such as the culturagram can assist in understanding each family's unique heritage and belief system. Chapters in this book that deal with children from minority, immigrant, or mixed cultures include the cases of Jacob and Damien (Chapter 1), José (Chapter 2), Sally (Chapter 9), Maria and Mario (Chapter 10), Ahmed (Chapter 13), and Alexa (Chapter 15). Each of these children lived in a home in which language, beliefs, values, and connections with the community were influenced to varying degrees by the cultural history of his or her particular family. Sometimes the children of immigrants serve as interpreters for their parents, thus reversing usual parent–child roles. At other times, the parents' expectations about acceptable child behavior differ from the prevailing norms; this puts undue pressure on the children, who are caught between two worlds. The culturagram provides a structured method for recording a family's cultural history and beliefs, and as such it is an essential resource in assessment and intervention with culturally diverse families.

❖

In the case of the Smith family, information about the ethnicity of the family was incomplete. The school program Barbie attended obtains data about languages spoken in the home, and about the ethnicity of various family members. Barbie's school record identified her as a native-born English speaker, with only English spoken in her home. With respect to ethnicity, the Lapp, Lettish (Latvia), and Jamaican categories were checked as applying to "spouse partner," but we do not know whether these applied to Barbie's father or to other men in the home. No categories were checked as applying to Mrs. Smith's ethnicity. Barbie's light blonde hair, blue eyes, and pale skin were similar to her mother's and sister's coloring, and seem characteristic of persons with northern European origins. We have no information about the family's religious or cultural practices.

Person-in-Environment

The Person-in-Environment (PIE) classification system describes and classifies difficulties in social functioning, such as problems in social roles and environmental problems (Karls & Wandrei, 1994). Although this tool was originally hailed as documenting the problems that are the primary focus of social workers (Williams, Karls, & Wandrei, 1989), it has become redundant for social workers who use DSM diagnoses, now that the DSM-IV includes psychosocial problems on its Axis IV. On the other hand, social workers in schools such as that attended by Barbie Smith, and many in child welfare agencies, do not use the DSM classification. Workers in such agencies may find the Person-in-Environment useful in identifying the specific environmental systems and problem areas, such as housing and medical needs, with which a family is struggling.

DSM-IV

The DSM-IV, the latest edition of an assessment tool produced by the American Psychiatric Association (1994), is a system of classifying observable symptoms and behaviors into discrete diagnostic categories. Many practitioners (Johnson, 1993a; Rapoport & Ismond, 1990) are concerned about the affixing of diagnostic labels to children, whose development is in flux and whose "disorders" may be reactive to family and environmental stress, rather than indicative of intrinsic pathology. Furthermore, scientific validation is lacking for many of the DSM categories used in practice with children, and some concepts applicable to adults have been extended to children without adequate recognition of the essential biological and psychosocial differences between children and adults (Johnson, 1994).

These reservations notwithstanding, DSM classifications are widely used in clinical practice, and probably will become even more so in the current environment of managed care, in which DSM diagnoses are required for reimbursement. Johnson (1993a), points out that "neither social work nor any other discipline, so far, has produced [an alternative to the DSM] that has gained wide acceptance" (p. 144). Therefore we must use it "by default" until a more satisfactory system emerges.

My own view is that the DSM is a very useful assessment tool for identifying and understanding certain psychological disorders and other conditions. I would never employ *only* the DSM, however, in formulating an assessment, because the genogram and eco-map provide essential information that is not included in the DSM.

A DSM-IV assessment involves the following five "axes" (American Psychiatric Association, 1994, p. 25) each of which covers a different domain of information that may assist the practitioner in specifying the nature and scope of the difficulty under examination, so that appropriate interventions may be planned:

Axis I   Clinical Disorders
           Other Conditions That May Be a Focus of Clinical Attention

Axis II   Personality Disorders
           Mental Retardation

Axis III   General Medical Conditions

Axis IV   Psychosocial and Environmental Problems

Axis V   Global Assessment of Functioning (GAF)

❖

Had Barbie Smith's school social worker used the DSM at the time of Barbie's entry into the school, the following multiaxial diagnosis could have assisted in formulating an appropriate treatment plan:

Axis I   315.00   Reading Disorder (pending formal tests)
           315.2   Disorder of Written Expression (pending formal tests)

Axis II   V71.09   No diagnosis

Axis III   Deferred, pending medical exam

Axis IV   Problems with primary support group (parental divorce; past physical abuse by father; erratic contact with father)
                       Problems related to the social environment (inadequate social support)
                       Educational problems (academic problems)
                       Occupational problems (mother's unemployment)
                       Housing problems (homelessness; unsafe neighborhood)
                       Economic problems (poverty; inadequate welfare support)
                       Problems related to interaction with the legal system/crime (mother on probation)

Axis V   GAF = 50   (current and past year)

It is my belief that pulling together the information obtained at intake within a DSM framework would have alerted the school staff as to specific problem areas that might have been contributing to Barbie's learning difficulties. Although the main function of school is to educate, a special program targeted to homeless children must, of necessity, attend to the basic needs of the students and their families before the children's education can proceed. Barbie's special needs would have been listed explicitly on DSM Axes I and IV. Axis V would have indicated that Barbie's general level of functioning was fairly low, both currently and during the past year (estimated at 50, with the range from 0 to 100). Because this child's problem situation had not changed during the past year, the important question about the chronicity of her difficulties would have been highlighted. Barbie's mother stated at intake that Barbie had received special education services within the past 3 years, so these records would have had to be obtained in order to compare Barbie's present academic functioning with her former level, and to maintain some continuity with regard to the educational focus.

Educational and Psychological Testing

The following types of tests commonly used with children (Barker, 1995) may be recommended either by the intake worker or by the child study team, in order to obtain more detailed information about the child:

> Tests of academic attainment
> Intelligence tests
> Personality tests
> Behavior checklists
> Tests assessing specific psychological conditions, such as anxiety, depression, self-esteem, and sustained attention

The social worker does not test the child, but must understand when to make a referral, and how to explain the need for specialized testing to the child and the parent(s). We do not know which, if any, of these types of tests were completed with Barbie at the time of referral.

Tests of academic achievement are usually part of children's regular school records, since they are often performed on an annual basis in order to determine the children's appropriate class placement. Intelligence tests are not performed routinely in most schools, and they have been criticized in the past decade as being culturally biased. Nonetheless, they give a "rough" estimate of a child's native ability, and are especially useful in suggesting the need for additional specialized testing for possible learning disabilities when there is a sizable discrepancy between the verbal and performance subsections. Personality tests such as the Children's Apperception Test (CAT) attempt to elicit responses that reflect the child's inner world and mental state. This is a projective test, adapted from the adult Thematic Apperception Test (TAT). Both present the client with a series of ambiguous pictures, onto which the client "projects" his or her personal meaning.

Another assessment measure sometimes employed as part of the assessment process is the Child Behavior Checklist (Achenbach & Edelbrock, 1983), on which a parent or teacher responds to questions about his or her perceptions of a child's behavior. This results in several different opinions, which may be useful in pinpointing a particular setting or person with which the child's behavior is considered most troublesome. Conners (1969, 1970) has developed another behavior checklist with separate forms for parents and teachers.

An intake worker who is concerned about a child's depressed mood may ask the child to fill out a questionnaire about the level of his or her depressed feelings (the Children's Depression Inventory; Kovacs, 1978). Of course, this presumes that the child can read or that the child is willing to respond to questions read by the worker. Pfeffer (1986) lists a series of questions to ask in evaluating a child's risk of suicide. In situations when I have serious questions about a child's depression and possible suicide risk, I communicate this to the parent and strongly suggest an immediate psychiatric consultation. Another self-report checklist, the State–Trait Anxiety Inventory for Children (Spielberger, 1973), assesses children's anxiety, and other scales exist for assessing the preschool child's home environment (Caldwell & Bradley, 1979).

In my own practice, I rarely use these various checklists. I prefer to base my assessment on my observations of the interactions among the child, the parent(s), and myself, as well as on the actual statements of the child and the family, and on the various reports from collateral sources. When social workers begin their work with a child and a family, the workers must focus on getting to know them as people; requests to fill out forms can feel rather impersonal and cold. However, since these checklists and tests may be used by school psychologists, it is important for workers to know about their contents and purpose. A manual of typical tests in child assessment (e.g., Goldman, Stein, & Guerry, 1983) can serve as a useful resource.

Children's Drawings

As previously discussed, I routinely invite children to complete several drawings during their assessment sessions. Since I am a social worker and not a psychologist, I do not "score" these drawings, as would a psychologist analyzing a Draw-A-Person test or a Kinetic Family Drawing. Whereas the psychologist examines the child's drawings and evaluates them with respect to the child's personality and developmental level, I follow the guidelines used by art therapists in using drawings in assessment and therapy (DiLeo, 1973; Oster & Gould, 1987, pp. 21–28, 41–43, 47–48). Some of the elements to be noted in the child's drawings include the size and position of the figures; the absence or exaggeration of body parts; the use of color and shading; the nature of facial expressions; and the general mood of the drawing. In addition, the child's attitude in producing it (e.g., labored, rushed, perfectionistic, or self-critical) should be noted.

Projective Questions

Commonly used by social workers and others in initial sessions with children, projective questions seek to elicit a child's feelings about his or her family and life. Examples of typical projective questions are as follows:

1. "If you had three wishes, what would you wish for?" (When a savvy child responds that he or she would want a thousand more wishes, the worker needs to specify that this will not be possible, and that the child must specify what he or she wants.)
2. "If a baby bird fell out of the nest, what might happen?" (The child is expected to complete the story.)
3. "If you were going on a rocket trip to the moon, and you could take only one person with you, who would that person be?" (The child's response is expected to reveal the most important person in his or her life, but it may also reflect the child's judgment about who would be most helpful in this special situation.)

The child's responses to these and other projective questions should be explored by the worker in an unhurried, interested way. The child should be given the explicit message that there is no one "right" answer, and that the worker is asking the questions in order to get to know the child better.

SUMMARIZING THE RELEVANT DATA

During the process of gathering information about a child and family, the worker continually weighs the significance of his or her findings, and immediately starts to generate hypotheses about what is wrong and how to help. This analysis, synthesis, and speculation constitute an ongoing process that continues *throughout the life of the case*. However, during the early evaluation of a case, most agencies expect the worker to formulate a biopsychosocial assessment summary in writing. According to Kadushin (1995), "Gathering data does not in itself yield an assessment. Data must be organized, interpreted, integrated with theory, and made meaningful to derive an assessment" (p. 63). The three tripartite assessment forms (Tables 4.3–4.5) will help the worker organize the data, preparatory to formulating a summary statement regarding the significant features of the case.

Hepworth and Larsen (1993, p. 192) recommend a multidimensional assessment summary, covering five distinct categories. I follow their general outline below in a retrospective assessment summary for Barbie Smith, during the period of her enrollment in the First Place School program, with special attention to factors relevant to a *child* assessment. The dimensions suggested by Hepworth and Larsen are as follows:

- The nature of the client's problems
- The coping capacities of the client and significant others
- The relevant systems involved in the client's problems
- The available or needed resources
- The client's motivation to work on the problems

A SAMPLE BIOPSYCHOSOCIAL ASSESSMENT SUMMARY: BARBIE SMITH

Date of birth: 6-6-82
Date of evaluation: 2-10-93 (hypothetical)
Age at time of evaluation: 10 years, 8 months

Reason for Referral

The family was referred to the First Place School, a special education program for children in transition, by the shelter in which they were currently residing. The mother was seeking schooling for Barbie, then in third grade. The family had moved seven times in 6 months and had been befriended and videotaped by a filmmaker, Kathryn Hunt, during this period. Ms. Hunt had also recommended this school program to Mrs. Smith.

Family Description

This female-headed household consists of a mother and three children, all born of different fathers. The mother has a history of imprisonment for the possession of firearms and methamphetamines, but claims to have been "clean" since her release 3 years ago. She is estranged from her family of origin and has no contact with the children's fathers, one of whom is deceased, and another of whom lives out of state (Barbie's father). The family receives public assistance and has been living in various shelters and welfare motels. They move because of inability to pay the rent and dissatisfaction with the neighborhood, which the mother describes as populated by addicts and pimps.

Family Composition

Lori (mother)	Age 34, unemployed (former bartender).
Donna (daughter)	Age 18, school dropout, in and out of home (living with boyfriend, when away).
David (son)	Age 16, school dropout.
Barbie (daughter)	Age 10, third grade.

The Nature of the Client's and Family's Problems

This homeless family seems beset by one crisis after another. The mother, a former addict, appears to be highly motivated to help her younger daughter obtain schooling, but her ability to organize her life in a way that will achieve this goal is questionable. Although the mother is not seeking help for herself, she clearly plays a pivotal role in this child's ability to pursue a normal developmental course. Therefore, it is essential to engage and help the mother with her numerous problems. The mother's energies are totally absorbed in searching out places for the family to reside.

Mrs. Smith alludes (on the Hunt videotape) to serious problems with her family of origin. She herself has been abused, and although we know no details about this, she appears to have suffered emotional damage that requires attention. This mother is trying to the best of her ability to hold her family together, but she seems to be under great stress, and may be at risk for depression and/or resumption of drug abuse.

Mrs. Smith, while professing "distrust of the system," nonetheless maintains an open attitude toward persons on the periphery, such as the filmmaker and myself (telephone). This suggests that despite her feelings of anger and hurt, she has not closed herself off completely and may be still reachable.

Barbie's problems are secondary to the situation of her family. Her delay in academic performance is understandable in view of her extremely erratic school attendance. If Barbie spends a consistent period of time in one school, we can better evaluate her true ability. With regard to the housing situation, Barbie's mother states that the girl sleeps with her lights on because of roaches, and that she is beginning to have nightmares.

Coping Capacities of Client and Family

Both Barbie and her mother demonstrate an unusual ability to deal with the uncertainties of their lives. We lack in-depth information about how they deal with stress, but the video portrayal suggests both resignation and determination on Mrs. Smith's part. At one point, she questions whether she may have brought her difficulties upon herself—a statement that demonstrates some capacity for self-reflection, despite its exaggeration.

Both Barbie and her mother make it clear that they do not like the uncertain quality of their life. Persons who live in a continual state of crisis are sometimes described as "borderline," but we have insufficient information on which to base this or any other diagnosis. However, the possibility of a mental disorder, in addition to a diagnosis of drug addiction, will need to be considered in evaluating Mrs. Smith's coping methods. She has a lot of strength, but she also seems to be under great stress.

Barbie's coping capacities are more difficult to determine. She is about 2 years behind her expected grade level, which probably has a negative impact on her self-esteem. After Barbie's first 2 months at First Place, her teacher wrote as follows:

> Barbie seems very defensive about her low skill level. She often seems angry and wants to control others. She may need counseling. *She really is a sweet little girl. She needs a lot of nurturing and patience.* (emphasis added)

Everything in the teacher's comments is understandable, in view of this child's life experience. Her lack of academic skills makes her anxious and defensive, and she responds with anger and an attempt to control others. So much of her own life has been beyond her control that she tries to exert whatever influence she can on others.

Despite Barbie's harsh past and present life, she still elicits positive feelings in adults, indicating a probability that she will be able to respond to a helping relationship.

Relevant Systems Involved in Client's and Family's Situation

A number of different agencies are involved with this family, but there is no evidence that they are in contact with one another to coordinate the case planning. The housing authority was instrumental in making Barbie's referral to the school. Mrs. Smith has ongoing contact with the public assistance agency, and also with the corrections department, since she is on probation. Both of Barbie's siblings also have had special school affiliations, and her sister reports monthly to a medical clinic for chronic kidney and heart problems.

Barbie's school records have not yet been obtained. She has changed schools so often that the records have not kept up with her. This presents serious problems in terms of academic planning targeted to Barbie's specific needs.

Available or Needed Resources

1. The family's most pressing need at this time is for decent housing in a safe neighborhood. The housing should afford a quiet place for Barbie to do her homework and read.

2. Case management/coordination is essential to bring the various helping agencies into contact with one another. The school could appropriately assume this role, since Barbie's academic success will depend on various family circumstances, including her mother's ability to remain drug-free and supportive to her children.

3. Academic tutoring is needed for Barbie. This should follow a review of previous tests, and completion of current tests to target Barbie's special needs.

4. Counseling is also indicated for Barbie. Ideally, this should occur on both an individual and a group basis. Barbie should benefit from individual counseling to deal with her feelings about her past traumatic experiences, such as being in foster care, the abuse by her father and in foster care, and her father's apparent abandonment of her. Group therapy with other homeless children will serve the function of mutual support and self-esteem building. The group members can identify themselves as "survivors" and reinforce one another's positive coping strategies.

5. Job counseling and training are needed for Mrs. Smith. [Note: Suggestions regarding approaching Mrs. Smith about this are discussed in Chapter 3.]

6. Individual counseling is also indicated for Mrs. Smith. (The success of this will depend on the worker's establishing a positive relationship pertaining to a concrete service, such as putting Mrs. Smith in contact with a resource for housing or job training.) Mrs. Smith has many issues to work out, including her conflictual relationship with her family of origin, her problematic relationships with men, and her history of addiction and homelessness. It is important to highlight how hard Mrs. Smith is trying

to keep her family together, since this is her strength and the key to motivating her. Basic trust in the helping relationship will build slowly.

7. Mrs. Smith should be encouraged to attend Narcotics Anonymous, or other group counseling focused on addiction. In order to maintain her sobriety, Mrs. Smith needs to establish new friends and activities that are not drug-related.

8. Educational and/or occupational counseling may well be needed for Barbie's older siblings. We do not know enough about either one to suggest specifics, but neither appears on the Hunt videotape to be headed toward a productive work career.

Client's and Family's Motivation to Work on Their Problems

Motivation is unknown at present. The problems as listed here are not recognized as such by Mrs. Smith or Barbie. The key to progress with the members of this family will be to engage them in a trusting relationship, based on Mrs. Smith's interest in providing schooling for Barbie and on keeping her family together.

Note. This assessment is based on observations from the videotape (Hunt, 1992) and on reports of various individuals who had contact with the Smith family. It is *not* based on any play sessions with Barbie, or on first-hand contact with her or her family.

———————— ❖ ————————

FEEDBACK/REVIEW WITH PARENTS AND OTHER PROFESSIONALS

Engaging the Parent(s) in the Feedback/Review Process

It is the responsibility of the person formulating the assessment to share it with a child's parent(s) and with other professionals involved in the case. In the case of Barbie Smith, I am assuming that the school social worker might have taken the initiative in engaging Mrs. Smith and in convening a case conference, in order to involve all the concerned professionals in establishing mutually agreed-upon goals and a plan for collaboration.

Maintaining contact with Mrs. Smith would have been essential to engaging her, both for Barbie's education and for the potential overall benefits for the Smith family. The worker would have had to stress that "the educational *team*" planned to pay special attention to Barbie's situation because she was a new student, and that the team would convene a meeting to make specific recommendations for Barbie. The worker would also have had to emphasize that the *parent's* input into this meeting would be very important, and that he or she would thus need Mrs. Smith's help to prepare for the meeting.

Often parents are intimidated by child study meetings in which "professionals" use unfamiliar language in talking about *their* children. The worker would have had to emphasize that he or she would need to meet with Mrs. Smith several times to prepare for this meeting, and might have suggested that Mrs. Smith could ride the school bus to come to these special individual planning meetings. The purposes of the individual meetings with Barbie's mother would have been to establish a relationship with her; to learn more about Barbie's history; and to give Mrs. Smith a private review of the recommendations about her daughter, prior to the case review meeting. The worker could have offered to record and summarize the various recommendations for Mrs. Smith after the meeting.

Releases for sharing of information among the numerous agencies involved with a family are routinely signed when a child enrolls in a special school program such as First Place. During the one or two individual meetings with a child's parent(s) prior to the case conference, the social worker emphasizes how important it is for all these separate people to cooperate on behalf of both the child and the family.

In the event that a parent does not keep the agreed-upon appointment with a social worker, a note should be sent home with the child stating the worker's concern and repeating the necessity of the parent's input with respect to the upcoming meeting. The note should offer the prospect of a home visit if the parent is unable to come to the next scheduled meeting. Actually, a home visit is often very helpful, because of the opportunity it affords the worker to see the environment in which the child is living.

The Case Conference

The case conference provides the opportunity for professionals involved in separate aspects of a case to meet in person to discuss the multidimensional elements of a given family's situation. In the case of the Smith family, had such a conference taken place, the probation officer and the housing authority worker might have put their heads together to resolve the prejudice Mrs. Smith faced in obtaining housing because of her history as a felon. Furthermore, the probation officer and the school social worker might have explored Mrs. Smith's employment prospects, with the possibility of recommending testing for her to ascertain her interests and abilities.

Once such a meeting has taken place, it is much easier to coordinate the case through ongoing telephone contact. The impact on Mrs. Smith if such a meeting had taken place can only be guessed, but it would, of necessity, have been self-affirming with regard to the time and care these numerous professional helpers would have devoted to helping her and her family.

CONCLUDING COMMENTS

Assessment is a complex and systematic process, requiring discipline, patience, the ability to apply a body of professional knowledge, and a sensitivity to clients' strengths and their unique individual and cultural profiles. Depending on each situation, varying attention must be given to biological, psychological, and social factors that interact and merge into a particular situation of human need. The case of Barbie Smith emphasizes the social factors of homelessness and poverty, as these contributed to the psychological distress associated with family dysfunction, abuse, addiction, imprisonment, and school failure.

The purpose of assessment is to point to needs that require intervention. The next chapter deals with establishing goals that flow from the needs identified in the assessment. One aspect of Barbie's case about which more information was needed was the possibility that a learning disability (biological factor) was interfering with her educational progress. Special testing could have provided details about this. I have noted that Barbie seemed to possess a resilient temperament, which had helped her cope with a non-nurturing environment. This strength, similar to her mother's, would have provided a basis for optimism about the prospects of moving beyond the assessment to a series of helping interventions that would have a positive impact on this family's future.

DISCUSSION QUESTIONS AND ROLE-PLAY EXERCISE

1. Discuss the implications of the shift in social workers' vocabulary away from the use of medical terms such as "diagnosis" and "treatment." Consider *both* the pros and the cons of this shift, from the client/patient's perspective, and with regard to working on an interdisciplinary team.

2. How can the worker deal with his or her negative feelings about parents who are overwhelmed with multiple problems and who seem oblivious to their children's needs?

3. Discuss the advantages and the disadvantages of using the DSM in assessing children. Consider the impact on Barbie Smith's family of employing this classification. How would you proceed in prioritizing the problem situations noted on Axis IV of Barbie's DSM diagnosis?

4. Examine the four drawings in this chapter (Figures 4.2–4.5). What elements in the children's drawings do you find of interest in terms of possibly conveying information about the children? After obtaining these drawings, what other play materials would you introduce?

5. Role-play a session with Mrs. Smith in which a worker attempts to engage her and prepare her for the case conference about Barbie.

CHAPTER 5

Contracting, Planning Interventions, and Tracking Progress

Every case situation is different, yet human needs are very similar despite these individual differences. Maslow's hierarchy of needs remains as pertinent today as it was over 25 years ago, when Maslow (1970) first maintained that we all have certain basic needs that must be met in order for us to reach our full potential as humans. The first level of needs includes the fundamental necessities of life, such as food, water, and shelter, which assure our physiological survival. The second level of needs consists of safety considerations; the third is to feel loved and to belong; the fourth is the need for self-esteem. The culminating achievement of "self-actualization" occurs after the lower-level needs have been met and the individual realizes the fulfillment of his or her potential as a person.

CONTRACTING: ENGAGING CLIENTS AND IDENTIFYING THEIR NEEDS

According to Maslow's schema, Barbie Smith's life (see Chapters 3 and 4) was characterized by unmet needs on every level. Any helpers involved with the Smith family, however, would have had to consider carefully where to start and how to involve Mrs. Smith in the decision-making process. It certainly would have been contraindicated for other people, no matter how good their intentions, to seem to "take over" and disempower Mrs. Smith in regard to decisions about her own family. In fact, until a school social worker engages a mother like Mrs. Smith and presents an offer to help her with matters other than her child's education, the mother is not a *client*, but mere the parent of a student. *A person becomes a client after an offer to help has been made and accepted.*

Chapter 3 has emphasized the importance of focusing on the client's perception of his or her needs, and has presented some strategies that could have been used to engage Mrs.. Smith in job-related counseling for herself, tying this to the mother's important role as an identification model for Barbie. A commitment to help the family locate decent housing would have been equally important, and this would ideally have coincided with the effort to upgrade Mrs. Smith's employment prospects. Like the job training offer, the housing issue would have had to be couched in terms of *Barbie's* needs, in order to capture Mrs. Smith's attention successfully. This mother's willingness to discuss her family problems and needs would have depended on repeatedly emphasizing the essential connection between the family circumstances and Barbie's learning situation. For example, if the school social worker had mentioned to Mrs. Smith the importance of Barbie's having a quiet place to do her homework, this topic would inevitably have brought up the issue of the family's poor housing and lack of privacy. Discussing the family's housing needs in the context of *Barbie's* academic requirements might have been more acceptable to Mrs. Smith than a direct offer of assistance, which she might have perceived as the worker's prejudgment that she was incompetent to take care of this matter herself.

It is not unusual for parents who live in ghetto or substandard environments, such as that in which the Smith family resided, to feel misunderstood by and alienated from middle-class helpers whose life experience differs drastically from theirs. Combrinck-Graham (1989, p. 235) points out that

> poverty is more than just a low income. Rather, it is an encompassing lifestyle of opportunism and survival . . . and a dangerous life. Poor families, when they ask for help, need acceptance of their situation, recognition of their efforts to make life livable, and assistance in identifying and connecting with any additional resources the sociopolitical system may have to offer them.

When the gap between worker and client appears too great, the client reacts to the perceived lack of empathy by missing appointment, which the worker may subsequently label "client resistance."

Engaging poor families in treatment makes special demands on the worker to understand the problem *from the clients' point of view*. This task

> requires that the clinician understand the *context* in which the problem is embedded . . . [and pay] attention to the concrete needs of the family, lest the reality of its world be invalidated and the therapist lose all cred-

ibility. Immediate intervention in this area is possibly the most power-ful and most connecting engagement skill, regardless of the discipline of the clinician. (Parnell & Vanderkloot, 1989, p. 447; emphasis added)

It seems probable that Mrs. Smith would have responded positively to an offer to help Barbie through assisting her family to find better hous-ing, if the worker making such an offer had indicated respect for her and an understanding of how repeatedly frustrated she had been in her own efforts to accomplish this. Her criminal history as a felon made it diffi-cult for this mother to obtain housing in the absence of a sponsor who would vouch for her dependability in paying the rent regularly. The assist-ance of Mrs. Smith's public assistance worker and probation officer (with Mrs. Smith's permission) could have been very valuable in working out some form of guaranteed direct-deposit rental system.

In this multiproblem family, as in others, environmental interventions such as seeking new housing are generally implemented in concert with other interventions. Hepworth and Larsen (1986, p. 434) point out that "because problems are generally multidimensional and involve recipro-cal interaction among multiple systems and subsystems, interventions aimed exclusively at the environment may ignore dysfunction in individu-als, thereby addressing only part of a problem."

Mrs. Smith's psychological status was not assessed, despite the many stresses to which she alluded on the video. We do not know whether individual counseling was recommended to her. As reported in Chapter 3, Mrs. Smith chose not to become involved in the various opportunities at the school, which might have addressed some of her own needs in a group format (such as a parenting support group).

Even more troubling was the fact that Mrs. Smith did not make it possible for Barbie to attend school on a *consistent* basis. Despite the avail-ability of transportation, Barbie missed 15 out of the 31 school days dur-ing the 2 months she was enrolled in the First Place program. The family then obtained Section 8 housing, and Barbie transferred to a neighbor-hood school briefly before leaving for an extended stay with her father out of state.

A consultant with many years of experience in the addictions field expressed great skepticism that Mrs. Smith would have remained drug-free during the time shown on the video, which was when Barbie missed so many days of school. Many former addicts find it formidable to get up in the morning and organize their lives. The consultant also com-mented that Mrs. Smith may have actually *needed* Barbie and her brother to help her with various daily living tasks. The tape showed Barbie and David preparing and serving their mother a simple meal, and also assisting with the laundry. Of course, many children perform routine chores to help their parents, and we do not know for certain whether or not Mrs. Smith had returned to using drugs at this time. However, it is unfortunate that she was not sufficiently engaged by the school to avail herself of any of its potentially useful services for homeless families, or to obtain a referral for counseling services outside the school.

I would like to consider, in retrospect, how the school personnel might have successfully engaged Mrs. Smith at the time of Barbie's first contact with them. I do not intend this to be critical of what was done at the time, but rather to use hindsight as a way to learn from experience, so that we can highlight engagement methods that may be effective with other homeless and disenfranchised populations.

Mrs. Smith's request at the time of the school's initial contact with her was for schooling for Barbie. A wider-angle, ecological view of the child's situation would have challenged the helpers to broaden the mother's view of her daughter's needs, to include the notion that helping Barbie would require that she simultaneously help *herself* and the rest of her family.

Successful contracting, therefore, with Mrs. Smith would have involved (1) starting with the mother's request for schooling (i.e., starting where the client was), and then (2) expanding this request to include housing, job training, and supportive counseling, to help *all* family members cope with their past and current stresses. All of this would have had to be presented in a manner that recognized and validated Mrs. Smith's strong wish to be a good mother and to keep her family together. Thus, *successful contracting helps clients to want what they need*. It culminates in an oral agreement, which then becomes operationalized through putting specific goals in writing.

PLANNING INTERVENTIONS

The Unit of Attention

What would have been the appropriate focus of the Smith case? The people or their environment? The child (Barbie) or her family? A "person-in-environment" ecosystems perspective (Germain, 1973; Meyer, 1983) allows the worker to shift back and forth between relevant dimensions of the case, and to consider the degree of fit (or lack of fit) between the two.

Whenever a child is the reason for referral, involvement with the family is mandatory. However, the unique circumstances of each case determine the degree to which either the child or the family becomes the primary "unit of attention." In some situations, such as helping a child process and accept his or her placement or traumatic experience (see Chapters 10 and 14), work with the child is primary, and family counseling is secondary to helping the child. In other situations, work with the family is pivotal to understanding and helping the child. This is true, for example, in families where divorce (Chapter 11) or a substance use disorder (Chapter 13) is a major factor. Still another method of work involves conjoint sessions with the child and family members. Many variations may also be appropriate, including alternating among individual child sessions, parent–child sessions, and full family sessions. The circumstances of each case determine who is seen and in which combinations, and this may vary over the lifespan of the case.

In similar fashion, the worker must keep a wide-angle focus on both environmental considerations *and* the persons involved. In Chapter 1, a multifactorial diagram of problem situations (Figure 1.1) depicts the interplay of reciprocal influences between the child and his or her physical and social environment. Specific factors, such as the child's temperament and coping style, can mediate and counteract noxious conditions in an unsafe, nonsupportive environment; conversely, a fragile child with a very reactive temperament may respond poorly even in supportive environmental conditions. Therefore, we must always consider interactive factors —those pertaining to the "fit" between persons and their environment— in assessing problem situations and planning interventions.

Setting Goals and a Time Frame

The establishment of goals follows directly from the client's recognition that help is needed, and from his or her agreement to focus together with the worker on amelioration of the particular difficulties.

The goals may be outlined for individual family members and/or for the family as a unit, depending on the situation. When a time frame is established for completion of certain goals or tasks, this increases motivation. Goals may be listed as "long-term," requiring a protracted period of time (possibly 9–12 months) for their completion, or as "short-term," with a designated target date for completion (possibly in 1 month). *It is essential for the client to participate in the setting of the goals and the time frame, and it is usually advisable to put these in writing.*

Keeping Goals Manageable: A Sample Dialogue

A cardinal rule in setting goals is to draft them in a manner that promises achievable results. The worker wants the client to have an experience of success, no matter how small this may be. Furthermore, it is important not to overwhelm the client; therefore, it is essential to begin with a limited number of manageable goals, with the understanding that once success has been achieved with the initial list, others may be added.

———————— ❖ ————————

The sample biopsychosocial assessment summary for Barbie, given in Chapter 4, lists eight "needed resources" for helping the Smith family. This comprehensive list could have been converted into specific goals during a planning session with Mrs. Smith and Barbie. It would have been important to begin with goals for Barbie that centered around her educational needs, and to specify family or personal goals for Mrs. Smith that would also have an impact on Barbie. A dialogue for this hypothetical meeting follows.

WORKER: I know that you are both very eager to have Barbie get a good start and do as well as possible in her new school. We want to do whatever we can also, so the purpose of this meeting is to decide *together* how to help Barbie achieve up to her fullest potential.

MRS. SMITH: Unfortunately, Barbie is behind where she should be for her age. We've moved so much, and she's been in so many different schools. It's not her fault.

WORKER: Of course it isn't her fault. (*To Barbie*) There are other children in this school who don't have permanent homes, and who have changed schools a lot. In fact, this school was designed exactly for kids like you, and we have some special ways to try to help.

BARBIE: Like what?

WORKER: Several different programs and activities that you will find out about as you go along. The first way is to try to find out just what you do know, so we can help you catch up, wherever you may need to. So I'm going to start a list of what the school will do, and what each of you can do. (*The worker divides a sheet of paper into three columns, and heads the first column "The School," the second section "Barbie," and the third section "Mrs. Smith."*) Under "The School," I'm going to write "1. Academic tests" and "2. Special tutoring." Barbie will be given a special teacher, who will work individually with her to help her in whatever areas the tests show she needs help. How does that sound?

BARBIE: Will I have a lot of homework?

WORKER: We don't expect you to get caught up the first week, or the first month! Yes, you will have homework, but it probably won't be more than an hour or, at most, two a day. (*To Mrs. Smith*) Would you be able to help Barbie figure out a quiet place and a time to do her homework?

MRS. SMITH: That's not so easy. We're in a one-bedroom motel, and the only table is where we all eat.

WORKER: Lots of kids do their homework on the kitchen table. The trick is to cut down on the distracting noise level, like from a TV. Do you think you could set aside a regular time each afternoon that would be "quiet time" for Barbie, and for you also, when there would be no TV and no distractions?

MRS. SMITH: That would be a miracle. But I'll try. Sometimes Barbie doesn't want to go to school when she doesn't do her homework, or if she doesn't get it right.

WORKER: In this school you don't always have to get it right, but you do have to try. So, Mrs. Smith, I'm writing this in your section: "1. Make a family rule for 1 hour of quiet time every afternoon, when there will be no TV and no noisy talk." The other thing is that you must be sure Barbie comes to school every day. She can't learn or catch up if she isn't here. So I'll write "2. Be sure Barbie comes to school every day."

Now we have to think about what to put in Barbie's section of this agreement. What do you think, Barbie?

BARBIE: I have to do my homework.

WORKER: Yes, You have to try. And your special teacher will help you. So I'll write this for you: "1. Do homework at least 1 hour each day." I also think you have to promise to come to school every day unless you are sick. I'm going to write that down as number 2. Actually, I think you'll like it here and *want* to come. We have some special groups for kids to get to know each other, and I'll see you tomorrow and tell you about those.

Sometimes the three of us will meet together, like today, and other times I'll meet alone with each of you. Let's make an appointment when we can all meet together again, so we can see how things are going with everybody's goals. I'd also like to set a separate appointment for Mrs. Smith to give me some background about Barbie.

Obviously, this would have been only the beginning of the contracting process. The next conjoint meeting (which ideally would have been scheduled within a week) would have provided an opportunity for reports of success in implementing the two goals of Barbie's regular school attendance and the homework routine. Later, separate individual meetings with Barbie and Mrs. Smith could have been used to introduce the offer of individual counseling as well as support groups for each.

Both the process of participation in formulating goals, and the experience of achieving success, are very ego-enhancing and increase self-esteem. Success in achieving goals, in turn, enhances clients' motivation to work on additional, more challenging tasks.

Various Intervention Options

Let us consider the range of intervention options that might have been pursued with the Smith family, both within and outside the First Place program. Within the school setting, support groups exist both for children and for parents. In addition, individual counseling is available for children, and case management for families. The latter includes networking and coordination with shelter providers, as well as referrals and follow-up to other services (housing, mental health, etc.). A flyer describing the range of services is given to each parent upon the child's admission, so this could have served as a nonthreatening way to review the available services with Mrs. Smith in a follow-up meeting. During this and subsequent sessions, the matter of the family's housing needs and Mrs. Smith's employment counseling/training could have been discussed, as could possible referrals for school/employment counseling for Barbie's siblings.

Individual counseling (therapy) for parents is *not* available through the school's professional staff, and therefore this very important referral for Mrs. Smith would have had to be made to an outside agency. Because this family was already involved with so many other outside agencies, it would have been understandable if Mrs. Smith were resistant to engaging with yet another person and place. Nonetheless, since help for Mrs. Smith would translate into potential help for her entire family, the matter of finding a counseling program for her that she could accept would have had to be pursued with utmost care and determination. It probably would have been best to make this referral after the relationship with Mrs. Smith was firmly established, through provision of other needed services.

Individual counseling for children is available through the school, and would have been a vital resource for Barbie. Her issues of past abuse and loss were probably continuing to create anxiety for her, and her family's ongoing lack of stability may well have made her vulnerable to loneliness, depression, and low self-esteem (Bassuk & Rubin, 1986).

In addition to a relationship with a counselor/therapist, Barbie might have benefited from a mentoring relationship. The literature reports the important role of such relationships in contributing to resilience in high-risk youths (Rhodes, 1994). Barbie's life was lacking in role models other than her mother. She had no known female relatives (other than her sister) and had never been involved in the type of extracurricular activities, such as Girl Scouts or team sports, that would provide her with other views of adult females she might choose to emulate. Studies in Great Britain (Rutter, 1979, 1987) and Hawaii (Werner & Smith, 1982) found that children living in developmentally hazardous settings who sought support from nonparental adults had a lower risk of psychiatric disorders and were more resilient than children living in similar settings who did not seek such support. Anthony's work on "the invulnerable child" also confirms the significance of one positive relationship in the lives of children growing up in very hostile home and/or community environments (Anthony & Cohler, 1987).

Finally, because of her family's frequent moves, Barbie had never had the opportunity to establish friendships with peers. She may have lacked socialization skills, and would probably have benefited from being in a group with other children in similar circumstances. Issues discussed in these school-based groups include friendships, conflicts with classmates, loss of former friends and schools, and domestic violence. It is very supportive for children to learn through being in such a group that they are not the only ones who have difficulties such as these.

Teamwork within and between Agencies

Professional collaboration would have been the key to success in the Smith case, since the clients' motivation and ability to work on their own behalf might have been limited. This would probably have been a "labor-intensive" case, requiring a major input from staff members to maintain the clients' motivation. Within the school, it would have been essential for the special education teacher working with Barbie to be aware of the physical limitations of the child's home environment, and to know about the agreed-upon contract for protected homework time. In addition, the regular classroom teacher would have needed to know about Barbie's history of extensive school changes, which may have interfered with the girl's ability to make friends and participate in social exchanges appropriate for a 10-year-old.

Regular pupil review conferences could also have alerted all staff members to significant developments in the family that might affect Barbie's ability to concentrate and learn. Examples of such developments might include Mrs. Smith's becoming involved with a new man, or Mrs. Smith's arguing with Barbie's sister, Donna, over Donna's choice of boyfriend.

Parnell and Vanderkloot (1989) state that they cannot work with poor, multiproblem families without a team of professionals:

> For members of the team, the involvement of the other members spells relief from the recurrent crises, the chronic problems, and the many occasions when it is necessary to devote whole days to individual clients. Furthermore, the team members function as a support group to one another, and as the nucleus of a resource network. (p. 452)

This kind of collaboration is also necessary among staff members in different agencies who are working with a multiproblem family. Certainly it would have been within the purview of Mrs. Smith's probation worker to help arrange adequate housing. It would *not* seem appropriate for someone with a history of addiction and possession of drugs to be living in an environment populated by substance users. Similarly, it would seem inappropriate for someone like Mrs. Smith to obtain employment in a bar, where she would probably be thrown into contact with many alcohol-addicted individuals. We do not know how much (if anything) Mrs. Smith's probation officer knew about her life at this time, but a case conference, coordinated by the school, would have provided the opportunity for *all* the professionals involved to meet with Mrs. Smith to share information and to coordinate planning on her behalf.

TRACKING PROGRESS AND TERMINATING

Tracking Progress

Once relationships have been established among the various professionals involved in a case, the process of keeping abreast of developments becomes easier. Ideally, the case conference establishes clear areas of responsibility, so that each member of the "team" knows his or her focus of duty, and no one person feels overburdened by attempting to work alone with *all* the various facets of the case. In the case of the Smiths, the school social worker might have become the case manager, with the understanding that new developments and the concerns of other agencies could be funneled through him or her. Although this might appear to be a major responsibility in and of itself, if others shared the tasks of helping Mrs. Smith find permanent housing, job training, addiction counseling, and mental health counseling, the school social worker would then have been freed from having to become involved personally in each of these tasks. The school, after all, was the primary contact point for the child, and the other agencies (probation, department of social services, housing, mental health, etc.) could share the responsibility of trying to rehabilitate the Smiths and help point them toward a more productive life.

Of course, the danger of having so many different people involved with the Smiths would have been that they could become scattered and frustrated because of having too many people to relate to. They also might confuse the appropriate functions of each, unless they were given direct guidance to avoid this.

Case review conferences should be held periodically, to track the progress of each case. The timing of such reviews should be determined during the original conference. Because of the rapidly changing elements in the Smith case, a plan for a review in 6 months might have been impractical, although in other case situations this is a reasonable period of time.

Actually, when the Smith family found Section 8 housing after Barbie had been at First Place School only 2 months, her records were transferred to a regular public school, and the case management role of the special school ceased to exist. In retrospect, a fallback plan to prevent the family's becoming "lost" would have helped keep both the helpers and this family on track.

Termination

The concept of "termination" is really not applicable in dealing with young children whose development is in flux, or with families that have serious and ongoing problems. What happens is that some families drop out of sight for a period of time and later come to the attention of other agencies, which may be unaware of previous efforts to help the family.

The term "termination" assumes that the difficulties presented at intake have been resolved and that there will be no further contacts. It certainly cannot guarantee that similar or different problems will not resurface at a later time. It is quite likely that a child who shows sufficient difficulties to come to the attention of a school social worker in third grade will again present problems in middle school, when physiological development creates stresses that make the individual less able to cope. The fact that a child has a confidential record related to the earlier difficulties may assist the counselor/social worker who meets this child for the first time at age 12. In my opinion, the availability of records offers great aid to professionals who enter a case after much work has already been done, but about which the parent(s) may give an inadequate report.

———————————— ❖ ————————————

UPDATE ON THE SMITH FAMILY

The following summary of what happened to the Smiths after the end of the *No Place like Home* videotape (Hunt, 1992) is based on information from the filmmaker, Kathryn Hunt; on my telephone conversation with Mrs. Smith; and on various conversations with the First Place School personnel, who had signed releases from Mrs. Smith to share this information.

The end of the video announced that Barbie had been sent a one-way ticket and that she had gone to visit her father. Her mother told me that Barbie remained with her father for an extended time (almost a full school year), although the original plan had been for a summer visit only. When Barbie eventually returned to her mother, she told the filmmaker that she had not gone to school during the previous year. However, the school records do indicate an out-of-state registration. The facts about this remain unclear.

The summer following Barbie's stay with her father, I attempted to contact the family in order to obtain releases for this book. The filmmaker had prepared Mrs. Smith for my call, and Mrs. Smith had indicated her willingness to give me her permission. I spoke to Barbie and David before finally reaching Mrs. Smith. My conversation with her took place the night before they were to be evicted from the apartment in which they had lived for more than a year following Barbie's transfer out of the special school program. Mrs. Smith gave me permission over the phone, and indicated her willingness to sign releases, which I said I would send to Kathryn Hunt

Following their eviction, it took 4 months after my phone call for the personnel at the school and Ms. Hunt to locate the family. During this time, Mrs. Smith evidently had some trouble with the law and was imprisoned again briefly (I do not know any details). Because I continued to press the school to locate the family, they eventually did so, through the department of social services. I had assumed that if the Smiths were still in the same state, they would be receiving public assistance. The fact that Barbie was *not* enrolled in school (which had been verified) constituted grounds to report Mrs. Smith, and this information was conveyed to her through a note to her public assistance worker.

Mrs. Smith soon after reappeared at the special school program to enroll Barbie. Barbie remained there for a full 6-month period, during which time Mrs. Smith accepted a referral and involved herself in counseling provided by the mental health system. Barbie made considerable academic gains during this period, was tested, and was found *not* to have a learning disability. In other words, her considerable academic delays were attributable to her irregular school attendance. As of this writing, Barbie was eligible to continue at that school program for one more year, after which she would be too old. However, the availability of this special school program for Barbie was contingent upon her family's continuing homeless status. Were she to transfer to a "regular" public middle school, it would be unlikely that there would be any special services to accommodate her special needs.

Barbie's sister, Donna, was once again living apart from Mrs. Smith and Barbie. She had had a baby, and was living alone with her child, since the baby's father was in prison. Barbie's brother had also moved out, and his whereabouts were unknown. As of this writing, Barbie had her own room in the motel where she resided with her mother.

CONCLUDING COMMENTS

Contracting assumes that a client has the motivation and ability to follow through with an agreed-upon plan. Sometimes a plan that seems logical and feasible on one day can become invalid when the client's circumstances change and the plan becomes unworkable. Therefore, the time frame of contracts with multiproblem clients and families should be short, and there should be frequent monitoring.

The case of Barbie Smith graphically illustrates the impact of homelessness on school attendance and child development. This population of children clearly requires special services such as those described here. However, the lack of follow-up after a family obtains housing and a child leaves the program can have serious consequences if the child goes for protracted periods of time without schooling. This state of affairs needs more careful monitoring by public assistance programs that provide financial support to families. Computerization should permit tracking of homeless children's school attendance, in order to insure that such children do not fall between the cracks.

DISCUSSION QUESTIONS

1. Discuss the ethical issue involved in trying to broaden a client's views of what he or she needs, as described in the beginning of this chapter. To what extent should the contract reflect the worker's vision about the client's potential for growth and change, and how does this conform to the principle of client self-determination?

2. What intervention(s) do you think would have been appropriate to encourage Barbie's more regular school attendance? If the school social worker suspected that Mrs. Smith had resumed drug use, how might this have been handled?

3. Consider the concepts of "risk" and "resilience" as they apply to Barbie Smith. Suggest some factors that may have contributed to her resilience. What do you predict for her future, and on what do you base your prediction?

4. Discuss the pros and cons of providing a *separate* school program for homeless children. How would you address the important issue of integrating children who have been in a separate program into a regular school program at a later date?

PART III

Different Methods of Helping Children

CHAPTER 6

Working with the Family

Children and their families are interdependent. Therefore, when one member of a family system experiences difficulties, the stress reverberates to all members of the family. Although a child may be singled out as having a "problem," the practitioner must look beyond the individual and think about the meaning and significance of that problem to *all* the family members, in order to understand the problem's source and to determine how best to focus helping efforts.

TWO DISTINCT HELPING APPROACHES: CHILD-CENTERED AND FAMILY THERAPY

Practitioners with different theoretical orientations define problems differently. If the child's "problem" is viewed as inherent in the *child*, individual play therapy is usually recommended as the treatment of choice, with adjunctive counseling for the parents/family. Alternatively, if the child's problem is considered as reactive to dysfunctional *family* interactions, then the assumption follows that the child's difficulty will resolve itself when the family's communication improves. These two polar views mirror the distinctive historical roots and different philosophical underpinnings of practice in the fields of child and family therapy. The manners in which practitioners with different theoretical orientations define the problem lead to distinctively different helping methods.

Systems Thinking and the Exclusion of Children from Family Therapy

Believing that the *real* problem is a troubled marriage and/or dysfunctional family communication, many family therapists work diligently in the first few sessions "to redefine the problem as systemic, rather than that of the individual child" (Wachtel, 1994, p. 2). Instead of seeing the family, *of* the patient, the family is regarded, *as* the patient (Bloch & LaPerriere, 1973). This focus on the family unit has resulted in a neglect of children within many approaches to family therapy. Indeed, in their zeal to remove children from the position of "symptom bearers," many family therapists have gone to the extreme of eliminating young, nonverbal children altogether from their therapy sessions (Chasin & White, 1989). Of course, sometimes a child's dysfunction *is* in fact reactive to parental conflict, and then the focus should properly be on the marriage and not the child. At other times, however, when children have bona fide troubles (e.g., their own identity issues, peer and school problems, or intrinsic conditions such as physical or learning disabilities), they need and deserve one-to-one work to help them. The danger in the family systems approach is that it may ignore children's needs as individuals. Treating the child *only* as a "pawn in the game-playing between adults" (McDermott & Char, 1974, p. 425) seems not only adultcentristic, but also simplistic and neglectful of children's rights.

The Exclusion of Parents from Child Therapy

With a different view of etiology and a different perspective about how to help, many therapists espousing the "child-centered" approach exclude parents from the playroom and do not believe that work with parents is essential for successful child therapy (Axline, 1947; Landreth, 1991). Because these therapists consider the relationship between the child and the therapist to be so growth-enhancing and healing, they believe that this present, here-and-now therapeutic relationship is more important than the impact of the child's past history and other relationships. Similar to the traditional child psychiatry model, child-centered therapy focuses on treatment of the identified child patient, with minimal contact with the parents.

A famous child-centered therapy case that excluded the parents is the one described by Virginia Axline (1964) in her book *Dibs: In Search of Self*. Every time I use this case for teaching purposes, I am in awe of Axline's work: She managed to develop a trusting relationship with a mute, oppositional 5-year-old child, whose parents and teachers were beginning to consider mentally retarded. Axline helped Dibs reveal his exceptional potential as a person in weekly sessions over an 18-month period, without any regular involvement of the child's parents.

Nevertheless, despite the remarkably successful outcome of this case, I am troubled by any approach that appears to elevate the *practitioner*'s relationship with the child to a more important position than the parent–

child relationship. Granted that the outcome for Dibs was very positive, and that his mother became more responsive to him and to the therapist once the boy's behavior began to change, his therapy took a fairly long time to achieve and would probably have been infeasible within a modern-day managed care system. Even more troubling, from a theoretical standpoint, was Axline's willingness to permit Dibs's mother to distance herself from her child, while Axline as the "expert" made him "better." The therapist thus inadvertently reinforced the mother's feelings of incompetence, as well as of contempt for her child's problems. A family therapist working with this case would have tried to validate the mother's essential role in her child's future life, and thereby helped to make an inadequate mother feel instrumental in her son's spectacular change from a mute, oppositional 5-year-old to a responsive, charming 7-year-old.

AN INTEGRATED CHILD AND FAMILY MODEL

Not all practitioners who work with children subscribe to either a child-centered or a family-centered approach. As far back as the 1960s, Guerney (1964) developed a form of parent–child therapy called "filial therapy," which has since been renamed "child relationship enhancement therapy." It is based on teaching parents to become empathic and accepting of their child in a manner similar to the role of a play therapist (Guerney, 1964; Guerney & Guerney, 1994).

More recently, other practitioners have begun to blend individual and family approaches. For example, Wachtel (1994) employs an integrated "child-in-family approach," and O'Connor (1991) proposes an ecosystemic model. Two recent books on the topic of family play therapy (Gil, 1994; Schaefer & Carey, 1994) provide many useful examples of successful integration of child and family therapy. Gil states (1994, p. 33) that "the integration of play with family therapy strengthens both therapeutic approaches."

In my own work, and in the various examples presented in this book, I try to employ whatever helping method seems to make sense for a particular child and family, rather than rigidly following either a child-centered or a family-centered approach because of allegiance to a particular method of working. A quote from an article that was first published more than 30 years ago expresses my own ideal of practice:

> It is true that treatment of only the parents (McNamara, 1963), the entire family (Bell, 1961), or only the child (Blanchard, 1946) may produce beneficial results. There is no good theoretical reason why one particular approach should be used on all problems. . . . *Effective treatment should*

be designed for whatever problems are recognized and should involve family members in ways that will ameliorate those problems. (Straughan, 1964/1994, p. 99; emphasis added)

DIFFERENT LEVELS OF FAMILY INVOLVEMENT

As I emphasize repeatedly in this book and demonstrate in various examples, work with children *always* includes some sort of work with their parents when they are living and available. Whether siblings are seen depends on the nature of the presenting problem and on conflicts in relationships that become evident in the course of the work. For example, in a previous publication (Webb, 1993), I have included several cases involving sibling and family work following deaths and parental separation.

Sometimes it is appropriate for a babysitter, or a member of the extended family (e.g., a grandmother), to be included in sessions with the child. Often I see the entire family together for one or more sessions, in order to assess the nature of the family members' interactions and to involve them in thinking about how they might get along better. I refer to myself as a "child and family social worker," thereby indicating to the family my ability to work flexibly with the various family members in different combinations, as well as in a unit.

Parent Counseling/Guidance

Parent counseling or guidance typically occurs once a month when a child is being seen on a weekly basis. The main purpose of these parent meetings is to give and receive feedback about the child's progress. The meetings also offer the worker the opportunity to ask questions about matters the child may have raised, to reinforce a parent's positive efforts with the child, and to support the parent in his or her continuing frustrations.

The issue of confidentiality always comes up in family work. Because of my belief that it is important to foster parent–child communication, and to convey the sense that the parent(s), child, and practitioner are all working *together* to try to alleviate the problem situation, I do not want to overvalue the importance of a child's relationship with me and leave a parent feeling like an outsider. Therefore, I share my impressions about the child openly with the parent, and, without quoting the child verbatim, I give the parent a sense of the nature of the child's participation in his or her sessions with me. Since this is a two-way street, I also share with the child, discreetly and appropriately, concerns that the parent may have brought to my attention. Sometimes the parent meeting indicates the need for a family session, which I then schedule, after clarifying with the child the potential positive outcome from such a meeting.

Practitioners in agency practice sometimes encounter parents who are reluctant to come to parent or family meetings. These parents may not be aware that their child has a problem, or they may prefer to let the school or someone else handle it. Often such parents may be burdened by work and home responsibilities and worries; they may view their child's difficulty with anger and resentment that yet another demand is now being placed on their time. Practitioners, in turn, sometimes become resentful when parents are unwilling to put the necessary effort into trying to help their own children. *It is the professional's responsibility to reach out and make the extra effort to connect with parents who are resistant to becoming involved.* Often, doing this requires stretching one's empathic sensitivity, to try to understand and feel what a particular mother's or father's life must be like. Offering to make a home visit may have a positive effect, as may trying to schedule an appointment in a restaurant near a parent's workplace during his or her lunch hour. A practitioner who sincerely believes in the importance of parents' involvement, and backs up this conviction with both words and action, has a better chance of engaging parents.

Parent–Child Sessions

It is appropriate to see a child together with a parent under certain circumstances. First, there may be no choice when the child has separation problems of such severity that he or she cannot tolerate being separated from the parent (usually the mother). Second, it is essential to have the parent present during at least part of the session when a behavior modification program has been set up; the therapist will need to encourage the parent to praise the child for gains, or to discuss with both the child and parent certain alterations of the program if the child is not achieving success with it. The use of parent–child sessions in connection with a behavior modification program is described in greater detail later in this chapter (see the case of Tim).

When a child is experiencing separation anxiety, as in the case of Tammy (Chapter 7), the issue becomes one of helping mother and child learn to separate from each other. The session itself serves as a training opportunity. It is advisable for the practitioner to have a separate session with the mother, or a telephone conference with her before the joint session, to coach her in an overall plan for gradual separation and increase her willingness to carry out the plan. Depending on the child's tolerance level and other possible contributing factors (such as the mother's own need to cling to the child), a plan can be established for the mother to sit in the doorway of the playroom, watching but not playing actively with the child. When the child appears to have established an adequate level of comfort with the practitioner, the practitioner will suggest to the mother that she take a look at an interesting article in a magazine in the waiting room. The mother should then leave without a big goodbye scene, since this may raise the child's anxiety again. This planned leavetaking may need to be repeated several times before the child can eventually begin the session in the playroom without the mother. This protocol for gradual separation can also be applied to a day care or nursery school situation in which the child cannot tolerate separation from the mother, and, with modification, to bedtime separation problems.

Sessions with Siblings

Sessions with siblings may be appropriate in cases where the nature of the presenting problem constitutes a shared family experience—for example, the death of a relative, or an upcoming parental divorce (Webb, 1993). Such sessions may also be useful when the practitioner becomes aware of intensive sibling conflict in the course of working with one child in the family.

Other children in a family *always* have some reaction to the fact that one of their siblings is in therapy. When the family considers the necessity for treatment as a weakness on the treated child's part, the sibling who has not been singled out may feel superior to the brother or sister who needs individual help. However, sometimes certain privileges accompany therapy, such as additional attention from the parents, and a dinosaur sticker or a food treat from the therapist at the end of a session. This can make the treated child appear to be the recipient of special "goodies" that are not accorded to other siblings in the family.

I try to alert parents to this possible source of strain, and suggest that they use the situation to emphasize that each brother and sister is different, and that the siblings will all have different positive and negative experiences in their lives. This discussion can prove to be a window into how each child is perceived in the family, as well as how the child in treatment views himself or herself in comparison to the other children.

When siblings are seen together, it is important to model this respect for individual difference as a principle of interaction. Certain guidelines and rules need to be made explicit, just as in group or family sessions. I have found it especially important with siblings to establish the ground rule that, differences or arguments that may emerge during the session must not continue when the siblings leave the office. They may repeat positive things about one another, but not negatives.

It is sometimes necessary to separate siblings when they are arguing and unable to take turns speaking and listening to one another. This happened in the case of the Martini sisters, ages 8 and 10 (Webb, 1993), whose anger toward each other became excessive and out of control following the closely timed proximity of their parents' separation and their uncle/godfather's death. Unable to express their rage at their grieving parents, they took it out on each other. When I attempted to see them together, the sessions were dominated by arguments, name calling, destructive putdowns, and some tears of frustration.

Realizing that the joint work was becoming counterproductive, I began splitting the sessions and seeing each girl individually. Prior to doing so, I told the girls that I could see how angry they both were, and that they had a right to feel angry, but that I could not let them take their feelings out on each other. I also advised each parent to echo this principle, and to separate the girls physically when they fought at home. In individual sessions, one girl drew a frightening werewolf with his teeth bared, and the other pounded, poked, and aggressively rolled out various lumps of clay. After several months of these split sessions during which each child was permitted to express her angry feelings symbolically through play, the parents reported noticeably reduced fighting at home, and I was able to resume some conjoint sessions with them.

Sessions with the Entire Family

The purpose of seeing the entire family together is twofold: (1) to see first-hand how family members relate to one another, and (2) to help the family find and use more positive and gratifying ways of relating.

Seeing the Parents First

Whole-family sessions provide wonderful opportunities to observe family members' interactions, but they also can seem very intimidating to the practitioner, who may feel outnumbered and quite uncomfortable in the role of outsider. Hepworth and Larsen (1993) recognize that work with the entire family requires advanced skills; they suggest that students and practitioners with little experience in family work begin by seeing the parents without the children. This permits the practitioner to become familiar with the overall problem situation, and to begin establishing an alliance with the parents, prior to introducing the children into sessions at a later date.

In Chapter 4, I have described three reasons for seeing parents alone before seeing children: establishing the alliance, obtaining the developmental history, and preparing a parent to prepare a child for the first session. Wachtel (1994) notes another interesting and important advantage of seeing the parents alone first. Wachtel points out that many parents who come for help in regard to their children's problems have developed some very negative feelings of resentment toward the children, because, in essence, the problems appear to expose the parents as "failures." Parents need to "unload" these negative feelings, including their fears that there is something drastically *wrong* with their children. Obviously, it would be contraindicated for them to do this in the children's presence. Therefore, the cathartic value of having the practitioner listen and respond appropriately to the *parents'* concerns helps strengthen the alliance with them, and also permits the practitioner to offer hope and therapeutic optimism that the situation can improve in time.

The "Joining" Process

When the practitioner meets the entire family together for the first time, it is essential that he or she find ways to "join" (Minuchin, 1974) with the family. "Joining" refers to efforts on the practitioner's part to become accepted, and "to establish an alliance with the family as a whole, with the key subsystems, and with each individual" (Chasin & White, 1989, p. 17). It is the process through which the practitioner moves from being an outsider to being an insider. This process relies on the practitioner's individual personality and style, as well as on his or her ability to establish enough of a feeling of comfort and connection with various family members that they will be able to tolerate having a stranger know about aspects of their lives not usually revealed to public scrutiny. Different authors suggest different techniques for joining, including small talk; mimicking the family's affect and style (Hepworth & Larsen, 1993); and commenting on a child's clothing, jewelry, or hairstyle (Chasin & White, 1989).

Setting Ground Rules for Family Sessions

Regardless of the particular subject of a "joining" conversation, the family session usually soon moves toward dealing with the important matters that are causing concern. Because the family has its own characteristic method of communicating (which may well include members' interrupting, shouting, and insulting one another), it is incumbent upon the practitioner to set ground rules early in the first session, in order to establish this meeting as different from interactions that occur in the family living room or kitchen. Sometimes, in the middle of a shouting match, I have found it effective to stand up and offer to leave the room, stating that the family members obviously do not need me to carry on their battles. I point out that if they continue to fight in my office the same way they do at home, then they are wasting their money and all of our time. This can be a prelude to establishing a rule that only one person speaks at a time, and that family members may disagree with one another, but not insult other persons or put them down because they have different opinions. Setting such ground rules as these in the first session establishes a climate of safety that models respect for the right of different individuals to express themselves without being heckled.

I introduce and enforce the following ground rules in family sessions:

- Only *one* person talks at a time.
- No insults, cursing, or putdowns are permitted.
- Disagreements/arguments are not to be continued outside the office.
- Children deserve the same respect as do adults.
- Everyone has the right to "pass" (i.e., not to answer or speak).
- Parents are in charge of limit setting for children.

Some Practical Guidelines for Working with the Entire Family

When the worker has had a preliminary meeting with the parents prior to the first session with the entire family, he or she will have a sense of the parents' personalities, as well as some background information about the various family members. Depending on the nature of the problem and the ages of the children, the practitioner should prepare to have toys or activities that are age-appropriate and that will permit the family to interact nonverbally through play, as well as verbally. During the preliminary meeting with the parents, I tell them that we cannot expect their children to sit and talk during the entire family meeting, so I will have some toys and activities that will make it easier for the children. I also tell the parents that I may ask them to participate in playing with their children. I make it clear that although I will be responsible for providing some play materials, I expect them, as the parents, to remain in charge of their children's behavior. In other words, if the children start whining and arguing, I want them to handle it as they would at home.

Some suggested activities for family sessions include paper and markers, puppets, clay, blocks, and selected board and card games. It is important, however, to avoid overstimulating the children through exposure to numerous toys. Since the purpose of the family session is to learn what *this* family is like, it is appropriate for the practitioner to take a directive stance—suggesting, for example, that the children draw a picture of their family doing something (i.e., Kinetic Family Drawing; Burns & Kaufman, 1970, 1972). Alternatively, the family may be asked to act out through puppet play something upsetting that happened in the family. The point is that the family session is not a "free-play" period; it is a time for understanding and discovering new ways of family interaction. The toys and play activities are used to facilitate this understanding.

Cultural Considerations

In some cultures, children are expected to be "seen but not heard." This view may present a strain between the practitioner's desire to permit the children to "have a voice" and the more traditional belief that "adults know best." For example, in the videotape *Tres Madres* the family therapist Harry Aponte (1990) conducted a family session with three generations of family members, including the 7-year-old girl who was the "identified patient." The child was rarely invited to participate in the adult conversation, and the tape showed her yawning and looking bored. Aponte clearly viewed the child's problem of sleepwalking as incidental to the girl's mother's unhappiness and inability to assert herself as a mother. Although this dynamic may indeed have been crucial to understanding the case, I question the need to have the child present during this discussion when she had no part in it. A play therapist, sensitive to the *child's* needs as well as to the mother's, would have provided paper and markers and suggested that the child draw a picture of her bedroom, of where her mother lived and where she lived, and of how she would like to have her family live. The conclusion that the child's symptom was related to the lack of a strong maternal presence could have also been deduced from a discussion centering around the child's drawings. The difference is that one approach meaningfully includes the child, and the other ignores her. When I have presented this example and viewpoint at workshops, however, some participants have responded that both Aponte and this Hispanic family might have been uncomfortable, for cultural reasons, in giving so much attention to a young child.

In my own practice with families of different ethnic backgrounds, I have learned to explore the parents' views about child involvement before including children in an entire family session. Sometimes the parents accept my offer to help them try a different way of relating to their children through play. However, this may be too difficult for others to attempt, and then I try to adapt my work to the reality of the clients' beliefs even when I may disagree with them.

What to Look For in Family Sessions

After a session with the entire family, the practitioner should try to answer the following questions:

1. Who seems to be the dominant parent? Do the children seem to accept parental rules, or do they try to split the parents?

2. Do parents share in the discipline, or is one or the other targeted for this role?

3. Which parent appears to set the limits for the children? Do the parents seem to agree, or is one more permissive and one more strict?

4. To whom do the children turn for affection and comfort?

5. Are any alliances between the children apparent? How is the symptomatic child treated by the other family members?

6. How does the symptomatic child relate to each parent? Do their responses to him or her differ?

7. How would the situation have to change in order for the family to feel better?

In a feedback session later with the parents, the practitioner will solicit the parents' reactions to the family session, and also share some of his or her own impressions. This can result in some important formulation of goals, with possible plans for another family meeting after a period of time during which the parents will have tried to implement changes.

A Note of Clarification

As evident in the preceding discussion, my view of "working with the family" is not the same as "family therapy" in the sense of seeking to change the family's roles and structure (Minuchin, 1974; Minuchin & Fishman, 1981). Rather, the integrated child and family approach presented in this book focuses on communication patterns and interactions among family members, in order to help them deal with the presenting problem in a manner that puts them in control of their own behavior. This systems view recognizes that when one person in a family has pain (which may show up in symptoms), all family members feel the pain in some way (Satir, 1983). This integrated child and family approach is similar to Satir's (1983) "growth model" of family therapy in focusing on clear communication among family members, which in turn promotes enhanced self-worth in each individual adult and child family member.

ETHICAL CHALLENGES IN FAMILY WORK

Because of its complexity, work with families places extra demands on practitioners, who must strive to be fair, objective, and self-aware in the midst of very intense emotional interactions. The goal of maintaining professional neutrality may be especially difficult when the lives of young children are at stake and the impulse to "rescue" them is ignited. Often people enter the helping professions because of a sincere, altruistic motivation to help those, like children, who for various reasons cannot help themselves. What is the danger, then, in wanting to "rescue" children? From whom or what are they being rescued? And what will become of them after the rescue?

There is a significant difference between helping and rescuing, because the implication in "rescue" is that the individual is being removed from a dangerous situation. In my opinion, a "child-rescuing mentality" serves to establish a barrier, rather than a bond, between a practitioner and a parent. When the worker becomes judgmental toward the parent, this greatly reduces his or her ability to work effectively with the parent, and ultimately the child suffers.

Work with children requires the ability to relate to children's parents. This relationship, however, inevitably stimulates memories and overtones from a practitioner's own family of origin. In supervising child therapists, and in my own work, I have often traced a lack of empathy or other therapeutic impasses to experiences in the practitioner's own family of origin or present family (Webb, 1989). "Countertransference can be triggered by identification with one of the clients, the family, the style of communication, and similar events in the therapist's life" (Miller, 1994, p. 16). Therefore, it is incumbent on practitioners working with families to be self-aware and to receive regular supervision, to help them recognize areas of possible identification with the families with which they are working.

Efforts to help children without attention to helping their families are short-sighted and will have limited impact. Admittedly, the work in trying to empower a family to help itself may seem more formidable than that of spending time individually with a child. However, more attention must be focused on this essential larger task if we are truly to integrate child and family helping.

Confidentiality is another thorny issue that frequently comes up in the context of family work. I have noted in Chapter 2 that children really do not have the right to confidentiality with respect to their parents, whose role affords them power to demand that a child reveal certain matters, or who may require that a child's medical (counseling) records be shared with them. When these matters come under dispute, the court may appoint a guardian *ad litem* to represent the child's best interests, but even then the child's position may be ambiguous and conflictual if he or she is caught between the demands of two hostile parents in a divorce proceeding. This situation is discussed more fully in Chapter 11.

Consistently in this book, I present the position that confidentiality between parent and child is neither feasible nor in the child's best interests. I argue for open communication between parent and child, for the purpose of increasing their understanding of each other's needs and feelings. When the child and parent treat each other with respect, confidentiality will not be a concern. Practitioners must consistently help families work toward this goal.

WORKING WITH CHILDREN WITH ATTENTION-DEFICIT/ HYPERACTIVITY DISORDER AND THEIR PARENTS

A diagnosis of Attention-Deficit/Hyperactivity Disorder (ADHD) usually follows some years of the parents' increasing awareness and growing concern because their child is difficult to manage, has a very high energy level, and is very distractible. This disorder is more common in boys than in girls, and is found in approximately 6–17% of children (Barker, 1995). The onset of the hyperactive behaviors is usually before the age of 3, but many children do not come to professional attention until they start school and cannot meet the additional demands placed on them in that setting.

The Nature of ADHD

ADHD is a biologically or constitutionally based disability of unclear etiology, although there is some evidence that genetic factors contribute to it (Barker, 1995; Bernier & Siegel, 1994). According to the American Psychiatric Association (1994), the characteristics of children with ADHD may include symptoms of inattention (e.g., easy distractibility, forgetfulness, lack of follow-through, difficulty organizing tasks and activities, and making careless mistakes) and/or symptoms of hyperactivity–impulsivity (e.g., fidgeting, excessive talking, seemingly "motor-driven" activity, interrupting others, blurting out answers, and difficulty taking turns). A formal diagnosis of ADHD requires at least six out of nine possible behavioral characteristics in one of these two subgroups (or 12 out of the total of 18 in both) "that have persisted for at least 6 months to a degree that is maladaptive and inconsistent with developmental level" (American Psychiatric Association, 1994, p. 83).

Interventions

Bernier and Siegel (1994, p. 143) report that a multimodal approach is most effective in helping children with ADHD and their families. Specific interventions include psychostimulant medication, usually methylphenidate (Ritalin); behavior management skills training for the children's parents and teachers; cognitive, supportive, and play therapy to enable the children to develop self-esteem; and supportive counseling for parents. Several of these methods were employed in the case of Tim (see below).

Dane (1990) points out that effective work with parents of children with learning disabilities requires that the social worker understand what such a disability means to a family. "Only by understanding the specific limitations of the individual child and the child's behavior within the context of its fit within the family and cultural group can the social worker begin to design appropriate strategies for intervention" (Dane, 1990, pp. 137–138). Certainly this statement also applies to work with ADHD children and their families. The tripartite assessment (see Chapter 4) assists the social worker in pinpointing the particular meaning of the child's disability in a given family.

Among various interventions recommended by Dane (1990, pp. 139–140) as helpful for families of children with learning disabilities are the following:

- Educating parents about the special developmental needs of their children (e.g., offering more stimulation and attention to areas in which their children may need extra practice).
- Helping parents anticipate the critical stages of their children's maturational process (e.g., advocating to promote their children's special needs with each new teacher or recreational group leader).
- Assisting parents and their children to determine the appropriate degree of parental intervention (e.g., moderating parental protective behavior toward the children, and encouraging the advocacy skills of the maturing children to intervene whenever appropriate on their own behalf).

Family Considerations

The impact of living with a "hyped-up" child with many distractible and agitated behaviors cannot be minimized. Children with ADHD do not slow down, and even when watching TV they may bounce on the couch, poke or tickle a sibling, or laugh raucously and fall on the floor. Bernier and Siegel (1994, p. 146) state that "the child's noncompliant, disruptive behavior contributes to chronic stress in parents, which in turn produces unproductive parenting behaviors that exacerbate the ADHD symptoms." The cycle of negative parent–child interactions that often characterizes a family with an ADHD child results in fewer gratifications in the parental role and reduced parental self-esteem. These factors in turn sometimes precipitate or aggravate parental problems, such as depression (Bernier & Siegel, 1994). A focus on the parents and the family system, therefore, is essential when working with an ADHD child. If the practitioner can effectively support the parents, this may help to prevent a negative cycle of behaviors that could become worse as the child gets older (Hallowell & Ratey, 1994). The case discussion that follows illustrates some behavioral approaches in work with a 7-year-old boy with ADHD and his family.

——————— ❖ ———————

THE CASE OF TIM, AGE 7

Family Information

Mother	Kathy Marino, age 35, nursery school teacher.
Father	Tony Marino, age 37, music store owner. Plays in band several nights a week and on weekends.
Sister	Chris, age 3, attends nursery school (but not in Mrs. Marino's class).
Child client	Tim, age 7, second grade; plays hockey and soccer. ADHD diagnosed at end of first grade.
Paternal grandparents	In 60s, babysit two or three times per month.
Maternal grandparents	In 60s, live out of state.
Maternal uncle	Age 38, live out of state; had ADHD.
Son of uncle	Age 10, has ADHD; on Ritalin.

The Marinos are a white family, of Italian descent; they are Catholics.

Presenting Problem

The parents sought help in connection with Tim's recent diagnosis of ADHD. The school had wanted to retain Tim at the end of first grade, and the parents, who disagreed, had had Tim tested and put Tim on Ritalin, and were concerned about how to handle this with him. The mother also wanted guidance about how to manage Tim's difficult behavior at home.

Assessment and Plan for Intervention

I saw the parents for an initial meeting, followed by three play assessment sessions with Tim. I requested and received the report from the psychologist, who stated that Tim's "principal dysfunction appears to be in the inattention component, somewhat less in the impulsive component, and even less in the hyperactive factor." (The hyperactive and impulsive components are now combined into one symptom group in DSM-IV; see above.) The psychologist recommended Ritalin, tutorial assistance, parent counseling, and cognitive-behavioral therapy for Tim.

My evaluation, which I shared with the parents in the feedback session, was that I found Tim to be a charming, very likable child who demonstrated in the sessions with me many of the characteristics of ADHD that would probably cause him difficulty in school. Specifically, I was concerned about the rushed, "slapdash" manner in which Tim made several drawings, without apparent care as to details (see Figures 6.1 and 6.2). The figure of the person (Figure 6.1) was very distorted, with enormous arms, and none of the figures in the family drawing (Figure 6.2) had hands or feet. These drawings were immature for a 7-year-old.

Moreover, in playing some board games with Tim I noticed that he had a great deal of difficulty waiting for his turn and following rules, and I wondered how this might affect his social interactions. Curiously, when I asked Tim about friends, he was not able to remember any of their names. Tim also seemed to have a very distorted concept of numbers, telling me that his mother was 103 years old and that there were 93 children in his class at school!

FIGURE 6.1. Tim's Draw-A-Person.

FIGURE 6.2. Tim's Draw-A-Family.

The parents, especially Mrs. Marino, were very open about feeling "overwhelmed" by Tim. He was going to begin Ritalin soon, but even if it helped, they wanted some assistance in how to manage him. Because of Mr. Marino's long work hours, the mother often felt unsupported and unable to endure Tim's constant talking, night fears, and excessive demands in the evenings. We agreed on a plan for parent counseling, some mother–child sessions, and some work with Tim alone.

Interventions

Sessions with Tim

My first goal was to establish a positive relationship with this boy, which had already begun during the assessment phase. I had referred several times to the fact that I helped children and families with their troubles and worries. When Tim could not think of any worries, I let him know that his mother had told me that she lost her temper and yelled at him sometimes. He acknowledged that this happened, but seemed incapable of recalling an example of when this happened or of thinking about what might help.

Sessions with Tim and His Mother

I suggested to Tim that we invite his mom into the session, and together the three of us would come up with some techniques to use when they were beginning to lose control, so they wouldn't end up screaming at each other. I asked them to think of a signal they could give each other that would mean they had to stop talking and separate for a while. They came up with a hand movement across the mouth, which was supposed to signify "Zip your lip." Mrs. Marino was afraid that Tim would try to use this every time she told him to do something he didn't want to do, so I emphasized that this was meant *only* to keep them from screaming at each other. The next week, both Tim and his mother were happy to report that the signal had worked. There had been less negative interaction between them.

Mrs. Marino next wanted to figure out a way for Tim to be able to spend some time alone. She stated that he usually hung around her every minute when she was home, and that she needed some quiet time to herself. I asked Tim to think of some things he could do by himself in his room. With Mrs. Marino's help, we made a list. Realizing that Tim would need an incentive to carry out these solitary behaviors, I introduced a graph and suggested a star system for every day Tim succeeded in staying by himself for 10 minutes, and then a reward at the end of each week if he got at least four stars. Tim became very animated as he thought about the rewards he would want, and he finally settled on a particular computer game, which he would be able to "earn" at the end of a month.

The concrete nature of the graph and the stars proved to be an excellent technique for motivating Tim, although there were some disagreements about whether time spent playing with his sister would count, and whether he had to check with his mother *before* spending the time alone, since he sometimes would claim that he had completed a 10-minute period when his mother was not home or aware of his behavior. Tim wanted to put more stars on the graph than he had actually earned, but his mother, with my support, was able to set appropriate limits. At the end of the month Tim earned his reward, and immediately *asked* to start a new graph. (See Figure 6.3 for Tim's first graph.)

Another control technique that was useful for Tim was to have him construct a stop sign out of construction paper and hang it up in his room. With his mother, we talked about Tim's need to "slow down." His teacher

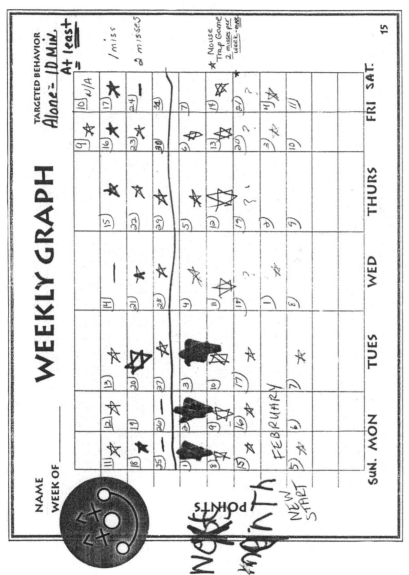

FIGURE 6.3. Tim's weekly graph for the first month of the graph/star system intervention.

133

had written this on his report card, and I thought that a tangible, visible reminder might be useful, since this had been effective with the graph. I also began to use some verbal directives during play sessions, when Tim appeared to be rushing. I would say to him, "You're going too fast. Close your eyes and imagine the stop sign. Count to five; then you can open your eyes and proceed *slowly*."

Parent Counseling

The parents had a good understanding of the biological component of ADHD, so it was not necessary for me to educate them about that. Nonetheless, Mr. Marino was not entirely happy with the idea of giving Tim a pill to help him concentrate better. He was afraid that this might mean that Tim would stop trying to help himself. I used the example of wearing glasses to help see better; this improves the focus, but it doesn't change the person's basic vision. Similarly, Ritalin does not change the underlying neurological condition, but it gives an immediate benefit for the person's ability to concentrate.

In discussing the graph with Mr. and Mrs. Marino, I emphasized that it motivated Tim because it gave him an immediate reinforcement that he knew would "pay off" at a later time. I emphasized that it was very important for them to give Tim consistent praise whenever he behaved appropriately. I stated that the stars, for now, were an additional reinforcement, but that the most important thing was for them to praise Tim when he showed control. Since it was not possible to know exactly how much Tim really *could* control his behavior, even when he tried, it was necessary to set small, reasonable goals that he could achieve, so that neither he nor they would become frustrated. I pointed out that this was why I had suggested a 10-minute period of solitary play, rather than 30 minutes. I suggested that after consistent success with one goal, they could extend it in small increments, such as trying a 15-minute period after Tim seemed comfortable with the 10-minute period.

Tracking Progress

I followed this child and family on a weekly basis over a school year, with several breaks because of holiday vacation periods. There was steady improvement in the mother–child relationship, to the point that Tim no longer wanted his mother present during his sessions. His mother also confirmed during the parent sessions that she was feeling much better, and that the tension between her and Tim had diminished substantially.

I believe that this improvement was the result of several factors working together for this child's benefit:

1. The medication, which Tim took on school days only, and which improved his ability to concentrate and complete his schoolwork.
2. The various behavioral methods geared toward helping Tim control his own behavior, and the tangible rewards he received when he succeeded.
3. The increase in Tim's self-esteem, which resulted from his having success experiences and receiving positive reinforcement from his parents.
4. The parents' ability to work together and support each other. In the parent meetings, Mr. Marino became more aware of his wife's need for more support in managing Tim. Mornings were especially difficult for her: She had to get to her job on time, and Tim was often noisy and resistant to getting dressed, which added to her stress. Although Mr. Marino had trouble getting up because he worked late in the evenings, the couple was able to work out a "tradeoff" of days on which each parent would be responsible for Tim in the mornings, and this relieved Mrs. Marino from feeling that she had to manage him entirely alone.

I expect to follow up with this family periodically, but I do not anticipate that they will need ongoing weekly meetings, because they achieved such impressive gains in a relatively short time.

Discussion

This case demonstrates how a child and family under the stress of a recent ADHD diagnosis can be effectively helped. The Marinos seemed to feel out of control and unable to function well, despite their many strengths and areas of achievement. The interventions helped them to assume control of their lives once again, and to feel better about one another.

The specific behavioral interventions demonstrated in this case that are applicable to other children with ADHD and their families are the following:

- Hand signal to stop arguing
- Graph and star system, charting *one* goal
- Solitary time/quiet time for parent and child separation
- List of solitary activities
- Stop sign (construction, display, and discussion)

- Tangible, agreed-upon reward for achieving goal
- Parents' use of praise to reinforce positive behavior
- Play therapy to promote/enhance Tim's self-esteem

The members of this family were remarkable in their ability to help themselves, once some limited guidance was offered to them. Other families may require longer and more extensive help. However, the principle of supporting the parents so that they can be more effective in supporting their own children is the key to working with families of ADHD children.

I did not contact Tim's teacher to collaborate with her, because Mrs. Marino assured me that the school was also employing behavior modification techniques with him, and her descriptions of his teacher's approach seemed appropriate to me.

There probably will not be a true "termination" in this case for many years, since ADHD typically continues at least until adolescence and sometimes later. It is important for the parents to know that they can contact me in the future, according to their perceived need.

CONCLUDING COMMENTS

This chapter has reviewed various ways of working with families for the purpose of helping children. Although some practitioners follow a child-centered approach, and others focus primarily on the family, I prefer an integrated child and family model because it offers the flexibility to suit the helping method to the particular needs of each case situation.

It is assumed in this integrated approach that the practitioner will *always* involve the parents to the fullest extent possible. However, different helping approaches may be appropriate, such as parent counseling, working with a parent and child together, sibling sessions, and sessions with the entire family. Within a particular case, different members or subsets of the family may be seen, according to need.

This work places special demands on the practitioner, who must endeavor to remain objective, and try to understand the problem situation from the different perspectives of various family members. Ethical considerations arising from expectations of confidentiality and issues of cultural differences between clients and the practitioner require careful self-monitoring and regular supervision.

The strength of the family becomes the practitioner's ally, once the helping relationship has been formed and mutual goals have been established. In work with a family with a child with ADHD, certain guidelines can help the family offer appropriate support to the child, once the parents feel that they are supported and respected by the worker.

DISCUSSION QUESTIONS

1. How can a practitioner prepare to meet with an entire family for the first time? What information is essential to insure the success of the meeting, and how can the practitioner best obtain this?

2. If children become silly and out of control during a family session, what kind of response from the worker is appropriate and helpful? If the parents are unable to control the children, what options does the practitioner have?

3. Discuss how the child's therapist can effectively involve resistant parents in the treatment of their children. How can the therapist manage his or her own feelings of resentment toward the parents for their lack of involvement?

4. How should the practitioner respond when a child with ADHD and the family do not experience success in using a hand signal or the graph? If the parents want to punish the child, should the worker suggest another alternative? Discuss both in terms of whether the worker *should* intervene, and if he or she does so, what form the intervention might take.

5. Make a list of potential positive reinforcements for a child whose parents cannot afford costly incentives, such as computer games and bicycles. How does the worker respond to the parent who thinks that offering rewards is "just bribery"?

❖ CHAPTER 7 ❖

One-to-One Work
with the Child

"Working" with a child usually means that a social worker or other clinician engages the child in play activities for the purpose of helping the child recognize and overcome his or her anxieties. Because children have limited verbal abilities, we cannot expect them to adapt to our adult style of communication. The social worker must "meet the (child) client where he or she is"—namely, on the level of *nonverbal* communication. It has been said that play is the child's work, so the therapist's work is the child's play.

The preferred method of working with children under 12 years old is play therapy. In this approach, the social worker/counselor uses the child's language of play as the primary helping method, with the degree of verbal communication dependent upon the child's age and ability to use words. When the child *can* talk, the worker/therapist talks with him or her, but usually in play therapy the child is more comfortable and fluent in the language of play, so the therapist must accept the challenge of "speaking" and responding to the child through the child's symbolic language. Thompson and Rudolph (1992) state that in play therapy "the assumption is that children will translate their imagination into symbolic play action rather than words" (p. 197). Numerous examples in this book illustrate play communication with the child client.

Because this chapter focuses on one-to-one work with the child, it covers some of the basic techniques and approaches used in play therapy, distinguishing between directive and nondirective methods, and between open-ended and planned short-term treatment of children. To illustrate the blend of nonverbal and verbal helping methods in work with an older child with verbal ability, a case is presented in which behavior modification and parental support helped a 10-year-old girl gain control over her sleep disturbance.

As stated repeatedly in this book, helping a child *always* includes work with the parents/caretakers and other significant family members. It also frequently involves contacts with teachers, the family physician/

pediatrician, and other professionals who have had contact with the child and who have relevant information to share. Although this chapter focuses on one-to-one work with the child, this work *never* occurs in isolation, and often (as in the cases to be discussed) entails tandem work with the parents. When the clinical social worker/counselor has established a cooperative relationship with the parents and has formulated a plan for individual work with the child as a result of the series of assessment interviews, he or she then proceeds to work with the child in separate sessions. Parental contact then typically occurs on a monthly basis, sometimes with the child included in the parent sessions.

RATIONALE FOR WORKING SEPARATELY WITH THE CHILD

Like adults, children experience anxiety, and this can arise from both internal and external sources. Defensive responses (i.e., defense mechanisms) can effectively ward off anxiety (A. Freud, 1937). However, when the defenses are immature or inadequate—as is true for many children— the anxiety may be converted to symptoms that "bind" the anxiety, but at a cost that interferes with day-to-day functioning.

――――― ❖ ―――――

The Case of Anna, Age 5

An example of this can be seen in the case of Anna, age 5, who developed excessive clinging to her mother during the month following a fire that destroyed the family's apartment in the middle of the night. Although Anna could ride the school bus and attend school as usual, when she was in her new home she could not tolerate having her mother out of her sight. She followed her mother into the bathroom and from room to room in the family's new three-bedroom apartment. Anna's symptoms of clinging were specific to the home situation, indicating that the fire had destroyed her sense of safety and ability to play by herself or with friends in the apartment after school. When she was in her mother's presence, Anna felt secure. However, her need to keep in her mother's proximity interfered with her age-appropriate task to develop increased autonomy and peer relations. Anna's symptoms decreased after several play therapy sessions in which I directed her to draw pictures of the fire and of her favorite stuffed animal that perished in the blaze.

――――― ❖ ―――――

The use of drawings to help "debrief" children following traumatic experiences is discussed more fully in Chapters 12 and 14. The next case illustrates the use of puppets in individual work with a child.

❖

The Case of Tammy, Age 4

Tammy, age 4, was very fearful about having her mother leave her at nursery school. Her mother gave Tammy a picture of the two of them together, which Tammy carried in a little purse attached to her waist. Whenever she missed her mother, she could look at the photo. This "concrete" method of keeping her mother close worked successfully, until one day another child started crying and the teacher took the child on her lap, trying to console her. Tammy began sobbing and crying for her mother and could not be comforted by any of the adults present in the classroom. They had to call her mother to come pick her up. The next morning, when it was time to leave for school, Tammy said she had a stomachache. She began crying and subsequently vomited. This "symptomatic behavior," fueled by anxiety, lasted only until Tammy's mother, thinking that the child might have a virus, permitted Tammy to remain home; the stomachache anxiety disappeared as soon as the separation from the mother was no longer threatened. This was repeated for several days, and although the mother recognized the meaning of Tammy's symptoms, she did not know how to cope with her daughter's separation fears.

During the assessment phase, after the referral to the social worker, it became apparent that the mother was quite depressed over her inability to become pregnant. Tammy's age-appropriate separation concerns were thus magnified because of the child's worry and confusion about her mother's sadness.

This case was successfully treated through parent counseling and individual play therapy sessions with Tammy. Tammy's fears had escalated to the point that work with the mother alone could not reassure the child that it would be safe for her to spend a few hours each day away from home, playing with peers. In play therapy sessions, Tammy played out her mother's concerns about becoming pregnant through her choice of a spider puppet who laid "thousands and thousands of eggs." It was evident that Tammy understood her mother's wish to get pregnant, even though the mother denied her daughter's knowledge of this. In directed play therapy, I took the role of a honeybee puppet who offered to babysit for the spider's children, so the mother spider could go shopping and buy food for her hungry spider babies. Tammy and I (as the spider and bee) played repeatedly the "goodbye"/leavetaking of the mother spider, and her subsequent return to her children. During the mother's absence, I (as the babysitting bee) encouraged the spider children to have a good time playing and enjoying themselves. In effect, I gave both mother and child permission to pursue their own developmental needs. After less than 3 months, Tammy's separation fears at nursery school had totally abated.

About a year later, the mother and Tammy came back to show off Tammy's new baby sister!

This example demonstrates the necessary tandem work with *both* the child and the parent in order to relieve the child's symptoms. Individual work with either the mother or the child would have been insufficient. Although counseling the mother to reassure her child that she (the mother) was "all right" was an essential part of treatment, it is unlikely that this reassurance alone would have diminished Tammy's anxiety, which seemed rooted in her conflict about whether to be a "big girl" or whether to remain "Mommy's baby." Individual work with the child moved things along more rapidly than would have occurred if I had intervened only with the mother. Through play communication, Tammy received the message that it was all right to play and have fun with peers in her mother's absence. The work with the mother emphasized my encouragement that she could "let Tammy go," even as the mother spider left her children safely in the care of the babysitting bee.

Situations Calling for One-to-One Work with the Child

When a child has developed symptoms, or when the child's behavior is so extreme as to interfere with his or her ability to interact with others and to proceed with age-appropriate social and cognitive tasks, then individual work is necessary to alleviate the child's anxiety and/or to help the child modify the behavior that is interfering with the normal push toward growth.

Other situations in which individual work with a child is recommended include instances in which the child has been abused, neglected, or abandoned by a parent. Children in these situations will benefit from the opportunity to express their confusion, rage, and neediness with a play therapist/social worker who validates their feelings and gives them the implicit message that what happened was not their fault. These communications often occur through the metaphor of play, with emotions expressed by puppets or doll figures. It is tricky work for the play therapist to confirm such a child's feelings without "blaming" the abusive/ neglectful parent. The child needs to feel that the parent loved him or her, despite the hurtful behavior. The social worker/play therapist dealing with a child in this type of situation usually benefits from an opportunity to deal with his or her *own* feelings in supervision, since the tendency of the worker to join with the child and "blame" the parent for the child's difficulties must be recognized and held in check.

Sessions with a child alone also serve an important function when the child has low self-esteem because of a physical or cognitive disability. A one-to-one relationship with an adult strongly benefits the disabled child, who comes to feel valued as a person, despite the disability. Of course, in such a situation the social worker is simultaneously counseling the parents, to insure that they are also attempting to enhance the child's deflated self-esteem. However, children sometimes discount their parents' attempts to praise them, whereas they can more easily accept an expression of genuine positive regard from an unrelated adult.

Yet another circumstance that merits one-to-one intervention with a child is exposure to traumatic events. When children have witnessed or been victims of violence, they require prompt "debriefing" in order to avert later development of symptoms. This debriefing gives them the opportunity to reenact in play what they witnessed or experienced in real life; it thus gives them a sense of control over a situation in which they were helpless. This controlled repetition puts distance between the frightening event and the present circumstances. The role of the social worker supports and emphasizes a child's survival of such a frightening experience.

Thus, children in a variety of situations gain from a one-to-one helping relationship with a social worker or other clinician who is dedicated to understanding and spending time to help them. It is not surprising that such therapy almost always is "therapeutic," despite the good intentions of family therapists who wish to remove the child from the role of "identified patient." When the opportunity for individual play sessions is presented in a thoughtful and appealing manner, most children flourish through the experience, after they get to know the play therapist and understand the special opportunity for self-expression that the play therapy sessions provide.

However, the fact that something helps does not necessarily argue for its universal application. The realities of economic and time constraints may prevent many families from committing themselves to bringing children for unlimited play therapy appointments, unless the children's symptoms urgently motivate them to seek help. Almost always, the parents will also be expected to attend some counseling or family therapy sessions, so seeking help for children may result in a major commitment of time and resources that is difficult for many families. Because of these realities, time-limited contracts that are problem-focused are generally better understood and accepted by parents than are treatment goals geared to more general and vague objectives, such as "improved self-esteem."

In summary, children with the following type of presenting problems will benefit from one-to-one sessions with a play therapist (in addition to whatever intervention may be occurring simultaneously with their parents and/or families):

1. *Children whose anxiety has escalated to the point that they are not functioning appropriately at home or at school.* They may have developed symptoms; the course of their normal development may have been arrested; and/or they may appear to be "stuck."

2. *Children who have been abused, neglected, and/or abandoned.* As noted above, children need to express their confusion, rage, and other feelings about why this happened to them; they also need to understand that it was not their fault. Because their ability to trust adults may be impaired, work with these children may require more time than work with children whose development has not been so seriously compromised.

3. *Children with disabilities that engender feeling of low self-esteem.* Often these children are painfully aware that they are "different" from their peers, and this difference may cause them pain and anger. Work with these children proceeds well when the social worker/counselor can identify some genuinely likable qualities and/or talents in which the youngsters can begin to take some pride. These children's ability to accept themselves as persons with disabilities frequently follows the experience of mourning (through play therapy) for the qualities/abilities they never had.

4. *Children who have been traumatized.* Depending on the circumstances, individual play therapy may be a valuable option, in addition to group and/or family approaches. The more violent the trauma, the more likely it is that victims will require individual intervention. Ideally, this should be offered *before* the emergence of symptoms, as a preventive strategy. Unfortunately, this type of preventive intervention is far from routine. See Chapter 8 for an example of group debriefing following a disaster, and Webb (1991) for numerous examples of individual work with children after crises of various types.

SELECTED PLAY THERAPY TECHNIQUES

It is ironic that many social work students have contact with young children during their internships and are expected to interact helpfully with them, yet their coursework may not have prepared them regarding basic play therapy techniques appropriate for work with their child clients. A few years ago I sent a survey to all baccalaureate and master's-level programs in social work, to learn details about curriculum content related to direct intervention with children. Although 48 out of 84 returned responses from B.S.W. programs indicated that their courses contained content related to providing services for *children*, about half (24) of the respondents stated that they did not think there was a need to teach *play therapy* content in their curricula. The reasons given for this were the beliefs that play therapy content is "too specialized" and "not relevant to the work of B.S.W. practitioners." The two negative responses out of a total of 48 from the M.S.W. programs stated that (1) their curriculum was not "therapy-oriented," and (2) that their curriculum was based on a "family systems" model.

Although I do agree that play therapy is a specialized field, I nonetheless argue that social workers at *all* levels can and should be able to use some basic play therapy techniques in their work with children. Generic practitioners need this knowledge and skill just as clinical specialists do, and clearly familiarity with play therapy techniques is essential for social workers using a family systems perspective.

Terminology

Let us not be afraid of the word "therapy." I suspect that some of the negative responses in the survey about including play therapy in the social work curriculum reflect a backlash against the medical (clinical treatment) model, and a preference to cast social work in a broad context that sees the individual in terms of family and social influences. (See my discussion of this topic in Chapter 4.) Although I share a wide view of social workers' professional identity, I do not exclude the concept of therapy as a legitimate helping method *within social work* for individuals (of any age) who are in pain and need of service. My word processor's thesaurus lists "care" as a synonym for "therapy."

What Is Play Therapy?

The term "play therapy" refers to caring and helping interventions with children that employ *play* techniques. Clinicians who refer to themselves as "play therapists" come from many disciplines in addition to social work, and all have had specialized training and supervision on an advanced level. The list of child-related professional organizations in the Appendices includes the Association for Play Therapy, which regulates post-master's-degree training in this field. Some social workers may wish to obtain this advanced training. However, social workers at *all* levels can learn to utilize selected play therapy techniques in their work with child clients.

The choice of particular activities will vary according to the child's age and responsiveness to different options; therefore, each social worker's office should contain a range of play materials from which the worker and the child can make selections. (See Figure 3.3 for a list of basic supplies.) The following subsections discuss selected basic play therapy techniques and necessary supplies.

Play Therapy Materials

Figure 3.3 and Table 4.1 of this book list play therapy equipment that I recommend for *every* social worker's office. Even a worker specializing in gerontology may be called upon, for example, to intervene with a school-age grandchild of a terminally ill woman being transferred to hospice care. Providing this child with some drawing paper and markers, and suggesting that she draw her happiest memory about "Gramma," will not only occupy the child and permit the worker to speak with the child's mother about necessary plans for convening the family; it will also serve an anticipatory grieving function for the child and the mother, who can recognize in the picture a concrete portrayal of the grandmother's significant role in the family. The grandchild can communicate her feelings through concrete images rather than in words, because young children have limited abilities to express emotions in language.

Art/Drawing

In my experience, plain white paper, colored paper, and colored markers are the most useful of all play therapy supplies. Children as young as 3 and as old as 18 can express themselves meaningfully through art and drawings, especially when the play therapist/social worker makes it clear that "drawing here is not like drawing in school; you don't have to be good at it in order to be able to show how you feel." Furthermore, family members can work on drawings or collages together, when given the opportunity to express themselves in this manner.

Chapter 4 has discussed how the Draw-A-Person and the Draw-A-Family can provide useful information in assessing how a child sees himself or herself and his or her family. I usually keep these drawings in a special folder with the child's name on it, so the child and I can examine them together at different points in our work. I often ask the child to repeat both these drawings after several months, in order to note the changes over the course of time.

When the child refuses to draw or says that he or she can't draw, the "squiggle game" (Winnicott, 1971a, 1971b) almost invariably intrigues the child, even as it loosens up his or her inhibitions. In this game, which is essentially a technique of communication through drawings, the child and worker/therapist take turns closing their eyes and then making some kind of "scribble/squiggle" line on the paper, which the other person then has to turn into a figure or object. Each drawing receives a name, and after several have been completed, the child is asked to pick his or her favorite and make up a story about it. An example of the use of this method with a 9-year-old girl who friend had died tragically can be found in Webb (1993). This child, who could not bear to talk about her dead friend, made up a "squiggle story" that was replete with danger and threatening death themes. See DiLeo (1973), Oster and Gould (1987), and Rubin (1984) for guidance in understanding and interpreting children's drawings.

Clay and Play-Doh

Also of compelling appeal across the age span, modeling materials allow a child to create something completely original. Play-Doh is soft and malleable, and thus more appropriate for use with the preschool child; modeling clay is stiffer and requires some manual strength to mold into shapes, therefore making it more suitable for school-age children. In a video demonstration of play therapy techniques (Webb, 1994b), a 4-year-old child who was completely uninterested in drawing enthusiastically created dragons and monsters with Play-Doh, thereby suggesting some of his own fears about uncontrolled aggression. On the same video, a 12-year-old girl created a sun with clay as she reflected on how her earlier therapy using clay had helped her gain control over her anger. See Oaklander (1988) for specific suggestions about using clay in group, family, and individual work with children.

Dolls/Puppets

Miniature, bendable family dolls readily lend themselves to reenactment of scenes from a child's family. Preschoolers eagerly engage in this type of play, which can be facilitated by the use of dollhouse furniture representing the kitchen and bedroom(s). These supplies can be stored in a small container, such as a lunch bag or satchel. I mention this to emphasize that the minimum supplies for play therapy are easily portable and do not require extensive storage space. A fancy dollhouse, for example, is neither necessary nor appropriate, since many children live in small apartments, whereas the typical dollhouse represents a suburban upper-middle-class home. Children are very creative about adapting objects in the office to their play needs (e.g., using tissues for blankets or a turned-over ashtray for a kitchen table). *A worker does not need to offer elaborate play materials to engage a child in play activities.*

Animal and insect puppets appeal to boys and latency-age children, who may believe that dolls are "sissy" and only for girls or younger children. Woltmann (1951/1964) suggests that the selection of puppets should provide the child with the opportunity to express a variety of emotions. For example, an alligator puppet will almost always call forth aggressive, biting play, whereas a rabbit or duck is more "neutral." Assuming that the child and the worker/therapist can each hold two puppets at a time, Woltmann suggests (as a minimum) that the choices available to the child should include two neutral and two aggressive puppets. My own preference is to offer a choice of at least six puppets, so that the child who may not wish to select aggressive puppets will not be forced to do so. Again, I stress that hand puppets are neither heavy nor bulky, and can be easily stored in a desk drawer with other play therapy supplies.

Card and Board Games

Following the publication of *Game Play* (Schaefer & Reid, 1986), there has been growing awareness of the usefulness of board games with latency-age children in therapy. There has also been a virtual flooding of the market with "therapeutic" board games. Schaefer and Reid (1986) have pointed out the numerous ways in which child therapists can help children while playing board games with them. This understanding is crucial to knowing the difference between just playing with a child and playing *therapeutically* with a child. In numerous workshops on play therapy across the country, I have been asked, "How can playing checkers or Monopoly with a child be therapeutic?" My answer is that unless the worker/therapist has a purpose in mind and responds consistently to the child during the play according to this purpose, the playing of a game may *not* be therapeutic (apart from the opportunity it provides to build a relationship with the child). An example of a purpose that can help the child is to point out to the child during the play that the child seems to have trouble following the rules, and that this must cause problems when the child plays with other children. The therapist can then offer to help the child slow down and wait for his or her turn, so that he or she can "be a better player."

Because I am focusing on *basic* play therapy techniques and the necessary supplies for these, I limit my recommendations to two games that I have found especially useful in work with elementary school-age children: the Talking, Feeling, and Doing Game (available from Creative Therapeutics, Cresskill, NJ) and the card game Feelings in Hand (available from Western Psychological Services, Los Angeles, CA). (Full addresses for these and other suppliers of play resources and materials are provided in the Appendices.) These games have certain features that make them attractive to school-age children. In common with commercial board games, they feature the possibility of winning (and losing), and this characteristic enables a worker/therapist to see and talk with a child about how he or she wins or loses in the course of daily activities. In contrast to commercial board games, however, these *therapeutic* games require a discussion of feelings as an integral part of playing. They give the worker/therapist the opportunity to model "feeling" responses that the child may initially consider inappropriate. For example, when a card in a game asks "What is the worst thing that someone can say to someone else?", and the therapist responds, "That you are stupid," the child learns that talking about embarrassing issues is all right. Chips are awarded for each response, further motivating the child to respond to each question.

USING THE CHILD'S PLAY THERAPEUTICALLY

Playing therapeutically with a child takes training, experience, and the special ability to relate to the child both playfully and with respect. It is not my intention to suggest that simply by acquiring some play materials, a worker can then, as if by magic, successfully carry out play therapy. In fact, having the necessary supplies is only the beginning of a process that will take hours of persistent relearning of the language of play, and struggling to communicate through this symbolic language.

At first, the work feels awkward and confusing. Social workers with many years of experience have said to me, "At least when I speak to adults, I usually know that they understand me; with children, it can be very puzzling. How do I know that I am playing helpfully/therapeutically with a child?"

This is, of course, the $64,000 question. We do *not* know initially whether our work with children is helpful. We do know that it will not harm children to spend time with adults who are interested in them. Just as in adult therapy, the *relationship* is the key to being helpful, not whether a worker invariably makes the "right" response. And progress takes time, whether with adults or with children.

Letting the Child Direct the Play

As an experienced play therapist, I feel comfortable asking a child what he or she wants me to do (or say). Letting the child direct the play can reveal far more than a response that *I* might guess to be appropriate. I have also found that if the child continues to play (whether or not I immediately understand the underlying meaning of the play), this can serve a purpose for the child. Usually it is only by reflecting about the *themes* of the child's play retrospectively over several sessions that I begin to comprehend its significance.

Ultimately, improvement of the problem or the symptoms suggests that something beneficial has happened. Occasionally, a parent credits the child's play therapy. However, this evaluation (no matter how flattering) cannot be accepted as the exclusive reason for change: The parent or parents have also been interacting with the child in a different way as a result of parent counseling or family therapy, and it is important that the worker/therapist attribute some of the child's improvement to the changes in the *family*. Almost always, progress is multidetermined.

Steps in the Therapeutic Work with the Child

Work with a child can be divided into the following phases:

1. Establishing the relationship with the child
2. Observing/listening to the child
3. Identifying themes in the child's play
4. Formulating a dynamic understanding about the child
5. Responding to the child according to this understanding

These phases of child therapy may overlap. They are listed in order of both occurrence and difficulty, which explains why some workers who are new to working with children may be unable to respond using a child's play language, despite their ability to relate well to young clients. A *therapeutic* response within a child's play language requires that the worker first understand what the child is communicating, and then how this communication reflects interactions and/or feelings from the child's life. Sometimes the connection between the symbolic play and the child's life is obvious, but just as often it is not. The ability to connect the symbol to the child's life requires many hours of supervised practice experience with children. For example, probably most readers instinctively understood the underlying meaning of Tammy's selection of the spider puppet who laid "thousands and thousands of eggs." This could be viewed as the child's wish for her mother to have many babies. My quick response to the child's play scenario followed from the dynamic understanding that Tammy was afraid to leave her mother because her mother was sad and needed her; furthermore, I believed that Tammy needed practice in saying goodbye to her mother and permission to have fun in her mother's absence. This dynamic understanding formed the basis for my assumption in playing the role of the babysitting bee.

When this kind of connection is not readily apparent, it is important for the worker to be able to tolerate ambiguity and to exercise patience while letting the helping process evolve. Not knowing is all right, and is well tolerated by children (who often feel baffled themselves in trying to understand their world).

When the child has been given the explanation of who the worker is ("someone who helps children and parents with their troubles and worries") and how the child and worker will interact ("sometimes we talk, and sometimes we play"), then the child is free to begin revealing his or her concerns to the worker/therapist. Incidentally, social workers should avoid using the term "working" in referring to their interactions with children. Talking and playing do not qualify as "work" in a child's *literal* understanding of the word, and if a worker says that he or she is going to be "working" with a child, the child may become confused about what to expect.

DIFFERENT CHILD THERAPY APPROACHES

Brief Historical Synopsis

The practice of child therapy has been in existence since the 1930s and 1940s, when Melanie Klein (1937) and Anna Freud (1946/1968), working separately, adapted methods of adult psychoanalysis to child analysis. Despite disagreements between these two child therapists about certain theoretical and practice issues in work with children, both therapists agreed about the importance of the therapeutic relationship with the child, and they both relied on play as the primary method of therapeutic communication with children.

In the more than half a century since these beginnings of child therapy, many different helping methods have evolved. Social workers, counselors, psychologists, psychiatrists, and others have developed a wide range of therapeutic interventions. In fact, Kazdin (1988) lists more than 230 "alternative psychosocial treatments" for children and adolescents—a number that seems mind-boggling, even allowing for his inclusion of group and family interventions. Kazdin's list contains some treatments with similar names, suggesting overlap among various approaches; it also includes activities such as yoga and sports groups (not considered therapy in the usual sense), as well as some discrete play therapy *techniques*, such as Winnicott's "squiggle game" and the Talking, Feeling, and Doing Game (which as distinct techniques are always used in combination with other helping methods, and cannot therefore be considered as integrated psychosocial treatment methods). Thus, Kazdin's list of alternative "treatments" must be viewed with great reservations in regard to the numbers. Even with these reservations, however, it *is* evident that there has been a proliferation of treatment approaches geared to children. No longer are most methods guided primarily by the theoretical underpinnings of psychoanalysis; instead, various behavioral, cognitive, and client-centered therapeutic models have been adapted from adult treatment approaches to serve the purposes of child therapy. Three major approaches utilized by contemporary child therapists are (1) client-centered (child-centered) treatment, (2) psychodynamic child therapy, and (3) cognitive-behavioral treatment.

Client-Centered or Child-Centered Therapy

The basic tenets of the client-centered approach with children, as described by Axline (1947), are as follows:

- Establishment of a warm rapport with the child
- Empathic understanding and respect for the child's ability to solve his or her own problems
- A nondirective stance on the part of the therapist, who lets the child lead the way without directing the child in any manner, for as long as the child needs treatment

In *Dibs: In Search of Self*, Axline (1964) demonstrated the child-centered approach, using play therapy with a 5-year-old boy who was on the verge of residential placement because of his mutism and his teachers' inability to make contact with him. Dibs flourished in nondirective play therapy with Axline, in which he developed and achieved his exceptional potential, in large measure because of Axline's ability to convey her genuine positive regard for him.

The child-centered approach has changed very little since its inception in the 1940s, with Axline's (1947) text continuing to be "the single best guide for client-centered psychotherapy with children" (Johnson, Rasbury, & Siegel, 1986, p. 130). Other past and current therapists/writers following the child-centered model include Moustakas (1959) and Landreth (1991).

In summary, child-centered therapy is permissive, nondirective, and open-ended. Because it proceeds at the child's pace, it tends to be long-term. It focuses on the person of the child, not on the child's problem. Its emphasis on the child's potential for growth is very appealing to social workers and others who wish to focus on clients' strengths, rather than on pathology.

Psychodynamic Child Therapy

Over the years, what began as child psychoanalysis has evolved into a less intensive, more practical approach to working with children—one that still recognizes the existence and power of instincts and conflicts in motivating behavior, but that now tends to focus on problems in the child's present life, rather than on the child's internal intrapsychic world. Because it is assumed that a child's behaviors and symptoms reflect complex, unconsciously determined meanings, work with the child relies on a thorough assessment to facilitate the therapist's understanding of the child's unconscious motivations, fantasies, impulses, and conflicts as reflected in his or her play. The therapist may utilize aspects of the relationship to make interpretations about the child's wishes and fears with respect to meaningful and significant relationships in the child's past and present life (Chethik, 1989; Johnson et al., 1986; LeVine & Sallee, 1992; Mishne, 1983).

Although therapists differ in the specifics of their approaches, psychodynamic child therapy as a whole is more directive than child-centered therapy. Especially when it is geared toward helping a child who has been traumatized, it may be very focused and of relatively short duration (Terr, 1983, 1989). Using a psychodynamic framework of understanding, the therapist engaged in crisis intervention helps the traumatized child reconstruct the traumatic experience so that the child can gain mastery over the trauma, acknowledge that he or she has survived, and realize that the trauma belongs in the past. This requires a high level of direction on the part of the therapist, who may provide particular toys to facilitate the play reenactment. This form of crisis therapy has been helpful for child victims of sexual and cult abuse, in addition to children who have witnessed violence and atrocities and who may be showing symptoms of Posttraumatic Stress Disorder. Bevin (1991), Strand (1991), and James (1989) provide examples of therapy with traumatized children that utilizes crisis intervention reconstructive techniques. This work is stressful and demands a high level of skill. *Therapists should not engage in this type of work without special training and supervision.*

In summary, psychodynamic child therapy focuses on helping the child cope with his or her everyday life. It relies on an in-depth understanding of the child's history and present circumstances, in order to make connections in play and/or in words that will relieve the child's anxieties and open up new possibilities to the child. When used in crisis intervention, this form of therapy is very directive. Concurrent parent counseling is an essential component of the one-to-one work with the child.

Cognitive-Behavioral Treatment of Children

By contrast with child-centered or psychodynamic therapy, in cognitive-behavioral therapy the child's thoughts (cognitions) and behaviors are the focus of work, not the child's feelings. There are many different forms of cognitive-behavioral thrapy, all of which employ learning principles in attempting to alter dysfunctional behavior. After a careful assessment of the presenting problem and of the environmental and/ or cognitive antecedents of the problematic behavior, an individual treatment program is tailored to the specific needs and situation of the individual child and family. When the therapist finds that the child's maladaptive thoughts are leading to maladaptive behavior, then the intervention emphasizes helping the child change his or her negative thoughts through self-instructional training, sometimes referred to as "self-talk." When environmental factors appear to be contributing to the persistence of a behavior pattern, then the intervention will target these reinforcing environmental responses through various techniques, such as positive reinforcement of desired behaviors, punishment, and the use of tokens (Johnson et al., 1986; LeVine & Sallee, 1992).

Because children are so dependent on the significant others in their environments, parents and teachers are often enlisted to help with children's behavior modification plans. According to Johnson et al. (1986), "the success of behavioral procedures is often highly dependent on the direct participation of significant members of the child's environment in the treatment program" (p. 184). The collaboration of a 10-year-old girl and her parents in a cognitive-behavioral treatment approach is described in the case of Linda, later in this chapter.

Synthesis of Approaches

It is possible and useful to combine therapeutic approaches where this seems indicated by the circumstances of the particular case. Wachtel (1994) recommends a integrated treatment approach that employs a combination of systemic, psychodynamic, and behavioral interventions simultaneously. Wachtel (1994, pp. 201–202) states:

> We do not wait until all systematic issues are resolved before attending to the psychodynamic aspect of the problem, nor do we attempt to fully resolve psychodynamic or systemic issues before introducing behavioral interventions. Instead, *psychodynamic and systemic understandings of the problem go hand in hand with behavioral methods targeted at the symptomatic behavior.* (emphasis added)

This philosophy recognizes that models of practice often overlap, and that the experienced practitioner learns to adapt practice to the client's needs rather than vice versa.

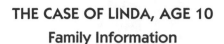

THE CASE OF LINDA, AGE 10
Family Information

Mother	Ann, age 34, buyer for department store.
Father	Jim, age 35, architect in building firm; recovering alcoholic (12 years).
Child client	Linda, age 10, fifth grade; on gymnastics team.
Sister	Amanda, age 8, third grade; very artistic.
Linda's godfather	Robert, age 35, former restaurant manager; recovering alcoholic (14 years).
Linda's godmother	Terry, age 34, secretary.
Robert and Terry's children	Susan, age 6, and Brian, age 4.

Linda was young Brian's godmother, and Linda and Amanda referred to Robert and Terry as "Aunt" and "Uncle." Robert was Jim's Alcoholics Anonymous sponsor; they generally attended meetings together three times per week. Ann had attended Al-Anon in the past (sometimes with Terry), and the girls had attended a group for children of alcoholics (Unicorn) several years earlier. At the time of intake, Ann was engaged in her own therapy, as was Jim.

This was a Catholic family of European cultural background. The family members observed major milestones such as First Communion according to the expected practice in their religion, but they did not attend church regularly.

Presenting Problem

Upon the recommendation of her pediatrician, Ann consulted me because of her concern about Linda's sleep problem of 2 months' duration. Linda was waking every night in the middle of the night because of bad dreams about robbers; she would turn on all the lights in the house, and then come into the parents' bedroom and stand by their bed until one of them awoke and returned with her to her bedroom. The parents reported that Linda's sleep difficulty had begun during the family's vacation with Robert and Terry and their children. Linda had awakened in the middle of the night and become panic-stricken when she mistakenly thought a "robber" was kidnapping her godson, Brian. Actually Robert was carrying his son to the bathroom, but in a strange location, Linda was disoriented and terrified. She had to spend that night sleeping in the room with her parents, and she had continued to awaken every night since then. The parents were at first sympathetic, assuming that Linda's problem would subside spontaneously, but they were now becoming tired, annoyed, and concerned about Linda's behavior.

Assessment

The parents were seen once, so that I could obtain their view of the problem and learn about Linda's developmental history and the family background. Linda was then seen for two assessment sessions in which we discussed the problem and several possible ways to deal with it.

In the meeting with the parents, I learned that Linda was functioning on a very high level in school and with peers. She was an excellent student and an enthusiastic member of the school gymnastics team. She had slept in her own room since age 2, and had not had separation problems; however, the mother considered Linda somewhat anxious and intense, and thought that she put a lot of pressure on herself to succeed. Through the years Linda had expressed some fears at night related to bad dreams, but she was easily consoled, and the parents had not been concerned until this current nightly problem. The father said he had recently lost patience with Linda, yelled at her, and shaken her when she woke him up in the middle of the night. Both parents were firm in feeling that "this just cannot continue."

In the two assessment sessions with Linda, I tried to understand the reason for the persistence of this problem. Linda said that she woke up because of a dream that a robber was going to "get" her. When this happened, she would get up and put on all the lights in her room, the hall, and the bathroom. Then she would walk into her parents' bedroom and stand by their bed until one of them woke up. She would tell them she had a bad dream, and then either her mother or her father would take her back to her room, reassuring her that it was only a dream and that she was all right.

Because of Linda's age, the work with her combined talking and some play (drawing). During Linda's discussion with me, I asked her to sketch a floor plan of her house and her bedroom, so I could get a better picture of her family situation (see Figures 7.1 and 7.2). I also wanted her to draw her dream, and I asked her to draw it in two different ways: the dream she was having now, and the dream she would have later when she was no longer waking up with the bad dream. Figure 7.3 depicts Linda's two dreams, in a "before" (i.e., current) version, with the alarm clock registering 2:00 and a male figure saying, "I'm going to get you"; the "after" dream shows her lying in bed asleep while having a happy dream of going down a slide and saying, "Whee!" I also asked Linda to draw a picture of herself showing how she would look after she had a good night's sleep, without waking up. She drew a figure with a smile, saying "Rise and shine," with the alarm clock indicating 7:00 A.M. (Figure 7.4).

In asking for the "after" drawings, I was deliberately conveying the positive suggestion to Linda that her bad dreams would end, and that she would feel better as a result. I also made several references to how brave she must be to be able to perform back flips on the balance beam in gymnastics. I wanted to emphasize Linda's strengths in a manner that would help her feel confident and assured that she could successfully master her nightime fears.

Knowing that it was developmentally unusual for a 10-year-old to be going into her parents' bedroom every night, and also having heard from the father than his patience was wearing thin, I made the decision

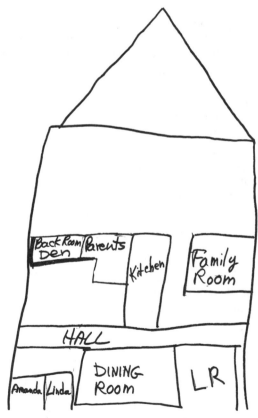

FIGURE 7.1. Floor plan of Linda's house.

FIGURE 7.2. Floor plan of Linda's bedroom.

to begin work immediately on "extinguishing" Linda's going into her parents' bedroom at night. I tried to make this behavior seem inappropriate (ego-dystonic) to Linda by saying to her in a sympathetic tone, "It must be *very* embarrassing for a 10-year-old to have to go to her parents at night! I know that many 4- and 5-year-olds do this, but it certainly is not what most 10-year-olds want to do. We need to think together about what you can do for *yourself* when you wake up to help you feel better." I then involved Linda in making a list of substitute behaviors, such as listening to her Walkman radio, drawing, writing in her diary, and so forth. A family meeting was planned for the next week to talk about some of the ways Linda's parents could help her, as well as to obtain everyone's input and agreement to a behavior modification plan.

Family Meeting

The meeting was attended by Linda and her parents. I began by stating a common purpose—that of our working together to help Linda get control over her "nightime problem." Everyone wanted relief in this situation, and each would have a part in helping.

FIGURE 7.3. Linda's drawings of her "before" and "after" dreams.

FIGURE 7.4. Linda's "good night's sleep" drawing.

First, we agreed that Linda was old enough to take care of herself at night without involving her parents. She couldn't control her dreams or the fact that she woke up, but there was no need for her to go into her parents' room and wake them up. I encouraged Linda to tell her parents that she would not disturb them, but that she wanted their permission to put on the lights when she woke up. I suggested that the parents close their door so the lights would not disturb them.

I mentioned that Linda was going to try hard to control her anxiety and that we needed to figure out a way to reward her, because this might take a lot of effort. Together we decided on a time frame for successful completion of the desired behavior (Christmas, which was 6 weeks away) and a reward for succeeding. Linda said she wanted some new bookshelves and some drapes for her room, and that she was hoping for a bicycle for Christmas. I suggested that we set up a token system of rewards, with the drapes to come after 2 successful weeks, the bookshelves after 4 weeks, and the bicycle after 6 weeks. I also suggested a gradual tapering of the lights at night: The first week, Linda would be permitted to put on as many lights as she wanted; the second week, all the lights in her *own* room; the third week, only her bedside lamp; and after a month, only a flashlight. The family was enthusiastic about the plan, although the father wanted to know how they would handle "slip-ups." I suggested that if the problem returned for more than two nights out of seven, the reward system should slow down accordingly. I also planned to see Linda every week, and wanted her to report her progress to me.

Treatment Summary

Within 3 weeks there was complete symptom alleviation, and Linda was sleeping through the night with no more bad dreams. Two weeks after the family session, Linda had to cancel her appointment because she had hurt her foot in a gymnastics injury. The pediatrician was giving her anti-inflammatory medication and wanted her to stay off the foot for 3 days. During our phone conversation, I asked Linda how she was doing at night. She said that she was still waking every night, but she just turned on her bedroom light and then went right back to sleep. I suggested that perhaps the medication would cause her to sleep through the entire night (positive suggestion). The next week Linda reported that she was now sleeping through the night. I kept in contact with the parents, to insure that they would carry through with the agreed-upon rewards. During the gradual tapering of sessions on a monthly basis after Christmas, Linda experienced no further nighttime difficulty.

———————— ❖ ————————

Discussion

The rapid improvement in this case could be attributed to several factors. First, I framed Linda's behavior in a way that was distasteful to her, by suggesting that it was typical of younger children; second, her parents removed whatever secondary gratification Linda may have derived from receiving their attention in the middle of the night, and instead rewarded her for her strengths (bravery). A third factor may have been the implicit message to Linda that her parents were serious about wanting her to manage her own anxieties. The short-term time frame (6 weeks) was appealing and manageable to all.

It is obvious that this situation required simultanous involvement of both the child and the parents in a mutually agreed-upon plan. My role as the therapist was that of catalyst and facilitator. In retrospect, the improvement may seem "too good to be true." I took a risk in suggesting that such a rapid change of behavior could occur. I based this on my knowledge of child development (i.e., most 10-year-olds do not have bad dreams that cause them to go into their parents' bedroom for help), plus the indications from this girl's developmental history that her development had been proceeding normally until this unusual event. It is fortunate that the parents sought help before the problem escalated and a spiral of negative interaction was set into motion.

CONCLUDING COMMENTS

One-to-one work with the child gives the social worker an opportunity to know the child in a manner different from that when the child is seen together with the parents. When the worker encourages the child to play, and conveys to the child that he or she will help through *both* playing and talking, the worker relieves the child of the obligation to communicate in the adult's verbal mode. Meeting the child on his or her level respects the child's individuality in a way that is unusual in child–adult relationships.

In one-to-one work, the therapist/worker uses play to interact with the child for the purpose of understanding and helping. This conforms to the commitment of the social work profession to meet clients at the level where the clients are comfortable. Therefore, *all* social workers must be prepared to use play in their interactions with children.

DISCUSSION QUESTIONS

1. Discuss the dynamics of the separation problem as depicted in the case of Tammy. Why was it necessary to see *both* mother and child in order to

resolve this? If you were the social worker, what information and advice would you give to Tammy's teacher in regard to her management of Tammy's separation difficulties?

2. Why is it important for family therapists to be familiar with play therapy techniques? Give an example of when it might be appropriate to use play techniques in a family session. How can the family therapist go about implementing this?

3. Imagine that you are working with a child who has very low self-esteem because of physical and cognitive disabilities. Discuss how the treatment of this child might differ, depending on whether you were to follow a child-centered, a psychodynamic, or a cognitive-behavioral approach.

4. Discuss the reasons for using play in work with children under 12 years of age. How can the social workers become more comfortable in using play techniques?

❖ CHAPTER 8 ❖

Group Work with Children

Many children feel more comfortable interacting with a social worker or counselor in the company of other children then in a one-to-one counseling situation (Rose, 1972; Schiffer, 1984). Whereas the prospect of working with six to eight children at the same time may challenge or even intimidate the counselor/worker, the group format has the opposite effect on the child group members, who experience mutual support and energy according to the "strength in numbers" principle. The group situation, by comparison with one-to-one counseling, gives a child greater freedom to speak and participate when he or she feels inclined to do so, since other members share the spotlight and can fill an uncomfortable silence. Of course, most children do not *choose* the helping methods through which adults offer them assistance. Even children who feel distressed and worried about some aspects of their lives usually have no idea about either who can help or what means are available for doing so. When such children find themselves in a group with peers who have similar worries, they feel a sense of relief that they are not "the only ones," and hopeful about the prospect of peer understanding and support.

RATIONALE FOR USE OF GROUPS

Children live and must be able to function as social beings. Their initial experience in their family group gradually broadens to include peer relationships when they enter day care or preschool, and eventually formal schooling. Some children, in addition, are exposed to group programs in religious settings, and others benefit from participation in recreational groups (e.g., Boy or Girl Scouts and team sports). Indeed, whether or not they are involved in other group activities, children in latency typically and spontaneously form their own neighborhood cliques, "gangs," and clubs. Children's intrinsic need for belonging and peer acceptance attests to the importance of group experience for their developing sense of personal identity. It is therefore quite logical to employ a group format to

162

help, treat, or counsel children who are experiencing personal, emotional, or behavioral difficulties that interfere with their optimal functioning.

A helping/counseling/therapy group provides children with a social experience in a "safe," nurturing environment that encourages emotional expression and problem solving in the process of demonstrating different individual styles of interacting and coping with common problems. Depending on the type of group and its composition, each member will inevitably be exposed to a variety of responses beyond his or her individual repertoire. Therefore, a counseling group constitutes a learning experience, in addition to providing support and acceptance.

There is general agreement about the rationale for treating children in groups, which Johnson, Rasbury, and Siegel (1986) summarize as follows:

> Groups provide socialization experiences that cannot occur in individual psychotherapy; specifically, the child is exposed to a wider range of relationships. Group treatment is often more appealing to the child than individual treatment because there are more varied activities and experiences, and for some children it is often less emotionally threatening than individual treatment. (p. 266)

The power of the group to promote behavior change can be far greater than generally occurs in individual treatment, because of the members' strong motivation for peer acceptance. For children, the peer system can be "either supportive or assaultive" (Papell & Rothman, 1984, p. 1), with corresponding impact on the youngster's sense of self-esteem and identity. A structured group involving both activity and verbal interaction can, through the influence of the peer culture, assist the children with their individual problems and growth needs (Kolodny & Garland, 1984). During the beginning phases of the group, protection may exist for the shy, tentative individual who fears "exposure," but the balance soon shifts in the form of group pressure or individual members to take risks and make changes in their usual ways of relating. Ideally, such a group combines confrontation and acceptance, serving as a behind-the-scenes cheering squad for individual members.

DIFFERENT TYPES OF GROUPS FOR CHILDREN

The guest editorial for a special issue of the journal *Social Work with Groups* refers to group work with children and adolescents as "a neglected stepchild of the profession" (Kolodny & Garland, 1984, p. 3). The editors of the special issue lament the very cursory mention of work with children and adolescents in many of the group work texts authored by social workers, and they also note with disapproval the tendency to distinguish between "therapy groups" and "activity groups."

The history and implications of this dichotomy reach beyond the scope and purpose of the present chapter, and are not discussed in detail here. However, my strong commitment to offering developmentally appropriate services to children leads me to support the provision of activity groups for children, because of the opportunities they provide for socialization and ego development. My experience with children from 6 to 12 years of age argues for using activities, whether in group or in individual work. Use of activities to supplement verbal discussions meets the children's needs for concrete representations of their experiences, and therefore contributes to a "therapeutic" outcome. For example, a group of children in foster care were guided over several weeks in a project "Write Your Own Life Story/Picture Autobiography" (Brandler & Roman, 1991). The structured drawing and personal storytelling actually became "a tool to address the terrible grief these youngsters [felt] about the loss of family" (Brandler & Roman, 1991, p. 128). Hence, an activity can become therapeutic, even as the "therapy" involves an activity; the distinction between "therapy groups" and "activity groups" overlooks the basic interrelationship between the two.

Historical Overview

An excellent review of the development of group psychotherapy with children can be found in Johnson et al. (1986), from which the following discussion is loosely drawn.

In the early 1930s, activity groups were initiated at the Madelyn Borg Child Guidance Institute in New York as an adjunct to individual therapy for children who appeared to require socialization experience. Over a period of 8 years, Samuel Slavson (1943) studied and worked with more than 750 children in 55 separate group treatment programs. He stated that

> in group therapy, we work with children who are directly rejected by parents, family, school, street gangs and community center. . . . They are either excessively aggressive or excessively withdrawn; obsessed with great fears or guilt, they overcompensate for them by nonsocial or antisocial behavior. . . . What a child needs in such circumstances is a haven of relief, a sanctuary where these distressing, threatening, and hostile pressures can be removed and relief supplied. (Slavson, 1943, pp. 2–3)

The appropriate treatment environment, according to Slavson, is a permissive, noncontrolling setting that provides children the opportunity to express their thoughts and feelings through play and action. The role of the therapist, in Slavson's model, is nondirective or client-centered, although grounded in psychoanalytic theory.

Adaptations of Slavson's "activity group therapy" were developed by Redl (1944), Axline (1947), and Ginott (1961) in approaches stressing ego development through play activities and personal accomplishments. Axline and Ginott employed nondirective methods in which the therapists verbalized and reflected the children's feelings as these emerged in the context of play.

Because the nondirective and noninterpretative format of activity group therapy requires some capacity on the part of the children for self-regulation and emotional control, Slavson later developed a more structured and interpretation-oriented group for disturbed children who needed and benefited from external control and guidance from the therapist. This modified approach, called "activity–interview group psychotherapy," was pilot-tested with latency-age children and subsequently adapted for use with prelatency and early latency-age children in the 1950s by Slavson and Schiffer (1975). For further information about both of Slavson's approaches, see Schiffer (1984).

Behavioral group treatment models emerged in the 1960s as an alternative to psychodynamic and client-centered approaches (Rose, 1967). Focusing on behavior rather than personality as the target of change, behavioral group therapy is highly structured, with specific tasks and goals set for the members. Learning and reinforcement principles, such as behavioral contracting, rehearsal, extinction, modeling, and systematic desensitization techniques, help children to acquire skills in making friends, to reduce their aggression and anxiety, and to learn about the impact of their behavior on others (Rose, 1972).

Current Range of Children's Groups

As we approach the 21st century, we find a veritable plethora of groups for children. These vary according to the nature of the problem situation, the children's developmental stage, and the philosophy and theoretical stance of the helping personnel regarding the appropriate type of intervention.

Numerous group models target children who have experienced loss, either through parental divorce (Kalter & Schreier, 1994) or through the death of a family member, teacher, or close friend (Vastola, Nierenberg, & Graham, 1986; Tait & Depta, 1993; Doster & McElroy, 1993; Hickey, 1993). Other reports in the literature include school-based support groups for children of cancer patients (Call, 1990), groups for siblings of handicapped children (Block & Margolis, 1986), groups in a shelter for battered women and their children (Roberts & Roberts, 1990), time-limited groups for children with a variety of problems (Rose, 1985), and crisis "debriefing" groups for children in a shelter following a natural disaster (Hoffman & Rogers, 1991). Most of these groups employ a structured, time-limited format.

Accounts of groups that utilize cognitive and behavioral methods with children include a play group for a 5-year-old boy who had difficulty with peer relationships (Boulanger & Langevin, 1992) and a skills training approach in working with depressed children (Stark, Raffaelle, & Reysa, 1994). With the existence of groups so ubiquitous, one might ask whether there are any situations in which the referral of a child to a group would be contraindicated. This question is discussed further in the next section.

An Integrated Model for Children's Groups

As previously mentioned, there has been and still is strain in the helping professions between practitioners who provide group *therapy*, focused on helping individuals within a group format (termed the "remedial" model; Papell & Rothman, 1966; Vinter, 1959) and other practitioners who focus on the group as an entity unto itself, believing that the individuals benefit in such a group both through providing assistance to others and through receiving support from the other group members (the "mutual aid" model; Schwartz, 1977; Gitterman & Shulman, 1986; Shulman, 1984, 1992). For reasons related to children's immature development and special need for adult protection and guidance, neither model in its pure form seems apt for application to children. Rather, I recommend an approach that integrates elements of both models. Children are narcissistic, and will not participate in a counseling group (even when they are required to do so) unless they believe that it serves a purpose they deem personally relevant. At the same time, however, they are social beings, and they benefit greatly from the feeling of acceptance and belonging generated by group membership.

Perhaps a new model of social group work merits consideration with regard to children. I suggest that we refer to this model as the "integrated model." With the dual goals of helping each child group member toward greater appreciation of individual *and* group (social) awareness, this approach would meet the children on their level (through providing activities) and would increase their sense of self-esteem through the experience of group sharing, acceptance, and bonding. The definition of group work formulated by the American Association of Group Work in 1948 seems especially applicable to work with children within the integrated framework just described: "Group Work is a method by which . . . both group interaction and program activities contribute to the growth of the individual, and the achievement of socially desirable goals" (quoted in Sullivan, 1952, p. 420).

A Children's Group Therapy Association, founded by social workers in the greater Boston area in 1977, holds an annual conference in New England in May. Many of the presentations in this conference reflect an integrated approach to group work with children, although none are explicitly labeled as embodying such an approach. Let us hope that the tide is turning with regard to the neglect of children among social group workers. It is reassuring to find two chapters on the topic of mutual aid and children in Gitterman and Shulman's (1986) text, as well as similar articles in Alissi and Casper's (1985) special issue of *Social Work with Groups*.

Work with children is different from work with adults, and it does not conform to structures adapted for adults. Group work with children is a promising and rewarding field of practice for social workers. The discussion and case examples in this chapter and elsewhere in this text attest to the viability and versatility of this helping method.

CONSIDERATIONS IN PLANNING A GROUP FOR CHILDREN

Group Composition

In planning a group for children, the following factors must be evaluated in a screening interview with each child that provides the opportunity to determine the child's suitability for placement in the group:

- The purpose of the group
- The degree of homogeneity–heterogeneity among members
- Ages and gender of members
- Level of maturity and attention span
- Type of problem situation
- Leadership (a single leader vs. coleaders)

Tait and Depta (1993) describe a bereavement group that included 10 children, both boys and girls, between the ages of 7 and 11. There were two group leaders, thereby assuring adult support that permitted each child maximum participation in the structured group activities. When there is only one leader, when the children have Conduct Disorder or Attention-Deficit/Hyperactivity Disorder, or when the group is not structured, a more feasible size would be four to six children. Children in kindergarten or first grade, who often have difficulty focusing for longer than 20 or 30 minutes at a time, probably will do better in a group limited to three or four children. Thompson and Rudolph (1992) and Johnson et al. (1986) recommend that the age range and/or grade span among child group members not exceed 1–2 years. Obviously, individual circumstances take precedence over these guidelines, as in the bereavement group described above, in which the age range of members (from 7 to 11 years) permitted siblings to participate in the same group.

Since each child deserves the opportunity to participate in the group, the leader(s) must weigh all factors impinging on the comfort level of the members. Usually, the degree of homogeneity with regard to the nature of the problem situation provides a unifying bond, referred to by Schwartz and Zalba (1971) as "the common ground." For example, a child who has HIV may feel tremendous support in a group of peers with the same diagnosis, and the mixing of genders in such a group would not be contraindicated, since the significance of the diagnosis outweighs the possible importance of gender commonality. On the other hand, a mixed-gender group would *not* be appropriate for children who have been sexually abused and whose discussion might be constricted in the presence of members of the opposite sex.

According to the "Noah's Ark" principle (i.e., two by two), each child in a group should share certain identifying characteristics with at least *one* other group member. Thus, it is not advisable to put a single boy in a group with all girls, or a single white child in a group with all black children. Children have a need to belong and to fit in, and because they tend to think concretely, they pay close attention to physical characteristics.

The leader(s) must also consider the personality attributes of prospective members in order to form a balanced group. Children who present in an extreme way—for example, as excessively self-absorbed, domineering, or unable to give attention to the concerns of peers—probably would be ostracized by a group, with negative consequences for both the individuals and the group as a whole. Yalom (1985) cautions against admitting a potentially "deviant" member into a group because of probable negative responses that will be detrimental to all. In situations where a leader questions whether or not a prospective group member will "fit," better results may be obtained through arranging a period of individual counseling, rather than risking the possible demoralizing experience of rejection. Of course, it might be argued that a "misfit" desperately needs socialization experience. A period of individual counseling might help such an individual to reach a point at which group contact would be beneficial.

In addition, group membership may be contraindicated when an individual has been exposed to a stigmatizing or traumatic event that may be difficult for the prospective member to discuss among others, and/or that may be too horrific for children in general to hear. The treatment of choice in these cases is individual rather than group therapy. The child who has been bereaved by suicide falls into this category (Eth & Pynoos, 1985; Webb, 1993), as does the child who has witnessed or been victim of a traumatic experience (Eth & Pynoos, 1985). Guided reenactment of the trauma experience must be facilitated on an individual basis, as will be discussed in Chapter 14. However, when a *group* of children (e.g., a school class or club group) has undergone a traumatic experience (e.g., a natural or human-made disaster), a crisis debriefing group is helpful and can serve a preventive intervention purpose. Crisis intervention group debriefing is discussed more fully later in this chapter.

Group Format and Structure

A major consideration with regard to the structure of the group is whether it will be open-ended or time-limited. An open-ended group is ongoing, and permits members to remain as long as they perceive the need to do so. When old members withdraw from the group, new individuals are added; this permits more seasoned members to orient, and serve as role models for, the newer members. An example of this type of group is a group for children living in substance-abusing families. Some groups targeted for these children follow a structured approach, using a curriculum within an 8- or 12-week format, during the course of which the group membership remains constant. Other programs for children of alcoholics or drug abusers follow the Alcoholics Anonymous model, in which the membership may change from week to week, but some members attend indefinitely as a core group.

Either the open-ended or the time-limited group format can be useful, depending on the purpose for which the group is being formed. Since children's sense of time is guided by school semesters, vacations, and holidays, a time-limited framework can conform naturally to their lives. A 12-week group, for example, can be completed between Labor Day and the Christmas vacation. If the group will be repeated during the spring semester, some of the same children may choose to enroll again. In this situation, the leader(s) should evaluate in advance whether to extend a reenrollment offer to previous group members. Sometimes there are more children than can be accommodated in the available groups, and "triage" decisions must be made to insure that all needy children receive service.

The optimal length of the group meetings also needs to be planned, with practical matters usually dictating decisions about this. When a group meets during the school day, for example, the length of the class period determines the length of the meeting. However, if the group meets after school, the age of the members and the size of the group influence the amount of time needed to assure members full participation. In general, the larger the group and the older the members, the longer the meeting time. For a group of older (11- and 12-year-old) children involved in a structured activity, 1½ hours would be the suggested time period, whereas a 20-minute group meeting may be appropriate for a group of 5- and 6-year old children.

The frequency of meetings depends on the setting and the purpose of the group. In residential settings and hospitals, group meetings may be convened daily or several times a week. Outpatient settings, such as clinics, community recreational settings, and schools, more typically hold group meetings on a weekly basis.

Leadership Considerations

The question of whether to have a single group leader or coleaders deserves reflection, although in many settings coleadership is not an option because of limited staff availability. There are many advantages to coleadership, especially when one leader is male and the other female, since this simulates parental roles and provides the opportunity for role modeling. Coleadership also permits the leaders to share impressions about the group, as well as to divide responsibilities related to collaboration with other professionals involved with the children, keeping records, and maintaining contacts with the parents/guardians, according to the expectations created and agreements made when the group was initiated.

However, coleadership can become problematic if the leaders become competitive with each other, cannot agree about goals, or cannot work comfortably together because of personality or philosophical differences. These possibilities need to be discussed prior to the beginning of the group, so that if they cannot be resolved, another leadership plan can be implemented.

When a leader works alone, it is important that he or she receive supervision, because the process of reviewing the group's progress and impasses will assist the leader in maintaining the necessary degree of objectivity. The leader will also benefit from systematic thinking about the nature of his or her leadership role with the group.

Necessary Ground Rules for Children's Groups

In order for a children's group to function effectively, the children must understand the expectations involved in membership. Often part of the first group meeting is devoted to the establishment of rules, which the children draft for themselves with the leader's assistance. A basic expectation relates to attendance. Children are urged to attend every session, and if they disagree or disapprove of something that happens in the group, they are advised to bring it up at the time. Some group leaders ask children to sign a contract in the first session, agreeing to come for the planned number of group meetings.

Kalter and Schreier (1994) mention these other typical rules in children's groups:

1. Listening (i.e., only one person talks at a time).
2. Right to pass (i.e., members have no obligation to speak or respond).
3. No putdowns (i.e., there is to be no teasing or name calling).
4. Confidentiality (i.e., members can report outside the group only what they and the leaders have said in the group, *not* what other group members have said).

The Particular Importance of Confidentiality

Probably no issue is more critical than confidentiality. Children may not understand the rationale for keeping what is discussed by others private, and even if they do understand, they may not have the self-control to maintain the promised confidence. Some group leaders use a "confidentiality contract" to emphasize the importance of this issue (Stark et al., 1994). Figure 8.1 illustrates such a contract.

Because of the limits to the worker's promise of confidentiality, these should be mentioned in the initial group meeting during the orientation

---

CONFIDENTIALITY CONTRACT

It is important for me to respect the rights of others to confidentiality, just as I want them to respect *my* right to confidentiality.

I hereby promise not to tell ANYONE outside the group what any other group member says during our meetings.

WHAT IS SAID IN THE GROUP MUST **STAY IN THE GROUP**.

This promise lasts even after the group is over.

Name_____
Date_____

FIGURE 8.1. A sample confidentiality contract.

discussion of group members' responsibilities to one another and to the group. Specifically, the worker/counselor states that there are three circumstances in which he or she will be obligated by law to reveal what members say in the group. These are situations in which members discuss their intent to hurt either themselves or others, or when members disclose that someone is hurting them.

The following case example illustrates the serious problems that occurred when the leader was obliged to break confidence in connection with a member's disclosure of attempted sexual contact in a school-based group of latency-age girls.

———————— ❖ ————————

Case Example: A Mutual Support Group for Children of Divorce

A group was formed of five girls, ages 9–11, whose parents were divorced. The purpose of the group was to provide a source of peer support in the form of mutual aid for students who were confronting similar problems, such as divided loyalties, visitation, and future or current parental remarriage and adjustment to a stepparent and stepsiblings. Permission was obtained from the custodial parents for their children to participate in this group. The group leader was a social worker who had recently received her M.S.W.

The first two group meetings consisted of beginning issues. Each student introduced herself and described her "predivorce" and current family structure. The nature of each girl's relationship and degree of contact with each parent was also discussed; the focus was on each student's feelings about the changes in her life brought about by her parents' divorce.

In the third group meeting, the discussion turned to confidentiality. The leader repeated the circumstances under which she would be obligated to break confidentiality, which she had briefly mentioned during the first meeting.

After this group session, one girl, Barbara, stayed behind with her friend, Mary. Barbara said that she wanted to tell the leader about an incident between her and her father. In Mary's presence, Barbara revealed that her father had said to her during a recent visitation: "Let's play Barbie and Ken; I'll be Ken, and you be Barbie." The father then began hugging and kissing Barbara, pushed her on the bed, and allegedly stated that he "wanted" her. When Barbara kicked her father, he stood up as if nothing had happened, and the matter had been ignored by the two since then.

The worker telephoned to report the alleged abuse to child protective services (CPS). The CPS investigated and found the claim to be unfounded. Barbara's parents found out that the social worker had made the call, threatened to sue her, and refused to permit Barbara to continue with the group.

Barbara, no longer a group member, felt no need to preserve confidentiality. She told classmates who were not in the group about matters that had been discussed, as well as some allegations of serious physical abuse that had not in fact been discussed in the group. Some children, worried about the stories, spoke to their parents, who in turn were justifiably concerned about the rumors being spread by Barbara about their families. Several parents withdrew their children from the group because of all this confusion.

This case demonstrates how quickly matters can get out of control in group situations. The social worker, aware of her responsibility to report allegations of sexual abuse, unfortunately did not anticipate the aftermath when she did so. Perhaps both Barbara and the other group members felt that when Barbara withdrew from the group, they no longer were obligated to respect confidentiality. We can also speculate that Barbara's feelings about the outcome of the CPS investigation provoked her to act out against the other group members by making up false stories about what group members had said in meetings. Still another possibility is that none of Barbara's "disclosures" had any basis in fact.

The social worker, looking back on this situation, believes that it is important to stress with group members that "confidentiality is forever"; the fact that a member withdraws from the group does not mean that other members are free to discuss any details about that person. In the future, she will employ a confidentiality contract to try to avoid unfortunate breaches of members' confidences. The matter of confidentiality's continuing even after death has been litigated in court (National Association of Social Workers, 1994).

CRISIS INTERVENTION GROUPS FOR CHILDREN

Both natural and human-made disasters (e.g., natural disasters; explosions; bus, airplane, and train crashes; and random shootings) occur with distressing frequency and unpredictability in our world. The "normal" responses to such "abnormal" events include a range of anxiety reactions related to the stress and associated with the perceived threat to personal and physical safety. Children, like adults, experience fear and anxiety when they witness "unthinkable" events, such as the collapse of a building, the flooding of their home and community, or the random shooting of classmates on their school playground.

Our growing knowledge about the impact of trauma on the lives of children (and adults) has led to intervention models focused on timely outreach to the survivors of the crisis situation. The intent is to facilitate expression of feelings associated with the crisis, so that underlying anxiety will not continue to create discomforting symptoms. When a community or group of individuals has experienced a crisis, the preferred method of intervention is to conduct a crisis debriefing group. The group format permits individuals to offer support to one another, even as they identify reactions in other survivors that are similar to their own.

The state of California has pioneered the use of crisis groups with children following earthquakes. These groups employ a format and procedures that can be adapted to various crisis situations (see Federal Emergency Management Agency, 1991b, 1991c; Santa Clara County Health Department, 1990).

Tasks in a Crisis Group for Children

In any crisis situation, rumors abound. Children are particularly vulnerable to anxiety related to incorrect information or a partial or total lack of information; indeed, adults may unwisely seek to "protect" them by withholding information. Furthermore, children trying to understand puzzling events will often create their own explanations of why something happened and who was to blame. When children have experienced a frightening event together, it is advisable to convene them as a group to talk about, or "debrief," each child's experience of what happened. Clearly, the first task of the leader in such a crisis group is to give information. In language appropriate to the age of the individuals, they should be told about what happened, and about the efforts to help survivors like themselves.

A second step in crisis intervention groups with children is to encourage each child to tell his or her own story, giving details and providing vivid descriptions. The leader should ask for specifics related to the individual's perceptions in all five senses. In other words, the child should be asked about what he or she heard, smelled, felt, and tasted during the crisis experience, in addition to describing his or her visual memories. Traumatologists (e.g., van der Kolk, 1987; Eth & Pynoos, 1985; Lindy, 1986) have learned that the detailed and timely recall of traumatic memories helps in the prevention of Posttraumatic Stress Disorder. Because children have limited ability to articulate their experiences in words, drawing and play activities can be utilized to assist them in externalizing their feelings about traumatic events. An excellent videotape illustrating school-based interventions with children following earthquakes

FIGURE 8.2. Child's drawing in a debriefing group following an earthquake. Drawing courtesy Katharyn E. K. Ross, National Center for Earthquake Engineering Research, State University of New York College at Buffalo. Used with permission.

is available from the Federal Emergency Management Agency (1991a). This tape demonstrates a classroom debriefing that includes drawing activities in addition to class discussion. Figure 8.2 shows a sample drawing made by a child in a debriefing session following an earthquake.

The individual storytelling and the drawings provide the leader of the crisis group with the opportunity to universalize reactions to the crisis, so that group members do not feel peculiar or stigmatized because of the nature of their feelings. Sometimes parents and other adults unwisely minimize children's feelings, thereby depriving them of the opportunity for validation that occurs in a debriefing group. This validation is supportive and helps children put the frightening experience in the past so that they can move on with their lives.

A final task of the crisis group is to help the children identify the strengths resulting from their having survived the experience. Implicit in the circumstances of both natural and human-made disasters is a sense of helplessness. Although it would be unrealistic to assure children that they can *always* survive future disasters, it is helpful to assist them in identifying what they have learned from this experience, and even to indicate ways in which they may feel stronger and better prepared to meet frightening experiences in the future.

In summary, the following tasks guide the work of leaders in crisis debriefing groups with children:

1. Give information about the crisis in language comprehensible to the children.
2. Encourage detailed recounting of the crisis experience by each group member.
3. Universalize and normalize personal reactions to the crisis.
4. Identify strengths and new coping abilities learned as a result of the crisis experience.

———————— ❖ ————————

Case Example: The World Trade Center Bombing

In a previous publication (Webb, 1994a), I analyzed and made recommendations regarding the intervention of a school-based crisis team following the February 1993 terrorist attack on the World Trade Center in New York City, during which 17 kindergarten children were trapped in an elevator for 5 hours. Although I was not a member of that crisis team, I read numerous accounts about their interventions and spoke to various school personnel who were involved in the aftermath of this crisis. For the purposes of this chapter, I want to invite the reader to attempt to apply the principles of crisis debriefing to this event.

The facts of the situation are as follows. The children, from nearby Brooklyn, were on a school-sponsored field trip to the second tallest building in the world; they had enjoyed the view from the observation deck on the 107th floor, finished their lunches, and gone to the bathroom. As they were descending in the elevator, preparing to take the bus trip back to their school, the elevator suddenly stopped between the 36th and 34th floors. No one in the elevator knew that there had been a bomb blast; however, the lights and ventilation went off, and the children could smell smoke. There was no communication between the elevator and the outside world for several hours. Upon the eventual rescue and safe return of the children to their school, many hours later, the bus was greeted by camera crews and the crisis team carrying balloons. Several parents were described as "hysterical," and most parents preferred to take their children immediately to the safety of home for the weekend, rather than accept the invitation of the crisis team to attend a group meeting when they descended from the bus. Only a few families attended this first debriefing session.

The next involvement of the crisis team took place in the kindergarten classroom the following Monday morning (the bombing had occurred the previous Friday). According to the oral reports and accounts of teaching personnel, the team members spent approximately half a day in the classroom; they engaged the children in play activities, using blocks and other play materials to reenact the explosion in the building, which had been repeatedly portrayed on TV over the weekend. The crisis team also encouraged the children to draw pictures of their experiences.

—————— ❖ ——————

Was this intervention sufficient to relieve the tension and fears these children may have experienced during their 5-hour ordeal of being trapped in a dark, hot elevator? For some children it may have been, since we know that simple exposure to a traumatic event does not automatically result in traumatization for all individuals. In fact, the available research indicates that "even after extreme trauma, . . . only approximately 40% of an exposed population develop Posttraumatic Stress Disorder" (McFarlane, 1990, p. 74). However, there is no way to distinguish those who are vulnerable from those who are not, so a group intervention targeted to the entire exposed population offers the most prudent means for a prevention of severe reactions at a later date.

Ideally, such an intervention should involve every child in a verbal and play reenactment of what he or she experienced. We do not know about the specific meaning of a crisis to each individual involved until we ask and listen. Since young children's verbal abilities are limited, play approaches (together with verbal inquiries) are necessary. Let us consider what could have been done in this case, using the four tasks described above as a guide.

1. *Give information about the crisis.* In this event, as in many crisis situations, there was a lot of confusion about what actually happened and who was to blame. In trying to explain these circumstances to 5-year-olds, a simple statement such as "Something very bad happened, and we don't know yet who or what caused it" would have conformed to the truth; it would also have permitted a reassuring follow-up about the fact that they were safe now and the police would take charge of the situation. Such an explanation, in language children can understand, permits the children to leave the matter in adult hands to that they themselves can proceed with their lives.

2. *Encourage detailed recounting of the crisis.* Each of the 17 children should have been given the opportunity to describe what he or she experienced. Although it probably would not have been feasible for each 5-year-old to listen to the accounts of 16 other children, it would have been possible to divide the group in half, so that each child would have heard about the experiences of seven or eight other children. In view of the children's young ages, their accounts would probably have been rather brief; nonetheless, they would have offered a trained observer an insight

into the degree of each child's perceived stress in this situation. Children appearing to be seriously stressed could have been identified for further follow-up on an individual basis.

3. *Universalize and normalize personal reactions.* After several children had expressed their feelings, either verbally or through drawings or play, the leader could have begun to draw parallels (where appropriate) and to ask whether others felt the same way. Even when expressed feelings were not shared, the leader could have validated each child's individual experience.

4. *Identify strengths and new coping abilities.* The sense of helplessness and dependence on adults, typical of young children, may actually have helped these kindergarteners. Whereas with older children the ability to control their anxiety might have been most important, the younger children in this case who were able to lie down on the floor (at the adult's instructions) and go to sleep may have fared better than some others, who tuned in to the anxiety of the adults and began to cry for their mothers and experience somatic reactions. The crisis group leader would have needed to emphasize that *all* the children survived a difficult situation, even those who were very worried. Feelings of gratitude about being rescued and about cooperating with the rescue personnel would have helped restore a sense of security to these young children.

CONCLUDING COMMENTS

This chapter, emphasizing the wide applicability of groups with children, recommends a helping approach that combines play and art activities as a means of furthering communication with young clients. The group modality appeals to youngsters, who benefit from the sense of belonging and peer support intrinsic to an effective group. In group work with children, activities are considered as therapeutic tools, so the distinction that is sometimes made between "activity groups" and "therapy groups" does not apply. Instead, I have proposed an integrated model that joins both approaches.

It is important for the success of a group that the leader or leaders plan its composition and involve the members in adopting certain guiding principles that will assure each person confidentiality and respect. When these procedures are followed, the group can result not only in improved social interactions, but also in increased feelings of self-esteem among individual members.

The special circumstances and guidelines for conducting crisis debriefing groups have been presented. Unlike other groups, which require prior screening of members, a crisis group consists of all individuals who shared a traumatic event. Timely and detailed attention to the emotional state of each individual helps prevent future possible symptom development, even as it helps group members realize that many of their feelings are shared by others.

I hope that this chapter will encourage more social workers to use groups with children, and will thereby reduce the neglect of this helpful modality in work with young clients.

DISCUSSION QUESTIONS

1. Review some of the advantages of group interventions for children. What is the appropriate manner for preparing a child to enter a group?

2. Imagine that in a group for children with divorced parents, the male and female leaders disagree about the issue of visitation with the noncustodial parent. Consider the ideal way for the leaders to resolve their differences, and speculate about the possible repercussions in the group if the matter remains unresolved.

3. Critique the response of the social worker in the mutual support group for latency-age girls in the school setting after a student made an allegation of attempted sexual contact by her father. Other than reporting this allegation, what other action could the worker have taken that might have prevented the disruption of the group?

4. Identify a crisis event involving a group of children that was reported in the news media. Outline a model preventive intervention approach that would utilize group debriefing with the child survivors.

❖ CHAPTER 9 ❖

School-Based Interventions

Next to the family, the school is probably the biggest influence on a child's life. In fact, since the school assumes responsibility for students during the time the children are on the school premises (i.e., the majority of children's waking hours), the school's role has been described as *in loco parentis* (Allen-Meares, Washington, & Welsh, 1986). This shared responsibility for the well-being of the dependent child makes the liaison between school and home both logical and essential.

SCHOOL–HOME–COMMUNITY PARTNERSHIPS

In addition to the natural link between school and home, an even broader liaison exists between the school and community agencies. This reciprocal community–school relationship includes, on the one hand, school-initiated efforts to involve the community in matters related to children's safety and well-being, and, on the other hand, the community's vested interest in obtaining the school's participation and involvement in projects outside the school that have an impact on children. Examples of the former efforts are school-initiated programs that link latchkey children with senior citizens, so that these children have regular, planned telephone contacts with adults after school. Conversely, an example of a program initiated in the community and later implemented in the schools is the "Good Touches/Bad Touches" curriculum (Turkel & Fink, 1986), which was developed in a mental health agency because of community concern about sexual abuse of children. It subsequently received state approval, and is required in all New York State elementary schools.

Thus, school-based interventions necessarily include work with the community and with parents, in addition to individual and group work with children. Helping children through school-based interventions includes work "from the outside in" (collaboration initiated by professionals outside the school system), as well as work "from the inside out" (efforts initiated in the school and reaching out into the family and community).

"From the Outside In": Essential Communication with the School

Any attempt to help a child must *always* consider the nature of the child's functioning in school. Because learning requires psychic energy, a kindergarten child's preoccupation with her mother's impending surgery, for example, may cause the child to have trouble concentrating and appear "spacey" to the teacher. (See Chapter 12 for details about such a case.) Ideally, the medical social worker, knowing that the mother has a young child, would obtain the mother's permission to contact the school, in order to inform appropriate personnel about the impending surgery and hospitalization. This information would permit the school to connect changes in the child's behavior to her worries about her mother. Referral to the school social worker would insure that the child would receive support during this difficult period.

Professional helpers working with a family in distress must *routinely* ask for permission to contact the school for information about the child's past and current functioning. Sometimes parents (and even professionals) do not perceive the need for this, especially in situations that may appear to be non-school-related (e.g., following a death or some other traumatic family event, such as a house fire). It is the obligation of helping professionals in the community to clarify for the parents the relationship between a child's emotional state and his or her ability to concentrate and learn. In addition, parents need to understand that when *they* are worried, the child usually intuits the parents' concerns, even in the absence of direct information. Social workers in family and child welfare agencies, hospitals, and emergency crisis clinics must recognize the important preventive implications of informing the school about a child's exposure to an upsetting event. Relationships with relevant school staff members pay dividends by expediting referrals and facilitating future feedback regarding the status of the case.

Additional "Outside" Influences on the School: Legislation

Because schools receive their funding from federal, state, and local appropriations, the services offered to children depend on the availability of resources and on legislation approving specific programs. The establishment of these programs, in turn, affects the role of the school social worker. Hancock (1982) summarizes the significance of legislation on school social work practice as follows:

> School social work practice is affected by federal and state legislation and by the resultant school policies. School social workers must become familiar with present laws relating to education and be alert to new legislation. . . . The effectiveness of school social work practice can be greatly diminished by the failure to acquire basic knowledge of legislation pertaining to education and [to keep] up with new developments. It is also essential to be thoroughly acquainted with the policies of the school and sensitive to the need for changes in policy. (p. 41)

Reviews of legislation influencing services to children in schools appear in Hancock (1982) and Costin (1987). The present discussion focuses on two specific laws that have an impact on school social workers: the Education for All Handicapped Children Act (P.L. 94-142, 1975) and the Improving America's Schools Act (P.L. 103-382, 1994).

Education for All Handicapped Children Act (P.L. 94-142)

P.L. 94-142, passed in 1975 with no expiration date, guarantees all disabled children between the ages of 3 and 21 years of age the right to an appropriate public education in the "least restrictive environment." This law "requires that an individualized education program (IEP) be developed for every handicapped child and that the IEP specify the educational and related services to be provided." The law specifies that these services are to be provided by qualified social workers, psychologists, guidance counselors, or other qualified personnel (Newton-Logston & Armstrong, 1993, p. 187; see also Assistance to States for Education of Handicapped Children, 1991).

As a result of this law, social workers have assumed a visible and important role in the schools of many states as case managers. Hancock (1982) points out that it was very significant to the field of social work when Congress specifically mentioned the tasks and services social workers would perform in connection with this legislation. Social workers typically coordinate an array of interdisciplinary school personnel in developing the IEP for each student classified as disabled. They also prepare the social history, make sure that all relevant information is considered in formulating goals, and include the parents as equal partners in the educational planning for their child. The recommendations of an IEP for a classified child are discussed more fully later in this chapter, in connection with the case of Sally.

Classification of disability occurs following a comprehensive evaluation by a team of specialists who gather and review extensive information regarding the child's academic achievement, learning characteristics, social and physical development, and management needs (New York State Department of Education, 1991). Table 9.1 lists and defines the classification of disabilities according to the latest federal regulations (*Code of Federal Regulations*, 1993). A full discussion of each of these disabilities is beyond the scope of this chapter; however, Turner (1989) provides a complete review of child psychopathology, including chapters on mental retardation, autism, and various emotional disturbances of childhood. A section on children with special needs, and a case example involving such a child, appear later in this chapter.

Improving America's Schools Act (P.L. 103-382)

P.L. 103-382, passed in 1994, calls for more involvement of pupil services personnel in helping disadvantaged children; it specifically names school social workers with master's degrees in its list of pupil services personnel (National Association of Social Workers [NASW], 1995). An article about this act was prominently featured on the front page of the *NASW News* in January 1995, together with an announcement about the creation of NASW's first specialty membership section in school social work. Both the new legislation and the school specialty section spotlight the role of school social workers, both within the social work profession itself and in the perception of the public at large.

OVERVIEW OF THE ROLE OF THE SCHOOL SOCIAL WORKER

"From the Inside Out": Working within the School

Social workers have provided school-based services since the turn of the century, when they were called "visiting teachers" because they made home visits to help orient immigrant families to U.S. culture and the role of the school (Costin, 1969, 1987). The nature of the school social worker's role has varied since then, with emphasis shifting from providing casework services to the individual child, to focusing on the problem rather than on the person, to the more recent conceptualization of facilitating home–school–community relations. Ambiguity about their role continues to plague many school social workers, however. Sometimes administrators expect social workers to teach health classes and even to serve as attendance officers of a sort, checking up on the status of children who are chronically truant. Although some teaching assignments may be relevant to the social worker's role, and many truant children may be in drastic need of social work services, social workers may resent these job

TABLE 9.1. Classifications of Disabilities

Classification	Definition of the disability
Autism	Autism is a behaviorally defined syndrome that may occur in children of all levels of intelligence. It significantly affects verbal and nonverbal communication and social interaction, and is generally evident before age 3. There is usually difficulty in responding to people, events, and objects. Responses to sensations of light, sound, and feeling may be exaggerated, and delayed speech and language skills may be demonstrated.
Deafness	Deafness means a hearing loss so severe that it prevents processing linguistic information through hearing. The severity of this hearing loss usually necessitates the use of specialized training through an alternative means of communication or use of speech sounds.
Deaf-blindness	Deaf-blindness means concomitant hearing and visual impairments that cause such severe communication and other developmental and educational problems that the student cannot be accommodated in special education programs solely for deaf or blind students.
Emotional disturbance	This term means a condition that is demonstrated in difficulties in school that cannot be explained by intellectual, sensory, or health factors. Over a long period of time, the student is usually unable to build satisfactory relationships, may be generally unhappy, may develop physical symptoms or have fears associated with his or her school experience, or may have inappropriate behaviors or feelings.
Hearing impairment	This term refers to an impairment in hearing that adversely affects a student's educational performance. The hearing loss may or may not be permanent. The student may have difficulty following instructions or have difficulty in other areas relating to the hearing loss; he or she may have problems discriminating speech sounds, or have speech and/or language difficulties, as well as frequent middle ear infections.
Learning disability	This term refers to a psychological processing disorder that causes a problem in understanding or using spoken or written language. A child who is learning-disabled has difficulty listening, thinking, speaking, reading, writing, or doing arithmetic. This child's disability results in a severe discrepancy between his or her ability and achievement. A learning disability is not primarily due to a physical, mental, or emotional disability, or to environmental, cultural, or economic disadvantage.
Mental retardation	This term means significantly subaverage general intellectual functioning that exists concurrently with deficits in adaptive behavior. This condition adversely affects a child's educational performance.

(continued)

TABLE 9.1. (Continued)

Multiple disabilities	This term means concomitant impairments that result in multisensory or motor deficiencies and developmental lags in the cognitive, affective, or psychomotor area. The combination of these disabilities causes educational problems that cannot be accommodated through a special education program designed solely for one of the disabilities.
Orthopedic impairment	This term means a severe orthopedic impairment that adversely affects the child's educational performance. Included are the impairments caused by congenital anomalies, impairments caused by disease, and impairments from other causes (e.g., cerebral palsy, amputation, and fractures or burns that cause contractures).
Other health impairment	This term refers to having limited strength, vitality, or alertness due to chronic or acute health problems that adversely affect educational performance. These problems may include a heart condition, tuberculosis, rheumatic fever, nephritis, asthma, sickle cell anemia, Tourette's syndrome, hemophilia, epilepsy, lead poisoning, leukemia, or diabetes.
Speech impairment	This refers to a communication disorder such as stuttering, an inability to correctly product speech sounds, a language impairment, or a voice disorder that adversely affects a child's educational performance.
Traumatic brain injury	This term means an acquired injury to the brain due to open or closed head injuries caused by an external physical force or by medical conditions such as encephalitis, stroke, aneurysm, anoxia, or brain tumors. The injuries result in mild to severe impairments in one or more areas, including cognition, language, memory, attention, reasoning, abstract thinking, problem solving, sensory/perceptual and motor abilities, psychosocial behavior, physical functions, information processing, and speech. The term does not include congenital injuries or impairments caused by birth trauma.
Visual impairment	This term means an impairment to vision that, even with correction, adversely affects educational performance.

Note. Adapted from New York State Department of Education (1993, pp. 16–17, section 200.1 (mm)) and from the *Code of Federal Regulations* (1993, section 300.7).

assignments when they occur haphazardly rather than in a preplanned, agreed-upon manner. If school social workers *themselves* feel uncertain about the boundaries of their role, it is understandable that administrators and other professionals are similarly confused about it. Hancock (1982, p. 247) describes this lack of role clarity as follows:

The role of the school social worker is difficult for others to grasp for it varies in some ways from one school social worker to the next and is susceptible to many interpretations. In addition, school social workers themselves are seeking clarification of their roles. School social workers are not vague about what they are doing in the school, but many of them probably wonder whether they are doing what they should be doing.

This anxiety can be fueled by teachers who expect the social worker to "fix" children, yet fail to understand and accept the necessity to take the children from their regular schoolwork for counseling sessions.

The parameters of the school social worker's role are specified by Costin (1987), who identifies the following roles and tasks:

- Identification of children in need
- Extending services to pupils
- Work with school personnel
- Educational planning for disabled children
- Work with parents
- Community services

All of these important responsibilities are carried out within a "host" setting in which social work is *not* the dominant discipline. Because the main purpose of the schools is education, social workers in school settings must help fulfill this educational purpose. According to Hepworth and Larsen (1982, p. 283), the goals of the school social worker "center upon helping pupils attain a sense of competence, [and] a readiness for continued learning. . . . Increasingly, the focus of school social work is on cognitive areas—learning, thinking, and problem-solving—as well as the traditional areas of concern, i.e. relationships, emotions, motivation, and personality."

In order to facilitate the child's learning, the school social worker serves as a liaison *within* the school system between the children and the school staff, and *outside* the school system with the parents and community personnel. This role may include, but is not limited to, the following tasks:

- Collecting information about a child for a social history
- Conferring with teachers, school nurses, and other staff members about methods for helping a child
- Planning meetings for parents, with speakers and discussions focusing on topics of child behavior, parenting techniques, and relevant community concerns

- Working with community agencies to establish Big Brother/Big Sister connections for children in need
- Collaborating with foster care, family, welfare, probation, and other social service agencies that are involved with the child and family

Necessary Knowledge and Skills

The multidimensional role of school social workers requires both generic and specialized knowledge and skills. The *generic* base of knowledge and skills includes the ability to do the following:

- Think systemically
- Formulate a comprehensive biopsychosocial assessment
- Appreciate ethnic diversity and its effects on children's socialization
- Establish and maintain relationships with parents and with personnel relevant to the work with a child
- Help all parties formulate specific goals
- Link the family system to community resources
- Monitor the progress and involvement of the child and others with respect to the goals

The core of *specialized* knowledge required for competent practice as a school social worker includes the following:

- An understanding of special education and of the laws related to education
- Knowledge about children's rights and parents' rights
- The ability to work on a team and to communicate effectively with professionals who are not social workers
- The ability to work within the bureaucratic structure of the school system
- The ability to implement cognitive-behavioral treatment with children, families, and teachers
- An understanding of the impact of physical, sexual, and emotional abuse on a child, and knowledge of how to respond appropriately when children are affected by these and other traumatic situations
- The ability to provide therapeutic intervention with children and families in both one-to-one and group formats
- The ability to apply crisis intervention theory appropriately, including an understanding of when to utilize appropriate community agencies in a crisis situation

The school social workers I have interviewed about the nature of their role stress the necessity of being able to "think on their feet" and to be able to respond quickly and directly. For example, a teacher in the cafeteria may make an unexpected request for help, or a fight may break out in a corridor that demands prompt intervention by the social worker, who just happens to be in the vicinity. Ginsburg (1989, p. 87) states that "the school social worker should not be hiding in an office. Rather, it is important to be visible and well aware of the school's agenda and of what is happening there."

ISSUES IN INTERPROFESSIONAL COLLABORATION

Teamwork

Social work with children *always* involves interactions with family members, as well as with others who know the child and who may be able to offer a perspective on the child that enriches the worker's solitary view. Teamwork is fundamental in providing services to the child in the school. The members of the team vary in different settings, but often include the school psychologist, the child's regular teacher and/or special education teacher, a school administrator, and a specialized therapist, in addition to the child's parents.

——————— ❖ ———————

The Case of Johnny, Age 5

Johnny was referred to the social worker when the child's kindergarten teacher became concerned about his short attention span, aggression toward other children, and impatience about having to take turns on the playground equipment during recess. The teacher asked the social worker to contact the parents, to see whether family stress might be contributing to the child's difficulties. In discussions with the child's mother, the school social worker obtained permission to observe the child in the classroom. She also gleaned important information about the family. The parents were actively seeking to adopt a baby; in fact, they had recently left Johnny abruptly to go to a hospital in another state, where a prospective adoptee had just been born. When the birth mother changed her mind, the parents returned home and told Johnny that "the mother decided to keep the baby." Johnny, who knew that he himself had been adopted, became very confused about this sequence of events, as well as about his mother's sadness, irritability, and repeated statements about wanting to "get another baby sooner or later."

Several counseling sessions with Johnny and his mother together provided the opportunity to reassure Johnny that his adoptive parents loved him very much and would never give *him* up, as he had begun to fear. It also permitted both Johnny and his mother to voice their mutual wish to have a little baby in the house, so Johnny could experience being "a big brother." Finally, the mother (with the social worker's guidance) reassured Johnny that if she and his father had to go away again to try to adopt another baby, they would tell Johnny first and say goodbye, even if it was in the middle of the night.

This short-term, school-based intervention brought dramatic improvement in Johnny's peer interactions in school. His ability to focus on his learning also improved, since he was no longer worried about his mother and father's sudden disappearance, and about being displaced by a new baby.

This example portrays social worker–teacher collaboration in the ideal situation—one in which the professionals work together to understand the child's problem, and the parent openly shares the family's concerns with the school social worker. Unfortunately, this ideal state of trust, communication, and cooperation does not always exist.

Ethical Dilemmas

Social workers are sometimes uncomfortable with the team concept because of the expectation to share information about families. In fact, social workers may feel caught in an ethical bind about disclosing information that was given to them in confidence. Garrett (1994) points out that school social workers may have difficulty determining who the "client" is, since the school, the child, and the family all have a stake in the designated "problem situation." Whereas the NASW code of ethics states that "social workers [should] respect and promote the rights of clients to self-determination" (NASW, 1996, section 1:02), the application of this principle in school settings requires a concept of the "client" that encompasses the triangle of child, family, and school. Even with this conceptualization, however, the social worker may think it unnecessary and inappropriate to divulge to a child's teacher all the intimate details of the parents' marriage and other sensitive family matters.

Professional discretion regarding sharing of information with other members of the school team, in my opinion, must be guided by the "best interests of the child" and by what will best serve the child's learning experience. Therefore, it may be unnecessary for a teacher to know about a mother's substance abuse background when the mother is in recovery. However, it may be helpful for the teacher to know that this child's working mother leaves her in the care of a babysitter in the evening, since the teacher has noticed that the child yawns a lot and seems tired in school. It is important for the teacher to tell the mother that her child seems tired, so the mother will be able to impress on the child's sitter the need for a regular, specific bedtime.

Parents are often concerned about the nature of the information in their children's school records. As already discussed in Chapter 2, the federal Family Educational Rights and Privacy Act (P.L. 93-380, 1974) gives parents the right to inspect their children's school records. Therefore, all school personnel should be both factual and discreet regarding the information they write in the record. As parents are increasingly encouraged to take an active role in their children's educational planning, school personnel must learn to view parents as partners.

Interprofessional Communication

Because professionals with different backgrounds and training must collaborate on behalf of the pupils in their schools, it is essential that these professionals understand enough about one another's respective areas of specialization to communicate effectively. For example, the school social worker needs sufficient knowledge about educational and psychological tests to comprehend their significance in the school psychologist's reports. Similarly, the school social worker should understand the possible contribution of the special education teacher, the speech therapist, and the physical therapist in assisting children with Attention-Deficit/Hyperactivity Disorder, especially when the parents are fearful that medication may become "addictive" and therefore be harmful to their children.

Few school social workers are knowledgeable about the assessment and appropriate intervention for all conditions listed as disabling. However, school social workers who become involved in working with such children can build incrementally in their knowledge base in order to communicate effectively with their colleagues, as well as with the children's parents about the children's disabilities and the recommended educational interventions. Because the team approach is inherent in school social work practice, there can be no sense of personal "ownership" of any case; rather, there must be a sharing of responsibility. This mandates interprofessional collaboration, cooperation, and communication.

Working with School Administrators

The role of the school principal has been compared to that of a captain of a ship, insofar as he or she has ultimate responsibility for what happens or does not happen in the vessel/school building. Parents, the school board, and the community expect the principal to be "in charge" and knowledgeable about the curriculum, about after-school activities, and about children who are having difficulties (and the helping plans for such children). Hancock (1982) points out that principals are public figures without job tenure who are vulnerable to pressures from various factions in the community, and whose position may subject them to intense scrutiny and even litigation.

These diverse pressures on principals explain their interest in and need to know about the activities of school social workers and other school employees who interact with parents and agencies in the community. Of course, every principal functions according to his or her unique personality and his or her history of relations with past "helpers" (both within the school and without). Also influencing the principal's attitudes may be the attitudes in the community about social workers and their appropriate role and function in the school.

It is incumbent upon school social workers to develop harmonious working relationships with their principals. During the initial phase of their contacts, both parties should articulate and discuss their respective expectations regarding the social work role, to avoid future ambiguity and confusion about this. The common goal of wanting to facilitate the educational experience of the children in the school can serve as the foundation for a solid social worker–principal relationship, which will promote the best interests of the children in the school.

SPECIAL NEEDS CHILDREN

Terminology

The Education for All Handicapped Children Act (P.L. 94-142), as noted earlier, protects the right of children with disabilities to a free, appropriate public education in the least restrictive environment. Before I describe the process of classifying such children, I must first review the variety of general terms used currently and in the past to refer to children with special needs. They have been referred to as "handicapped children," "exceptional children," "disabled children," "defective children," and "children with individual learning differences." When children have more than one special needs condition, they are referred to as "multiply disabled."

Hancock (1982) points out that a child may be born with a disabling condition, or may become disabled through an accident or injury. Attitudes toward children with disabilities have gradually become more accepting, with emphasis on what the children *can* do rather than on their limitations. Those who prefer to focus on strengths rather than on limitations argue for use of the term "special needs children." However, the law refers to "handicapped children," and the classification system uses terms such as "emotionally disturbed," "speech-impaired," and "learning-disabled" for various categories; such terms emphasize the losses or disruptions created by different physical, emotional, and cognitive conditions. In view of the pejorative connotations of most of these labels, the terminology of educators seems appropriately sensitive to these children's feelings of being "different" from other children. Thus, being in "special education" classes, or leaving a "regular" classroom to go to the "resource room," does not *ipso facto* imply inferiority (although the children themselves and their classmates often attach their own negative connotations to these terms).

Parents of Special Children

Despite efforts to destigmatize children with special needs, the parents of such a child suffer greatly upon learning definitively about their child's specific condition. All parents want their children to be well and to possess the necessary innate abilities to deal effectively with life. When parents are told (either at birth, or later by a pediatrician or other specialist) that there is something wrong with their child, this information stirs up a barrage of feelings, including anger, denial, guilt, and tremendous sadness. Olshansky (1962) coined the expression "chronic sorrow" to refer to the grief of parents in response to the diagnosis of their child's disability, and to the recurrence (i.e., chronicity) of that grief throughout the child's life, when it becomes repeatedly apparent that the child's condition requires special assistance from a variety of professionals. Although this view of the long-term, recurring reactions of parents of disabled children has been disputed by some (Wikler, Wason, & Hatfield, 1981), social workers who have ongoing contact with parents of classified children tend to support the view that these parents' grief is chronic and requires sensitive response from school personnel (Rothschild, 1986). The social worker's goals in counseling the parents of a special child, according to Rothschild (1986, p. 42), are these: (1) to increase the parents' acceptance of living with and adjusting to their disabled child; and (2) to help the parents develop the tools they need to increase their child's skills, through "translating" the processes of children's education to the parents.

Some special education programs offer support groups for parents of special children. Such groups give these parents the opportunity to listen to and discuss both positive and negative feelings, and to contribute to and benefit from the solutions of other parents who have similar frustrations and pressures. Dillard, Donenberg, and Glickman (1986, p. 50) point out that "just as a child may experience negative affect and feel separated from the mainstream of school life when placed in a special education class or program, parents may experience similar negative feelings." Examples of both long-term and short-term parent groups are described in Hawkins (1986).

The Classification Process

New York State follows a specific procedure in assessing children who have been referred to a committee on special education (CSE) for a comprehensive evaluation. Figure 9.1 illustrates the steps involved in classifying a child in New York and following the child's progress, from the referral stage to the follow-up evaluations every 3 years. Because school attendance is mandatory in New York State for children between the ages of 6 and 16 (and may extend until age 21 for a child who is classified as disabled), the school and the parents must periodically reevaluate the child's needs for special education. Figure 9.1 and the two tables in this chapter come from a guide for parents (New York State Department of Education, 1992) that presents a complete, "user-friendly" description of the special education process, in order to provide parents with the knowledge they need to insure appropriate educational programs for their children with special needs. Involvement of the parents is basic to the various procedures, beginning with the referral, which requires parental consent before the evaluation can proceed.

Components of a Comprehensive Evaluation

Once a request for an evaluation has been received, and the parents have given their consent, a team of specialists prepares a comprehensive assessment of the child's skills and abilities. The areas that are assessed and the staff members who will conduct the specific evaluations are outlined in Table 9.2. A CSE arranges to obtain the necessary information in a timely manner and to schedule discussion of these findings at a CSE

STEP 1
Referral: Identifying Children Who May Need Special Education

STEP 2
Evaluation: Collecting Information Through Assessment

STEP 3
Recommendation: A Plan for Children's Needs

STEP 4
Implementation: Arranging for Programs and Services

STEP 5
Annual Review: Updating the Program

STEP 6
Triennial Evaluation: Updating Tests and Evaluative Information

FIGURE 9.1. The special education process in New York State for children and youths ages 5–21. From New York State Department of Education (1992, p. 10).

meeting, in which parents are encouraged to participate. The goal of the evaluation is to arrive at a recommendation that summarizes a child's current skills and abilities, establishes educational goals and objectives for the school year, describes programs designed to meet these goals, and lists ways to check the child's progress periodically.

A child may be found ineligible for special education when the committee finds that the student cannot be classified as having one of the disabling conditions defined in Table 9.1. Such "ineligible" children may, however, qualify for educationally related support services (e.g., short-term counseling) or speech and language improvement services, which must be specified on a child's IEP.

On the other hand, when a child is found to be eligible for special education, the IEP details the specific nature of the recommended classes and services, following the principle of the "least restrictive environment."

TABLE 9.2. Components of a Comprehensive Evaluation

Type of evaluation	Areas that may be assessed	Staff who might conduct evaluations
Physical examination	Vision, hearing, physical development, medical needs, and physical factors which affect school progress.	School physician Nurse practitioner Physician's assistant
Psychological assessment and psychological evaluation (as deemed necessary by the school psychologist)	General intelligence, learning strengths and weaknesses, instructional needs, social interactions and relationships.	School psychologist
Social history	Social development, current social interactions, factors within home, school, and community which may contribute to student's difficulties.	Social worker Guidance counselor School psychologist School administrator School nurse
Observation in the classroom	Performance in the current educational setting, relationship to teachers and other students, learning styles, and attention span.	School administrator Teacher Reading specialist Guidance counselor CSE member School psychologist
Appropriate educational evaluations	Educational achievement, learning strengths and weaknesses, vocational and academic needs.	Teacher Reading specialist Guidance counselor Vocational counselor
Assessments in all areas relating to the suspected disability	Specific assessments relating to health, vision, hearing, social–emotional development, general intelligence, communication skills, motor abilities, and academic performance.	School nurse Speech therapist Audiologist Physical therapist Occupational therapist Specialist with knowledge in area of suspected disability
Vocational assessment	Possible areas of future employment; work-related skills, interests.	Counselor Psychologist Work site evaluator Vocational counselor Rehabilitation counselor

Note. From New York State Department of Education (1992, p. 14).

This means that if a child's abilities in a particular area (e.g., math) qualify him or her to participate in a "regular" math class, this must be implemented. Special class instruction, when indicated, will specify the student–teacher ratio, with students grouped according to the similarity of their needs.

The Role of the Social Worker in Special Education

Some school social workers work primarily or exclusively in special education programs, but the job descriptions of most school social workers include work both with children who have been classified as disabled and with children in the general school population. The specific responsibilities of the social worker related to special education includes contact with parents; counseling parents through the evaluation period (and afterward, when indicated); obtaining and writing children's social histories; participating in CSE meetings; advocating for the children; and working with the teachers, special education staff, principal, and families to implement the goals of children's IEPs. Sometimes the social worker provides individual counseling with a child, and/or parent/family counseling (which may include home visits); in addition, the worker may provide group interventions with children, as well as with parents who have similar needs.

In summary, the role and functions of the social worker in special education programs are similar to those of any school social worker. However, the special education social worker must also have specialized knowledge regarding classification categories and procedures, and the skill and sensitivity to implement this knowledge with other professionals and with parents. Some of these functions are illustrated in the following case.

———————— ❖ ————————

THE CASE OF SALLY, AGE 11

Family Information

Family Members in Child's Household

Maternal grandmother   Mrs. Jones, age 85.
Brother   Michael, age 16, sophomore in high
                                          school.
Child client   Sally, age 11, fifth grade (see below for details
                                          of classification and educational placement).

Other Family Members

Mother (deceased)   Laureen, died of lung cancer at age 35 when
                                          Sally was a baby.
Father   .   Sammy, age 45, truck driver.
Siblings   Four brothers and five sisters, all older than
                                          Sally.
Stepmother   Mary, age 37.
Half-siblings   Two, younger than Sally.

This was an African-American family of the Baptist faith. The grand-mother and Sally attended church regularly, whereas those living in the father's household and the children living with him were not particularly observant.

Presenting Problem

Sally was referred at age 11 to the school social worker for counseling, because of the girl's "many angry feelings," "mood swings," "poor self-image," and "uncooperative and argumentative behavior toward author-ity figures." A psychological evaluation described Sally as "immature in her social–emotional functioning" and as revealing "feelings of inferior-ity" related to being "less bright than others."

Background

Academic Problems

Sally's school records indicated that she had academic problems in all areas in first grade. Her psychological evaluation at that time indicated borderline intellectual functioning (Full Scale IQ of 71), and she was clas-sified as a "mentally retarded" learner and placed in special education in second grade. Sally's reevaluation 3 years later (end of fourth grade) showed some growth in her nonverbal cognitive functioning. Her Full Scale IQ had improved to 78, thereby justifying the change of her classi-fication to "learning-disabled" and the recommendation for ongoing placement in special education.

In fourth and fifth grades, Sally's teachers reported poor academic skills but good work habits and social skills, up until the referral for coun-seling in the spring of Sally's fifth-grade year.

Family Situation

Following her mother's death when Sally was a baby, Sally and her older siblings were taken care of by her grandmother and her father in her father's home. The grandmother lived separately, but within walking distance; she provided routine care for this large household of children, returning to her own residence when the father came home from work. The father remarried within a year of the mother's death, and a new baby was soon born, followed by a second a few years later. There was increas-ing friction between the grandmother and the stepmother; Sally, demonstrating loyalty to her grandmother, opposed her stepmother, adding to the family conflict. This culminated in a custody hearing in family court, at which the judge awarded custody of Sally (then 8 years old) and one of her older brothers to the grandmother. This arrangement continued in the intervening years, with Sally visiting her siblings at her father's house on Saturdays, when she often accompanied her father on shopping and other errands.

The apartment in which Sally resided with her grandmother and brother consisted of three rooms over a garage. She shared a bedroom with her grandmother and helped her with cooking and household chores. It was notable that the grandmother did not read or write (she had been raised in the South and received little or no schooling). The brother attended regular high school classes and was a popular member of the basketball team.

Summary of Social Work Interventions

Weekly counseling with Sally, home visits and telephone contacts with the grandmother, meetings with the father, and teacher conferences over a 2-year period contributed to marked improvement in Sally's classroom behavior and to more appropriate family interactions. With Sally's approaching adolescence, her grandmother's strict discipline was beginning to create stress between them. The social worker helped the grandmother relax her firm stance enough to permit Sally to participate in selected after-school activities that were age-appropriate. Furthermore, the social worker arranged a Big Sister for Sally, and convinced the grandmother to permit Sally to serve as a volunteer classroom helper at a local day care center. This last activity contributed greatly to Sally's feelings of self-esteem, since she had to undergo an interview to become accepted for this position, albeit as a volunteer.

In counseling, Sally revealed her fears that her grandmother would die. Believing that Sally needed reassurance and a plan related to this possibility, the social worker taught Sally how to dial 911, and she also asked the grandmother's permission to have Sally and herself attend the grandmother's next routine visit to her doctor. This proved to be very helpful: The doctor reassured Sally that her grandmother was presently quite well, and he invited Sally to call him in the future if she became worried or had questions about her grandmother's health.

The individual counseling with Sally focused on some of the girl's losses, as well as on age-appropriate concerns about her appearance and developing interest in boys. Aware of Sally's receptive and expressive language deficits, the social worker invited Sally to draw. However, Sally rejected this and other play materials as "babyish." In contrast, she agreed to read some books with the social worker in which the main characters were girls of Sally's own age who were experiencing a variety of life problems (e.g., the death of a parent, relationships with a new stepmother, or not being popular). Sally could join with the social worker in verbalizing the feelings of the characters in the books, without necessarily acknowledging the similarity with her own life.

Despite the overall improvement in Sally's relationships with her family and teacher, the girl's emotional vulnerability and pervasive neediness continued in moody and unpredictable reactions that caused ongoing difficulties. For example, Sally sabotaged the Big Sister relationship when she became more and more demanding of the older girl's time. Similarly, a relationship with a special education teacher turned sour when Sally seemed "ungrateful" and unresponsive, after the teacher had given Sally some clothing and invited her to her home.

—————— ❖ ——————

Discussion

This case demonstrates the crucial role of the school social worker as liaison between the school and the home. It is doubtful that individual counseling alone, without the intensive family interventions utilized here, could possibly have been sufficient to help this child. Indeed, an argument could be made that these interventions should have occurred much sooner, before the youngster began showing difficulties. A strong case could be made for Sally's unresolved mourning for her mother as the source of her volatile relationships with female teachers, her Big Sister, and her stepmother. However, the fact that Sally had a strong positive relationship with her grandmother laid the foundation for the girl to accept the social worker, who provided very concrete services, balanced with discussion of feelings in a displaced manner.

The case rather vividly portrays a child in special education as having much the same emotional needs and problems in response to life crises as might have been experienced by *any* child her age. Although Sally's limited intellectual functioning may have interfered with her ability to understand the nuances of social interactions, her pain over loss, her frustration in having to adjust to a stepmother, and her reduced self-esteem over her school work were reactions that any 11-year-old might have had. Therefore, the necessary social work skills for helping this special needs child included the generic skill base for helping all children.

CONCLUDING COMMENTS

The complexity of the role of the school social worker demands great versatility, the ability to think on one's feet, and awareness of the reciprocity of multiple interacting systems. Liking children and wanting to advocate for their best interests in the school are only the beginning of the job qualifications of a school social worker. In addition, as illustrated in this chapter, the school social worker must understand and be able to communicate and collaborate with parents and with the various professionals who also participate and contribute to the child's educational experience.

The whole range of social work knowledge and skills is epitomized in the role of the school social worker, whose regular activities in the course of a week may include such diverse responsibilities as obtaining data and writing a social history; attending and participating in a CSE meeting; identifying and reporting sexual and/or physical abuse; counseling children on an individual and/or group basis; conducting a "Good Touches/Bad Touches" kindergarten class; conferring with teachers about specific children; working with outside agencies and making referrals; conducting parent group meetings; and consulting with the principal about special programs in response to parent concerns about community violence. This demanding role includes the satisfaction of being a child advocate in a manner that seeks to help not only the individual child, but also an entire school community of children.

DISCUSSION QUESTIONS

1. Discuss some of the special challenges related to working in a "host" setting, such as a school. How can the social worker maintain a strong sense of professional identity when working with professionals from many different disciplines?

2. What is meant by "the best interests of the child," and how does this apply to the work of school social workers?

3. How can the school social worker create and maintain harmonious and effective relationships with the principal?

4. Consider the various issues that might be raised in an ongoing support group for parents of children with special needs. What is the ideal role for the social worker in such a group?

5. Discuss how reading works of fiction can assist in counseling/therapy with a child. How can a child be helped when the child refuses to discuss his or her *own* feelings?

❖ PART IV ❖

Helping Children in Special Circumstances

❖ CHAPTER 10 ❖

Children in
Out-of-Home Placements

Once upon a time, everyone assumed that children would be raised in a home with their mothers, fathers, brothers, and sisters, and that they would remain at home until they married and moved away to start a family of their own. Is this a true story that reflects real life, or is it a fairy tale? If true, does it apply to *all* children or mainly to children in economically secure families, in which the "traditional" roles of father as breadwinner and mother as homemaker permit the children to grow up in a tight circle of nuclear family, church, school, and community? How is this view of children in the nuclear family currently altered because of the high incidence of never-married and divorced working mothers, who must arrange out-of-home child care for their children? How strongly do we continue to subscribe to the ideal that children *should* be raised, whenever possible, by two biological parents?

THE BEST INTERESTS OF THE CHILD

Times have changed, but many people still adhere to values specific to a particular lifestyle in the past that may no longer conform to current reality. The portrayal of children as safe in the bosom of the home certainly did not apply to many poor and immigrant families at the beginning of the 20th century, when many mothers worked in factories, farms, or sweatshops, sometimes bringing their dependent children to work with them. This belief about the importance of raising children within their family and cultural groups also did not prove true for the thousands of immigrant children in New York who were removed from their homes between 1854 and 1930, and sent to the country in order to offer the children the benefits of fresh air, good food, and a "wholesome" atmosphere—factors supposedly not present in their urban environment (Hall, 1992). Finally, this fairy tale does not apply to the single mother today who relies on Aid to Families with Dependent Children to meet the costs of raising her children, and who, in the political climate at the end of the 20th century, fears the unthinkable prospect of having her children placed in orphanages because she cannot obtain employment. The references made in 1994 to placing children in institutions because of the "inadequacies" of their mothers echo ominously the birth of the foster home movement in 1855, when the New York Children's Aid Society, under the direction of Charles Loring Brace, removed thousands of children from their homes and placed them in homes in the West (Hall, 1992). The essential question, in the 1990s as in the 1850s, pertains to the relative importance of parental bonds as compared with environmental factors in determining the best interests of the child.

Although some parents become overwhelmed and voluntarily place their children out of the home, and others relinquish their infants for adoption, the majority of children in residential and foster placements are there because their parents have been found by the courts to be abusive or neglectful (Kinard, 1987). Brieland, Costin, and Atherton (1985) state that "children who are found to be neglected, abused, or at high risk in their family situations require specialized protective services from the community and its social agencies. . . . *neglect and abuse constitute the major reason for placement of children in foster care*" (p. 240, emphasis added). Exercising the principle of *parens patriae* (which can be roughly translated as "the state as guardian"), the court uses its power to protect a dependent child by removing the child from home and placing him or her in a foster home or institution.

Although the percentage of children in foster care and group care is relatively small (less than 1%, according to Whittaker, 1987), approximately half of these children are from minority groups, and many become recipients of social work services. Because of the growing numbers of children being orphaned by the AIDS epidemic (Michaels & Levine, 1992), and the large number of children essentially abandoned by substance-addicted parents, it seems inevitable that the populations of children in foster care and in group and residential care will increase in the next decade, despite all countervailing efforts of mandatory permanency planning to keep children in their own homes. In fact, during the late 1980s and early 1990s, the number of U.S. children in foster care increased by 23% (National Association of Social Workers, 1993). In short, children may have no home of their own and no parents available for rehabilitative work. The best interests of such a child point to adoption; yet a suitable adoptive home may not be available. This is illustrated later in this chapter, in the case of Maria and Mario.

Although the focus of this chapter is on methods of helping children who are already in foster care or residential placement, we must not overlook the importance of family preservation services that might have averted the necessity for placement in the first place. Intensive family preservation services, such as the Homebuilders model (Kinney, Madsen, Flemming, & Haapala, 1977; Whittaker, Kinney, Tracy, & Booth, 1990), serve families in which children are at risk of imminent placement. These services offer intensive, brief, home-based interventions on a 24-hour, 7-day-per-week basis; their goals are to stabilize these families so that the children are no longer in danger of being placed out of home, and to link the families to professional and natural support services. Between 70% and 90% of children who received this form of intervention remained in the home at the time of termination of services, according to the National Resource Center on Family-Based Services (1983). The values base of family preservation programs includes the belief that the family is the best place to rear a child, and that the entire family is the client, rather than the individual child or parent (Hodges, Morgan, & Johnston, 1993).

Although these values and outcome findings are impressive, the high cost of funding such programs may limit their wide application. Another concern is whether the gains can be sustained over the long term when families continue to experience stress. Brieland et al. (1985) point out that protective intervention through social services comes at a late stage of a family's problems, after heavy stresses have culminated in neglect or abuse. These authors also maintain that foster care institutions and small group homes may not necessarily have devastating effects upon children, as traditionally believed. Certainly when a child has no family, foster placement is essential.

This chapter presents ways to help children and their families when the children are already in care. Whenever family members are available, they must be included as partners in the helping process; when they cannot be located or when they do not exist, methods to help children identify and resolve their feelings about lost/absent relatives should be encouraged. A child's sense of identity is connected to his or her family background, and the process of helping the child requires that the family be included in work with the child, either in reality or symbolically.

DETERMINING THE NEED FOR PLACEMENT

What is the meaning of relocating a child to another family for foster placement or to a group setting? Mishne (1983) mischievously points out that many wealthy parents voluntarily send their children to boarding school, with no expectation that the young people will be harmed by the experience of separation from home. Obviously, it is not primarily the *separation* that threatens a child, but the circumstances that precipitated the separation in the first place. If, as previously indicated, the main reason for involuntary placement is parental abuse or neglect, a separation can be viewed as the culmination of *many* past experiences of emotional and/or physical distress because of adult behavior. The separation is frequently the outcome of a long, sad history, which often leads the child to mistrust adults. These life experiences of abuse or neglect also contribute to the child's poor ego development and reduced ability to deal with even the everyday difficulties of life, let alone situations of extreme stress. Since every placement decision is different, the interacting influence of many factors must be weighed in determining the specific meaning of the placement to each individual child and family, and in outlining a realistic treatment plan.

Evaluating Placement as Crisis: The Use of Tripartite Assessment

In two previous publications (Webb, 1991, 1993), I have presented the use of "tripartite assessment" as a method of evaluating the impact of a particular crisis or bereavement experience on a child. As noted also in Chapter 4 of the present book, tripartite assessment looks at the interaction of three groups of factors: those related to (1) the individual, (2) the situation, and (3) the support system of family and community. When used by child welfare practitioners, tripartite assessment will assist in evaluating the need for the placement and in weighing the prospects for returning the child to his or her family.

An out-of-home placement qualifies as a "crisis" as defined by Gilliland and James (1993, p. 3), insofar as it is usually perceived by both the child and the family as "a situation that exceeds [their] resources and coping mechanisms." The involuntary placement of a child stirs up many feelings in the child and the family, including varying degrees of shame, guilt, and anger. The parents have been publicly exposed as unfit to care for their own child, with the result that the stage is set for a tragedy of "loss of face" and accompanying loss of self-respect. The child, in turn, may feel guilty about his or her role in precipitating the placement. This form of loss generates a state of "disenfranchised grief" (Doka, 1989), because the stigma associated with the child's placement can be neither openly acknowledged nor mourned. These suppressed, complicated feelings must be recognized and understood by child welfare professionals who work with the child and family. The use of tripartite assessment facilitates this understanding, especially of the complex factors that precipitated the placement decision. Workers who recognize the importance of the multiple factors culminating in the child's placement will be better able to help the child and the family acknowledge the loss experience that the placement represents, in order to plan realistically for the future. In Figure 10.1, I have diagrammed the particular factors that apply to the out-of-home placement of a child.

Determining the Factors Precipitating Placement

The decision to move a child from his or her own home to another setting merits careful deliberation and review of all relevant facts. Whittaker (1987, p. 677), citing the U.S. Children's Bureau (1983), states that three-fourths of children in foster care enter care because of family problems, over three-fourths of which are related to abuse and neglect. Table 10.1 is a form

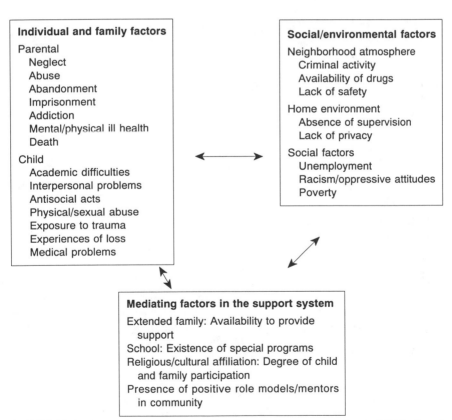

Individual and family factors

Parental
  Neglect
  Abuse
  Abandonment
  Imprisonment
  Addiction
  Mental/physical ill health
  Death

Child
  Academic difficulties
  Interpersonal problems
  Antisocial acts
  Physical/sexual abuse
  Exposure to trauma
  Experiences of loss
  Medical problems

Social/environmental factors

Neighborhood atmosphere
  Criminal activity
  Availability of drugs
  Lack of safety

Home environment
  Absence of supervision
  Lack of privacy

Social factors
  Unemployment
  Racism/oppressive attitudes
  Poverty

Mediating factors in the support system

Extended family: Availability to provide
  support
School: Existence of special programs
Religious/cultural affiliation: Degree of child
  and family participation
Presence of positive role models/mentors
  in community

FIGURE 10.1. Interactive components of a tripartite assessment when a child is placed out of the home: Webb.

TABLE 10.1. Factors Precipitating Placement Decision: Webb

1. Parental behaviors (list all that apply, identify relevant individual, and give dates):
Abuse(describe) _____
_____

Neglect (describe) _____
_____

Abandonment (describe) _____
_____

Imprisonment (reason) _____

Addiction (describe) _____

Physical/mental ill health (describe) _____
_____

Death (give date and cause of death, including child's involvement) _____
_____

2. Child behaviors (describe in detail) _____
_____

Frequency _____
Responses of adults _____
_____

Child's reactions to adult interventions _____
_____

3. Environmental/social conditions (describe the environment in which the child lived
prior to placement) _____
_____

Presence of after-school activities/sports/recreational programs _____
_____

Neighborhood atmosphere (check applicable items):
    Safe _____   Unsafe _____
    Presence of drugs: Yes _____   No _____   Not sure _____
    Influence of peers: Positive _____   Negative _____
    Presence of positive role models: Yes _____   No _____   Not sure _____

(continued)

TABLE 10.1. (Continued)

4. Traumatizing experiences in child's history (list all that apply):
Physical abuse (specify perpetrator, frequency, and form)

_____

_____

_____

Sexual abuse (specify perpetrator, frequency, and form)

_____

_____

_____

Other traumatic experiences, either witnessed or experienced

_____

_____

_____

_____

that allows the child welfare practitioner to record in detail the key factors contributing to the placement, based on the tripartite conceptualization.

Factors related to the family itself and to its ability to nurture the child are often critical in precipitating placement. Some children (e.g., those with Attention-Deficit/Hyperactivity Disorder) make excessive demands on their families because of their special needs and the difficulty they have in controlling their emotions and behavior. Other children may have the misfortune to be born at a difficult time in their parents' relationship, or the added demands of child care may prove too much for immature parents who themselves feel needy and unfulfilled, and who may take out their frustrations on their dependent children. For example, a father who has recently lost his job and whose wife has been diagnosed with cancer may vent his fury on his innocent 9-year-old son, who reminds the father of everything he hoped for in his own life that he now believes has been taken away from him. When the boy asks for money to buy a baseball mitt, the father tells him scornfully that money doesn't grow on trees and that he'd better begin to think about ways to obtain his own money for the things he wants.

Clearly, one isolated episode like this is not likely to propel a boy into a life of crime. However, when it and others like it are combined with pressure from older neighborhood youngsters who serve as drug runners and decoys for drug dealers, it is comprehensible how the boy could become involved in a life of petty crime—one that later may result in placement in a residential treatment facility.

Evaluation of significant influences in child placement often hinges on an understanding of interacting individual and family factors. Table 10.2 is a form for recording these specific influences on the placement decision.

TABLE 10.2. Individual and Family Factors Related to Placement: Webb

Relevant information from genogram
    Position of child in family _____
    Extended family (location and degree of involvement) _____
    _____

Status of parents (current, and at the time of child's birth)
    Ages: Mo _____   Fa _____
    Quality of parental relationship _____
    _____
    _____

    Employment: Mo _____
                    Fa _____
    Medical: Mo _____
                    Fa _____
    History of addictions:
                    Mo _____
                    Fa _____
    History of court involvement:
                    Mo _____
                    Fa _____
    Religious/cultural affiliation:
                    Mo _____
                    Fa _____
    Achievements/ego strengths:
                    Mo _____
                    Fa _____

Status of child
    Age and date of date of birth _____
    School grade and adjustment _____
    _____

    Educational testing results _____
    _____

    Psychological testing summary _____
    _____

    Peer involvement (describe in detail) _____
    _____

    Names of and relationships with siblings _____
    _____

    Medical history _____
    History of physical/sexual abuse (describe in detail) _____
    _____
    _____
    _____

(continued)

TABLE 10.2. (Continued)

History of exposure to trauma _____
_____
_____

Separation history (including moves and previous placements)
_____
_____

Past coping/strengths/typical defenses _____
_____
_____

Home environment
   Physical conditions (describe in detail, especially regarding child's sleeping arrangements)
_____

   Persons living in the home (give names and relationships to the child, if any) _____
_____
_____
_____

Length of time in current residence _____
Previous residences:
   Length of time _____
   Reasons for moving _____

DIFFERENT LEVELS OF CARE

Although it is beyond the scope of this chapter to analyze the wide range of child welfare programs for children, it is important to know that there is a continuum of services for children who are dependent and/or who have emotional or behavioral difficulties. Because of space limitations, I focus here primarily on foster care and on residential treatment programs, which are illustrated through references to the case of Maria and Mario (to be described in detail later).

Foster Care

Foster care implies a *temporary* arrangement for child care in a substitute home when the parents cannot take care of their own children because of some serious situation. The expectation is that the children will return to their parents' home when the conditions precipitating the foster placement have been corrected.

Unfortunately, although foster care is supposed to be temporary (limited to 18 months), it is often long-term. Commonly, children are moved from one foster placement to another, with resulting negative effects on the children's sense of security and identity. Brieland et al. (1985) state that the longer a child stays in foster care, the smaller the child's chances of obtaining a permanent home. In the case under discussion, 10-year-old Maria was placed in two foster homes after her mother died when she was 6 years old. Because of her HIV-positive status, she had few prospects of finding a permanent home; finally, her second set of foster parents agreed to adopt her. Issues for the foster parents of an HIV-positive child (and others in similar circumstances) include medical and confidentiality concerns, and the need to deal with a diverse group of care providers and health and welfare professionals (Boyd-Franklin, Steiner, & Boland, 1995).

Group and Institutional Care

Whittaker (1985), referring to the Child Welfare League of America (1981), identifies six different types of group care settings for children: residential treatment centers, group homes, crisis centers, shelter facilities, children's psychiatric facilities, and respite care facilities. Child welfare researchers and clinicians (Whittaker, 1985; Ford & Youksetter, 1981) note that there are fewer orphans and dependent children in residential settings, and more children with complex behavioral/psychological problems, such as the following:

- Poorly developed impulse control
- Low self-image
- Poorly developed modulation of emotion
- Deficiencies in forming relationships
- Special learning disabilities
- Limited play skills

Maria's half-brother, Mario, age 13, entered residential treatment when his behavior in the foster home became unmanageable. It included fire setting, rock throwing, slashing of the foster father's tires, and verbal hostility toward the foster parents. Significant factors in Mario's history, in addition to his mother's death, include his father's terminal illness with AIDS and his own lack of contact with his unmarried 20-year-old sister, who lives out of state with her two preschool children. At this writing, Mario comes for day visits with Maria twice a month; the foster parents permit this visitation, but worry about possible further hostile or abusive behavior on Mario's part.

THE CASE OF MARIA, AGE 10, AND MARIO, AGE 13

Case Summary

Three years ago, Maria and her brother were brought to the social service agency by the foster mother who had had custody of them since their mother's death 18 months earlier. The foster mother, in the role of homemaker, had taken care of the children in their home during the period of their mother's terminal illness. When the foster mother later moved out of state with the children, she forfeited financial assistance, since she was not a blood relative. Unable to support the children on her own small income as a homemaker, she returned the children to their previous location and abruptly left without waiting to make appropriate arrangements. She has had no further contact with the children during the intervening years.

The children were subsequently placed with Mr. and Mrs. Ramos, who have a daughter the same age as Maria and two younger children. As indicated earlier, Mario had great difficulty adjusting to this foster home. His behavior became steadily less acceptable, finally precipitating his placement in a residential treatment center.

Current Issues

As noted earlier, Maria has been freed for adoption, and Mr. and Mrs. Ramos have indicated their interest in adopting her. Previously they had considered adopting both Maria and Mario, but because of Mario's acting-out behavior toward them, they no longer plan to adopt him. Maria feels strongly about maintaining contact with her brother, and the Ramos have agreed to let him come for day visits twice a month. Earlier, when he came for an overnight stay, there was a big argument involving missing money; Mario ran away in anger, necessitating police involvement to return him to the residential treatment center.

Mr. and Mrs. Ramos have known about Maria's HIV diagnosis since shortly after her placement. Maria herself was informed about it when she began to question why she had to take so much medication (14 pills each day). She had not asked how she contracted HIV; yet she referred to her mother dying very young of heart disease. In fact, there is no information about how Maria contracted the illness. Her father is unknown, and there is no confirmation of her mother's medical history. Mario, who has a different father, does not have HIV.

Mr. Ramos had some concerns about the possibility of his own children's becoming infected through contact with Maria. However, a conference with Maria's doctor reassured him, so he says he is no longer fearful. The foster parents' 10-year-old daughter does not know about Maria's illness, and this remains an unresolved issue.

———————— ❖ ————————

Case Discussion

This case highlights the question of permanency planning for children with special problems and needs. The intent of the Adoption Assistance and Child Welfare Reform Act (P.L. 96-272, 1980) is to provide permanent homes for children in the foster system, either by returning them to their biological parents or by placing them with relatives; the third best alternative is a legally permanent adoptive family, and the fourth best placement is a reasonably permanent foster family (University of Kentucky College of Social Work, 1989; Whittaker, 1987).

It is unlikely that Mario, at age 13 with a history of problematic behaviors, will qualify for adoption. However, a tripartite assessment of his background may shed light on the factors contributing to his antisocial behavior, so that helping interventions can be planned accordingly. For example, we do not know enough about how Mario was functioning in school and in other areas of his life prior to his mother's death, which occurred when he was 9 years old. We also do not have information about the boy's relationship with his father, or when his father moved away. Finally, we need to know about Mario's relationship with the first foster mother. The facts of this case history reveal that this boy witnessed his mother's decline and eventual death (with or without the support of his father); he then was taken away by the homemaker/foster mother, who subsequently abandoned him and his sister with no follow-up contact. McFadden (1985) states that placement should be planned carefully to minimize the traumatic effects on the children. We can only imagine the feelings of these two young children who were virtually "dumped" by the person designated to take care of them following their mother's untimely death.

This and the other events in these children's lives represent serious loss experiences, which would have a negative cumulative effect on anyone. There is no evidence that either Mario or Maria was given the opportunity to mourn these losses. Mario's anger and his inability or unwillingness to become attached to a new family are understandable, since he probably has not resolved his feelings about the sad events in his nuclear family. In the absence of intervention focused on grief work and resolution of personal identity issues, Mario cannot risk the emotional closeness implicit in family living. In all likelihood, he will "graduate" from residential placement to a group home for adolescents, where his prognosis will be guarded. However, if Mario receives appropriate intervention focused on helping him ventilate his anger and come to terms with the unfair circumstances of his life, his negative identity and negative life trajectory may be altered.

On the other hand, Maria's prospects for a positive adjustment seem more hopeful. For reasons that may have to do with her younger age at the time of her mother's death (and other possible family factors about which we do not have information), Maria continues to be open to relationships. She relates well to the school social worker who sees her for weekly counseling, and she appears to be especially bonded to the Spanish-speaking caseworker who has managed her placement for the past 3 years. Although Maria is not as angry on the surface as her brother, she has similar needs to mourn for her mother's death and her subsequent losses. In my work with her once a month, I have been amazed at how readily she *spontaneously* refers to her mother's death and to the rupture this created in her family. Guided assistance with her grief work needs to continue.

It appears that Maria has been able to attach herself to the foster family she has known since age 7. Although she is sometimes tempted to join with Mario and confront the foster parents in the same angry manner as her brother, on another level she appreciates their acceptance of her, and she refrains from doing so. The fact that no other prospective foster families came forward during the year since she was freed for adoption probably increases Maria's feelings of dependence on Mr. and Mrs. Ramos. As Maria enters adolescence and the implications of her life-threatening illness become more apparent to her, she will need intensive help focused on her feelings about her illness.

INTERVENTIONS TO ASSIST CHILDREN AND FOSTER PARENTS

I will continue to use the case of Maria and Mario to illustrate possible interventions with children in out-of-home placements and with foster parents. Both Maria and Mario, like many other children in foster care and in residential treatment, will benefit from interventions specifically aimed to assist them with their unfinished grief work and with issues related to their identity. In turn, foster parents who assume the care of children with multiple losses need assistance in understanding the children's needs and responding to them sympathetically and realistically. The range of intervention methods to meet these diverse needs includes family, group, and individual approaches.

Interventions with the Foster Parents

Mr. and Mrs. Ramos will need ongoing support in integrating Maria into their family. Although they maintain that they treat her "equally," this is unlikely, and probably is an unrealistic ideal. HIV/AIDS often creates anxiety in others, who react by distancing themselves rather than drawing close. Although Maria's condition is presently stable, Mr. and Mrs. Ramos are well aware of her prognosis. They need to arrive at some understanding related to her uncertain future and the limited time she will be with them, and to learn more about how they can assist her to have as normal a life as possible during this period.

A group of parents with children who have HIV would provide essential support to Mr. and Mrs. Ramos, as well as assisting them with parenting. They have already had trouble dealing with Mario's rebelliousness, and it may prove difficult in the coming years for them to have two girls in adolescence at the same time. A parenting support group could provide an outlet and a resource for them, which may be critical in enabling them to provide the support to Maria that she will need during her adolescent years.

Interventions with the Children

Most (if not all) children in foster care and in residential treatment have experienced losses, ranging from multiple moves to parental separation, death, or abandonment. The fact that these experiences are frequent does not minimize their significance in the life of a child. When a child has to enter a new school several times in his or her elementary school years, this requires repeated efforts to make friends and establish "credibility" among children who have already formed peer relationships and who may not openly welcome newcomers. Some schools routinely have time-limited "newcomers" groups in the fall of each year to help integrate new students into the school, and also to provide them with a ready-made group of peers with whom to establish friendships. These would be helpful to foster children who have been transferred to another family. Unfortunately, these transfers do not always occur at the beginning of the year, and therefore may not be available when most needed. In any case, the school social worker should be notified when a foster child enters a new school, so that this professional can try to provide an appropriate service to the child.

Specific Methods for Helping Children with Grief Work

Some of the following interventions have been or will be used with Maria and Mario, to help them mourn their losses. They may be used either in individual sessions, in tandem meetings, or in a group of bereaved children. See Webb (1993) for specific case illustrations of the use of many of these methods.

Lifebooks

A "lifebook" is a document that an individual creates to record his or her unique life story (Aust, 1981; Backhaus, 1984). When used by children in placement, it contains stories and/or factual accounts dictated or written by the child, and it also contains the child's own drawings. The use of "time lines" in the lifebook helps the child depict the significant events of each year of his or her life, clarifying various moves and the significant people at each location (Doyle & Stoop, 1991). The purpose of making the lifebook is to help the child understand his or her own history, and simultaneously to provide the opportunity for validation and release of feelings connected to the powerful memories.

In my second meeting with Maria, I asked her to draw a picture of one of her memories of her mother. Figure 10.2 is her depiction of her mother in the casket, with the three children (Maria, Mario, and Mario's older sister) crying, and no adult present. My comments to Maria conveyed how sad this was for all of them, especially for Maria, who was such a *little* girl to have to experience such a terrible loss! I plan to return to Maria's drawing at a later time in our work together, to elicit more feelings, and also to point out that no father or other protecting adult was present.

Another time, she told me that she never knew her father, because he was in prison when she was born. However, Maria stated that she had a stepfather, and she included him in the family drawing she made in her first session with me (see Figure 10.3). In this portrayal of her family (which she also included in her lifebook), Maria put herself in the middle, not touching any other family figure. She placed her mother and stepfather on one side of her, and her half-brother and half-sister on the other. She explained that she drew the "girls" (females) in one color and the "boys" (males) in another. Since this drawing was made at the very be-

FIGURE 10.2. Maria's drawing of her mother's wake. The ages on this drawing are inaccurate and reflect Maria's confusion at the time of her mother's death, which continues to affect her accurate recall of ages.

FIGURE 10.3. Maria's Draw-A-Family.

FIGURE 10.4. Maria's optional drawing of her mother (as a bride).

ginning of my relationship with Maria, I did not make any comments about it that the child might consider critical or evaluative. I said that we would keep the drawing for her book, and that I hoped she would make other drawings to add to her book in the future.

We have not as yet begun work on a time line, because of more urgent concerns regarding Maria's adoption, Mario's visits, and Maria's difficulties with her schoolwork. Work on this in the future will open up discussion about the first foster mother, and about Maria's understanding about why that placement ended.

Maria uses drawing in each session to reflect on her past and to touch upon important elements of her life. For example, she voluntarily drew a picture of her mother in her wedding dress, mentioning to me that her mother was married when she was only 15 years old (probably inaccurate; Figure 10.4). Maria's drawing was possibly connected to her feelings about women being married and having babies at a young age, as happened with both her mother and her half-sister. Maria has told her foster mother that she does not plan to get married, and that she hopes she can adopt some children. Of course, the issue of her illness is relevant here, and it will be an important focus of our future work.

At this writing, I have not had the opportunity to meet Mario. (However, see "Addendum," below.) I believe that it will be useful to have some joint sessions with these siblings, for the purpose of helping them recount their history together. It will also be important to have some joint sessions with Maria and her 10-year-old foster sister, with whom she shares a bedroom. As noted earlier, this girl does not yet know about Maria's medical diagnosis, and careful thought and planning need to be devoted to the questions of when and how to divulge this information. The girls are somewhat competitive, and Mrs. Ramos is concerned that her daughter might use Maria's diagnosis against her in an argument.

Letters to Absent or Deceased Family Members and Others

An essential part of grief work involves relieving the bereaved of "unfinished business." Often when a death or other loss occurs, the remaining family members are left wanting to see the person again so that they can ask or tell them something important. This sometimes consists of expressing anger at being left. Writing letters to the missing or dead person and reading these aloud in an appropriate setting can relieve the individual of the burden of sadness, guilt, or anger. This may be relevant for foster children who feel unfairly treated or who have been abused, as well as for children (and adults) who have suffered a loss through death. The healing dynamic in writing such a letter relates to the individual's taking *action* in a situation in which he or she previously felt powerless. It is not necessary for the letter to be delivered for the positive effects to result.

In the course of my work with Maria and Mario, I intend to invite each of them to write several letters individually. These will include a letter to their mother, telling her something important about their lives, and expressing whatever feelings they have when they think about her today. (Again, see "Addendum," below.)

With regard to Maria, I expect that in the future she will inevitably conclude that she acquired HIV from her mother. This will be very hard for her to accept, since she tends to idealize her mother's memory. As she gets older and her understanding of HIV/AIDS increases, she may seek to learn how her mother contracted the illness; unless she finds out that her mother received a blood transfusion, this search may disillusion her about her mother and/or her father. She will need support at this time.

The second important letter for Maria to write will be to her unknown father. She must have many questions about his identity and about the nature of his involvement with her mother and the family. Maria thinks that Mario can tell her about her father, as could her absent half-sister.

There are no other known relatives on either side of the family. Whatever information Maria receives will leave her with many unanswered questions.

A third letter that will be important for both Maria and Mario will be one to the first foster mother. She cared for them for 2½ years, and yet she deserted them, as if they meant nothing to her. Both children must be full of anger, guilt, and confusion related to this. Much remains to be resolved, and they each need to realize that what happened was not their fault. Since children are narcissistic, they generally believe that they cause bad things to happen. Some of Mario's acting-out behavior could be construed as his need to be punished for his imagined "crimes."

Visit to Grave

At this writing, neither Maria nor Mario has visited their mother's grave, although it is located within the greater metropolitan area in which the children currently reside. Maria spontaneously mentioned when she drew the casket picture that she would like to see where her mother is buried; she wants to see "the dates of when she was born and when she died." If we consider that children require concrete representation of experience, it is understandable that a child who is now 10 years old would want confirmation of an event that occurred when she was 6.

I shall try to fulfill Maria's request by taking her to the grave, together with Mario (if he so chooses) and the caseworker who has been involved with the children since the placement with Mr. and Mrs. Ramos. I will suggest that each child bring his or her letter to their mother and read it (and possibly bury it) at the gravesite. I will offer to take pictures of each child separately and together at the gravesite, in order to give them a tangible memory of their visit. (This visit has now actually taken place; see "Addendum," below.)

Looking toward the Future

Again, the work with Mario and Maria is ongoing and includes many unknowns, especially with regard to Maria's health. Although we cannot guarantee a secure future for these children, we can give them the best possible resources with which to face that future. I believe that this can be done in this case by giving the children continuing opportunities to understand their past history and to grieve for their losses, so that they can proceed with their development within their current realities. The ghosts of the past will continue to haunt them until they have been closely examined and repositioned *in the past*.

Another plan for Maria is to locate a support group of children/ young adolescents who have HIV. The existing groups in her geographic area consist of older adolescents who contracted HIV through sexual contact or drug use. Although many of their issues are similar, the disparities in age and types of life experiences are obstacles to Maria's feeling comfortable in such a group. This requires ongoing exploration.

Addendum

Six months after this chapter was written, Maria and Mario went on a visit to their mother's grave. Their social services caseworker and I (as the therapist/consultant working with Maria on a monthly basis) accompanied them. Prior to the 45-minute car trip to the cemetery, I met with both young people to explore their expectations about the visit, and to invite them to write letters to their mother that they could read aloud or to themselves at her grave. The letter had an opening instruction format, as indicated in Figure 10.5. Their separate letters, reproduced as written, follow.

Mario

Dear Mom,

How the life upstairs? Is it better than earth, like they say with angels?

I wish I could see you one more time to say goodbye because I didn't have a chance.

Maria

Dear Mommy,

I really miss you. I can't tell you went I have been. I am very big and fat. I go to school allready, gone away from are babysitter. We are living in _____. We love Miss _____ [caseworker]. I am 11 years old and I am in 5 grade. I now your dead but I just went you to know how I am doing. I really went to now how did you get sick. That all wen I have to say. Who is my Father? Went he's name?

Love,

Your Sweet Pie
Maria

P.S. Who is my Father? How old is he? Were does he live? I miss you a lot.

On this page, write a letter to the person who died. Tell this person all the things you wanted to say but never had the chance. Tell him or her all that is in your heart. Tell the person what you miss about him or her, and what you don't miss, too.

Dear _____,

_____
_____
_____
_____
_____
_____
_____
_____
_____
_____
_____
_____
_____
_____
_____
_____
_____
_____
_____

FIGURE 10.5. Form for a letter to a person who died.

THE ROLE OF THE SOCIAL WORKER IN CHILD WELFARE

Social workers in child welfare settings have a multifaceted role—one that includes direct work with culturally diverse children and families; work with the family court and the department of social services; and the necessity of functioning on an interdisciplinary team. A social worker often serves as a case manager, coordinating the progress reports of a child's cottage staff, educational and psychological reports, and all matters related to setting goals and evaluating the child's progress.

It is important for social workers in this field of practice to have a solid knowledge base in child assessment, including diagnostic classifications, family systems assessment, substance abuse assessment, and evaluation of the impact of trauma on children (especially that resulting from physical and sexual abuse). An administrator of a large residential treatment center identified the issues of substance abuse, HIV/AIDS, neglect, and physical abuse as typical of about 80% of the center's population in 1994 (Webb, 1995). Since many children in foster care and residential treatment have experienced multigenerational losses because of

AIDS, it is imperative that social workers who attempt to help these children understand the impact of disenfranchised grief (Doka, 1989) and have a knowledge of methods for assisting with mourning. Because of HIV/AIDS, it is increasingly common for multiple siblings in a family to enter care simultaneously. It may become the social worker's responsibility to coordinate the work with these siblings, which will be greatly facilitated when the children's care is managed by the same agency rather than by several agencies. Social workers need skills in conducting sibling sessions in order to maintain the children's family ties.

Special Challenges

Some of the special challenges to the social worker in child welfare settings relate to the need to work with very resistant and overwhelmed families in a political climate in which funding is decreasing. Sometimes the worker's own feelings of discouragement can be an obstacle, especially when the worker assumes too much responsibility for a child or family, and in the process fails to respect appropriate professional boundaries. The worker who shares *all* the pain with his or her clients will soon suffer burnout and become ineffective.

Special Rewards

The child welfare worker does experience moments of great satisfaction in his or her work, despite the difficulty and heart-wrenching circumstances of so many cases. One positive response to my survey question about satisfaction in this work (Webb, 1995) was as follows: "Seeing children go from depression and hopelessness to trust and belief in the possibility of a happy future." Another respondent referred to "clinical moments" when children are able to verbalize important understandings about their lives, as in the case of a child who finally developed enough trust in his caseworker to tell her how ashamed he felt because no one in his family wanted him! These significant moments help the child welfare worker appreciate the importance of his or her role, and (let us hope) will lead to retention of competent workers in the system. There are probably few settings that make as many demands on social workers, or in which dedicated workers are more desperately needed. Our profession must acknowledge more fully the vital importance of this work.

CONCLUDING COMMENTS

The case of Maria and Mario illustrates many of the typical problems related to children in foster care and in residential treatment. Through no fault of their own, such children grow up without the security of a stable family, and the lack of extended family members thrusts them into the child welfare system. Unresolved mourning is a vital issue for these children, as it is for many in foster and residential placement. Children who are moved from one family to another, and who may lose contact with their biological parents through either death or abandonment, need assistance to put their experience into perspective and to realize that they were not to blame.

Some useful techniques to help children resolve these matters include creation of a lifebook, writing letters to absent or deceased persons, and visiting the gravesites of significant family members. When a child has HIV, this personal reconstruction of his or her family history is essential to help the child connect the past with the present, so that he or she can move beyond the past and thereby proceed with his or her present reality.

DISCUSSION QUESTIONS

1. Discuss the pros and cons of including a preadolescent who contracted HIV as an infant in a group with adolescents who acquired the illness through sexual contact or drug use (sharing needles). Would the advantages outweigh the disadvantages?

2. Consider the matter of a family secret involving a foster child who is HIV-positive. Do you think it would be appropriate to share this information with the other foster children in the family? If so, at what age? Give reasons for your response.

3. What are some of the key personal issues for the social worker who is employed in a child welfare agency? Describe some ways in which to avoid burnout.

4. Discuss the implications of the position that clinical issues and larger societal issues overlap in child welfare.

CHAPTER 11

Children in Nontraditional Families

Children in the mid-1990s come from many different types of families. No longer can teachers or others working with children assume that a child lives in a nuclear family with his or her biological father and mother and the siblings from that marriage. In 1985, only about 58% of children lived in such "traditional" two-parent biological families. Other family structures included two-parent reconstituted families (i.e., stepfamilies—15.8%); children living with their mothers (20.9%); children living with their fathers (2.5%); and children in "other" family arrangements (2.7%) (U.S. Bureau of the Census, 1989). The last category included children living with relatives, and children in foster and adoptive families. Children living in gay or lesbian families were probably categorized as living with either their fathers or their mothers. Thirty-six percent of "single" parents had never married, and the absent parent was the father in 86% of single-parent situations. Thus, although all children begin life as the result of the biological union of a man and a woman, many of them do not grow up with these two individuals, and some never even know the identity of one or both of their biological parents.

This chapter focuses on helping children who experience stress and difficulty as a result of living in such nontraditional families. Some children and their families cope effectively with the stress of their nontraditional status. However, despite society's growing tolerance of divorce and of single parenthood by choice, the children living in these and in various other family structures often suffer multiple stresses that are not usually experienced by children in intact, "traditional" nuclear families. Some of these stresses include the following:

- Lower socioeconomic status
- Custody battles

- Divided loyalties
- Changes of school and home environments
- Reduced or absent communication with the noncustodial parent
- Adjustment to a stepparent and stepsiblings
- Divergent rules and lifestyles
- Uncertainty about information that they are permitted to share with others
- Confused feelings about where they belong
- Prejudice/disapproval related to a family's lifestyle

Of course, every family is unique, and it may seem inappropriate to group together children from drastically different backgrounds (e.g., children of never-married mothers and children of divorced, remarried, or lesbian/gay partners). However, I believe that these children all have some important issues in common because of the nontraditional status of their families. We need to be aware of these issues in our efforts to help. The most important issues relate to experiences of loss and multiple stressors.

ISSUES OF LOSS AND MULTIPLE STRESSORS

Issues of Loss

Children who live in nontraditional families realize at a fairly young age that their families are different. Because our society features various portraits of the traditional nuclear family with mother, father, and children in popular books and on television, children learn before they begin school that everyone has a mommy and a daddy. When there is no father in the home, a preschooler will usually ask about him; depending on what the child is told, he or she may either accept the explanation, or continue to mull it over and wonder when Daddy is going to appear. If a never-married mother speaks disparagingly to her child about the man who impregnated her and then disappeared, the child picks up the underlying message that his or her father was "bad." This perception may have an ongoing influence on the child's feelings about men and relationships, as well as on his or her own sense of identity.

On the other hand, the preschool child in a blended family with a stepfather, and ongoing contact with his or her biological father, may accept the mother's statement that the child is lucky to have *two* daddies. However, as this same child grows to school age, he or she may intuit differences in the manner in which the stepfather treats him or her and his own children; the child may then begin to want more time with his or her "real" father, beyond the usual once-a-week visitation. This child may question both parents about why they don't get married or live together any more.

"Lost" (absent) parents remain significant presences for children in divorced, single, remarried, and homosexual families. The "ghosts" of missing parents also continue as important influences among adopted children who do not have information about their biological parents (LeVine & Sallee, 1992). My own experience with children in nontraditional families confirms that absent parents play important symbolic roles in these children's lives, and that the children actively grieve for the lost parents on significant holidays (e.g., Mother's Day or Father's Day, the child's own birthday, Thanksgiving, and other major holidays when rituals emphasize family togetherness). In psychodynamic terms, such a child has suffered an "object loss," meaning the loss of a major attachment figure. Feelings of longing and anger about this loss may persist indefinitely. This imagined presence of a "lost" parent can in fact serve an important comforting role for a child, similar to the manner in which a child may retain and benefit from the memory of a deceased parent (Silverman & Worden, 1992). The unfortunate aspect of the child's loss in a family with a missing parent, however, is the child's inability to speak openly about it, because the adults with whom the child currently lives usually prefer to deny or minimize the child's feelings of longing or positive connection with this person. The child is unsupported in his or her grief, which cannot be openly acknowledged or worked out. As noted in Chapter 10, Doka (1989) refers to this type of mourning as "disenfranchised grief."

Other losses experienced by many children in nontraditional families relate to the reduced economic status and possible changes in schools and living arrangements that often accompany divorce, remarriage, and single-parent status. Furthermore, when a parent's marital status changes, relationships with the kinship network also usually alter; in fact, a child may lose contact with a group of grandparents, uncles, and aunts, because the custodial parent no longer feels comfortable in their presence. This was true in the case of Monica, to be discussed later in this chapter.

In a single-parent home, a parent may work long hours and want to devote some time to adult relationships without the child (or children). This can cause a child to feel resentful and lonely. A child in a single-parent household may also be expected to do chores, and/or to accompany the parent to the supermarket or laundromat. Sometimes the single parent unwisely begins to confide in the child, almost as if the child were an adult. This blurring of parent–child boundaries causes the child to worry about adult concerns prematurely. When this happens, the child is losing his or her very childhood.

Issues of Multiple Stressors

Children do not like to be different; as early as elementary school, many want to dress in a certain way to resemble their peers, and to participate in after-school activities with their friends. A parent's reduced income, and/or lack of time to go shopping with the child or to attend a school event, may mean that the child dresses differently from peers and misses out on activities with them. This may contribute to a feeling of alienation or of "difference" from friends, whose parents are able to focus and spend more time and money on their children.

A child's worry about finances may preclude his or her even asking to participate in certain after-school activities (e.g., baseball or cheer-leading, which would involve expenses for a uniform). In times of financial prosperity, many schools have scholarship funds to accommodate the needs of children who cannot, without assistance, afford to participate in sports and other after-school activities. Unfortunately, in times of fiscal constraint, these special funds are not available in many school districts, and children are expected to pay for even basic school supplies. The impact of tighter economic conditions at home and in the community means that children whose family incomes are limited are deprived of certain "extras" that might enrich their lives. It would be understandable if this deprivation, together with the other stresses and losses in these children's lives, resulted in reduced self-esteem and increased anger and alienation.

Sometimes children in divorced families are "put in the middle" (Garrity & Baris, 1994) and asked by one parent to convey messages or to keep secrets from the other. This behavior creates disturbing feelings of divided loyalties in the children. Wallerstein and Kelly (1980) comment that

> school age children particularly appeared to conceptualize the divorce as a struggle in which each participant demanded one's primary loyalty, and this conception greatly increased the conflict and unhappiness of [such a] child. For, by its logic, a step in the direction of one parent was experienced by the child . . . as a betrayal of the other, a move likely to evoke anger and further rejection. (p. 49)

Other stresses that may preoccupy children in nontraditional families relate to worries about their parents' happiness and their own uncertain futures. Rather than assuming that their lives will continue on a certain course, children in nontraditional families know that conflict can lead to ruptured relationships and major life changes. Custodial parents may be angry or depressed, and thus may lack energy to focus on their children. The children may worry about both the parent with whom they live and about the absent parent, in addition to their own futures. These children have personally experienced the fragility and the complexity of life; this experience, while strengthening the coping capacities of some, may also lead to premature suffering and strong feelings of personal vulnerability.

Even children in *stable* single-parent households, and in homosexual families that are not suffering economic hardship, may experience stress related to the intolerant curiosity, prejudice, and disapproval expressed by some adults and peers about the nontraditional structure of their families. These children, although secure within their home environments, may experience a painful sense of being stigmatized because their families do not conform to society's norm.

ASSESSMENT OF THE IMPACT OF FAMILY CIRCUMSTANCES ON THE CHILD

Many distinctive factors interact to affect any given child's reaction to a parent's unmarried status, divorce, gay/lesbian lifestyle, or remarriage. It is not the parent's status itself that causes stress for the child, but rather the many factors associated with it that may affect the child adversely. Because children are self-centered, the overriding issue for them is how much their lives are inconvenienced. Certainly, not all children in nontraditional families develop problems. A child's temperament, a family's overall functioning, and/or the presence of an effective support system can all balance the negative effects of stress on the child.

As discussed in Chapter 10 with regard to the interactive components of child placement, a tripartite conceptualization (Webb, 1991, 1993) can help us understand the reactions of an individual to a specific situation, based on analysis of three groups of factors that interact and determine the outcome of a particular crisis state: (1) the nature of the crisis situation, (2) the idiosyncratic characteristics of the individual, and (3) the strengths and weaknesses of the support system. Whereas I originally developed this tripartite model with regard to crisis situations, and later adapted it to bereavement, I now propose to adapt it further to make it specifically relevant to children living in nontraditional families. In Figure 11.1, I have diagrammed the factors to be considered in the tripartite assessment of children in nontraditional families. This diagram may help the practitioner understand why one child has difficulties adjusting to a nontraditional family, whereas another does not.

Table 11.1 presents a form to facilitate the practitioner's use of tripartite assessment to organize, summarize, and understand the unique

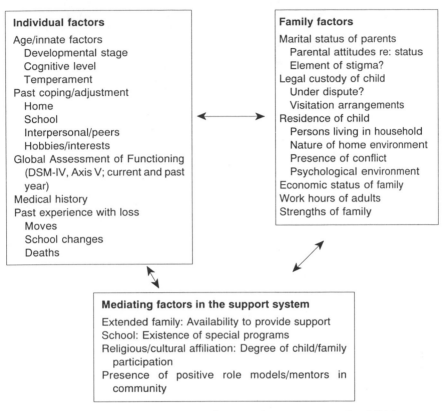

Individual factors

Age/innate factors
  Developmental stage
  Cognitive level
  Temperament
Past coping/adjustment
  Home
  School
  Interpersonal/peers
  Hobbies/interests
Global Assessment of Functioning
  (DSM-IV, Axis V; current and past
  year)
Medical history
Past experience with loss
  Moves
  School changes
  Deaths

Family factors

Marital status of parents
  Parental attitudes re: status
  Element of stigma?
Legal custody of child
  Under dispute?
  Visitation arrangements
Residence of child
  Persons living in household
  Nature of home environment
  Presence of conflict
  Psychological environment
Economic status of family
Work hours of adults
Strengths of family

Mediating factors in the support system

Extended family: Availability to provide support
School: Existence of special programs
Religious/cultural affiliation: Degree of child/family
  participation
Presence of positive role models/mentors in
  community

FIGURE 11.1. Interactive components of a tripartite assessment of a child in a non-traditional family: Webb.

circumstances pertaining to a particular child living in a nontraditional family.

The practitioner fills out this form on the basis of information available in the family's record and interviews with various family members. Use of the form, together with information from the child's developmental history, will help identify sources of possible stress for the child (and, therefore, areas for possible intervention).

GOALS IN HELPING CHILDREN IN NONTRADITIONAL FAMILIES

Depending on the circumstances of each case, individual, family, or group methods can help children in nontraditional families express and resolve

TABLE 11.1. Tripartite Assessment of Family Circumstances: Webb

Marital status of parents
    Mother: Never married ____ Divorced ____ (date) ____ Remarried ____ (date) ____
    Father: Never married ____ Divorced ____ (date) ____ Remarried ____ (date) ____
Parental attitudes re: status
    Mother: Accepting ____ Angry ____ Ashamed ____
    Father: Accepting ____ Angry ____ Ashamed ____
Family composition
    With whom is child currently living? (check all that apply)
    Mo ____ Fa ____ Stepmo ____ Stepfa ____ Mo's boyfriend ____
    Mo's lesbian partner ____
    Fa's girlfriend ____ Fa's gay partner ____ Grandparent(s) (specify) _____
    Siblings: No ____ Yes ____ Ages ____
    Stepsibs: No ____ Yes ____ Ages ____
    Half-sibs: No ____ Yes ____ Ages ____
    Others living in family with the child _____
With whom does noncustodial parent live? _____
    Are there children from this relationship? No ____ Yes ____ Ages ____
Child's contacts with parent(s)
    Does child have contact with mother?
    Yes ____ How frequently? _____
    No ____ Why not? _____
    Does child have contact with father?
    Yes ____ How frequently? _____
    No ____ Why not? _____
What child has been told about whereabouts of absent parent(s)
    Does child know where parent is? Yes ____ No ____
    If no, has child asked about the absent parent? No ____ Yes ____
    If yes, at what age? ____ What was child told? _____
_____

Contacts with extended family
    Does child have contact with members of the extended family?
    No ____ Yes ____
    If yes, with whom? _____ How frequently? _____
Changes in child's life over past year
    Has there been a change in the family's economic status during the last year?
    No ____ Yes ____ If yes, explain _____
_____
    Has there been a change in the custodial parent's work hours? No ____ Yes ____
    If yes, give details _____
    If yes, does this affect the child's schedule? No ____ Yes ____
    If yes, give details _____
Child's housing history
    How long has child lived in current residence? _____
    Where did child live previously? _____
    How long lived there? _____ Why moved? _____
    Does child share a bedroom? No ____ Yes ____ If yes, with whom? _____
    Did child share a bedroom in previous residence? No ____ Yes ____
    If yes, with whom? _____

(continued)

TABLE 11.1. (Continued)

Child's school history
   Current grade ____ Appropriate grade for child's age? Yes ____ No ____
   If no, explain _____
   Current academic performance: Good ____ Fair ____ Poor ____
   How long has child been enrolled in present school? _____
   Was child enrolled in a different school last year? No ____ Yes ____
   Child's academic performance in previous school: Good ____ Fair ____ Poor ____
   Why has child changed schools? (give details) _____
   _____

Custody issues
   Who presently has legal custody of the child?
   Mo ____ Father ____ Other (specify) _____
   Is the child's custody under dispute? No ____ Yes ____ If yes, give details _____
   _____

Presence of conflict
   Are the child's parents in conflict? No ____ Yes ____ If yes, give details _____
   _____
   _____
   Is there conflict in custodial parent's home? No ____ Yes ____ If yes, give details _____
   _____

Psychological environment of custodial home
   Level of custodial parent's functioning: Good ____ Fair ____ Poor ____
   Give details
   _____
   Strengths in custodial family (give details) _____
   _____
   _____
   Problems in custodial family (give details) _____
   _____
   _____

some of their feelings of loss and stress. Regardless of the particular method, the work must emphasize that the adults are responsible for creating and resolving the family difficulties. Children must be reminded repeatedly that they did not cause the situation, and that because they are children, they cannot remedy it. The adults involved have to free the children to proceed with their lives and to leave adult concerns to adults. This is generally easier said than done, both for the adults and for the children, who become accustomed to sharing adult conflicts and worries.

Wallerstein (1983) and Wallerstein and Blakeslee (1989) describe six "psychological tasks" that children of divorce must successfully resolve. I propose that these same tasks, with minor adaptations, also apply to children of single (never-married) parents, children in remarried families, and children living with homosexual parents. The tasks are as follows:

1. *Acknowledging the reality* (of the marital rupture, of a parent's re-marriage, or of a parent's single or homosexual status). Children may deny the reality, or fantasize about a status or outcome they would prefer. The adults can help the children by providing them with information, including (in terms that the children can comprehend) the reason for the current living situation. This should be done with consideration for the children's feelings and for their limited ability to understand complex adult motivations.

2. *Disengaging from parental conflicts and distress, and resuming their own customary, age-appropriate pursuits.* As mentioned above, it is contraindicated for children to spend their time worrying about their parents. This worry takes energy, and consumes time and effort that the children otherwise would be able to put into schoolwork or social activities. Single parents who may (knowingly or unknowingly) use their children as confidants need to be helped to find peers with whom to share their concerns.

3. *Resolving the loss.* This refers to a child's feelings of confusion and rejection about an absent parent. Children should be encouraged to talk about their feelings, in group or individual counseling, as well as with their parents in parent–child sessions. In situations where a child has grown up in a single-parent family and has never known his or her father, the child needs to acknowledge that he or she has a father, but that for many complicated reasons his or her parents decided not to live together. The emphasis should be on the fact that this was an *adult* decision. A similar explanation should be given to a child in a gay or lesbian family—namely, that at one time (however briefly), the child had a mother and a father, but that now the mother or father prefers to live with a same-sex partner. Again, this should be presented as an *adult* choice.

4. *Resolving anger and self-blame.* It is very common in situations of divorce for children to feel great anger toward one or both parents. Even when they have witnessed years of painful conflict between their parents, many children still cling to the belief that the divorce was preventable. Some children also blame themselves for causing or contributing to the divorce, because their parents argued about them or because they did something that upset the parents. Sometimes a child in a single-parent family feels that he or she is a burden to their parent, and possibly the reason for the parent's not remarrying. In a remarried family, the child's anger may be projected onto the stepparent, who is viewed as the cause of the divorce and of all subsequent difficulties.

Resolving children's anger and self-blame takes time. The parent(s) have an important role in this, and the children may require additional help in the form of group, parent–child, or individual counseling. There are numerous books written for children of various ages, to help them realize that other children have struggled with many of the same complicated, disturbing feelings.

5. *Accepting the relative permanence of the parental status* (divorce, remarriage, single or homosexual life). This goal encourages children to give up their hope of magically remaking their families into the forms they would prefer. Although as adults we know that nothing in life is truly permanent, children who hang onto a fantasy that their parents will reunite, or that their father or mother will leave a gay or lesbian partner, are depriving themselves of the opportunity to invest emotionally in the family in which they presently live. If we are always hoping for something different, we lose what we have.

6. *Achieving realistic hope regarding future relationships.* Some of the longitudinal research on children in divorced families (Wallerstein & Blakeslee, 1989; Guidubaldi, 1989) reports that the children of divorced parents have difficulties later in adjusting socially and in establishing trusting relationships themselves. Because they have witnessed unsuccessful marriages, they fear that they will have similar marriages themselves; as a result, they have difficulty with intimacy. With regard to children in homosexual families, there is no evidence that they are concerned about their own future relationships (Hare, 1994). However, this topic has not been studied extensively, nor has the question of the personal future expectations of children who grow up in single-parent, never-married households.

CUSTODY DISPUTES: CHILDREN "CAUGHT IN THE MIDDLE"

Approximately 10–15% of divorcing parents take their struggles to court in the form of disputes about visitation, financial support, and custody of the children (Wallerstein & Kelly, 1980). In such a case the parents are usually angry and embittered toward each other, and each turns to the court in an adversary proceeding designed to "win" a judgment that will force certain concessions from the former partner. These proceedings prove absolutely contrary to the recommendations discussed above for assisting children in adjusting to this major change in their lives. Frequently, according to Wallerstein and Kelly (1980), one or both parents will deliberately attempt to sway a child to *their* side; each does this by denigrating the other parent, and questioning that parent's interest in and love for the child.

Under these circumstances, it is no surprise that children often become upset and anxious. They are *encouraged* to take sides, which then interferes with any of their own attempts to disengage from the parents' hostility. One child graphically referred to the experience as similar to "being cut down the middle with a hatchet." Another said, poignantly, "My mother doesn't realize that when she shoots arrows at my father they have to go through my body before they reach him!" (Wallerstein & Kelly, 1980, p. 71).

Effects on Children

In these sad situations, many children develop such problems as deteriorating schoolwork, aggression toward siblings and peers, sleep disturbances, and somatic complaints. Regression is common but is not always present, because mediating influences may exist in the extended family, the child's school, and the community. Figure 11.1 and Table 11.1 can help practitioners identify children who are at risk because of intense family hostility and lack of compensatory supports. These children often come to the attention of social workers and other practitioners through the recommendation of the court, when it becomes evident that the children are reacting to an embattled family situation, and the family court judge orders that the children receive counseling. In some cases, the judge may also appoint a guardian *ad litem* to represent a child's best interests. The case of Monica, to be described below, was referred for counseling under these circumstances.

The Court-Appointed Guardian

Sometimes referred to as a "mediator" (Rice & Rice, 1986), and in many states as a "guardian *ad litem*" (literally, "guardian at law"), an individual may be hired by the court to represent the best interests of the *child* and to advocate for the child's welfare. The guardian, often a lawyer, may interview both parents and the child preparatory to making recommendations to the judge. In addition, the guardian may recommend psychological and psychiatric testing of the child and the parents, in addition to counseling for the child.

At best, the guardian remains neutral and objective, and helps a child feel protected from the warring parents. At worst, a child may be intimidated by the perceived power of this person to decide monumental issues in their lives, such as with which parent they will reside.

According to Koocher and Keith-Spiegel (1990), most states subscribe to the concept of "the best interests of the child" in making legal decisions in court custody cases. The following factors are considered in making such a determination:

- The nature of the child's relationship with each parent
- The capacity and willingness of each parent to care for the child
- The presence of a stable environment, and the length of time the child has spent in that environment
- The likelihood that the home will serve as a family unit
- The nature of the child's adjustment at school and in the community
- The moral fitness of each parent
- The physical and mental fitness of each parent
- The child's own preference

The next section describes how the guardian and I attempted to weigh these factors in the case of Monica.

THE CASE OF MONICA, AGE 10

Family Information

Father	John Ross, age 38, plumber (own business).
Stepmother	Debbie Ross, age 32, at home.
Half-sister	Terry Ross, age 2.
Child client	Monica Ross, age 10, fifth grade.
Mother	Janet Baker, age 36, real estate agent; living out of state.
Stepfather	Don Baker, age 36, tennis instructor (own business); living out of state.

Presenting Problem

Monica's mother was seeking custody of her daughter, after having relinquished it voluntarily to her former husband 4 years previously, when she was seriously depressed. The mother claimed that she was now fully recovered, and she wanted Monica to join her and her husband in their new home out of state (approximately 4 hours by car from the father's residence). The father was unwilling to give custody to his former wife, whom he still considered mentally ill.

Background

Monica's parents were divorced 5 years earlier, having been separated 2 years prior to that. Since age 6 Monica had resided with her father, with frequent overnight visits with the paternal grandparents, who lived nearby. During the 2-year period prior to the divorce, Mrs. Baker would often leave Monica (then 4 years old) with her mother-in-law while she worked as a waitress or looked for another job. Everyone agreed that this was a difficult time for Monica's mother, and that she lost a great deal of weight and became seriously depressed. She was not taking good care of either herself or Monica; when the divorce became final, she asked Monica's father to take custody of Monica on a temporary basis while she tried to pull her life together. Mr. Ross went to court and obtained permanent legal custody. Although Mrs. Baker never intended the arrangement to be permanent, she did sign the necessary court papers, because she claimed that her lawyer convinced her it was all right to do so.

During the 4 years following the custody decision, Mrs. Baker made steady improvement in both her physical and her mental state, with the aid of therapy. At this time, she was no longer depressed. She had steady employment, and she had recently married a man who was moving his business to a neighboring state, where the couple had bought a house and planned to reside.

Mrs. Baker seemed hurt and perplexed because her former husband would not return Monica to her, and because Monica herself was uncertain about whether she wanted to move away and live with her mother. Although Monica had seen her mother on short visits over the past few years, and was a bridesmaid at her mother's wedding, she had been told repeatedly by her father and grandmother that her mother was "crazy" and unable to take care of her.

Realizing that this family was at an impasse, the judge appointed a guardian *ad litem* to represent the child's best interests. The guardian, in turn, ordered psychiatric evaluations of each parent and of Monica; she also arranged for Monica to begin counseling.

Assessment and Plan for Intervention

I decided to see Monica alone initially, to establish a relationship with her. I then planned to see her with her father and stepmother, and to see her with her mother and stepfather. I realized that both Mr. Ross and Mrs. Baker would probably try to present themselves as the preferred custodial parent, and I also realized that Monica herself must be in turmoil over the dilemma of having both parents pulling her in separate directions.

In my initial meeting with Monica, she confirmed my expectations. When I asked her to draw a person, she drew a figure with "nerves" exposed on her arms and legs, the face crying, and the brain verbalizing great distress and anguish (see Figure 11.2). My response to Monica's vivid portrayal of a child in agony was to empathize with how terribly difficult her situation was, and to let her know that I would try to help her, regardless of the outcome. I also stated that there would be good and bad things about living with either parent, and that if her parents could work out a cooperative agreement, then it might be possible for her to continue to be in touch with both of them, regardless of where she lived. I emphasized that the judge, not she, would make the decision; it would be unfair for her to decide, since that would mean that either one parent or the other would be upset with her.

I tried to make arrangements to see Monica with each parent–stepparent pair, but the father's wife did not want to be involved. I spoke with the father about refraining from saying disparaging things about Monica's mother to her, but he insisted that "she would never change," and that "she is only putting on an act now because it suits her purposes." I stated my experience that people *can* change through therapy, but Mr. Ross was unwilling to alter his perception of his former wife. He also made it clear that he did not believe in therapy, citing this belief as the reason his current wife did not want to come to see me. I tried to form an

FIGURE 11.2. Monica's Draw-A-Person.

alliance with Mr. Ross through crediting him with taking such good care of Monica all these years, but he conveyed a sense of duty, not pride, associated with this. He did agree to bring Monica for her weekly appointments, knowing that the guardian had recommended the counseling.

In a session with Mr. and Mrs. Baker and Monica, I used some drawing exercises from a scrapbook/journal for children living in stepfamilies (Evans, 1986). I asked each of them to draw a picture of the interior of the Baker home, showing the members of the family engaged in some activity. After some initial awkwardness about their drawing ability, Mr. Baker drew a picture of a living room with three people sitting on a couch watching television; Mrs. Baker drew herself and Monica in the kitchen making cookies (Mr. Baker was at work, she said); and Monica drew herself alone in her bedroom. I commented that the pictures perhaps showed how they were expecting their family to function, if Monica were to join them in the future. I pointed out to Monica that while she was perhaps still cautious and keeping herself alone, her mother envisioned their doing fun things together, and her stepfather seemed ready for all three of them to participate in an activity.

I emphasized my role as that of helping Monica with her difficult situation, and hoped that I could be helpful to Mr. and Mrs. Baker also as time went on. Acknowledging that Mr. Baker was in fact a new father, I commented that regardless of the background situation, it always takes time for members of new stepfamilies to become comfortable with one another. I gave him a copy of "Guidelines for Stepfamilies" (Visher & Visher, 1979, pp. 261–267), and offered to discuss any issues that seemed relevant with him when we met again in the future.

Summary of the Next 7 Months

A psychiatrist met with both parents, and submitted a report to the guardian recommending that Monica be reunited with her mother. He did not find any evidence that Mrs. Baker was unfit, and he argued that it was important for Monica to resume living with her mother.

I continued to meet with Monica weekly, and to see her father briefly on these occasions. I also met once a month with Mr. and Mrs. Baker, who were increasingly open with me in discussing some interactional difficulties with Monica during her visits with them.

The guardian and I had recommended increasingly longer visits between Monica and her mother, in order to permit them to repair and build a relationship that had languished over the years. While subscribing to the goal of *eventual* mother–child reunion, we recommended that this occur at the end of the school year, after several months of anticipation. Even if she were to remain with her father, Monica would be changing to a middle school the following year. The father remained uncommitted to this plan. In fact, after Monica and I met with him to try to obtain his acceptance, he would not agree; moreover, he refused to bring Monica to further appointments, to return my phone calls, or to pay her outstanding bill.

Outcome of Case

At the end of the school year, Monica went for her planned summer vacation with her mother, and never returned to her father's house. She had grown slowly but steadily closer to her mother, and they appeared to be developing a fairly good relationship. Monica's relationship with her stepfather, however, remained cool. Mr. Baker, who worked with children and teens in his job, had been overly optimistic about being able to relate easily to Monica. He needed ongoing assistance not to rush their relationship, and he continued to use the guidelines I had given to him.

Monica's mother brought her for a termination appointment with me, at which time I implemented a referral to a child and family therapist in the area where they lived. I sent a birthday card to Monica a month later, which was never acknowledged.

Information that later came to me through the guardian revealed that Monica's father did not pay child support when she moved to live with her mother, and that the matter was complicated to litigate because of the child's move out of state. I never learned whether visitation with the father occurred. At this writing (5 years later), it seems likely that Monica is still "in the middle," with the difference now that her father is the "bad" parent. Furthermore, her association with her mother has probably resulted in lack of contact with her paternal relatives.

❖

Discussion

Despite the best efforts of most parties, this case did not have an outcome that permitted this child to have an ongoing, nonconflictual relationship with both parents. Certainly the goal of disengagement from parental conflict in order to resume age-appropriate pursuits would seem remote, in view of the continuing issue about child support.

Ideally, the new family therapist to whom I referred Monica and the Bakers would have helped Mrs. Baker refrain from expressing her anger about Mr. Ross in front of the child. Certainly Monica would have needed to mourn the loss of her father, grandparents, and familiar home environment before she could begin forming a relationship with her step-father. Monica's mother had previously expressed her willingness to in-vite some of Monica's friends to visit her over the summer, which would have helped with the transition to the new locale.

This case illustrates many of the issues typical for children in non-traditional families: multiple losses and stressors, custody battles, loyalty conflicts, changes of school and home environment, reduced or absent communication with the noncustodial parent, and adjustment to a step-parent. It also demonstrates the reality that help for a child may not be obtained until after years of family instability, stress, and anxiety related to parental conflict and parental depression.

The balancing factors in predicting Monica's future adjustment are her own and her mother's strengths, the ability of both to express their feelings appropriately, and (I hope) their continued willingness to engage in a helping process in order to obtain the support they need. My sincere hope is that Monica will continue to involve herself in counseling, since she otherwise will be vulnerable to problems in relationships herself when she is older. She may benefit from the opportunity to participate in a support group of peers who are also from divorced and remarried fami-lies. Monica and the Bakers should also continue with family counseling. A long-term goal would be for the family therapist to help Monica reach out to her father, to try to include him in her life again.

According to Garrity and Baris (1994), children who are pressured to "take sides" between their divorcing parents often pay the price of "denial of the sense of self" (p. 87). "Lacking the freedom to form their own opinions . . . children grow to doubt their own feelings. Therefore, the most important goal of therapy is to encourage the emergence of the child's separate sense of self" (p. 90). Older children can achieve this more easily, whereas younger children will have more difficulty understand-ing the divergent or contradictory positions of their parents. Because of these developmental differences, younger children "may require more time in therapy to accomplish the goal of claiming their own thoughts, feelings, and opinions" (Garrity & Baris, 1994, p. 90). The methods for helping these children "in the middle" include the range of play therapy techniques illustrated throughout this book.

ETHICAL ISSUES FOR PRACTITIONERS

Goldman, Stein, and Guerry (1983, p. 4) note astutely:

> In working with children, many ethical issues should be expected to arise. Because children are dependent upon others who are legally re-

sponsible for them, and because parents are often at legal odds with one another or with juvenile authorities, there are many times when the [practitioner] will be called upon to consider at what point the child is truly served.

The matter of access to the child's records constitutes one such problematic ethical issue. The question of who is entitled to see reports of a child's psychiatric/psychological evaluations and counseling sessions lacks clarity with regard to the legal rights of divorced parents. Often a custodial parent brings a child for an evaluation, hoping to use the resulting information on his or her own behalf in a subsequent divorce proceeding. The noncustodial parent, later learning of this evaluation, may demand to see the record. According to Goldman et al. (1983), both parents have the right to see their child's record in some states; in others, only the parent with legal custody of the child is legally entitled to the information. Practitioners should know the status of the law in their particular state.

I have argued previously against putting the ethic of confidentiality between parent and child, because of the unfortunate communication barrier this creates. Because it is virtually impossible to promise confidentiality, the practitioner must make process notes, with the assumption that these may become open to both parents or the court at a later date. In situations where families are involved in litigation, the practitioner must be prepared to have his or her notes subpoenaed. This may present great difficulty, for example, in a situation where a child has reported instances of verbal abuse and the practitioner wants to explore the matter further before taking action. The practitioner must exercise care in writing detailed notes about matters that may subsequently be used as part of a custody determination. Furthermore, the fact that the record may later be shared with others puts distinct constraints on the relationship, and the practitioner may need to discuss these with the child. In addition, according to the latest (1996) revision of the National Association of Social Workers (NASW) code of ethics, the worker has an *obligation* to clarify with all individuals the matter of "which individuals will be considered clients and the nature of the social worker's professional obligations to the various individuals who are receiving services" (NASW, 1996, section 1.06(d)).

Yet another matter that may cause an ethical conflict for the practitioner relates to the relationship between the practitioner and the guardian *ad litem*. When a child enters counseling, the guardian may expect the child's practitioner to offer an opinion regarding the child's and parents' mental state and attitudes. This can cause an ethical dilemma for the worker, because these matters often take considerable time and thought, and the outcome is so critical in terms of the child's future. Many social workers are not prepared to offer a firm opinion about with which parent a child *should* live, when they believe that the child's optimal adjustment depends on his or her maintaining an ongoing relationship with *both* parents.

These difficult ethical matters deserve more attention in schools of social work, in order to prepare practitioners who work with children for the likelihood that they will be faced with these dilemmas in their future practice.

CONCLUDING COMMENTS

Children who live in nontraditional families must cope with numerous stressors and losses. All children are responsive to the conflicts within their families, and to the negative attitudes of others toward their families. When parents divorce, remarry, decide to remain single, or decide to live in a homosexual partnership, their children are particularly vulnerable because of the internal conflicts or external negative attitudes associated with their nontraditional family structure.

Individual, family, and group helping methods can assist children with their confused feelings. However, in situations involving divorce and custody disputes, the children have often experienced years of conflict between their parents before they are referred for counseling. There are probably few other situations in which family therapy is more necessary; it is imperative to reduce the ongoing recriminations and hostility between partners, which continue to damage the child's relationship with each parent. Although the marriage may be beyond repair, the parents should be nonetheless enjoined to act in the best interests of their child or children, in order to prevent further pain to them. The court could play an important preventive role in this regard by insisting on a minimum of three sessions of counseling for divorcing parents, to attempt to orient them to and focus them on their children's needs.

Single parents need support of a different kind, in order to provide them with respite from the fatigue of full-time parenting. Peer groups, located in the community at day care centers and schools, could help connect single parents with their counterparts; this would enable them to offer both emotional and concrete help to one another.

Attention to the rights of children living in homosexual families must focus on respect for individual choice. Although the research on such families to date is limited, it is certainly true that children growing up in gay/lesbian families have the same needs for love and self-esteem as other children.

Regardless of the structure of nontraditional families, we must affirm that such families are different but not deviant. Because of our mission to respect individual differences, we must do everything possible to ease the stresses on the children in these families and to help them mourn their losses, so that they may continue with their age-appropriate development.

DISCUSSION QUESTIONS

1. How can a practitioner help a single mother tell her preschool child about the father who abandoned the mother when he learned about the pregnancy? (Imagine that the father is now in jail for crimes committed in connection with drug abuse, and the mother has not seen him since before the child's birth.)

2. Many schools offer "banana splits" groups to help children in divorced families talk about their experiences and offer support to one another. What kind of supports and/or programs would you suggest for children with never-married parents and children in homosexual families?

3. Consider ways in which the court might collaborate with a family agency to assist children and families in the midst of divorce proceedings. What guidelines would you propose in providing services to parents and to children? What would be the purposes and goals of such collaboration?

4. How can the practitioner resolve his or her own feelings of disappointment when a parent continues to put the child in the middle, as in the case of Monica?

CHAPTER 12

Children in Families Affected by Illness and Death

All children, in the normal course of their development, learn about being sick, and most, by the time they enter school, have at least rudimentary familiarity with the word "dead" through the experience of seeing dead insects and animals. However, when a young child lives in a family in which a parent has a recurring illness such as cancer, and in which an older sibling dies suddenly of a drug overdose, the child's confusion and anxiety about his or her own personal survival and that of the well parent are entirely understandable. In the case outlined below and described throughout this chapter, we see that this was the family context of illness and death in which young Sabrina completed kindergarten and entered first grade.

———————— ✤ ————————

THE CASE OF SABRINA, AGE 5¾

Family Information

Child client	Sabrina Rossi, age 5¾, completing kindergarten.
Mother	Lida Rossi, age 47, psychologist (currently unemployed).
Father	Dan Rossi, age 40, editor at publishing house.
Half-brother	John Sand, age 18, unemployed; former college student.
Paternal grandparents	In 70s, living nearby.
Paternal aunt	Carol, age 44, living nearby.

Cousins	Carol's children, Katie and Greg, ages 10 and 4.
Maternal grandmother	Age 70, living out of state.
Maternal aunt	Ann, age 45, living out of state.
Cousin	Ann's son, Steve, age 6.
Maternal aunt	Jean, age 43, living out of state.

Mrs. Rossi had been married previously; her first husband had died of a heart attack at the age of 45, when John was 14. She stated that her husband had a history of depression and alcoholism, and that they had been separated since John was 2½. Neither she nor John had contact with any of her first husband's relatives. In fact, she stated that she did not know their whereabouts.

Mr. and Mrs. Rossi have been married 8 years. They are of different religious backgrounds: The father and his relatives are Catholic and Italian, whereas the mother is Protestant and of northern European descent. However, neither Mr. nor Mrs. Rossi attends traditional religious services, and both have been interested in Eastern religions; they have a statue of Buddha in their living room.

Presenting Problem

Mrs. Rossi telephoned to request help for her family because she was facing major surgery, and she was concerned about how they would cope with her long postoperative period. Lida had a large tumor that required removal, necessitating both a colostomy and a vaginectomy. She stated that there was a lot of tension between her husband and her son, and that she was quite worried about how they would manage without her presence as a buffer. Although the operation was not considered life-threatening, Mrs. Rossi nonetheless wanted to work with a therapist who was experienced with both family and bereavement issues.

Assessment and Plan for Intervention

Since the operation was to occur in 10 days, time was limited. Mrs. Rossi had indicated on the phone her reluctance to include Sabrina in the initial family meeting, so I began by seeing the parents and John to address Mrs. Rossi's specific concerns. It was very evident that Mr. Rossi was angry about John's lack of employment or plans for his future. The boy, who looked more like a 14-year-old than an 18-year-old, had overdosed on cocaine 6 months earlier, and since then had dropped out of college. He spent most of his days sleeping, and his evenings out with friends, engaged in writing graffiti and drinking beer. There was a great deal of tension between Mr. Rossi and John; nonetheless, Mr. Rossi gave John money every week, in order for him to buy gas to go job hunting. Recently Mrs. Rossi had insisted that John enter therapy, and he had gone for two or three sessions at the time of the first family meeting with me. Mrs. Rossi herself had been engaged in individual therapy for several years.

I sensed that Mrs. Rossi seemed to be trying very hard to "put her house in order" before going into the hospital. She wanted John and her husband to promise to help her when she came home, when she herself would be too weak to go shopping or perform routine housekeeping tasks. During the session, we listed the chores and obtained agreements about who would do what. It was evident that everything related to John was a struggle; he resisted the idea of doing his laundry regularly rather than leaving it piled up, and he seemed equally reluctant to promise to feed his own cats or to meet Sabrina's school bus, because he "might be sleeping." He did agree to do the shopping, and Mr. Rossi agreed to vacuum and cook. I made an appointment to see Mr. Rossi and John together the day after Lida's operation.

I also expressed concern about Sabrina's reaction to the impending separation from her mother, especially after Mrs. Rossi told me that the child's kindergarten teacher had commented recently about Sabrina's "spaciness" and inability to concentrate. I encouraged Mrs. Rossi to bring her for one session, in order to prepare her for her mother's absence. We agreed that couple, family, and/or parent–child sessions would be planned later, depending on Mrs. Rossi's stamina and the family's needs after her operation.

Mother–Child Session

Sabrina brought a stuffed white cat named "Sassy" with her. At the beginning of the session she seemed quite anxious, as expressed in silly, teasing behavior in which she had Sassy crawl all over and tickle her mother.

I explained to Sabrina who I was. I then said that I knew her mother was going into the hospital next week, and that I wondered what it would be like for *her* without her mom at home. Sabrina said that she was "mad" because she had to stay at her grandmother's. She had her own room there, but it was dark at night and she didn't like it. Mrs. Rossi immediately said that they would get a night light for that room, just like the one she had at home. Sabrina seemed somewhat placated by this idea.

I asked Sabrina to draw a person. The drawing (see Figure 12.1) appeared to be very primitive and almost fearsome. The core body was in black, with parts of the hands, legs, and feet outlined in red. Sabrina also outlined the body and arms in purple. The features of the face were minimal, and the figure had no hair. Sabrina declined my invitation to tell me about this person. I considered that it might reflect the child's fantasy about surgery (the distinctive red color could signify blood). I decided to prepare Sabrina for the experience of seeing her mother hooked up to intravenous (IV) lines. I knew that Mr. Rossi planned to take her to the hospital to visit soon after the operation. Therefore, I made a crude drawing of a person in a hospital bed with the IV stand next to it, with connections to the patient (see Figure 12.2). I explained to Sabrina that after an operation people cannot eat as usual, and that their food and medicines are given to them in tubes that go into the veins in their hands and noses. Sabrina expressed disgust about the nose tube, but her mother reassured her that it was only for a short time and that it didn't hurt.

I then introduced a doll family and bedroom furniture, and suggested that we play out what it would be like to go to visit Mom in the hospital. We set up Sabrina's home in one location, with a toy telephone, and Mom's hospital bed in another, also with a phone. I invited Mrs. Rossi to role-play what it would be like after her operation, suggesting that she tell Sabrina that she felt very tired and weak, but that she would get stron-

FIGURE 12.1. Sabrina's Draw-A-Person before her mother's surgery.

ger later. Mrs. Rossi played this scene with Sabrina very effectively, and at the end Sabrina hugged her mother and said, "I'm glad it's not today!"

Summary of Next 8 Months

On the whole, the first several months after Mrs. Rossi's surgery were a period of hope and optimism. Mrs. Rossi had a good recovery from the operation, despite the considerable adjustment related to adapting to using the colostomy and urinary bags. No chemotherapy or radiation was prescribed, since Lida had previously undergone a course of radiation in an earlier attempt to shrink the tumor. Mr. Rossi was very supportive of his wife, and hopeful that they could resume some form of sexual activity, adapted to his wife's limitations. Mr. and Mrs. Rossi and Sabrina went on a vacation together, and Lida was making plans to resume her professional career. John had obtained employment, with the intention of getting his own apartment and returning to school the next semester.

FIGURE 12.2. Worker's drawing of a person in a hospital bed with IV stand and tubes.

FIGURE 12.3. Sabrina's Draw-A-Person (a princess), 2 months after her mother's surgery.

Sabrina was doing well in her first-grade class; she drew a picture of a "princess" (see Figure 12.3) 2 months after she had drawn the primitive, insect-like drawing prior to her mother's hospitalization. Comparing the two drawings now, I believe that the earlier figure reflected the child's regression caused by her anxiety about her mother's upcoming operation and the anticipated separation.

During this period I saw various members of the family at 2-week intervals in different combinations, including the parents together, Sabrina alone, Mr. Rossi and John together, and Mr. Rossi alone. John was continuing sporadically in individual therapy with another therapist. The family mood was positive, despite the ongoing concern about John. Because Sabrina was doing so well in school and at home, it was not necessary to see her weekly.

Eight months after Mrs. Rossi's operation, this period of optimism and hope for the future came to an abrupt end. John was found dead of a heroin overdose in a friend's apartment. My initial thought upon hearing the news was that it was a suicide, but both Mr. and Mrs. Rossi stressed that John had gotten a job and was in good spirits, talking about getting his own apartment and returning to school. They regarded the death as an accident, and believed that John had not used heroin previously. They also believed that the friend who had given it to him was irresponsible in failing to notice that John passed out and remained in a drugged state long beyond the usual expectations. Members of both Mr. and Mrs. Rossi's extended families attended the funeral, as did many of John's friends; Sabrina sat in the front row between her parents.

Again, I shall use the Rossi family's state at the time of John's death to illustrate a number of points throughout the chapter.

———————— ❖ ————————

DEVELOPMENTAL INFLUENCES ON CHILDREN'S UNDERSTANDING OF DEATH

The poet who described childhood as "the kingdom where nobody dies" (Millay, 1934/1969, p. 203) presented an idealistic picture that might have been true in the 1920s and 1930s when parents protected their children from exposure to death; however, it certainly is not true in this age of television, war, open discussion about AIDS, and growing awareness among teachers and parents that children should be included in death-related discussions and experiences. Kastenbaum (1991, p. 163) states that "developmental studies and observations made in natural and clinical settings all indicate that children are aware of death from an early age. The child, however, does not begin with the realization that death is inevitable, universal, and final but quickly grasps the implications of separation and loss."

In an earlier publication (Webb, 1993), I presented a review of the child's gradual, progressive understanding about death as related to his or her cognitive development. Using Piaget's work as a guide (Piaget, 1955, 1968, 1972; Piaget & Inhelder, 1969), I connected children's developing ideas about death to the three major phases of cognitive development, as summarized in Table 12.1. The age references in the table should not be taken too literally, since development is an individual process, and variations occur depending on a child's unique life experiences. Chronological age is only a very general guideline, indicating the typical gradual progression in children's understanding about death.

Let us now apply the concepts in Table 12.1 to the case of Sabrina. Because of Sabrina's young age (6½) when her brother died, her understanding was still at the preoperational stage. She may have thought that something she did or said led her brother to take drugs or alcohol. She may also have thought that he would return, especially since her parents' religious perspective included the concept of reincarnation. This could have been confusing for Sabrina, because children her age are very literal; she could have become angry if she believed John would come back and he did not do so.

TABLE 12.1. Children's Cognitive Development and Understanding of Death

Age of child	Piaget's stage	Understanding of death
The young child (ages 2–7)	Preoperational Magical thinking Egocentricity	Temporary, reversible, caused by own wishes/deeds
The latency-age child (ages 7–10)	Concrete operational Reduced egocentricity Improved reasoning Awareness of time	Irreversible, final, inevitable (but in future, for "old," not selves); distinction between body and "spirit"[a]
The prepubertal child (ages 11–12)	Formal operational Logical thinking Abstract thinking Tolerance of contradictions and ambiguity	Mature understanding: Final, inevitable/universal, irreversible

Note. Adapted from the discussion in Webb (1993, pp. 4–7). Copyright 1993 by The Guilford Press. Adapted by permission.

[a]Most experts believe that children acquire a realistic perception of the finality and irreversibility of death at the *end* of this period, by age 9 or 10. This understanding is a *gradual* process.

THE TRIPARTITE ASSESSMENT OF THE BEREAVED CHILD

Although the child's age and developmental stage should always be considered in assessing the impact of a death experience, these are only a few of the many factors that must be evaluated. In my earlier publication (Webb, 1993), I presented the tripartite assessment of the bereaved child as a method for understanding the specific meaning of a specific death to a particular child. The discussion that follows is a further elaboration of the concepts I originally presented there.

As I have indicated in earlier chapters of the present book, a tripartite assessment consists of weighing the interaction of three groups of factors. When a practitioner is considering the reactions of a child following a death, these three groups of factors are as follows:

1. Individual factors
2. Factors related to the death
3. Factors in the support system (family, social, religious/cultural factors)

In some situations, individual factors, such as the child's past history of death and loss, may have a compelling impact on his or her response. In other cases, the element of trauma related to the death may exert an overriding influence on the child and family. Finally, regardless of the nature of factors related to the individual and to the death itself, the responses of family, religious/cultural, and social networks must always be considered as balancing factors that support the grieving individual. Figure 12.4 illustrates the specific components of and interactions among the three sets of variables.

I have developed four different forms to assist the practitioner in highlighting significant factors in the tripartite assessment of the bereaved child. Blank versions of these forms are provided in the Appendices; in the following discussion, I use filled-in versions to demonstrate their application to Sabrina and her family at the time of John's death.

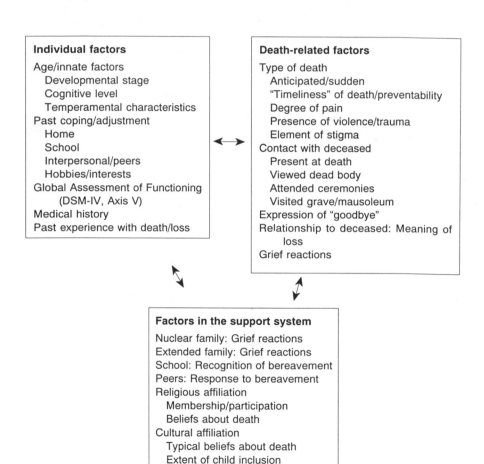

FIGURE 12.4. Interactive components of a tripartite assessment of the bereaved child: Webb. Adapted from Webb (1993, p. 30). Copyright 1993 by The Guilford Press. Adapted by permission.

TABLE 12.2. Individual Factors in Childhood Bereavement: Webb

---

1. Age _6_ years _6_ months   Date of birth ____
                                             Date of assessment ____

   a. Developmental stage: b. Cognitive level:
      Freud _Late Oedipal/early latency_   Piaget _Preoperational_
      Erikson _Industry vs. inferiority_   c. Temperamental characteristics:
                                                Thomas and Chess _Easy_____

2. Past coping/adjustment
   a. Home (as reported by parents): Good _x_ Fair ___ Poor ___
   b. School (as reported by parents and teachers): Good _x_ Fair ___ Poor ___
   c. Interpersonal/peers: Good ___ Fair _x_ Poor ___
   d. Hobbies/interests (list) _Brownies, ballet_____

3. Global Assessment of Functioning: DSM-IV, Axis V
   Current _75_____   Past year _90_____

4. Medical history (as reported by parents and pediatrician)—describe serious illnesses,
   operations, and injuries since birth, with dates and outcome _Some earaches and difficult_
   hearing because of allergies; neither problem is severe, according to parents. Otherwise, health is
   _good._____

5. Past experience with death/loss—give details with dates and outcome *or* complete
   Wolfelt's Loss Inventory _No known experience. Maternal grandfather died before she was_
   born. She may be aware that John's father died 5 years ago; however, Sabrina would have been
   _only a toddler of 18 months at the time._____

Note. This form is one part of the three-part assessment of the bereaved child, which
also includes an assessment of death-related factors (Table 12.3) and family/social/reli-
gious/cultural factors (Table 12.4). The form itself (not the responses) is from Webb (1993,
p. 31). Copyright 1993 by The Guilford Press. Reprinted by permission.

The first form (Table 12.2) facilitates the recording of information
about the child's life and general level of adjustment prior to the death.
A second form (Table 12.3) records information about the death itself, and
about the child's degree of involvement in ritual observances connected
to the death. A third form (Table 12.4) permits the recording of information about the extended family, about the child's school and peer contacts, and about possible religious and cultural influences on the child
following the death. A form for recording the nature of the child's grief
reactions (Table 12.5) can be filled out with the assistance of the parent(s)
or others who were present following the death. This form probes for
specific information related to the nature of the relationship between the
child and the person who died.

TABLE 12.3. Death-Related Factors in Childhood Bereavement: Webb

1. Type of death
    Anticipated: Yes ____ No ____ If yes, how long? ___ or sudden _x_
    "Timeliness" of death: Age of the deceased _19_
    Perception of preventability:
        Definitely preventable _x_ Maybe ___ Not ___
    Degree of pain associated with death:
        None _x_ Some ___ Much ___
    Presence of violence/trauma: Yes ___ No _x_
        If yes, describe, indicating whether the child witnessed, heard about, or was
        present and experienced the trauma personally. _____
        _____
        _____
    Element of stigma: Yes _x_   No ___
        If yes, describe, indicating nature of death, and degree of openness of family in
        discussing. _Since the death was caused by a drug overdose, the family felt ashamed._
        Sabrina's grandparents never discussed the death with Lida and Dan, although they did
        attend the funeral.

2. Contact with deceased:
    Present at moment of death? Yes ___ No _x_
        If yes, describe circumstances, including who else was present and whether the
        deceased said anything specifically to the child. _____
        _____
        _____
    Did the child view the dead body? Yes ___ No _x_
        If yes, describe circumstances, including reactions of the child and others who
        were present. _____
    Did the child attend funeral/memorial service/graveside service? Yes _x_ No ___
        Which? _____
        Child's reactions _Child cried at funeral; there was no graveside service, since the_
        body was cremated.
    Has the child visited grave/mausoleum since the death? Yes ___ No _x_
        If yes, describe circumstances. _____
        _____
        _____

3. Did the child make any expression of "goodbye" to the deceased, either spontaneous
    or suggested? Yes _x_ No ___
        If yes, describe. _Sabrina assisted in writing messages on the exterior of John's casket._
        The messages said, "Goodbye, John, we love you." She also drew hearts and flowers next
        to the words.

Note. This form is one part of the three-part assessment of the bereaved child, which
also includes an assessment of individual factors (Table 12.2) and family/social/religious/
cultural factors (Table 12.4). The form itself (not the responses) is from Webb (1993, p. 35).
Copyright 1993 by The Guilford Press. Reprinted by permission.

TABLE 12.4. Family/Social/Religious/Cultural Factors in Childhood Bereavement: Webb

1. Family influences

   Nuclear family: How responding to death? Describe in terms of relative degree of openness of response.

   Very expressive _x_ Moderately expressive ___ Very guarded ___

   To what extent is child included in family discussions/rituals related to the deceased?

   Some ___ A great deal _x_ Not at all ___

   Extended family: How responding to death? Describe, as above, in terms of relative degree of openness of response.

   Very expressive _x (Mother's)_ Moderately expressive_____

   Very guarded _x (Father's)_

   To what extent do the views of the extended family differ or agree with those of the nuclear family with regard to the planning of rituals and inclusion of child?

   Very different _Father's_ Very similar _Mother's_

   If different, describe the nature of the disagreement _Father's family is Catholic; the_ _service was conducted by a lay reader and held in a funeral home. Since John was not_ _their biological grandchild, this did not prove to be a major issue._

2. School/peer influences

   Child's grade in school _First_

   Did any of the child's friends/peers attend the funeral/memorial services?

   Yes ___ No _x_ (However, cousins her age were present)

   Was teacher informed of death? Yes _x_ No ___

   Did child receive condolence messages from friends/peers? Yes _x_ No ___

   Does child know anyone his/her age who has been bereaved? Yes ___ No ___

   Not sure _x_

   If yes, has child spoken to this person since the death? Yes ___ No ___

   Does child express feelings about wanting or not wanting peers/friends to know about the death? Yes ___ No ___ Not sure _x_

   If yes, what has the child said? _____

3. Religious/cultural influences

   What is the child's religion? _Father has recently been taking her to Catholic church with_ _his niece and nephew._

   Has he/she been observant? Yes _Only recently_ No ___

   What are the beliefs of the child's religion regarding death? _____

   What about life after death? _The Catholic religion believes in life after death. Further-_ _more, the Eastern religious beliefs that are part of the parents' views consider death as a_ _journey, and include the possibility of reincarnation. These latter views were expressed in_ _John's funeral service._

   Has child expressed any thoughts/feelings about this? _No_

Note. This form is one part of the three-part assessment of the bereaved child, which also includes an assessment of individual factors (Table 12.2) and death-related factors (Table 12.3). The form itself (not the responses) is from Webb (1993, p. 39). Copyright 1993 by The Guilford Press. Reprinted by permission.

TABLE 12.5. Recording Form for Childhood Grief Reactions: Webb

Age of child _6_ years _6_ months   Date of birth _____

                                                 Date of assessment _____

See the form "Individual Factors in Childhood Bereavement" [Table 12.2] for recording of personal history factors.

Date of death _____

Relationship to deceased _Half-brother_ _____

   Favorite activities shared with deceased _Playing with his cats_ _____

   What the child will miss the most _His jokes; his music_ _____

   If the child could see the deceased again for 1 hour, what would he/she like to do or say?

   "Why did you have to take that drug?" _____

Nature of grief reactions (describe) _Cried when mother told her that John had died. Now_

   every night when says her prayers, asks God to take good care of John. Mother listens to her

   prayers and tucks her in, and they cry together. _____

   Signs of the following feelings? Y = Yes; N = No

   Sadness _Y_ Anger _N_ Confusion _N_ Guilt _N_ Relief _N_ Other _N_____

Source of information on which this form has been completed

_x_ Parent _x_ Observation ____ Other

Note. This form is an extension of "Death-Related Factors in Childhood Bereavement" (Table 12.3), focusing specifically on the nature of the child's grief. The form itself (not the responses) is from Webb (1993, p. 38). Copyright 1993 by The Guilford Press. Reprinted by permission.

It appears from Table 12.2 that this child was developing well, without apparent behavioral or emotional difficulties. The mother's only concern about her was her seeming lack of assertiveness with friends; Mrs. Rossi had noticed that Sabrina was usually a follower, not a leader.

Table 12.3, which records information related to the death, shows that this family was in shock following John's death. However, the parents were concerned about Sabrina's reaction and tried to include her as much as possible in the family rituals. The presence of West Coast relatives and cousins who came for the funeral helped Sabrina engage with children her own age during this intensely stressful time.

On the whole, the members of this family were expressing their grief openly and fully, as Table 12.4 shows.

Sabrina's grief reactions are described in Table 12.5. Sabrina's teacher said that she was continuing to do well in school (she was now in first grade). However, Mrs. Rossi reported that Sabrina told her that she sometimes went into the bathroom at school and cried. Sabrina was also waking up in the night and sometimes sleeping on the couch. She denied that she had bad dreams, or that she was thinking about John.

ISSUES IN SIBLING DEATH

The death of *any* family member constitutes a crisis (Goldberg, 1973). However, when the death is untimely (Bank & Kahn, 1982; McGoldrick & Walsh, 1991), and/or when the circumstances of the death (e.g., a death from suicide, AIDS, or a drug overdose) cannot be openly recognized or socially supported (Doka, 1989), the impact on the family can be devastating. McGoldrick and Walsh (1991) point out that an untimely death in young adulthood may generate in the surviving family members "a sense of cruel injustice in the ending of a life before its prime" (p. 33); it deprives the deceased of the opportunity to fulfill his or her life plans, and causes the family members "pain and survivor guilt [that] may block [them] from continuing their own pursuits" (p. 33).

The responses of siblings to the death of a brother or a sister reflect not only their own unique reactions based on their personal relationship with the deceased sibling, but also the responses of other nuclear and extended family members, and of the community in which they live. A systems perspective views the reactions of individual family members as reflective of both those of the family and those of the surrounding environment. Therefore, a great outpouring of support from extended family and friends, expressed through attendance at the funeral and messages of condolence, can take away some of the lonely feelings of mourning.

The professional literature on bereavement in childhood tends to focus on the impact of a death of a parent (Bowlby, 1969, 1979, 1980; Furman, 1974; Gardner, 1983; Grollman, 1967) or on helping a dying child. A volume titled *The Child and Death* (Schowalter et al., 1983) does not contain a single chapter (among 29) devoted to the topic of sibling bereavement. Exceptions to this unfortunate neglect can be found in the work of Bank and Kahn (1982), McGoldrick and Walsh (1991), Raphael (1983), Rosen (1986, 1991), and Kaplan and Joslin (1993). Some of the main points emphasized by these writers include the following:

1. The death of a sibling creates a sense of vulnerability in the surviving siblings, who may begin to fear that they also may die (Rosen, 1991). However, the loss of a sibling does not present a child with the *intense* survival issues posed by the loss of a parent (Rosen, 1986).

2. Grieving parents have reduced energy and time to carry out their usual parental functions with respect to the surviving siblings. Therefore, a child in a bereaved family has lost not only a brother or a sister, but also parents who are emotionally available. "The fatality of the sibling casts a shadow across the parents' wounded forms, and thence upon the children" (Bank & Kahn, 1982, p. 273).

3. The child's reaction to the loss depends on how successfully the parents can continue to maintain their parental functions while they mourn (Rosen, 1991).

4. The child's developmental level has an important effect on his or her bereavement response. The existence of ambivalent and/or hostile feelings toward the deceased sibling may seriously compromise the mourning of survivors. A young, egocentric child may believe that some of his or her earlier hostile thoughts toward the sibling caused the death (Kaplan & Joslin, 1993).

5. The death of any family member requires role realignments and reorganization:

> After a loss, families must be restructured without the dead person, whose roles and functions must be taken over by others. The more important the deceased was to the ongoing emotional or practical functioning of the family, the more difficult it is for those remaining to adjust. When a child dies, family restructuring requires finding another focus for the love and care that previously went to that child. (McGoldrick & Walsh, 1991, p. 51)

In the case of the Rossi family, John's death had different significance to Mr. and Mrs. Rossi and to Sabrina. As a mother, Lida experienced a very strong reaction of anger and terrible sadness; Mr. Rossi was also angry; and Sabrina was very sad. John's death must be understood in terms of the family history and John's role in this remarried family.

Lida and John had lived alone together for about 10 years before Dan entered their lives, and they had gone through some difficult times together. Soon after Lida and Dan married, John was preparing to live with his own father; unfortunately, however, his father died at that time. John never accepted Dan's role as stepfather, and their relationship was always stormy. More recently, with John old enough to be on his own, Lida shared Dan's hope that he would find a job or a field of study that interested him. However, this emancipation process did not proceed smoothly. John's involvement with peers who drank and engaged in antisocial behavior worried Lida, especially after the cocaine overdose (which precipitated a short hospitalization), followed by months of daytime sleeping and nighttime alcohol use. Lida was concerned that John would become an alcoholic like his father, and she warned him repeatedly about the dangers of alcohol addiction. However, John continued on his own path; he responded with cursing and rude, self-deprecating remarks whenever either his mother or his stepfather tried to engage him in planning for his future.

In short, John had assumed the role of "black sheep" in this family, and Dan had given up on him. They would go for long periods without speaking to each other, and Lida would finally serve as intermediary. Dan kept telling Lida to "cut the cord," and in several counseling sessions I urged both parents to set reasonable limits and follow through on them. I was also concerned about John's possible depression, and urged Lida to speak with John's therapist about his father's history. She did so, and informed me that John's therapist did not believe that John was depressed.

Once John became employed, Lida gave him an ultimatum to move out by a certain date. John's therapist was supporting the plan, and an apartment was located and the deposit paid. Lida had hopes that "the therapy was working" and that John would finally achieve success in his life. Dan was planning to redecorate John's room for Sabrina, who up to this time had been sharing a bedroom with her parents.

John's death eliminated the universal dream and hope that Lida shared with all parents—the dream of seeing their children happy and successful. Lida had tried very hard to be a good mother, and now her only son's death of a heroin overdose seemed to point to her failure. Certainly John represented the end of a very difficult chapter in her life, wiping away all traces of her unhappy first marriage. As Raphael (1983) states, "a child is many things: a part of the self, and of the loved partner; a representation of the generations past; the genes of the forebears; the hope of the future; a source of love, pleasure, even narcissistic delight; a tie or a burden; and sometimes a symbol of the worst parts of the self and others" (p. 229).

Lida's rage was widespread; it was directed most intensely toward John's friends, but it also encompassed Dan, John's therapist, her own therapist, and myself. Sabrina was spared, as evidenced in Lida's statement to me that the only people who *really* cared about John were herself and Sabrina. I understood and accepted Lida's anger as a necessary aspect of her bereavement, and especially as related to her displaced rage because John had failed to validate all the years of their special relationship. In fact, the nature of his death shamed her and refuted her consistent belief that he could succeed.

An adolescent like John struggles with issues of identity, sexuality, and separation, which can become very complicated in a remarried family: "To the question of 'Who am I?' is added, 'Who am I in this new family?'" (Rosenberg, 1988, p. 225). It seemed clear to me that John did not want to be in this family, and that his life had taken a negative trajectory since the death of his father interrupted his own plans to remain with his father in the familiar neighborhood and school environment of his past. My view of John's situation was that his life had come to a standstill at that time, and that his inability to complete the tasks of adolescence without assuming a "negative identity" (Erikson, 1968) was related to the boy's incomplete mourning for his own father. John always impressed me, in both his physical appearance and his manner, as a *young adolescent*. I think he was "stuck" in the guise of a 14-year-old without a father, and unwilling to bond to the stepfather who was willing and waiting to take on that role.

Mr. Rossi's reactions to John's death were also dominated by anger, because the youth had not taken advantage of the numerous opportunities he had been given. In addition, part of Mr. Rossi's difficulties in being firm with John stemmed from his partial identification with him; he too had found it difficult to break away from his family of origin, and Mr. Rossi did not want to force the issue with his stepson.

Another aspect of Dan's anger related to the impact of John's behavior on the family. For example, Dan was completely intolerant of John's habit of returning home in the middle of the night and proceeding to cook hamburgers and other food, when the accompanying odors and noise woke other family members in their small apartment. This behavior continued even during Lida's postoperative period, and became the "straw that broke the camel's back," totally alienating Mr. Rossi from his stepson. Nonetheless, Dan felt some affection and admiration for the young man, as expressed in his spontaneous funeral tribute that focused on John's charm and potential, together with his unpredictability and self-centeredness.

For Sabrina, her brother's death converted her into the only child in the family. She told her mother that she was jealous of her cousin Katie, who had a brother. However, because of the big age difference between Sabrina and John, their lives did not overlap very much. Even on the weekends, when both were home, John usually slept until 2 or 3 in the afternoon, when Sabrina typically would be out of the house playing with friends or engaged in other activities. John rarely ate dinner or other meals with the family, so Sabrina's contacts with her brother were few, and possibly weighed toward overhearing arguments between him and her parents.

Raphael (1983) comments that "in losing a sibling the child loses a playmate, a companion, someone who is a buffer against the parents, someone who may love and comfort him, someone with whom he identifies and who he admires. In short, he loses someone dearly loved as well as perhaps envied and rivalrously hated" (p. 114). It was not at all clear how much of this related to Sabrina. In fact, because of the great age difference and gender difference, we might conclude that this sibling bond was not especially strong, and that since Sabrina had strong bonds with other family members, she might be able to tolerate this loss without undue developmental interference (Rosen, 1986). This actually proved true in Sabrina's case, as will be discussed later.

❖

SELECTED HELPING INTERVENTIONS
FOR BEREAVED CHILDREN

The goal in helping bereaved children and their families is to facilitate the mourning process, and to assist when needed with the necessary realignment of roles. Because the process of children's grief is different from that of adults (Rando, 1988/1991; Webb, 1993; Wolfenstein, 1966), the worker may need to help family members understand these differences, so that they do not misinterpret a child's interest in playing and carrying out his or her usual activities in the midst of the mourning period. Actually, it is *helpful* for the child to return to his or her routine as soon as possible, since children have a "short sadness span" (Wolfenstein, 1966) and cannot tolerate the pain of grief for sustained periods of time. Kliman (1989, p. 61) comments that "during latency, mourning is apt to be particularly silent and slow." This may be related to the fact that latency-age children consider crying to be babyish (Furman, 1974), so they try to act "grown up," which for them means being in control of their feelings.

Play Approaches

The rationale for employing play therapy interventions with a young bereaved child relates to children's reluctance to talk about their feelings, possibly because of the fear of being overwhelmed and then breaking down in tears. Through directed play with a worker/counselor, however, the child can express feelings in a displaced way, using dolls, drawing, games, and other techniques. The method of directed or structured play allows the worker/counselor to deliberately select and offer play materials that will encourage the child to project his or her worries onto the materials, and thus to experience cathartic relief, clarification of misunderstandings, and a corrective emotional experience (Enzer, 1988).

Play Materials

Many of the same play materials that should be available in any office in which children are seen for counseling can be employed in work with bereaved children. I have found that plain white and colored paper, markers, clay, family dolls, and some card and board games are very effective in helping children express their concerns in a displaced manner. Clay is particularly useful in encouraging the release of pent-up feelings of tension and anger; in addition, it permits the child the mastery experience of creating something and then obliterating it (possibly reflecting the child's feelings about having a loved person "disappear" through death).

Depending on the age of the child and the particular circumstances of the death, it may be useful to offer specific toys that will encourage reenactment of the circumstances of the illness and death. Toys in this category include toy ambulances, a doctor kit, and the board game Operation (available from Milton Bradley, Springfield, MA). A therapeutic board game, Gardner's Storytelling Card Game (available from Creative Therapeutics, Cresskill, NJ), contains a cemetery picture that requires the player to make up a story about that background scene. In a previous publication (Webb, 1993), I discussed the productive use of this game with a 9-year-old boy whose grandmother had died.

In recent years, a number of workbooks have been published that are designed to help children draw pictures and fill in their thoughts and feelings associated with death. Although these workbooks can serve as a guide for counselors who lack experience in and confidence about using drawing and play methods with bereaved children, I am concerned that if such workbooks are used by the lay public or given to children to fill in without supervision, the content might overwhelm young children. These workbooks should be used *at a very slow pace* that permits a child to reveal and cope with the feelings that will be generated. My advice to students and the workers I supervise is that "less is more," especially when working with the bereaved.

Two excellent exercises from the workbook *When Something Terrible Happens: Children Can Learn to Cope with Grief* (Heegaard, 1991) are (1) Feelings Faces and (2) the Body Map of Feelings. In the Feelings Faces exercise, the child is asked to draw faces showing different expressions on circles, with five different emotions named under each circle: "angry," "sad," "afraid," "worried," and "happy." I believe that these are too many different emotions for a bereaved child to have to draw at once. Therefore, when I use this exercise, I reduce the number of emotions to three at most; sometimes I ask a child to draw only the primary emotion that matches his or her feelings when he or she thinks about the person who died.

The Body Map of Feelings permits similar adaptations, which I recommend, to conform to a child's developmental and emotional capacity. The body map is an outline of a body, on which the child is asked to use seven different colors to indicate the places where seven different emotions are felt: "sad," "afraid," "guilty," "angry," "jealous," "nervous," and "happy." When I use this, I ask the child to choose which of three feelings he or she would like to draw, and generally this task proves to be sufficient for one time. It is also possible to go very slowly and request only one emotion each session. Because the practitioner and the child use the drawing as an opportunity to talk about a time when the child felt this emotion, it is not desirable to rush the experience. In fact, it may be more helpful to expand on the child's recollection by inviting him or her to draw a picture of that experience.

Individual, Family, and Group Approaches

Grief is a family experience, and the helping person must attend to the needs of the family unit, as well as those of the individual members. In Chapter 6 I have recommended an integrated child and family model, which is very apt for a bereaved family. Typically I offer to make a home visit when I learn about a death that pertains to a child client. Depending on the circumstances, I may attend the funeral. It is *always* relevant to see the entire family together soon after the death, to offer condolences and to assess the group and individual needs. Following the death of a child, the parents may benefit from some marital counseling, and at some point it may be useful to see individual family members alone (when this is practical). This latter approach permits the expression of frustration or anger toward other family members, without exposing the targets of these strong feelings to the added stress of being blamed when they are already in the throes of grieving. Often it is helpful to see the child with each parent, in order to observe differences in the child's reactions with different parents, and to determine each parent's ability to comfort and support the grieving child.

Whenever I see a parent with a child, or the family as a unit, I always invite the parent(s) to participate in whatever play activity I make available to the child. Most parents comprehend that their children are communicating symbolically through play, even though they may have difficulty in knowing how to respond. There are examples of this in the discussion about Sabrina's family that follows.

Referrals to grief support groups should always be considered, depending on the willingness of the family members to involve themselves in this type of counseling. Many schools offer bereavement groups for children, which can help a child realize that he or she is not the only one who has suffered a loss. Two examples of bereavement groups for children, with detailed process notes illustrating specific interventions and the children's responses, are described in Tait and Depta (1993) and Hickey (1993).

❖

Interventions with Sabrina and Her Parents after John's Death

Initial Interventions

In the month after John's death, I met with Mr. and Mrs. Rossi once, and Mrs. Rossi brought Sabrina for a conjoint session. The meeting with Mr. and Mrs. Rossi was very intense, because Mrs. Rossi was in the throes of grieving and needed to express her anger about John's death. She stated that she did not wish to involve herself with marital counseling because she planned to continue in individual therapy, and she had also joined a bereavement group. Although I knew that she was angry with me because I had been unable to mend the relationship between John and Dan, Lida did want me to continue to see Sabrina, and agreed to bring her alternately with Mr. Rossi.

Dan was very concerned about his wife's pain over John's death. However, he did not feel the same need as his wife did to process the events surrounding the death, or to examine how it personally affected him. He declined my offer to meet with him individually, stating that he "might look for a men's group." Perhaps taking his cues from Lida, Mr. Rossi agreed to bring Sabrina for individual play sessions, according to my recommendations.

In the first session with Sabrina after her brother's death, I asked her to draw a picture of John. Sabrina drew a colorful figure, appearing to float in air, with arms outstretched (see Figure 12.5). She declined my invitation to tell me about the drawing, but she did agree to think about some happy memories of John, mentioning sitting on a wall in a favorite park with John and some of his friends.

Individual Session with Sabrina

In a session a month later, Sabrina told me directly that she didn't want to talk about John or "anything else." I then produced a "new" game, Operation; this totally captured Sabrina's interest, insofar as it permitted her to assume a controlling role in regard to "operating" on a helpless patient. The game also permitted me to make connections to her mother's operation. For example, at one point during the play I asked Sabrina whether any of these operations were like those her mother had. Sabrina said, "No, that was *very* different!" I indicated that I knew about the operation, and asked Sabrina whether she was worried about her mother now. She said, "Sometimes," but she could not tell me more.

FIGURE 12.5. Sabrina's drawing of John.

Several times during the play, Sabrina went into the waiting room to say something to her mother. At the end of the session, Sabrina wanted to show her mother the game; she also gave her reward for winning (a wildlife sticker) to her mother.

Session with Sabrina and Her Father

During the first session with Sabrina and her father following the death (about 6 weeks following the session with the mother), I asked how it seemed in the house without John. Sabrina said that she couldn't say, so I suggested that she draw a picture of a face (showing her the Feelings Faces exercise). Sabrina said it was sad, and drew a very sad face (see Figure 12.6). The original drawing had one line to denote the mouth, which appeared to convey distress. I responded, "What do we need to help that sad face feel better?" (expecting to lead into a verbal discussion). Sabrina took the marker and drew a full mouth around the straight line she had previously created. I said, "Sometimes we put on a smile when we feel sad inside." Sabrina nodded and then looked toward the doll family and doll furniture she had played with previously. She then proceeded to reenact a scene with the mother doll in the hospital, because "she had to have an operation." The family, around the breakfast table,

FIGURE 12.6. Sabrina's drawing of a sad face.

read the newspaper, and Sabrina announced, "They wrote about Mom in the newspaper." She turned to me (in play) and asked, "What does it say?" I responded, "Mrs. Jones is in the hospital," and Sabrina interjected, "for a very serious operation." I continued, "She has a very good doctor, and we expect her to recover."

Sabrina then asked to go to the bathroom. During this interval, Mr. Rossi, who was in the room observing this play interaction, stated: "I don't know why she does this; she must associate coming here with Lida's operation." When Sabrina returned, she asked to play Operation.

Session with Sabrina and Her Mother
4 Months after John's Death

Prior to the next session with Sabrina and her mother, I had received a telephone message from Lida stating that one of John's two cats had died.

At the beginning of the session, I noticed how attractive both Lida and Sabrina looked. Lida had lipstick on (for the first time in months), and Sabrina was specially dressed for a birthday party immediately after this session.

Sabrina began by telling me that she forgot to bring the picture she had drawn for me last night in bed. I asked her to describe it, and she said it had "a sun, a house, and grass." She then said, handing me two quarters, that she wanted to give me some money "because you invite me to come here." I was very touched, and impressed by the apparent meaning of the sessions to Sabrina. I told her that her father already paid me (through insurance), but she insisted, saying, "I *want* to give it to you!" I thanked her very much, continuing to puzzle about the meaning of this behavior.

Telling Sabrina that I knew about the cat's death, and that I was sorry, I asked her whether she was surprised that he died. Sabrina said that she was not sure why he died, and Lida reminded Sabrina that the cat's X-rays had shown an enlarged heart. At this point, Sabrina could not tolerate any more words, and she began crawling around the floor acting out how the cat had wanted to sleep and stay by himself. I asked about how the other cat was responding since the death of her friend, and Sabrina again acted this out by crawling on the floor and making cat sounds.

I introduced the Body Map of Feelings (Heegaard, 1991), and suggested that Sabrina draw on the body in blue where she felt sad. First she thought this would be in her eyes, but then she said it was in her stomach. She drew a very large blue circle in the center of the body (see Figure 12.7). When I asked Sabrina if she could indicate where in the body she felt afraid, she put a black circle within the blue nucleus of the stomach. She drew orange (nervous) in the neck, and green (jealous) in the

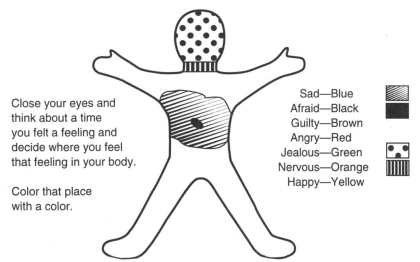

Feelings are something people feel in their body.

Close your eyes and think about a time you felt a feeling and decide where you feel that feeling in your body.

Color that place with a color.

Sad—Blue
Afraid—Black
Guilty—Brown
Angry—Red
Jealous—Green
Nervous—Orange
Happy—Yellow

FIGURE 12.7. Sabrina's Body Map of Feelings. The form is adapted from Heegaard (1991, p. 13). Copyright 1991 by Woodland Press. Adapted by permission.

head. She said that she couldn't do angry, and said that happy would be on the face, but she didn't want to mix it with the green color already there.

When we later played Gardner's Storytelling Card Game, one of Sabrina's stories had the theme of feeding a dog, then later calling the dog and he wasn't there.

———————— ❖ ————————

Comment

The accounts of these sessions graphically depict how this latency-age child used a variety of play materials to project her feelings of bereavement and confusion about the two major crises in her life that occurred within an 8-month span: namely, her mother's serious operation, and her half-brother's sudden death. Play, in the context of a therapeutic relationship, truly served as an outlet for this child to express her worries about her mother and her sadness about the loss of her brother.

It seems clear from these descriptions that Sabrina continued to be very concerned and protective toward her mother. For example, she presented her mother with her "reward" sticker at the end of a session. In fact, the death of her brother may have assumed major significance to her because it made her mother so very sad. Sabrina continued to be very concerned about her mother's health, which made Mrs. Rossi's prognosis very significant to this child.

Addendum

Approximately a year after John's death, Sabrina's mother died. Gradually, over a 4-month period, Lida's ability to walk and carry on her usual activities deteriorated. The local hospice provided the necessary nursing and home health care services.

Lida had difficulty accepting the reality of her impending death, which created concomitant difficulty in adequately preparing Sabrina. Ultimately, I told Lida that it was essential to tell Sabrina about the fact that she (Lida) was not getting better, despite all medicines and the best efforts of the doctors. Three days after hearing this from me, Sabrina's mother told her, "God wants me and God may be taking me soon." Lida also told Sabrina, "God will take care of you and Daddy, and I'll be watching over both of you." Eight days later, on her own birthday, Lida died.

Because of the coincidence of time, Sabrina may link the two major crises in her life. There is no evidence of this yet, but I will be alert for possible confusion in the child's mind that her brother's death may have led to her mother's deteriorating condition.

CONCLUDING COMMENTS

Children need the stability and security of knowing that the people who love them will remain constant in their lives. When illness and death take precedence over a child's needs, the child may feel abandoned. Actually, children *need* their parents in order to complete certain developmental tasks, such as integrating a firm sense of identity.

It is possible to help children and parents with "the work of mourning" after the death of a family member. These helping methods should be adapted to the age of the individual and to his or her ability to comprehend the reality of what has happened. When a young child is faced with the death of a sibling or the recurring illness of a parent, play techniques can provide the mechanism through which the child can express, in a displaced manner, the conflicts and anxiety he or she is experiencing internally but trying to suppress. The use of directed or structured play therapy can provide such children with relief and the reassurance that an adult comprehends their confused internal state.

DISCUSSION QUESTIONS AND ROLE-PLAY EXERCISES

1. Discuss the implications of young children's magical thinking and egocentricity for their ability to understand death. How can a worker assist a parent in helping a bereaved child who is under 7 years of age?

2. What issues in a remarried family are illustrated in the Rossi case? If you had been the worker, how would you have dealt with the long-standing conflict between Mr. Rossi and John? Role-play a session in which you attempt to modify their hostility toward each other.

3. Consider the pros and cons of having multiple workers involved in helping a family such as the Rossis. What recommendations would you make to avoid mixed messages and differing goals among the various workers?

4. How can the worker effectively assist latency-age children who do not wish to talk about their feelings after a death? What play materials might be useful?

5. Compare and contrast the use of individual, family, and group approaches in situations of bereavement.

❖ CHAPTER 13 ❖

Children in Substance-Disordered Families

Many children growing up at the end of the 20th century have been exposed repeatedly to the effects of substance abuse or dependence in their own families, schools, and communities. Television commercials and shows routinely portray scenes of a father drinking beer as he watches a football game, and news reports often feature drive-by shootings and crimes committed by drug addicts and dealers. In some families, children receive their first sip of beer or wine from a parent, and even children whose parents are not users of substances know that many teenagers brag about "getting loaded" on weekends, and that some get into trouble when they are drunk or "high." In urban settings, children may watch addicts buying drugs or "shooting up" in empty lots or the hallways of their own apartment buildings. Older siblings or neighbors may introduce 9- or 10-year-olds into the drug trade by making them "runners," thereby insinuating them into an adult antisocial world that welcomes them primarily because of their immunity from prosecution.

What is the impact of growing up surrounded by older people who regulate their moods through using chemicals and whose lives seem totally committed to this experience? And what are the effects on a child when one or both parents are abusing or dependent on drugs or alcohol?

CLARIFICATION OF TERMINOLOGY

Before I proceed further, it is essential to define some of the terms that are used in this discussion of drugs and alcohol, and to outline some of the differing effects of various mood-altering chemicals on the individu-

272

als who ingest them. The *Diagnostic and Statistical Manual of Mental Disorders*, fourth edition (DSM-IV; American Psychiatric Association, 1994) includes the category of Substance Use Disorders; these disorders are subdivided into Substance Abuse and Substance Dependence. The substance causing a disorder may be either alcohol or one of 10 other substances listed in the DSM-IV; Polysubstance Abuse or Dependence is of course also possible.

The DSM-IV term Substance Dependence refers to a dysfunctional pattern of substance use leading to clinically important distress or impairment over a 1-year period, during which tolerance and withdrawal increase, use of and desire to obtain the substance are also increased, and other activities are given up because of substance use. (See American Psychiatric Association, 1994, p. 181, for specific criteria.)

Substance Abuse is not as severe as Substance Dependence, according to DSM-IV. It refers to a maladaptive pattern of substance use in its early phases, with danger signs such as not fulfilling major role obligations at work or home, and continuing to use a substance despite frequent interpersonal or social problems caused by the substance's effects. (Again, see American Psychiatric Association, 1994, pp. 182–183, for specific criteria.)

Straussner (1989) classifies the psychoactive drugs in terms of their distinctive effects on the central nervous system, and thus on a person's thinking and behavior. Table 13.1 presents Straussner's categorization.

IMPACT OF GROWING UP IN A
SUBSTANCE-DISORDERED FAMILY/ENVIRONMENT

Multiple Stressors

When parents are abusing or dependent on depressants, stimulants, narcotics/opiates, or psychodelics/hallucinogens, their ability to focus on and respond to their children is significantly impaired. Straussner (1989, p. 149) states that "clinicians and researchers have only recently recognized that growing up with a drug- or alcohol-abusing parent is frequently a highly traumatizing experience with long-lasting effects." Among the multiple stressors faced by children in substance-disordered homes is the sad reality that a parent's disorder "is likely to take precedence over [a] child's basic needs" (Tracy, 1994, p. 535). Other stressors on these children, according to Tracy (1994, citing Feig, 1990, and Gittler & McPherson, 1990), include the following:

- Chaotic and often dangerous neighborhoods
- Poverty and homelessness or unstable housing

TABLE 13.1. Effects of Different Categories of Substances on Individuals

Category of substance: Effects on brain:	<u>Depressants</u> Slow down, sedate brain tissues; alter judgment and behavior; cause agitation (hangover) in coming off.
Names of substances:	Alcoholic beverages; barbiturates and sedatives/hypnotics; minor tranquilizers (Librium, Valium); low doses of cannabinoids (marijuana and hashish).
Category of substance: Effects on brain:	<u>Stimulants</u> Increase or speed up function of brain; can produce acute delirium and psychosis (symptoms may include hallucinations, paranoia, and hypersexuality); violent behavior may occur with use of potent forms of cocaine ("freebase" or "crack").
Names of substances:	Amphetamines; cocaine; caffeine; nicotine.
Category of substance: Effects on brain:	<u>Narcotics or opiates</u> Decrease pain; create a sedative and tranquilizing effect; may cause stuporous inactivity (daydreaming/fantasies); may cause physical agitation upon withdrawal (panic and violent behavior may occur at this time).
Names of substances:	Opium, morphine, heroin, codeine, paregoric, methadone; Demerol, Darvon, Prinadol.
Category of substance: Effects on brain:	<u>Psychedelics/hallucinogens</u> Produce gross distortions of thoughts and sensory processes (e.g., visual hallucinations, distorted body image); may produce depersonalization, depression, hostility; may lead to violence because of anxiety and misperceptions of reality.
Names of substances:	LSD; PCP ("angel dust"); DOM; STP; mescaline; psilocybin.

Note. Adapted from Straussner (1989, pp. 151–152). Copyright 1989 by New York University Press. Adapted by permission.

- Parents who lack an extended family and community support system
- Parents who may have been victimized themselves as children or adults
- Parents with poor parenting skills and few or no role models for effective coping

Johnson (1991, p. 276) points out that "in the chemically dependent family, the child is in a permanent state of crisis, with inconsistency and chaos being the norm."

Various forms of child maltreatment often occur in families with substance-disordered parents. These may include neglect, physical abuse, and/or sexual abuse. The concept of "maltreatment" (according to Gonzales-Ramos & Goldstein, 1989, p. 5) refers to *all* physical abuse or marked neglect of children. Specifically, an abused child has parents or caretakers who inflict or permit injury or protracted impairment of physical or emotional health, or allow the risk of such injury. A neglected child has parents or caretakers who fail to supply basic care, supervision, or guardianship, or who actually abandon him or her.

Numerous studies have found a correlation between child maltreatment and substance use disorders, ranging from 40% nationwide (Daro & McCurdy, 1991) to 80–90% in certain localities (Feig, 1990). The most common form of child maltreatment by substance-disordered parents is child neglect, according to Black and Mayer (1980). The nature of this neglect may range from a general lack of supervision to "total inattention to such basic needs of children as food and clothing" (U.S. Children's Bureau, 1978, p. 59). Tracy (1994) cites Besharov (1989) as reporting that in New York State over 73% of neglect-related child fatalities are attributed to parental alcohol and drug abuse.

Sexual abuse and incest are also common in substance-disordered families (Barnard, 1984; Copans, 1989; Johnson, 1991; Tormes, 1968), possibly because of the diffuse parent–child boundaries in such families, which are characterized by role reversals and inappropriate parental role maintenance. Wertz (1986) suggests that over 50% of physically and sexually abused children come from substance-disordered families. Straussner (1989, p. 151) points out that "any psychoactive substance that produces a state of intoxication . . . can affect parenting behavior," because of alterations in the individual's judgment and behavior. Indeed, substance-disordered parents are often unable to care for *themselves* adequately; thus, it is not surprising that they cannot meet the needs of young children.

However, despite this disturbing picture, we must emphasize that the relationship between child maltreatment and substance use disorders is considered correlational, *not* causal. Moreover, the incidence of maltreatment varies according to type of substance used and other factors. Child abuse has been found most frequently in families in which there is an alcohol- or opiate-addicted mother; in families in which parental violence is common; and in families with low financial status and poor living conditions (Black & Mayer, 1980). Clearly, many elements in addition to substance use contribute to the constellation of family stress in which a young child becomes victimized (Belsky, 1993).

The child born into a substance-disordered family is at risk of a range of problems in addition to maltreatment. Beginning *in utero*, for example, infants of cocaine-using mothers suffer a decreased growth rate, and their behavior as toddlers tends to be hyperexcitable, fussy, and impulsive. (Petitti & Coleman, 1990, as reported in Feinberg, 1995). Even more startling than this information is the finding that "children who were exposed to cocaine use in the *home* had more serious behavior problems than those exposed in the womb" (Youngstrom, 1991, as reported in Feinberg, 1995, p. 241; emphasis added here). In addition to behavior problems, lower intellectual and educational functioning has been found in children whose mothers use drugs of all types (Feinberg, 1995).

Multiple Losses

Because of the numerous problems in substance-disordered families, loss is an ever-present reality that threatens children's sense of security and safety. On the most basic level, these children are deprived of a structured, predictable routine, because of their parents' inconsistent moods and behavior. The children never know when they may have to take total care of themselves, in addition to their parents. This seriously interferes with the children's ability to become involved with peer activities, since the parents' need may take precedence over the children's wishes for more age-appropriate involvement. Often such a child feels embarrassed, "different," and even ashamed of his or her family circumstances. This can lead to social isolation, loneliness, and depression. The child's very childhood has been lost.

If a child is maltreated and comes to the attention of child protective services, separation of the child and parent may be mandated to protect the child from additional harm. This separation, unfortunately, constitutes an even more wrenching loss for the child, who must adapt to a foster family of strangers. The parent, in turn, may feel that the removal of the child is a punitive response to the addiction, rather than a remedial effort to help. Certainly this major loss to the family is one that may be very difficult to reverse in the future, since children from substance-disordered families have low rates of reunification with their biological parents once they enter placement, despite all efforts toward permanency planning (Tracy, 1994).

ETHICAL DILEMMAS AND PRESSURES ON PRACTITIONERS

Numerous ethical dilemmas and pressures confront practitioners who work with substance-disordered families. Because the use of many substances is illegal, and because many people consider drug or even alcohol abuse or dependence a psychological "weakness" rather than a disease, addicted individuals with substance use disorders tend to deny and hide their problems. In addition, denial is an unconscious defense that permits the individuals to continue their substance use. It is understandable that these persons respond with suspicion and rejection to well-meaning helping efforts, in view of society's tendency to denigrate and stigmatize them. Substance-disordered parents may be oblivious to the havoc of their lives. However, when their behavior puts their young children at risk, then society flexes the muscles of the legal system, challenges these parents' behavior, and insists on detoxification and change as conditions for their retaining custody of their children. These individuals' right to self-determination no longer applies when their disorders keep them from being effective parents, and therefore interfere with their children's rights.

In circumstances like this, many ethical dilemmas arise for social workers, who want to advocate for dependent children, yet do not wish to alienate the children's parents or to rupture, through mandatory placement, the attachment bond between children and parents. Sometimes workers agree with society's negative feelings about a *mother* who neglects her children, not fully understanding that a substance use disorder can seriously compromise an individual's judgment and behavior. Of course, the absent or neglectful *father* also shares responsibility for his children, but the sexist views of our society exact a higher standard for women; as a result, mothers are often penalized for neglect, while similar behavior in men is ignored (Feinberg, 1995; Goldberg, 1995). Of course, in many single-parent families headed by women, the fathers are unknown.

The "Rescue Fantasy"

In teaching, I have found that master's-level students working with substance-disordered families often progress from an initial strong stance of wanting to protect ("rescue") dependent children through filing complaints about neglect or abuse, to subsequent observation that the children's situations do not improve appreciably in cases where placement occurs. Furthermore, the students witness much bitterness and unhappiness connected with these placements. Seasoned workers learn through experience that the concept of "the best interests of the child" has to be weighed against that of "the least detrimental alternative"; this requires "a realistic appraisal of existing resources" (Kamen & Gewirtz, 1989, p. 180) as a basis for determining the choice of child care in a given situation. Sometimes *no* good alternative is available, and a concerted effort to help the family members remain together offers the best prospect for "rescuing" a child.

Weighing Differing Needs of Children and Parents

It may be very stressful for a worker to have to determine the degree of risk to a child in two alternative situations, neither of which appears desirable. As Tracy (1994) states, "although the emotional limbo of being in foster care carries its own set of risks, remaining in a substance-abusing home also carries risks" (p. 535).

The separation of a child from his or her family generates intense feelings for *all* parties involved. This serious move, which is intended to protect the child, allows the laws of the state to intervene in family life and to supersede the rights and authority of parents in situations of suspected child maltreatment. However, the goal of permanency planning as reflected in the Adoption Assistance and Child Welfare Reform Act (P.L. 96-272, 1980) is to provide intensive preventive services for families at risk, in order to reduce the need for placement and to reunify families in a timely manner when placement has occurred. Thus, the role of the social worker frequently consists of offering services to substance-disordered parents (even when they do not want this help), in order to prevent the out-of-home placement of their children. Tracy (1994) points to the need for demonstrating "reasonable effort" to provide services that address the family circumstances (such as parental substance use disorders) that put the child at risk of placement. Clearly, the critical assistance in these cases is to get substance-disordered parents into treatment.

In an ideal world, the removal of children from their parents would never be necessary. If parents were negligent or unable to carry out their child care responsibilities, some form of assistance would be offered to families on a temporary basis, to provide respite and insure the well-being of the children. In essence, this is the purpose of foster care: "not to rescue the child, but to offer respite for the family until life becomes manageable" (Minuchin, 1995, p. 253). However, there is a broad gap between the ideal and the real. Effective treatment for substance use disorders takes time, is costly, and is often characterized by recurrence of the addictive behavior. Social workers and others may doubt parents' ability to complete a detoxification and treatment program, and/or to sustain their sobriety after discharge. In truth, although treatment is initially costly, it is highly cost-effective *in the long run*.

Knowledge that a substance use disorder is a "family (i.e., intergenerational) disease" (Straussner, 1989) may perpetuate attitudes of determinism and powerlessness among workers who genuinely want to "rescue" children, and who view removal of the children from their "diseased" families as the preferred method of helping. Of course, a child should only be removed if a parent refuses treatment, and neglect or abuse continues.

Impact of Mandatory Reporting

Although only about 20% of all reported cases of child maltreatment actually result in court involvement (Kamen & Gewirtz, 1989), every report must be investigated, and the very presence of child protective services can have a profound impact on families because of its implicit challenge to the family's autonomy. It also has a strong impact on the worker, who realizes that his or her report to child protective services will threaten the helping relationship because of the client's resentment about being reported. A combination of empathy and authority is necessary in working with nonvoluntary court-referred maltreating parents. (See Chapter 14 of the present book, as well as Kamen & Gewirtz, 1989, for further discussion of this topic.)

Issues of Confidentiality

Confidentiality has specific limitations in situations where the court is involved. This can present a formidable additional obstacle in the worker–client relationship, since the client knows that the worker has a legal obligation to report any incidents that indicate recurrence of maltreatment. In such cases, even when the worker informs the client that a report will be made, the parent often deeply resents the worker's actions.

———————— ❖ ————————

A brief case example illustrates this point. Mrs. Jones, a 25-year-old pregnant mother of three sons (ages 6½, 5½, and 1), was mandated to receive individual therapy with a focus on parenting skills. Her children had been placed in foster care for 8 months because of neglect when she allegedly left them alone for extended periods of time. A neighbor stated that Mrs. Jones took drugs and hung around with drug dealers, but she denied this allegation; she also denied that she had left her children unattended.

Mrs. Jones seemed distant and angry in counseling sessions. She often refused to engage in discussion, answer questions, or talk about her feelings or behavior, or about how she was managing now that the children had returned home. She also refused to discuss her pregnancy, stating that she didn't like to have other people "minding her business."

The worker felt that little progress was made in 3½ months, stating in a case summary that "this mother is unresponsive, distant, critical and punitive toward the children, showing them only occasional displays of warmth."

In supervision, the worker recognized that she and the client were both "trapped" in a relationship neither of them wanted. Although the worker admitted her feelings of anger toward the client, she was unable to move beyond this to recognize with the client how the issue of their *mutual* anger and need for control prevented their working together on meeting the children's needs for effective parenting.

This brief vignette illustrates the intense feelings generated by the removal of children from a mother's custody when her allegedly neglectful behavior put them at risk of potential harm. The possible or even probable substance involvement of a parent merits close attention, but it is not in itself grounds for evidence of child maltreatment in most states (Tracy, 1994, citing English, 1990).

Work with parents who have been charged with some form of child maltreatment requires great sensitivity and skill. Often such parents distrust "the system," and insofar as they view the worker as part of this system, they will be very difficult to engage. The key to effective helping is to discuss a parent's resistance openly, while also identifying the parent's strengths and attempting to form a mutually acceptable alliance.

Another situation that requires sensitivity and skill on the part of the worker is that in which a child reveals ongoing abuse, but asks the worker to keep this revelation a secret because of fear of destroying his or her family. The worker does not really have a choice in this case, since reporting of abuse is mandatory. *Confidentiality cannot be maintained when a child's safety is in jeopardy.* The worker must make this clear to the child, in a manner that assures the child's protection and keeps the child from feeling betrayed by the worker. The new revision of the National Association of Social Workers (NASW) code of ethics (NASW, 1996, section 1.01) points out that social workers' responsibility to the larger society and/or their specific legal obligations may supersede the loyalty owed to clients, and clients should be advised accordingly.

COMBINING INDIVIDUAL AND FAMILY HELPING METHODS

Because substance use disorders affect individuals, families, and communities, a broad approach to helping is necessary, using a combination of psychological, educational, behavioral, and environmental interventions. The primary focus in such a case must be on the substance use problem itself, because, as Copans (1989) has stated, "treating a family with [a substance-disordered] member without acknowledging, confronting, focusing on, and dealing with the [substance use] is generally doomed to failure" (p. 277). Furthermore, after treatment, the best chances for lifetime recovery are afforded by ongoing participation in one of the Twelve-Step self-help groups, such as Alcoholics Anonymous (AA), Narcotics Anonymous (NA), or Cocaine Anonymous (CA). Whereas the use of alcohol or drugs previously dominated the substance-disordered person's life, the focus after detoxification (if needed) and treatment must change to a commitment to remain drug- and alcohol-free. The disorder is not "cured," but, like diabetes, can be controlled if the individual initiates and sustains a certain lifestyle. This usually entails finding new friends who share the recovering individual's goal of maintaining sobriety. Contacts with the previous network of substance-using peers must cease. Moving to a new neighborhood, when this is possible, symbolizes leaving the past behind and represents a new beginning.

Helping Substance-Disordered Parents

Most specialists in the field of substance use disorder agree that few individuals enter treatment voluntarily. Because of the denial that characterizes the substance-disordered population, a family member usually must insist on treatment, or someone like a social worker must threaten to remove a child from parental custody unless the parent agrees to enroll in a detoxification and rehabilitation program.

Many detoxification programs (which are necessary for alcohol and opioid dependence, for instance) are carried out on an inpatient medical or psychiatric unit. This almost always requires a parent–child separation during a 5-day period. Moreover, detoxification is only the first step in treatment; intensive, ongoing educational and other programs are needed. Goldberg (1995) points out that few treatment programs provide accommodation for children with their mothers, and she believes that the high costs of these may limit the widespread development of such programs in the future. Ironically, the cost of such treatment is much less costly than is foster care.

One model program, in existence for more than 30 years, is Meta House in Milwaukee, Wisconsin. This program treats women and children *together*, with the average length of stay between 9 and 18 months. About 25 women complete the program every year (Feinberg, 1995). Treatment is multifaceted, and is successful in 90% of cases, with no recidivism. Components of this model program include educational/ vocational counseling and training, assistance with housing, monitoring of physical health, legal assistance, and treatment focused on parenting and improvement of the mother–child relationship. Unfortunately, the high cost per family probably precludes broad duplication of this model program, no matter how successful its methods.

Less costly treatment approaches to helping substance-disordered parents on an *outpatient* basis following detoxification include day treatment, intensive patient rehabilitation programs, ego-supportive individual treatment, various self-help groups, and intervention with family members (Goldberg, 1995; Straussner, 1989). Whatever the modality, attention must be paid to environmental factors, such as housing, employment, and health needs, in addition to counseling focused on building the parents' self-esteem and self-confidence.

Family Approaches

Just as addiction occurs over time, the response of a family to a substance-disordered member may vary over time, according to the changing individual and family life cycle stresses that occur during the onset and course of the addictive process (Krestan & Bepko, 1989). Often "the family, as well as the [substance user], develops a rigid system of denial in an attempt to avoid acknowledgment of the problem" (Krestan & Bepko, 1989, p. 486). However, when parents are at midlife (mid-40s to mid-60s), they are most likely to seek help for alcohol use disorders; this may be after the children have left home. The course of disorders related to the use of illicit drugs, which are more rapid in their addictive effects than alcohol is, probably creates an earlier and stronger family recognition and responses. See Straussner (1993) for a discussion of the impact of different substances on the family.

Some general guidelines set forth by Deutsch (1982, pp. 127–128) for the treatment of alcohol problems in the family may, with slight revisions, apply also to the family treatment of other substance use disorders. They are adapted here as follows:

• Make a careful assessment of substance use problems in the two prior generations (i.e., look for evidence of the intergenerational persistence of such problems).

• Insist on sobriety/abstinence as a precondition of treatment. Recommend the attendance of the substance-disordered person at AA, NA, CA, or (when relevant) Parents Anonymous (PA), and the attendance of family members at Al-Anon or Alateen, *at least six times*.

• Educate the family about substance abuse/dependence.

• Encourage open discussion of the problem among family members and other families with similar problems.

• Pay attention to the special needs of the children. If they have assumed a parentified role, they need permission to give this up in favor of more age-appropriate behavior; this may require ongoing work to accomplish.

Helping the Children of Substance-Disordered Parents

The following principles, proposed originally by Deutsch (1982, pp. 127–128) to help children in alcoholic families, have been likewise adapted to children of parents with other substance use problems:

• "You are not alone."
• "It's not your fault."
• "It's not the substance user's fault either."
• "Substance users can and do recover."
• "You need and deserve help for yourself."

It is notable that even this chapter, whose title is intended to reflect a major focus on *children* in substance-disordered families, emphasizes the addicted *parents* and the family system, without detailed mention of the stress on the children and on helping the children with this stress. Of course, helping the parents ultimately helps the children most effectively in the long run; nevertheless, a child with a substance-disordered parent deserves individual attention to his or her own considerable needs, which are frequently overlooked by family members and other helpers.

GROUPS FOR CHILDREN OF SUBSTANCE-DISORDERED PARENTS

A few programs in different parts of the United States do target the children of alcoholics, regardless of whether their parents are in treatment (Deutsch, DiCicco, & Mills, 1979; Zevon, 1990). These contrast with treatment approaches that focus primarily on substance-disordered adults. Traditional alcoholism treatment focused first on recovering alcoholics/ addicts, and second on their spouses or parents; children often were not included (Zevon, 1990). This pattern of bypassing children's needs, or subverting them to the overriding needs of adults, is endemic and very demoralizing to workers who are sensitive to children. Unfortunately, this issue is not unique to the field of substance use disorders, and professional consciousness-raising and advocacy efforts will be required to resolve it. This is discussed further in Chapter 15.

A School-Based Approach Combining
Prevention and Treatment

Deutsch (1979) pilot-tested a school-based primary prevention program (Cambridge and Somerville Program for Alcoholism Rehabilitation, or CASPAR) in a working-class community in Massachusetts. The purpose of CASPAR was, and still is, to educate *all* children about alcoholism early in their lives. Because this program was begun in response to community concerns about the high proportion of teens who were drinking heavily, teachers are trained to provide alcohol education as a prevention strategy. Children from alcoholic families (estimated to constitute half the school population) receive educational interventions alongside their peers from nonalcoholic families.

When, during classroom discussions about alcohol, some children reveal themselves as needing help, they are offered a therapeutically oriented alcohol education group. This is designed to help children cope with the emotional distress of living with family alcoholism and prevent them from using alcohol abusively in their teenage years or as adults (Davis, Johnston, DiCicco, & Orenstein, 1985). Each group consists of 8–12 participants with an age span of no more than 3 years; the groups meet during school hours for 45-minute periods over a 10-week time span. Group coleaders are guidance counselors, psychologists, or social workers experienced in providing treatment services to children of alcoholics.

The groups include specific activities for children that stimulate discussion of addiction. Among these are special games, movies, puppet shows, coloring books, storybooks, arts and crafts, and other activities, according to the curriculum format developed by CASPAR (1978).

The leaders take every opportunity to emphasize Deutsch's five principles for children (listed earlier), in order to help the children understand and put in perspective their experience of growing up in alcoholic families. Evaluation studies comparing responses of participants in the first and final group sessions show impressive changes in how the children understand alcoholism (DiCicco et al., 1984). Of course, the program originators realize that a 10-week group is likely to have limited effects. To the credit of this program design, alcohol education is *required* in 7th, 8th, and 10th grades, thereby reinforcing the earlier exposure during the elementary grades. In addition to the school-based program for the older children, there are after-school alcohol education groups run by trained high-school-age peer leaders. Referral to Alateen groups is an additional community resource appropriate for teens.

This admirable community effort to prevent alcoholism demonstrates the necessity of dealing with substance use disorders in families *over time.* It is not expected that one 10-week program in fourth grade will adequately address the stresses of a child who lives daily with alcoholism in his or her family. Davis et al. (1985) describe a network of services structured differently at each age level that all reiterate the same messages about alcohol use and alcoholism. The hope of the program formulators is that "children who receive support at one age level will be able to connect with similar services later and will know that help is available when they need it" (Davis et al., 1985, p. 363).

An Open-Ended Outpatient Approach

Another approach to helping children is exemplified by the Archway Program, run by Yonkers General Hospital in Mount Vernon, New York, which provides after-school groups for children of alcoholics and addicts (Zevon, 1990). This treatment program is licensed by the New York State Office of Alcoholism and Substance Abuse Services. A distinctive feature of the program is that children can continue to be served on a long-term basis, depending on their needs and family situation. Children can enroll even if their parents are not receiving simultaneous services, although the goal of the program is to provide recovery groups for each family member in parallel treatment tracks. Most parents are or have been in treatment.

Each after-school group consists of six male and female children within a 2-year age range between the ages of 5 and 18 years. As in the CASPAR model, the groups are structured around activities that facilitate open discussion of the impact of alcohol/drug use on family life. One such activity is called the Feelings-in-the-Bottle or Feelings-in-the-Drug-Syringe drawing exercise. The children are given large sheets of poster paper and instructed to draw a bottle, can, syringe, or vial, and then to indicate the "feelings" that come out of this container as the substance enters a person's body. Figures 13.1 to Figure 13.3 show some typical drawings that children using this exercise in a group have produced. After the drawings are completed, the group leaders post them on the wall and encourage each child to talk about what he or she drew. This group experience offers a great sense of validation and support to children in substance-disordered families, who up to this point may have felt very alone and isolated with their feelings.

Figure 13.1, for example, reflects an 8-year-old girl's ambivalent feelings—of sadness about a parent's drinking, yet also her feelings of love for alcoholic parent. Children younger than 8 years often have trouble reconciling two apparently contradictory feelings, such as being angry at someone they love. This would be an important clarifying point for the group leaders to mention as the child displays her drawing.

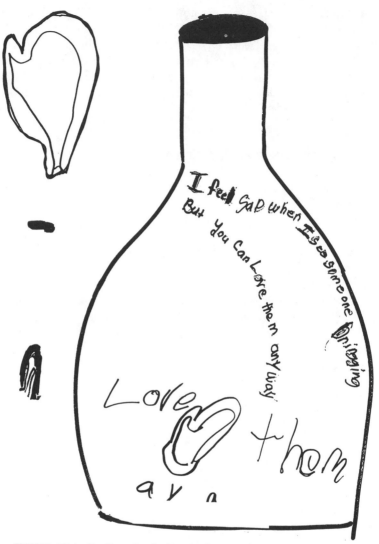

FIGURE 13.1. Feelings-in-the-Bottle drawing by an 8-year-old girl.

Figure 13.2, by a 12-year-old girl, is replete with a variety of feelings. She mentions "sad," "angry," and "ashamed," as well as "stupid" and "dumb." It's not clear whether these last two terms refer to herself or her alcoholic parent; however, this child recognizes the impact of the drinking on self-esteem. Another cause for concern is this child's phrase in the lower left corner of the bottle—"like I'm not a real person." This

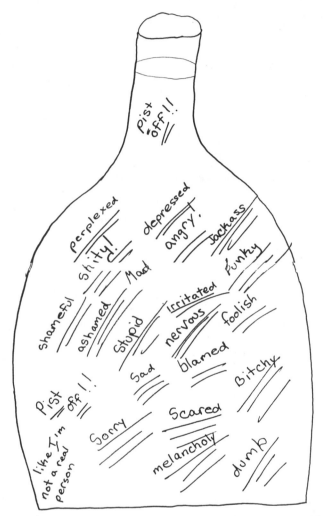

FIGURE 13.2. Feelings-in-the-Bottle drawing by a 12-year-old girl.

seems to refer to her awareness that the alcohol causes her parent to ignore her individual needs because the alcohol takes precedence in the
parent's mind. This child needs validation that her needs *are* important,
even when her parent ignores them. This recognition would be very supportive not only to the child, but also to others in the group who also
feel as if they are unimportant to their parents.

Figure 13.3, a 15-year-old girl's drawing of a syringe, contains many
typical emotions of an injection drug user, including the word "misfit"

on the needle. Other feelings mentioned reflect the unhappiness and disgust associated with drug use. Although this girl's age places her beyond the range covered in this book (which does not include the adolescent years), I have included this drawing here because of the probability that the drawings of teenagers who attend separate groups will be seen by younger children on the walls of the group room and the hallway of the agency. The intention is to have *all* children and their parents exposed to the wide-ranging effects of substance use disorders.

Videotapes, Workbooks, and Storybooks for Children

Video and written materials are useful in children's activity/support groups to stimulate discussion and sharing about the experience of growing up in a substance-disordered family. The Children of Alcoholics Foundation has produced an exemplary videotape, *Kids Talking to Kids*, which would be a wonderful resource for children's groups. The "Resource Materials" list at the end of this chapter provides sources of information for obtaining this and other videotapes, workbooks, and children's stories that would be useful to leaders of children's groups.

In using a videotape, workbook, or storybook, the group leader tells the children that other children in other places have also grown up in families with substance use disorders, and that the video or book tells about one (or more) such examples. The leader also mentions that after the planned activity, the children will have the opportunity to talk about their own experience. After trying to elicit from the group some of the

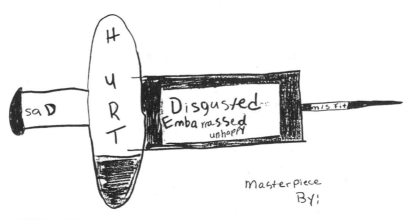

FIGURE 13.3. Feelings-in-the-Drug-Syringe drawing by a 15-year-old girl.

universal themes that emerge from the video or book, the leader invites the group members to make comparisons with their own life experiences.

Summary

In summary, the group experience combats the isolation and shame of each child, while making explicit the fact that many other children are going through similar experiences. The challenge to the leaders is to provide support to the children, while validating each child's need to live in a family in which he or she is the "apple of the parent's eye," rather than an unimportant family member who has to fend for himself or herself.

THE CASE OF AHMED, AGE 8

Family Information

Mother	Anna, age 33, European-American; recovering alcoholic (9 years).
Father	Josef, age 49, African-American; history of heroin and crack dependence and spouse abuse; Vietnam veteran; in prison for selling drugs (2 years).
Child client	Ahmed, age 8, biracial, third grade; acting out aggressively with peers and siblings since father was imprisoned.
Sister	Sena, age 7, biracial, second grade; some physical problems; not doing well in school.
Brother	Abdul, age 4, biracial; hyperactive.

Presenting Problem

Ahmed was becoming very disruptive toward his peers in his children of alcoholics (COA) group. The leader believed that the boy could not tolerate the emotionally charged issues that were discussed in the group, and that the group was not appropriate for him at this time. In addition, Ahmed had recently been transferred to a different school within his district because of his disruptive conduct within the school setting. At home, Ahmed's mother noticed that Ahmed was fighting more aggressively with his brother and sister than in the past.

Because of this regression in Ahmed's behavior, the decision was made to work with the boy on an individual basis, with the goal of returning him to the group at a later time.

Background

From the time he was a toddler, Ahmed had witnessed his father's physical abuse of his mother. At one time Ahmed had lived in a family shelter with his mother and siblings because of the serious family violence. During this period, Ahmed's father was arrested and sent to prison for selling drugs. The boy was 6 years old at that time, and he had not seen his father since then.

When Ahmed was born, his mother was in the early stages of recovery from alcohol use, and his father had recently undergone detoxification from heroin. The father's abstinence, however, did not last long, and he used crack heavily for several years prior to his arrest.

Ahmed suffered another loss about the same time that his father went to prison: His maternal grandfather died suddenly of a heart attack. Ahmed's mother stated that the boy had been very close to his grandfather, and could not understand why he did not come back for holidays such as Thanksgiving to be with the family.

Assessment and Plan for Intervention

Ahmed had suffered the simultaneous loss of his father and his grandfather, and had witnessed the physical abuse of his mother at his father's hands on many occasions. He was undoubtedly confused about aggression and love, and may even have believed, because of his young age, that something *he* did caused his father to abuse his mother or made his grandfather die.

In addition to his possible cognitive confusion about the losses of his father and grandfather, Ahmed had had to cope with chronic stress and inconsistency as endemic to growing up in a family with substance-disordered parents. Although in time Ahmed would benefit from the support of knowing that he was not alone with this experience, at the moment he needed help related to the absence of the two male figures in his life, and his possible misunderstandings about this.

The recommendation was for time-limited individual counseling with a male counselor, to work on issues related to the domestic violence and his father's and grandfather's absences from his life.

Interventions

Ahmed was assigned to a male M.S.W. student who worked with him for several months, using a variety of play therapy methods. The student mentioned to the boy in their first meeting that he would be seeing him for only "a few months," in order to avoid further abandonment issues when the student's internship was completed.

During several months of weekly play therapy sessions, Ahmed chose to play with a dollhouse and family dolls, which he would involve in very violent episodes. During the play, the student therapist would label the feelings of the child doll, thus validating the emotions of fear, helplessness, and anger. The fact that Ahmed repeated this violent dollhouse play suggested that it was very significant for him, and that through the play he was assuming mastery over a situation in which he had felt very helpless and hopeless. Sometimes, in the play, Ahmed would step in (as the male child doll) and protect the mother from being physically abused by the father. This made him feel powerful and effective; it also enabled the therapist to praise the boy doll for his *wish* to protect his mother, despite the fact that in reality little boys are not supposed to have this responsibility, since their parents are supposed to protect them.

During the play Ahmed also revealed his fear of losing his mother because she smoked cigarettes, and he thought that she would die as a result of her smoking. (His grandfather had been a heavy smoker.) The child's sensitivity to loss was explained to his mother by the therapist, who counseled the mother to reassure Ahmed that she wanted to take good care of herself so she could live a long time. The fact that Ahmed's grandfather had smoked was playing into his fears about his mother.

Other aspects of the work with Ahmed included educating him about the diseases of alcoholism and drug dependence, and clarifying that substances can make parents act in a hurtful manner. The therapist also referred from time to time to the COA group, reinforcing that other children also had to cope with similar problems, and stating that he hoped Ahmed would return to the group soon.

In fact, Ahmed did return to the COA group after 3 months of individual therapy. When the student therapist reminded Ahmed that he would be leaving the agency soon, Ahmed's behavior regressed temporarily. However, the therapist was able to help Ahmed verbalize his sadness and anger about losing the relationship, so the aftereffects of this loss did not seriously impinge on Ahmed's life.

———————— ❖ ————————

Discussion

This case demonstrates the multiple stresses on a child who witnessed physical abuse in the context of growing up in a family with a father who was actively substance-dependent. Ahmed lacked an appropriate male role model, and when his father abused the mother, he experienced conflict between his wish to protect his mother and his guilt because he was not able to do so.

Sometimes children such as Ahmed cannot tolerate a group format in which other children may discuss witnessing parent abuse. Often a period of individual therapy helps to clear the child's confusion and guilt, so that return to the group format is possible later. Certainly, it seems that a child like Ahmed would benefit from ongoing support on an indefinite basis.

CONCLUDING COMMENTS

Unlike many of the topics discussed in this book, substance abuse and dependence are lifelong problems with repercussions through the generations. Therefore, the first approach to helping must be education about substance use disorders. Children and adults alike need to understand the implications of having such a disorder, so that they will be able to make rational decisions for themselves and their family members.

Because a substance use disorder affects not only the individual, but all his or her family members and the community in which the individual lives, the approaches to helping must be comprehensive and long-term. Interventions must always begin with a commitment to remain substance-free, but that is only the beginning, since extensive life changes and ongoing treatment will be necessary to maintain sobriety. Counseling for the addicted individual and for the family members, and special programs for children are necessary to address this problem adequately. Groups—either Twelve-Step self-help groups or professionally led groups—help the addicted person and family members realize that they are not alone. The support given and received in groups can help build self-esteem, even as the group constitutes a new friendship network.

Preventive efforts in the schools have been shown to have positive results in reducing substance use disorders. Because of the serious consequences of such disorders, an argument can be made for implementing substance use prevention groups as part of *every* school's curriculum. In addition, every outpatient treatment program for substance use disorders should have a component for children, in order to help children understand the disease and, it is hoped, to prevent its recurrence in the next generation.

DISCUSSION QUESTIONS AND ROLE-PLAY EXERCISES

1. Discuss the implications of the statement that a substance use disorder is a family disease. How does this apply to the question of which family members to see, and to setting up short- and long-term goals?

2. Role-play a situation in which the child reveals recurring physical abuse to a social worker, but asks the worker "not to tell" because of fear of reprisal. First, demonstrate what you would say to the child; second, show how you would deal with the parent.

3. How can the worker best respond to a parent's anger at "the system" and tendency to view all helpers as critical and threatening?

4. Discuss the tension between "children's rights" and the rights of parents as this affects appropriate treatment for children in substance-disordered families.

5. Role-play a session in which the worker discusses with a parent the effects of the parent's substance use on his or her children, as preparation for the children's beginning treatment.

RESOURCE MATERIALS

Videotapes

Kids Talking to Kids
17 minutes ($75)
Children of Alcoholics Foundation
555 Madison Avenue, 20th floor
New York, NY 10022
800-359-COAF

Soft Is the Heart of a Child
35 minutes ($195)
Hazelden Foundation
Box 176
Center City, MN 55012-0176
800-328-9000

Books/Workbooks

Note: Ages are specified, when indicated.

Black, C. (1979). *My dad loves me, my dad has a disease: A workbook for children of alcoholics*. Newport Beach, CA: Alcoholism, Children, Therapy. (Ages 5–10.)
Brooks, C. (1981). *The secret everyone knows*. San Diego, CA: Kroc Foundation. (Older children.)
DiGiovanni, K. (1986). *My house is different*. Center City, MN: Hazelden Foundation. (Ages 6 and up.)
Hastings, J., & Typpo, M. (1984). *An elephant in the living room*. Minneapolis: Comp Care. (Ages 7–13.)

Jones, P. (1983). *The brown bottle*. Center City, MN: Hazelden Foundation.

Kenney, K., & Krull, H. (1980). *Sometimes my mom drinks too much*. Milwaukee, WI: Raintree Children's Books.

McFarland, R. (1991). *Drugs and your brothers and sisters*. New York: Rosen. (Ages 10 and up.)

Melquist, E. (1974). *Pepper*. Frederick, MD: Frederick County Council on Alcoholism. (Ages 5–10.)

Seixas, J. (1979). *Living with a parent who drinks too much*. New York: Greenwillow Books. (Ages 8–12.)

Snyder, A. (1975). *First step*. New York: Holt, Rinehart & Winston.

What's drunk, mama? (1977). New York: Al-Anon Family Group Headquarters.

Winthrop and Munchie talk about alcohol. (1983). La Jolla, CA: Operation Cork.

Woods, G., & Woods, H. (1985). *Cocaine*. New York: Watts. (Ages 10–14.)

CHAPTER 14

Child Victims and Witnesses of Family Violence

The idea of home as a sanctuary has long and deep roots. Even adults who accept the presence of violence on the streets of their community expect to feel safe behind the locked doors of their own homes. The poet May Sarton poignantly refers to "a house where every man may take his ease, May come to shelter from the outer air, A little house where he may find his peace" (1936–1938/1973, p. 43).

If only this were universally true! The idea of the home as a sanctuary simply does not apply to many children who are abused by their parents or caretakers, and whose hours in school represent a respite from the verbal and physical attacks that they witness and experience behind the closed doors of their homes. Gelles (1979), defining violence as "an act carried out with the intention of physically injuring another person" (p. 78), states that people are more likely to be hit, beat up, physically injured, or even killed in their own homes by another family member than anywhere else or by anyone else in U.S. society (p. 11). This suggests that home, far from being a sanctuary, is a place of danger and fear for many children.

DEFINITION AND SCOPE OF THE PROBLEM

In this chapter, the term "family violence" refers to verbal threats and behavioral assaults made by individual family members upon other individuals in the family and upon their pets and personal property. The fact that "a child may be extremely traumatized by violence exerted by an adult against the child's mother, a family pet, or personal property" has been noted by Miller (1989, p. 419). Pynoos and Eth (1985) warn that children who witness extreme acts of violence "represent a population at significant risk of developing anxiety, depressive, phobic, conduct, and posttraumatic stress disorders" (p. 19).

The topic of domestic violence has attracted growing media attention and increased public awareness and outrage since the mid-1970s. Traditionally, a patriarchal system condoned the battering of women, but the formation of the National Coalition against Domestic Violence in 1978 raised public consciousness and led to the development of shelters, support groups, and improved legislation for battered women. Nonetheless, the problem continues. In the United States in 1990, there were an estimated 85,800 arrests for crimes against family members (Federal Bureau of Investigation, 1991). Approximately one-fourth of all murders in the United States occur within the family, and one-half of those are spouse killings (Margolin, 1979, as reported in Gilliland & James, 1993).

Many children both witness and personally experience violence in their families. The *Harvard Mental Health Letter* (1991) reports that children witness 10–20% of the homicides in the United States, and that they either know about or witness 10% of the rapes. Furthermore, children, themselves can become the targets of uncontrolled rage. In 1989 there were an estimated 1,225 reported child abuse fatalities among the estimated 2.4 million cases of suspected child abuse and neglect reports filed (National Committee for Prevention of Child Abuse, 1990). From 1% to 5% of children may be victims of incest, and several times that number are subjected to serious physical abuse or see their mothers, brothers, and sisters being beaten.

Because children are helpless and terrified in the face of the violent acts of adults, the witnessing and experiencing of this behavior may result in "profound changes in the child's [belief] about the safety and security of future intimate human relationships" (Pynoos & Eth, 1985, p. 27). Unable to trust their parents to serve as protectors, children may be overwhelmed with a sense of fear, betrayal, and loneliness regarding their present and future security. Dread about the possible repetition of the abuse may cause defensive reactions in the children, such as distancing, wariness, and avoidance of the frightening parents and other adults. Some of these responses correspond to the criteria for Posttraumatic Stress Disorder (PTSD), which are discussed more fully later in this chapter.

> Psychological trauma is especially damaging when it involves a violation of trust and a distortion of family intimacy. For a child who is repeatedly abused physically or sexually, the stress is constant and the threat is always present. . . . *the source of terror is also the only source of comfort.* . . . abused children understand little of what is happening, since everyone around them is ignoring it or lying about it. They are systematically confused and misled; *incest is disguised as love, beating as discipline.* (*Harvard Mental Health Letter*, 1991, pp. 1–2; emphasis added)

The literature documents that children's present and future behavior may be adversely affected by exposure to domestic violence (Rosenbaum & O'Leary, 1981), and that both marital discord and punitive maternal parenting styles are related to children's behavioral and emotional problems (Hershorn & Rosenbaum, 1985).

THE ASSESSMENT OF THE ABUSED CHILD

This chapter deals with the child as both the victim and the witness to various forms of family violence. The topic encompasses both the physical and sexual abuse of a child by another family member, as well as the witnessing by a child of either form of abuse perpetrated by one family member upon another. The special stresses involved in *witnessing* violence are discussed and demonstrated later in the chapter, through a case example involving a child who witnessed her sister's alleged homicide.

After discussing the legal mandate to report suspected abuse, I review the specific signs and symptoms associated with physical and sexual abuse.

The Legal Mandate

The Child Abuse Prevention and Treatment Act (P.L. 93-247, 1974) mandates the reporting of child maltreatment in all states receiving certain federal funds. Social workers come into contact with children in a variety of settings. They may become concerned about the possibility of physical or sexual abuse of a child because of certain aspects of the child's behavior or attitude, or because of specific physical indications on the child's body.

It is the responsibility of every social worker to know the laws in his or her state about reporting suspected maltreatment, the information that is required in making such a report, and the agency that is responsible for investigating the report. Although reporting to the appropriate agency is *mandatory*, Lukas (1993) cautions about making the decision to report hastily or unilaterally, because of the inevitable complicated repercussions that such a report sets in motion (as already discussed in Chapter 13). It is often helpful to a worker to discuss the details of a case with a supervisor or with more experienced workers. Weighing the needs of the child and those of the family may generate ethical dilemmas and pressures on the worker. This is "a powerful responsibility . . . since both a child's safety and the well-being of a family may be at risk" (Lukas, 1993, p. 139). Also, the legal and protective interventions that often follow may be very perplexing and anxiety-provoking for the child (Gil, 1991). The worker must convince the child that he or she will do everything possible to insure the child's safety, even though this may mean that the child will have to live someplace else for a while.

If it is likely that the child will have to testify in court or to a judge, the worker can help prepare the child for this experience—*not* by rehearsing with the child his or her actual testimony (since this would be considered putting words in the child's mouth), but by briefly and simply explaining the court procedures. It is often helpful to use a workbook for children that has pictures of a courtroom, and descriptions of a child's participation in typical court procedures. (See Schwab, 1986, for a coloring book to prepare children ages 5–12 to go to court.)

Indicators of Physical Abuse

The indicators of physical abuse listed in Table 14.1 constitute a general guide, rather than positive proof of child abuse, since it is always possible that a child's injuries occurred through play or otherwise accidentally. Obviously, multiple and recurrent injuries, and those that do not seem congruent with the description of how they occurred, merit further investigation and close monitoring.

———————— ❖ ————————

A newspaper account of the death of 6-year-old Alisa Izquierdo in New York City (Bruni, 1995) illustrates that children who suffer chronic abuse show many physical and behavioral indicators that are noted by their teachers and neighbors. In Alisa's case, the principal of her school wrote a letter to the family court judge, outlining the school's suspicion that the child was physically and emotionally abused during weekend visits with her mother. Among the indicators noticed by school personnel and by neighbors were bruises and welts on the child's body, nightmares, vomiting, withdrawn behavior, fear of using the bathroom, and "walking strangely." Despite these concerns and the letter written to the judge, her mother was granted custody. A year and a half later, the child died of bleeding caused by a blunt impact wound to her head.

Alisa's case raises the question about whose rights take precedence—those of the child, or those of the mother. The newspaper account (Bruni, 1995) portrays Alisa's mother as an abused woman herself, addicted to crack, who took much of her rage out on Alisa because she thought the child was possessed by voodoo. Alisa was the third of six children, ranging in age from 2 to 9. Although the other children did not show indications of abuse, they certainly were aware that their sister was beaten. As witnesses to family violence, these children will need help.

———————— ❖ ————————

TABLE 14.1. Physical and Behavioral Indicators of Physical Abuse: Webb

Physical indicators	Behavioral indicators
Bruises and welts	Wariness of adult contacts
Marks on face, lips, mouth	Apprehension when other children
Marks on torso, back, buttocks, thighs	cry or get hurt
Symmetrical marks on both sides of body	Behavioral extremes
(suggesting that the child has been	(aggressiveness or passive
grabbed by two hands; accidental	withdrawal)
injuries are not symmetrical)	Obvious fear of parents
Bruises/welts in various stages of healing	Reluctance to go home
Clustered bruises indicating repeated contact	Reports of injury by parents
with an object	Frequent weeping in school
Patterned bruises that reveal the shape of an	Self-mutilating behavior
object, such as a belt buckle, electric cord,	
or hairbrush	
Marks on several different areas	
Marks regularly appearing after weekends,	
absences, or vacations	
Burns	
Cigarette burns, especially on palms, soles, back,	
or buttocks	
Immersion burns (matching injuries on both	
ankles or hands, suggesting that the child was	
immersed in hot liquid)	
Patterned burns in the shape of an iron or a	
curling iron	
Rope burns on arms, legs, neck, or torso	
Fractures	
Fractures to skull, nose, face, arms, and legs	
Fractures in various stages of healing	
Multiple fractures, with splintering (caused	
by pulling or twisting)	
Lacerations/abrasions/bites	
Tears in tissues	
Tears to mouth, lips, gums, eyes	
Lacerations to genitalia	
Bites to buttocks	

Indicators of Sexual Abuse

Table 14.2, which lists the physical and behavioral symptoms of sexual abuse, can serve as a general guide for workers who suspect that a child is being sexually abused.

The term "sexual abuse" refers to behaviors in which a child is used for a sexual purpose. This rather simple definition encompasses a broad range of sexual behavior—from exposing a child to pornographic pictures, to touching, to various forms of sexual behavior (including oral, anal, or genital intercourse). Lukas (1993) clarifies that the perpetrator may be a man or a woman, that the child involved may be a male or female of any age, and that the abuse can have occurred once or many times. Lukas also reminds us of two important facts about the sexual abuse of children: (1) "Sexual abuse occurs in every race, ethnic group, and economic class in society" (p. 145), and (2) "The perpetrator is most likely to be someone the child knows" (p. 145).

Serious repercussions follow a conviction of sexual abuse, and workers who suspect possible sexual abuse may have to go to court to present the reasons for their concerns. Some guidelines in preparing to document suspicions of sexual abuse include the following:

1. Use open-ended questions in obtaining information from the child (e.g., "Tell me more about that," or "Show me with the dolls what happened," rather than "Did Daddy come into your bed every night?").

TABLE 14.2. Physical and Behavioral Indicators of Sexual Abuse: Webb

Physical indicators	Behavioral indicators
Pain, bruises, bleeding, or itching in genitals or rectum, or recurrent urinary infections	Sleep disturbances
Venereal disease in mouth, genitals, or rectum	Oversexualized or seductive behavior (including excessive masturbation)
Bedwetting	Preoccupation with own or other children's genitals
Difficulty in walking or sitting	Unwillingness to change for gym or to participate in physical education class
Torn, stained, or bloody underclothing	Poor peer relationships or sudden social withdrawal
Offensive odors	Reports of sexual assault
Preteen or early teen pregnancy	Self-mutilating behavior or suicide attempts
Recurrent vomiting or stomachaches	

2. Record information about what happened in the child's own words, using as many specifics as possible.

The Tripartite Crisis Assessment

Even when there are multiple physical and behavioral indicators of physical or sexual abuse, and even when a child has verbally confirmed experiences of abuse, we still do not know the *meaning* of the abusive experience to the child. James (1989) points out that the child's experience of an event can differ significantly form what adults expect: "An event may or may not be experienced as traumatic by a particular child, and it may be traumatizing at one stage of a child's development and not at another" (p. 21). A basic tenet of crisis intervention is that it is not the event itself that constitutes the crisis, but rather the individual's *perception* of the event. A full assessment of the event, the child, and the surrounding environment therefore permits us to understand more completely the implications of a particular abuse experience in a particular child's life.

In previous publications (Webb, 1991, 1993), and in several chapters of this book (Chapters 4, 10, 11, and 12), I have utilized variations of tripartite crisis assessment to demonstrate the interactive influences among three groups of factors in evaluating the significance of a particular crisis event or events:

1. Factors related to the individual
2. Factors related to the crisis situation
3. Factors in the support system

Figure 14.1 illustrates the specific elements that must be considered in evaluating the impact of a particular crisis situation, such as physical or sexual abuse in the family. See Webb (1991) for a full discussion of this assessment. Two forms that can be used in recording the individual and situational components of the crisis assessment are reproduced in the Appendices. The eco-map (see Chapters 2, 3, and 4) is useful in assessing essential information about the support system.

When a child is being evaluated for abuse, special attention should be given to the child's history of loss, to recurring experiences of abuse, and to the possibility that the child believed that the abusive experience endangered his or her or another family member's or a pet's life. Fear of death or serious injury is an essential condition for the diagnosis of PTSD (see below).

In addition, a child's developmental and cognitive level will determine the manner in which the child interprets the abuse experience. For

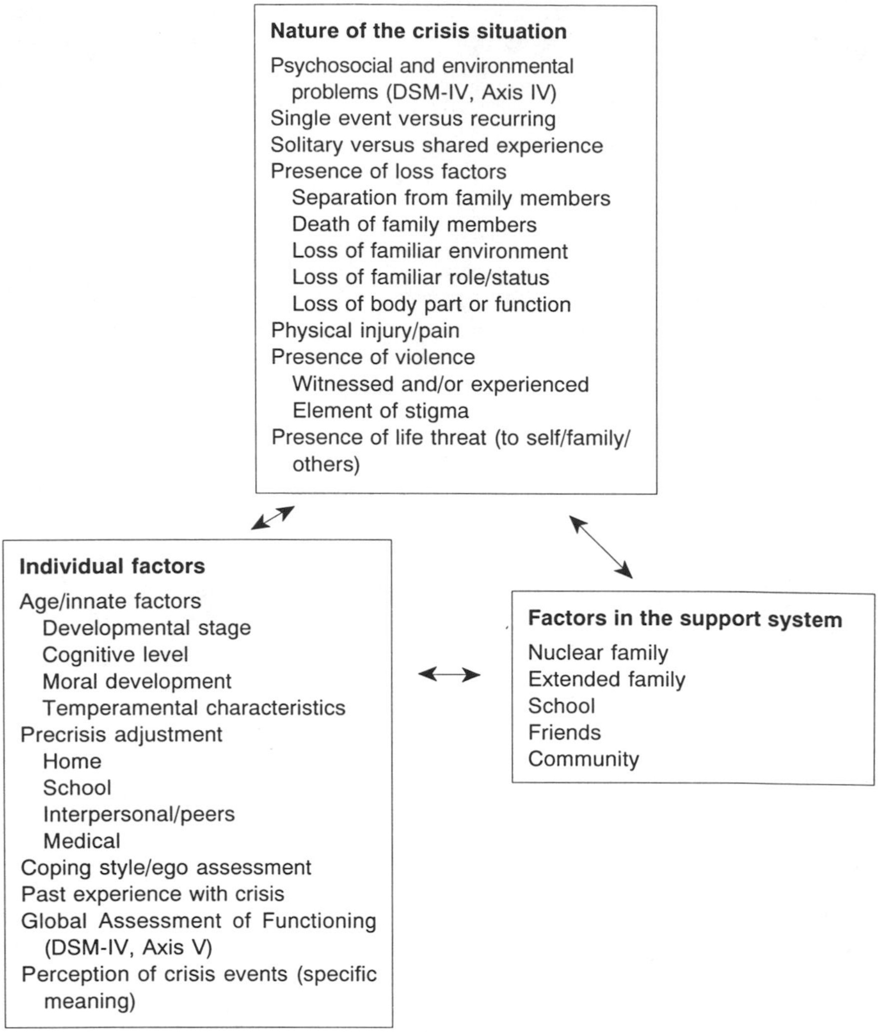

Nature of the crisis situation

Psychosocial and environmental
  problems (DSM-IV, Axis IV)
Single event versus recurring
Solitary versus shared experience
Presence of loss factors
  Separation from family members
  Death of family members
  Loss of familiar environment
  Loss of familiar role/status
  Loss of body part or function
Physical injury/pain
Presence of violence
  Witnessed and/or experienced
  Element of stigma
Presence of life threat (to self/family/
  others)

Individual factors

Age/innate factors
  Developmental stage
  Cognitive level
  Moral development
  Temperamental characteristics
Precrisis adjustment
  Home
  School
  Interpersonal/peers
  Medical
Coping style/ego assessment
Past experience with crisis
Global Assessment of Functioning
  (DSM-IV, Axis V)
Perception of crisis events (specific
  meaning)

Factors in the support system

Nuclear family
Extended family
School
Friends
Community

FIGURE 14.1. Interactive components of a tripartite crisis assessment: Webb. Adapted from Webb (1991, p. 6). Copyright 1991 by The Guilford Press. Adapted by permission.

example, the preschool or early latency-age child (up to approximately age 8) is still egocentric in his or her thinking, and may believe that he or she is "bad" and therefore caused the abuse. Of course, a perpetrator, playing into a child's normal narcissism, often reinforces these feelings by using guilt and secrecy tactics to keep the child from disclosing the abuse.

POSTTRAUMATIC STRESS DISORDER IN CHILDREN

The symptoms of PTSD (American Psychiatric Association, 1994) may develop in children who have been physically or sexually abused. It is important for child welfare workers and other social workers to be familiar with the signs and symptoms of this condition, because it is often confused with depression or conduct-disordered ("acting-out") behavior. Children with symptoms of PTSD require treatment from someone who is trained both in child therapy and in trauma counseling. Therefore, a referral to a child trauma specialist may be appropriate once the diagnosis has been made.

Components of PTSD

The foundation for PTSD is set when a person "experienced, witnessed, or was confronted with an event or events that involved actual or threatened death or serious injury, or a threat to the physical integrity of self or others" (American Psychiatric Association, 1994, p. 427), and that caused the person to respond with "intense fear, helplessness, or horror" (p. 428). In response to this traumatic event, the individual with PTSD demonstrates three different types of behavioral reactions over the course of a month or more:

1. *Reexperiencing the traumatic event.* In children, the reexperiencing often occurs through dreams that cause intense fear and helplessness resembling the emotions associated with the traumatic experience, even though the dreams may not reflect the *exact* circumstances of the traumatic experience. In addition to or instead of dreams, children sometimes engage in repetitive play that symbolizes the trauma.
2. *Avoidance and numbing.* Children may show a restriction in their ability to show positive feelings to others, or they may deliberately avoid people, activities, or places that are associated with the trauma.
3. *Increased arousal.* Children may have difficulty getting to sleep or staying asleep, may be more irritable, and/or may have difficulty concentrating in school or while doing homework.

More details about this diagnosis are available from the American Psychiatric Association (1994). Because the classification of PTSD originated with adult soldiers in the Vietnam war, its application to children is based on the work of child psychiatrists (Eth & Pynoos, 1985; Terr, 1983, 1988, 1989), social workers (James, 1989; Doyle & Bauer, 1989; Webb, 1991), and a child psychologist (Gil, 1991).

Incredible as it may seem, only a fraction of individuals exposed to traumatic experiences demonstrate behavioral responses indicative of PTSD. As previously discussed in Chapter 8, McFarlane (1990) states that "even after extreme trauma, only about 40 percent of an exposed population develop PTSD" (p. 74). We do not know whether this finding applies to children as well as adults, but its emphasis on the resilience of individuals in the face of terrible circumstances must not minimize the detrimental effect of these traumatic experiences on children's normal developmental course, whether or not they develop full-blown PTSD.

The Distinction between Victimization and Traumatization

It is important to distinguish between victimization and traumatization. Gil (1991) points out that a person may be victimized without being traumatized. That is, the person who experiences trauma is a victim during the traumatic event, but not every experience of being victimized qualifies as a traumatic experience in terms of causing responses of intense fear, helplessness, or horror. Thus, all children who are sexually abused do not experience this as a life-threatening event and react with intense fear. Furthermore, resilient children may not exhibit overt signs of disturbed behavior. However, the fact that children do not respond immediately and intensely to the experience of abuse does not mean it has had no effect on them.

THE CHILD WITNESS TO FAMILY VIOLENCE

Children who are exposed to violence in their families may respond with a wide range of behaviors, including somatic complaints, school-related problems, excessive crying and fear, withdrawal, clinging, aggressiveness, tantrums, anxiety, depression, and self-mutilation. (Carlson, 1984, cites numerous research articles documenting these findings.)

When children witness repeated violence between their parents, they learn that violence is a way to settle disagreements. This unfortunate and powerful lesson may affect their own present and future relationships, because these children have no experience of nonviolent methods of resolving controversies and conflicts. In addition, their observation of the failure of adults to restrain themselves may seriously jeopardize the children's confidence in their *own* impulse control (Pynoos & Eth, 1985, p. 26). This may be the operating dynamic when we see a child engaging in uncharacteristic aggressive, reckless, or self-destructive behavior after exposure to adult (especially parental) violence.

On an emotional level, child witnesses to family violence may experience a range of feelings, from fear to helplessness to violent revenge fantasies. It can be very helpful to them to draw and/or verbalize their wishes for revenge in a debriefing interview that "partially corrects the passive helplessness of the witness role" (Pynoos & Eth, 1986, p. 316).

Another typical reaction of children who witness family violence is posttraumatic guilt, connected to the children's imagined failure to intervene and prevent the violence. This response needs to be challenged with gentleness and reality testing, in terms of a child's size and role in a family by comparison with the size and controlling role of the parents. Bevin (1991), in a case demonstration, illustrates how to permit a child's *wish* for revenge on the man who raped his mother, while realistically questioning the possibility of a 9-year-old's being physically able to defend his mother against the attack of an adult male.

A particularly terrifying experience for a child witness is the death of a sibling, especially when it occurs through the neglect or intent of a parent in a family that routinely uses battering and other forms of violence to settle martial disputes and to "discipline" children. The case of 9-year-old Dorinda (described below), as well as that of the siblings of Alisa Izquierdo (Bruni, 1995), both illustrate the horror of alleged maternal homicide in families in which the deceased child was both physically and sexually abused by the parents.

Bereavement after homicide routinely generates a pathological response in survivors related to the nature of the death, which involves a combination of violence, violation, and volition, according to Rando (1993, citing Rynearson, 1987). The response of a child to a homicidal death in the family may be intensified by the "degree of identification with the victim" (Rando, 1993, p. 538). Thus, the closer in age and gender the child is to the victim, the more threatening the death.

---------- ❖ ----------

THE CASE OF DORINDA, AGE 9
Family Information

Mother	Susan, age 33; in prison for criminally negligent homicide re: death of daughter Jenny (see below); history of depression and suicidal ideation; raised in foster care.
Father	Jim, age 35; in prison for physical and sexual abuse of daughter Dorinda; also abused Susan; previous criminal background.
Two older siblings	Names, ages, and genders unknown; adopted out of state.

Child client   Dorinda, age 9; sexually abused by father; in resi-
                      dential treatment after a psychiatric hospitaliza-
                      tion following three different foster home place-
                      ments; was recently freed for adoption and started
                      going on preadoptive visits.
Brother   John, age 5; in foster care; abused by Dorinda.
Sister (deceased)   Jenny, died 5 years ago at 18 months of age in a
                      fall from a sixth-story window; the allegation
                      was that Susan threw Jenny out the window and
                      that Dorinda (then age 4) witnessed this; Susan
                      denied the charges and blamed Dorinda for Jenny's
                      death.

Note: Both parents have surrendered their rights to all their children.

Presenting Problem

Dorinda came into residential treatment from a psychiatric hospital,
where she had been admitted 8 months earlier after homicidal ideation
and two serious attempts to hurt her brother, John. The first attempt
involved trying to throw John down a flight of stairs, and the second involved trying to suffocate him by sitting on him. Previously, she had
slammed a door on the boy's hand, causing an injury that required am-
putation of one finger.

Other reasons for referral included "anxiety, self-abusive behaviors,
harming animals, and excessive masturbation." In addition, she was controlling and aggressive with peers.

Assessment

Dorinda's diagnoses at intake were PTSD, Dissociative Disorder Not
Otherwise Specified, and Oppositional Defiant Disorder. Psychological
testing indicated a Full Scale IQ of 87.

This child's traumatic history caused her to have difficulty trusting
people. Details pertaining to her early years were limited, but nonetheless revealed evidence of parental neglect, physical and emotional abuse,
sexual abuse, and the witnessing, at age 4, of her 18-month-old sister's
violent death. In addition, multiple foster home placements, and the subsequent "losses" of her parents and her older siblings, led Dorinda to
mistrust the motives of others.

Biopsychosocial Formulation

The combination of maternal psychiatric illness with parental domestic violence and sexual abuse resulted in Dorinda's lack of attachment to and empathy for others. Because she formed insecure bonds of attachment with her parents, she became unable to trust and bond with others. Furthermore, her traumatic experiences of both witnessing and experiencing violence and abuse resulted in emotional numbing (PTSD), which served to protect Dorinda from further hurt in personal relationships. Her immature and regressed behavior with peers (willingly playing "baby" with the girls in her dorm, allowing them to brush her hair and treat her like a much younger child) suggested that she still sought the nurturing experience she had missed as a young child. Other times, she would assume an authoritative stance and tell her peers what to do.

Treatment

Over the course of 11 months in a residential treatment center, Dorinda began to demonstrate some connection with her teacher and with the dorm worker, both of whom worked with her during the entire period. She was also able to form a relationship with her prospective adoptive mother, who took her on weekend visits, and with a second-year M.S.W. student, who worked with Dorinda in animal-assisted therapy as a method to enhance her empathy and to improve her identification and understanding of feelings. Dorinda's treatment is described in greater detail in the next section.

Dorinda's improvement in her life skills, her schoolwork, and her peer and adult relationships leads to a guardedly optimistic prognosis regarding her ability to adjust favorably to an adoptive home. She made considerable progress in her ability to trust and bond with others. However, Dorinda's underlying traumatic experience was not treated, nor was her history of multiple losses or their impact. These may require additional work at a future time.

❖

SELECTED METHODS FOR HELPING TRAUMATIZED CHILDREN WITH ATTACHMENT DIFFICULTIES

Some of the methods used to help Dorinda may be applicable to work with other children who have experienced multiple placements following abuse experiences, and whose behavior, like Dorinda's, shows evidence of attachment problems. Again, none of the methods used with Dorinda directly addressed the child's traumatic experience in the manner recommended by experts in the treatment of PTSD (Gil, 1991; James, 1989; Pynoos & Eth, 1986). Nonetheless, Dorinda's significant improvement in the nurturing environment of the residential treatment center suggests that her attachment difficulty, rather than her traumatic experiences, was fundamental to her presenting problems. Helping this child learn to identify feelings and to develop empathy through a relationship with an animal led to substantial improvements in her other relationships.

Identification of Feelings

Because of Dorinda's family background in which love and aggression were confused, and because Dorinda herself seemed uncertain about how to relate to peers and adults, the treatment review team recommended that Dorinda's therapy focus on helping her name and talk about a range of feelings, such as "sad," "angry," "happy," "guilty," and "proud." The task of the social worker and others involved with this child was to help her "own" her feeling reactions to the events in her *present* life, with the expectation that this would help Dorinda gradually sort out her confused feelings related to her past experiences.

Feelings Faces and the Body Map of Feelings

One method to help children identify and talk about feelings is to ask them to draw faces with different emotional expressions. An exercise that will facilitate this is the Feelings Faces exercise (Heegaard, 1991), discussed in Chapter 12. Starting with a circle to represent a head, and the word "happy" underneath, the worker invites the child to draw a happy face (see Figure 14.2). While the child is drawing, the worker asks the child about the kinds of things that make him or her happy, and lists these on a separate piece of paper. Next, the Body Map of Feelings (Gregory, 1990; Heegaard, 1991), also discussed in Chapter 12, can be introduced. This is simply an outline of a human body (see Figure 14.3). The worker asks the child to close his or her eyes and think about a time when he or she was very, very happy, then to open his or her eyes and draw with a yellow marker the places on the body where the child felt the happiness.

This three-step process (Feelings Faces, the list of associated feelings, and the Body Map of Feelings) can be repeated in other sessions for other feelings, such as "sad," "angry," "afraid," "nervous," "guilty," and "jealous." I recommend that initially only one feeling be addressed in each

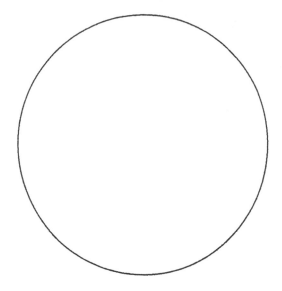

HAPPY

FIGURE 14.2. Outline for drawing a happy face in the Feeling Faces exercise.

session, especially for children like Dorinda, who tend to confuse different emotions. Later the worker can introduce the idea of more than one feeling at a time, by asking the child to pick two feelings that might coexist, and then asking the child to describe and draw a picture of a situation when that happened. The child needs to understand that he or she can have different feelings toward a person simultaneously.

If all the child's drawings are kept in a folder, the child can later be invited to make "a feelings book" by stapling the separate pages together and creating a special cover for the book.

Board and Card Games Dealing with Feelings

Therapeutic board games, such as the Talking, Feeling, and Doing Game and the Feelings in Hand card game (both of which have been mentioned in earlier chapters; see Figure 3.3 and Table 4.1), may also be useful in work with children like Dorinda. They provide structured activities that appeal to latency-age children, while also offering excellent opportunities to talk about different feelings during the course of the game.

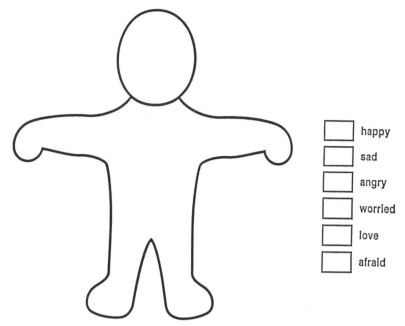

	happy
	sad
	angry
	worried
	love
	afraid

FIGURE 14.3. The Body Map of Feelings. From Gregory (1990). Copyright 1990 by the Family and Community Development Program, Lethbridge, Alberta, Canada. Reprinted by permission. (Although Gregory developed the Body Map of Feelings for use in working with children, neither she nor the Family and Community Development Program claims originality of the idea.)

Children who have problems with aggression may benefit from playing commercial board games such as Sorry (available from Parker Brothers, Springfield, MA) and Battleship (available from Milton Bradley, Springfield, MA), which provide structured methods for "attacking" the opponent while complying with the rules of the game. The worker uses the game to discuss aggressive themes during the play. Docker-Drysdale (1993) points out that children whose histories of deprivation and/or abuse contribute to severe developmental problems need an outlet for their aggression. In her school for "maladjusted children" she permitted ample scope for aggressive behavior, assuming that children would then devise their own forms of "restitution" for their aggression.

Dorinda's therapy focused on the full range of her feelings, including aggression. An emphasis on increasing her awareness of positive feelings of love and caring was also important to help her develop empathy.

Animal-Assisted Therapy

The use of pets in therapy with children dates from the pioneering work of the psychologist Boris Levinson, whose 1969 book describes his accidental discovery of the efficacy of his pet dog in stimulating the conversation of a difficult, previously noncommunicative child (see George, 1988, for a discussion). Levinson's work over the next decade convinced him and others that involvement with an animal helps children develop empathy, self-esteem, and autonomy, while also reducing their feelings of alienation (Levinson, 1978). He also emphasized the value of animal therapy for abused children who are afraid of human contact (Levinson, 1962).

In Dorinda's case, her treatment was greatly facilitated by the presence of animals at the residential treatment center. When the cat of Dorinda's prospective adoptive mother was found limping after one of the child's weekend visits, a specific goal was established: to help Dorinda bond with an animal of her choice at the farm center, in order to help the child learn appropriate interactive skills around this animal (which, it was hoped, would be generalized to relationships with other animals and people).

The M.S.W. student employee of the center permitted Dorinda to choose a particular animal to become the focus of their weekly therapy time together. Dorinda selected a female rabbit, and named her "Thumper." The following excerpt from a process recording conveys the worker's attempt to use the child's interaction with the animal as a way to sensitize Dorinda to feelings.

Worker's Process Recording

It was the first warm Monday of spring, and I suggested to Dorinda that we put Thumper in an enclosed area in the grass in front of the rabbit hutch. We sat on the grass and watched Thumper, who began to hop and thump almost as soon as she was put down.

WORKER: Look at her, Dorinda! She's thumping a lot today! Why do you suppose she's thumping so much? [I wanted to encourage Dorinda to recognize and label the rabbit's behavior. Thumper was excited, and might scratch Dorinda if she tried to hold her.]

DORINDA: She's happy that I take care of her.

WORKER: She's happy that she can leave her cage, and have you to take care of her. [Dorinda remained quiet, but was now looking at the other rabbits in the hutch.] The other rabbits are watching from the hutch.

DORINDA: The other rabbits *are* watching. So is Thumper's mother.

WORKER: You are right, Dorinda; even her mother is watching. I wonder what the rabbits are thinking. What does Thumper's mother think?

DORINDA: She is happy that Thumper is outside.

WORKER: I think you're right. And I bet she is happy that you take care of Thumper. [I wanted to connect mother, child, and caregiver.]

Dorinda's Stories about Thumper

Dorinda began making a storybook about Thumper. This is one of her stories:

> Once upon a time there was a rabbit named Thumper. She is a Rex. She is grey, brown and black. She likes to chew on people's shirts. She likes to look around at places. She also likes to climb all over people.
> She was born in October. That is when I got her. She likes to thump. Sometimes she is scared. She likes to put her head in people's arms. She likes to look at people. She likes to wiggle her nose. She likes her house. She says, "I love you." She likes this place.

Dorinda wrote the next story 6 weeks later after playing with Thumper on the grass:

> On one sunny day in spring, we played with Thumper. We gave her carrots. We played with her on a blanket. We put her in this big cage in the grass.
> She liked the grass because it tasted good to her. She ate it. She thought it tasted like food. She thumped a lot, and she jumped a lot because she was excited. Thumper was excited about coming out of her own cage.
> Other rabbits watched her. They were jealous. Her mother was happy because [Thumper] had *me* to take care of her. Her brothers and sisters were watching her, too. They were happy because their sister came out of the cage.
> Thumper said, "I'm happy!" She also said, "Are you happy?" She said that to me. I like Thumper. She is nice and she is special to me. She likes the sun. She loves her house.

Dorinda illustrated her book with a drawing of Thumper (see Figure 14.4).

❖

FIGURE 14.4. Dorinda's drawing of Thumper.

Comment

Through these excerpts from Dorinda's treatment, we can see the child's identification with the rabbit, as well as her own happiness at being cared for. Certainly, Dorinda's repeated statements about Thumper's liking her home suggested that the child too felt contentment in the residential setting. It is also notable that Dorinda expressed the mother rabbit's pleasure that someone else was caring for Thumper. We do not know any details about Dorinda's relationship with her own mother, but the child indicated, through the mother rabbit, the mother's permission to let another caretaker meet the young rabbit's needs. This acceptance of a substitute caregiver would, of course, be crucial to Dorinda's future adaptation to and development in an adoptive home.

It is often difficult to engage children who have experienced multiple placements during their formative years. (This was discussed previously with regard to Mario and Maria in Chapter 10.) Because of their lack of attachment and inability to form meaningful relationships, it may take from 3 to 11 months for therapists to engage attachment-disordered children in a residential setting, according to Doyle and Bauer (1989). In my opinion, the use of the rabbit in Dorinda's therapy helped considerably to enable her to name and understand a variety of feelings, and to develop a trusting relationship with the worker in the process of playing with the rabbit.

The process of establishing attachment in older children who have been traumatized may be long and difficult, according to James (1989,

1994). However, the effort put into this may be "the only hope for [the children's] ever forming an intimate bond with another person" (James, 1989, p. 141). "Children who have learned not to trust adults and who are intimacy-avoidant may not show signs of relationship development with the therapist for many months" (James, 1994, p. 61). Furthermore, when an individual has been subjected to abuse or trauma, he or she begins therapy full of doubts and suspicion about the therapist's motives and ability to help (Herman, 1992). Finally, the social worker/therapist trying to help children who have been traumatized and abused by their parents must consider the impact on these children of lack of parental empathy. This affects the children's developing ability to value themselves as persons, and to identify with the emotional state of others (Jordan, 1991).

WORKING WITH ABUSED CHILDREN IN SHELTERS

According to the *Harvard Mental Health Letter* (1993),

> there is no accepted formula for treating children and adults who are victims of incest or physical abuse. Since the symptoms vary a great deal, many kinds of psychotherapy and medication may be appropriate, and there are no controlled studies of outcome. . . . Surveys indicate[, however,] that professionals experienced in treating victims of child abuse prefer *group therapy* above all other kinds of treatment, especially for adult female survivors but also for men, adolescents, and *children*. . . . Group members with similar experiences are an ideal audience, certain to understand or sympathize. (pp. 2–3, emphasis added)

Group Approaches

Alessi and Hearn (1984) describe a six-session treatment group for children in a shelter for battered women. The children, ranging in age from 8 to 16, showed numerous symptoms of anxiety (e.g., nail biting, headaches, and stomachaches), as well as aggressive behavior toward other children. The group was structured around the following topics:

- Identification and expression of feelings
- Violence
- Problem solving (healthy and unhealthy methods)
- Sex, love, and sexuality (for the teenagers)

The two coleaders used each group session to encourage the children to reflect upon how their families responded in various situations and upon how they were personally affected by events in their families. The children were asked directly whether they thought that hitting is right, and whether they thought that they would hit others when they grew up. Role playing of possible family interactions (with both violent and nonviolent approaches to solving problems) helped the children to consider a range of alternatives other than the aggressive responses to which they had been exposed. The directive psychoeducational framework of this group provided a focus, whereas the mutual sharing of family experiences proved very supportive to children who had previously felt stigmatized and isolated because of their family situation.

Stories and Workbooks for Children Ages 4–10

The Bureau for At-Risk Youth (now located in Plainview, New York) has published a series of picture story workbooks (Alexander, 1992) intended for traumatized children and children who have witnessed and experienced family violence. These story workbooks include sketches of children in frightening situations; one such sketch depicts a small boy listening at night in bed to his parents fighting (see Figure 14.5). On the facing blank page, the child is encouraged to draw and color what happened in his or her own house. Another sketch shows a child talking and playing with a counselor who is pictured making helpful comments to the child, such as "Lots of people don't hit each other when they have angry feelings." The child, in turn, is pictured as saying, "I'm learning that I can use my words when I feel like fighting. I practice how with my counselor" (Alexander, 1992, p. 16). On the facing blank page, the child is invited to draw what he or she can do instead of fighting. These workbooks are available at discounted rates for bulk orders; they can be used in a group session a few pages at a time, or by an individual child and counselor at the child's own pace.

Another story workbook series focuses specifically on life in a shelter for women and children (Prato, 1984a, 1984b). Like the Alexander series, the Prato series openly discusses violence at home as the reason for the necessary separation of family members. It also validates the fact that a child may think about and miss his or her father, while making it clear that fathers are not allowed to come to the shelter.

PREVENTIVE APPROACHES TO FAMILY VIOLENCE

Helping children cope with their confused feelings related to family violence does not deal with the problem at its roots. Unfortunately, U.S.

I lie awake at night and try not to listen. Sometimes, I'm so afraid I can hardly breathe. And I wonder what will happen to me.

FIGURE 14.5. Child listening to parents fighting. From Alexander (1992, p. 28). Copyright 1992 by the Bureau for At-Risk Youth. Reprinted by permission.

society condones and even glamorizes (in movies and on television) the aggressive, abusive behavior of the strong toward the weak. The stage is set for violence when social values sanction the use of force against women and children, and when lack of preparation for parenthood or of knowledge about normal child behavior is combined with the endemic stresses of poverty, unemployment, substance abuse or dependence, and lack of social support.

The problem of family violence must be confronted on many levels. My emphasis in this chapter on the child witnesses and victims does not imply disregard for essential interventions on the societal and community levels. Chapter 15 discusses the need for clinicians and advocates on behalf of children to join forces and work toward common goals. Perhaps nowhere is this joining of purpose more essential than with regard to the child's right to grow up in a safe and nurturing home environment. However, we know that few adults who are disempowered and dissatisfied can function effectively as loving parents. It is therefore undeniable that to help children *in the long run*, we must focus on improving the life conditions of their parents.

Intensive Family Crisis Intervention: The Homebuilders Program

One program targeting the family at a time of threatened placement or institutionalization of a family member (child or parent) uses intensive short-term crisis intervention to help the family stay together. The Homebuilders program subscribes to the aims of P.L. 96-272, the Adoption Assistance and Child Welfare Reform Act of 1980, which provided financial incentives for states to develop family support programs to prevent out-of-home placements and speed the reunification of children already in foster care (Bishop & McNally, 1993; Hodges, Morgan, & Johnston, 1993; Whittaker, 1991; Whittaker, Kinney, Tracy, & Booth, 1990; McGowan, 1990).

The kinds of services provided by Homebuilders staff members are crisis intervention, case management, linkage, and collateral services. Behavioral and cognitive treatment approaches are provided in the home or in a convenient community location, such as a playground or fast-food restaurant. Because caseloads are very small, the counselors are available 24 hours a day, 7 days a week to meet families at times of crisis and to help parents learn problem-solving skills. The contact with a particular family lasts 4 to 6 weeks; it is assumed that the crisis will have been resolved during that period, and that the family members will have learned new coping skills and new resources to help them in times of future need.

The basic assumption upon which this program is based is that it is usually best for children to grow up in their own homes (Homebuilders, 1990). However, this ideal cannot always be realized. In some cases, it is simply not in the best interests of the children in a family to remain in the home. Kinard (1982, p. 88) points out that "mothers with emotional difficulties serious enough to warrant psychiatric help may be unable to give their children the nurturance and support necessary to foster positive self-images and appropriate handling of aggression." This was probably true in the cases of both Alisa and Dorinda. The situation of the child's father also merits attention, since a substance-disordered father who physically abuses the mother creates an environment that is potentially dangerous for the entire family.

Repeatedly in this book, I have presented the issue of the rights of children as compared with the rights of the parents. Balancing these two sets or rights is rarely simple. Social workers, however, must not sacrifice children to the "ideal" of family preservation.

Teaching School-Age Children
Conflict Management Skills

Children learn from examples at home, and what they learn is reflected in their own interpersonal responses with their peers. A school-based peer mediation program (Gentry & Beneson, 1993) attempted to teach anger management in fourth to sixth grades, in the hope that this learning would transfer to the home. This approach to conflict management helped children understand that tensions and disputes can be resolved through the following specific rules of mediation:

- Agreeing to solve the problem
- Not interrupting
- Telling the truth
- Avoiding name calling or putdowns

Trained peer mediators helped students deal with problems. The rationale for this program rested on the belief that the behaviors of children in one setting would transfer to another. This proved to be the case when conflict management was learned and practiced in the school: The skills appeared to generalize to the home setting, for use with family members, particularly siblings (Gentry & Beneson, 1993, p. 72).

Since all children go to school, the potential of this setting for interpersonal learning must be recognized and used to the fullest. Attempts to teach children constructive methods for dealing with intense emotions constitute a rich opportunity for interrupting the intergenerational transmission of family violence.

CONCLUDING COMMENTS

Most social workers whose practice puts them in contact with children will sooner or later become involved with a case of physical or sexual child abuse. Because of the magnitude of the problem, it is unavoidable. Some workers find it impossible to accept the evidence of abuse, joining in society's denial of the fact that parents, who are supposed to protect their children, can instead behave in a manner that threatens their children's mental and emotional health.

Many factors besides abusing parents contribute to child abuse. If we tackle this problem on a macro level, trying to address the *reasons* for the abuse, this wide-angle approach will ultimately reduce the numbers of abused children. Meanwhile, on a micro level, the abusive person has a face to the child, who needs help to try to understand how someone who loves him or her could do this. This is not an easy question to answer; let us hope that in the future there will be fewer children needing to know.

DISCUSSION QUESTIONS

1. Outline a treatment plan for the five siblings of Alisa Izquierdo, ages 2–9 (who as of late 1995 were in temporary custody, following the imprisonment of their mother for the murder of their sister; Bruni, 1995).

2. Consider the probable reaction of a 4-year-old who witnessed the sudden, violent death of a sibling. What interventions would be appropriate to help the preschool child witness?

3. What are some methods for helping children with their revenge fantasies after they have witnessed the physical or sexual abuse of a family member? Do you think that there is a danger that permitting a child to express these feelings may stimulate him or her to act them out? What can the worker do to avoid this possibility?

4. Discuss the effect on the worker of interacting with a child who has witnessed or experienced severe abuse. How can the worker deal with his or her own reactions?

CHAPTER 15

A Changing World's Impact on Practice with and for Children

The approaching end of this century compels social workers and other practitioners involved with children to assess their past and current efforts, as well as their future prospects for intervening helpfully in children's lives. The 20th century has sometimes been referred to as the "century of the child," because more serious study of children has been undertaken during this time than in the entire history of the world, according to LeVine and Sallee (1992). Certainly we would like to believe that we know more about how to help children, and that we are doing better as a society and as professionals, than we did in the early 1900s.

However, our enhanced knowledge has not prevented the fragmentation of the family and kinship network; nor has it countered the debilitating influences on children of poverty, substance use disorders, violence, and child abuse. There is a disturbing contradiction between the United States' view of itself as a child-centered nation and its fiscal policies, which reveal a "weak and eroding commitment to children" (Hewlett, 1991, p. 17). For example, the U.S. federal budget in 1987 allocated less than 5% of total expenditures on programs designed to benefit children (Hewlett, 1991, p. 17). Practitioners committed to working on behalf of children must avoid becoming demoralized by these double messages as they make decisions about how to respond to the needs of the children in their practice.

THE NEED FOR SHARED RESPONSIBILITY FOR CHILDREN

A philosophy of shared responsibility for the health and well-being of children becomes critical in the face of family breakdown, as I have pointed out in Chapter 1. Examples throughout this book have demonstrated the indisputable need for programs and services for children who are homeless, orphaned, maltreated, and disadvantaged. When parents and other family members are absent, addicted, poor, violent, and/or otherwise unable to help their own children, society has a moral responsibility to do so. The philosophy that "it takes a whole village to raise a child" should not be limited to Africa.

Factors Contributing to the Need for Services

Poverty

Children who grow up in poverty often suffer the associated problems of poor nutrition, inadequate health care, and substandard housing. Furthermore, race and ethnic minority membership often coexist with poverty, thus presenting additional obstacles to children's optimal growth and development. "When children are both poor and members of ethnic minorities, the negative and long-term impact of poverty increases significantly" (Gibbs, Huang, & Associates, 1989, p. 6).

The predictions of demographers that nonwhite and Spanish-speaking individuals under the age of 18 will constitute 30% of the nation's youth population in the year 2000, and 38% by 2020, demand our attention (Gibbs et al., 1989, citing 1987 U.S. government data). A multidimensional framework of assessment and treatment must include cultural, developmental, and environmental factors as essential to understanding and treating a child, in accordance with a person-in-environment perspective.

Homelessness

In 1991, 3 million people were homeless in the United States. Many homeless individuals are young children, who often fail to attend school while they are temporarily housed in shelters, motels, and welfare hotels. The acute shortage of low-income housing seems to be getting worse, as existing Section 8 federal housing programs expire and are not renewed (Hewlett, 1991). The era of fiscal constraint during the mid-1990s does not bode well for homeless families confronted not only with the lack of housing, but also with poor health care, disappearing Head Start and nutrition programs, and the threat to their children of violence and exposure to substances in their unsafe neighborhoods. The case of Barbie Smith (Chapters 3–5) illustrates the interweaving of environmental and psychological stressors, as well as the limitations on what practitioners can do in the absence of necessary programs.

HIV/AIDS

"By the end of 1995, maternal deaths caused by the HIV/AIDS epidemic will have orphaned an estimated 24,600 children in the United States. . . . by the year 2000, the overall number of motherless children and adolescents will exceed 80,000. . . . The vast majority of these motherless youth will come from poor communities of color" (Michaels & Levine, 1992, p. 3456). Because of the social stigma associated with HIV/AIDS, children in families that have been affected experience a sense of isolation and reduced self-esteem, in addition to the various stressful experiences associated with the medical treatment and terminal illness of a family member.

HIV/AIDS has been referred to as a "multigenerational family disease" because it crosses generational boundaries and infects many individuals within each family (Steiner, Boyd-Franklin, & Boland, 1995). Furthermore, the accompanying problems (such as homelessness, crime, unemployment, and drugs) that plague inner-city families with HIV/AIDS all call for a coordinated multisystem approach to helping, in order to avoid mixed messages among the different helping systems, overlapping case management efforts, and conflicting treatment plans and goals (Steiner et al., 1995).

Of course, direct work with affected children and families does not preclude advocacy efforts on behalf of funding for research and continuation of services for people with HIV/AIDS. Anyone who has worked closely with a child or family with this terrible illness understands the necessity of finding a cure in time to prevent loss of lives in the future.

Merging Goals of Clinicians and Advocates

Faced with the cruel realities of our changing world, practitioners who work directly with children realize that political and economic remedies are required to reduce poverty and bring about improved living conditions. All U.S. citizens who care about children and families must join together to raise the consciousness of the nation, and especially that of its political leaders, who allocate resources for programs and services. The National Association of Social Workers and the Council on Social Work Education, for example, teamed together to run a full-page advertisement in *The New York Times* (December 1, 1995, p. A-31) to protest cuts in a proposed federal welfare bill that would shift responsibility to the states, and inevitably would result in reduced benefits to needy families. When families suffer the combined throes of poverty, racism, unemployment, and lack of opportunity, its children pay the price. All of us must work together to try to correct this social injustice and help families that cannot help themselves.

A GLOBAL PERSPECTIVE ON CHILDREN'S RIGHTS

Social workers and other practitioners focused on promoting the best interests of the child cannot, in good conscience, limit themselves to U.S. citizens. Problems associated with the health and welfare of children extend to all nations.

The United Nations Convention on the Rights of the Child

In 1989, the United Nations approved the Convention on the Rights of the Child (U.N. General Assembly, 1989), covering three major areas of concern (summarized by Brieland, Fallon, & Korr, 1994, p. 132):

1. Entitlements
   The material provisions and basic services that all children have a right to expect from society.
2. Protections
   The means to safeguard children's well-being.
3. Affirmative Freedoms
   The right of children to think, decide, and act on their own, dependent on their capacities.

The full text of the Convention can be found in the U.N. General Assembly (1989). The United States has not yet officially ratified this document, although more than 180 other nations have approved it. In their essay, Brieland et al. (1994) urge the social work profession to "join with national organizations and private citizens to achieve American ratification of the U.N. Convention on the Rights of the Child" (p. 133). Ratification would affirm the United States' obligation to deal with child poverty, infant mortality, and child health. The objections to ratification relate to fears about state interference in family life, to the abortion issue, and to the concern that children's rights might give them power to "divorce" their parents (and thus erode parents' age-old right to "possession" of their children).

Immigration and Adoption of Refugee Children

Many children who are new arrivals in this country come from a background of political upheaval and family displacement related to their status as refugees. The child immigrant to the United States brings with him or her the "excess baggage" of family crisis associated with the often stressful reasons that led to the immigration. There can be many motives for immigration, but it seems obvious that families would not willingly leave an environment in which they felt safe and optimistic about their future. Moving a family to a new country may be the "least detrimental alternative" (i.e., better than remaining home in the middle of a war zone), or it may represent the father's or mother's wish for better family opportunities (Bevin, 1991).

Children who leave one country to establish residence in another, regardless of the reason for the major family move, have to cope with numerous losses, which are summarized by Ajdukovic and Ajdukovic (1993) in Table 15.1. Although a refugee child's vulnerability to stress is greatly increased by such losses, these negative effects can be reduced by a supportive family milieu and a supportive community (Ajdukovic & Ajdukovic, 1993). The ability of the family members to adjust in a new environment, moreover, relates to the degree to which the rules and norms of their own culture remain the same, and the extent to which role expectations, morals, and values are different and clash with the prevailing norms in the new locale (Bullrich, 1989).

The school is often the place where difficulties in adjustment become evident, since the child is thrust into a new situation that expects certain behaviors, even as the child is attempting to learn a new language and to establish some peer contacts. The role of the school social worker in serving as a bridge between two sets of values is illustrated in the case of Alexa, an adopted 8-year-old Romanian refugee with special needs.

THE CASE OF ALEXA, AGE 8

Presenting Problem

Alexa, an 8-year-old Romanian child in the second grade of a public school, was referred to an early intervention program (staffed by a local mental health agency) because of her aggressive behavior with other children, her failure to follow directions, and her immature behavior. She had been a student in the school for 2 years, and in first grade was suspended twice—once for slapping another student, and once for hitting a teacher. At the time of intake, she spoke English fluently, but she arrived in this country 2 years earlier without any English words.

Family Information

Alexa was adopted by Hungarian parents when she was 4 years old. She was orphaned during the first year of her life, when both of her parents

TABLE 15.1. Losses Confronted by Immigrant Children

- *Loss of important others*
  Many immigrant children have witnessed the death of one or both of their parents.
- *Loss of physical capacity*
  Children in war-torn zones may be injured or wounded.
- *Loss of parental support or protection*
  Many children become displaced and separated from their parents under war conditions. This can be very troubling to young children, who, as Garbarino (1992) noted, can cope with the stress of war if they retain positive attachments to their families, and if parents can project a sense of stability, permanence, and competence to their families.
- *Loss of home*
  The meaning of the term "home" is personal, and very significant to the child's sense of security; without this anchor children (and adults) may develop symptoms.
- *Living with distressed adults*
  The cumulative, negative effects of displacement produce high levels of distress among adults, which have disturbing reverberations for the children.
- *Family separation*
  Separation from loved ones results in emotional pain and in changes in the family structure.
- *Lost educational opportunities*
  Children in transition from one country to another lose not only the continuity of an educational experience, but they also need to acquire a new language and the accompanying set of educational expectations in the new environment.
- *Poor physical environment*
  Often refugee families live in crowded shelters with minimal space for play activities or learning. Lack of privacy, high social density, and poor housing are common in immigrant families.
- *Malnutrition*
  Dietary provisions in refugee settings usually are tailored to the needs of adults, not to the nutritional requirements of children.
- *Incarceration*
  Many refugee children are kept in refugee camps for prolonged periods of time. The stresses of an incarcerated environment can seriously interfere with the normal growth and development of children.

Note. Adapted from Ajdukovic and Ajdukovic (1993, pp. 845–846). Copyright 1993, with kind permission from Elsevier Science Ltd., The Boulevard, Langford Lane, Kidlington OX5 1GB, UK.

died as a result of civil unrest in Romania. She was placed in an orphanage with other displaced children at that time.

Alexa's adoptive parents are Hungarian, and multilingual in English, Romanian, and Hungarian. They are both employed in international business organizations. At the time of intake, the father was 42 years old and the mother was 37. Alexa is their only child.

Biopsychosocial Assessment

No developmental history is available regarding the first 4 years of Alexa's life. We know, however, that loss of the parents during the first year of life creates a sense of abandonment in the child, with resultant problems in lack of trust and attendant attachment difficulties (Remkus, 1991). We do not know the details about Alexa's parents' deaths, or whether she witnessed one or both of them. These facts may never be known, since the preverbal child lacks the language to convey traumatic experiences, which nonetheless may be imprinted on his or her visual memory (Terr, 1988).

We also do not know the conditions of the orphanage in which Alexa lived until her adoption at age 4, or whether she had any opportunity to form attachment bonds to one or more staff members there. It is likely that this child did receive enough attention and care from *someone* to benefit her development sufficiently that a couple seeking to adopt a preschool child found her appealing.

Alexa's anger and frustration when she was uprooted from her home in Hungary at age 6, and brought to the United States and enrolled in school, are understandable from the point of view of her isolated position because she did not know the language. Another possible factor contributing to Alexa's aggressiveness could be related to this child's sensitivity to change, and to her depleted ability to adapt to yet another loss of a familiar environment.

The facts that Alexa learned English in 2 years, and that she was able to make some friends, reflect her strengths and resilience. Her ongoing adjustment should be monitored closely.

Treatment Summary

Individual weekly play therapy with a second-year M.S.W. student provided a range of nonverbal methods for Alexa to express her frustrations symbolically, without the pressure to put them into words. Paper and markers offered a nonstructured method for Alexa to "draw out" her feelings in a safe environment. She sometimes referred to "a faraway place" in her drawings, which seemed to allude to some of the shadowy memories of her past. Unfortunately, the student therapist did not explore this further with Alexa. A dollhouse and family dolls were also available to the child, in addition to a variety of puppets and clay.

Group therapy was also an important part of Alexa's initial treatment, in order to offer her a socialization experience. She participated in a group of four children, two girls and two boys. Other members of the group also had difficulties with peer relationships. The goal for Alexa in this experience was to help her become aware that the other children also had to struggle to control their behavior. A second goal was for Alexa to receive a sense of being accepted by the group.

The involvement of Alexa's adoptive parents in counseling was and continues to be crucial in promoting the optimal development of their child. It is essential for the child's therapist to meet regularly and work closely with the parents, in order to guide and coach them so that they can support their child most effectively. The school initially focused on Alexa's troublesome behavior, which the social worker "normalized" with the parents in view of this child's traumatic life experiences. Until the worker presented this perspective to them, the parents were joining with the teacher in viewing Alexa as a "bad" child and responding to her punitively.

Another important goal in ongoing parent counseling is to help Alexa gradually understand her traumatic past. It is quite likely that she remembers some details of her experiences in the orphanage. Both the parents and the therapist must encourage and be willing to listen to the child's memories. Ideally, this recollection (crisis "debriefing") will first occur in individual therapy, with later family sessions to sensitize the parents to the ongoing influence of their daughter's early experiences in her present life. Eventually Alexa can be encouraged to construct a lifebook (see Chapter 10), in which she records the significant events of her life— both as she actually remembers them, and as her parents help supply missing information.

---- ❖ ----

Discussion

Alexa has experienced multiple traumatic events in her short life. However, the impact of Alexa's major losses during the first year of her life may be underestimated even by trained practitioners who are unaware of the impact of a child's preverbal experience. Terr's (1988) studies of children traumatized during their preschool years confirm that traumatic events create lasting visual images that "seem to last a lifetime" (p. 103). "When a trauma or series of extreme stresses strikes well before the age [of] 28 to 36 months, the child 'burns in' a visual memory of it, sometimes later becoming able . . . to affix a few words to the picture" (p. 103).

Terr's comments have direct treatment implications for Alexa and for other refugee children who may have witnessed multiple frightening events during their preverbal years. The recommended method of helping is to facilitate gradual recollection of the experience, in the belief that this recollection (in the context of the safety of the child's present reality and the support of a warm helping relationship) will reduce the child's anxiety about the trauma. This should enable the child to locate the experience in the past, and thereby to reduce its ongoing influence in his or her present life.

More research needs to be done on possible helping approaches for traumatized children. For example, when a child has witnessed one or both parents being murdered, it is difficult to conceive of *any* intervention that will help the child to accept this terrible reality. My own belief, based on many years' experience with traumatized children, is that a child's best interests lie in remembering the experience and then internalizing the memory, so that the child can carry on with his or her life in a way that honors the lost or deceased parent. In this manner the child holds onto the memory, while focusing on the present rather than the past.

TRENDS IN DIRECT PRACTICE WITH CHILDREN

In addition to the merging goals of clinicians and child advocates, and the greater sensitivity to children's rights in the international sphere, other trends are apparent in the work of practitioners who deal directly with children in the last decade of the 20th century. These trends include the following:

- Greater awareness of biological and environmental factors in the etiology of childhood problems
- Practice that recognizes the value of interprofessional collaboration and of parents as partners in their children's treatment
- Practice that is culturally sensitive
- Closer affiliation between child and family therapy
- Practice that utilizes cognitive and behavioral approaches, where appropriate

Greater Awareness of Biological and Environmental Factors

In a 50-year overview of child and adolescent psychiatry, Stella Chess (1988) stated that the most dramatic change in the past 20 years in our concepts of normal and deviant child development has been the "recognition of how much the *biological* mediates environmental stimuli and demands in shaping the child's behavior from birth onward" (p. 3; emphasis added). The work of Chess and Thomas (1986) on temperament made a significant contribution to our understanding of the innate temperamental characteristics that influence children's and adults' responses to the world.

In addition to the genetic reality of temperamental characteristics that we all possess, some children's biological inheritance predisposes them to certain conditions, such as schizophrenia, autism, alcoholism, Tourette's syndrome, Attention-Deficit/Hyperactivity Disorder (ADHD), and other emotional, learning, and/or behavioral disorders. These conditions are multidetermined, and we do not know the elusive reasons why one child in a family develops a disease or disorder, whereas another child in the same family with the same parents does not. Johnson (1989) states that

> some combination of intrinsic constitutional factors and environmental forces, in continuous interaction with each other, gives rise to conditions classified under disruptive behavior disorder. In some instances, biological factors play the major determining role, in others, environmental factors predominate, and in still others both biology and environment significantly contribute to an outcome identified as a "behavior disorder." (p. 91)

Furthermore, persistent psychosocial adversity, such as poverty, abuse, or neglect, increases the risk of mental illness in children (Institute of Medicine, 1989, cited in Johnson & Friesen, 1993).

Because of the complexity of conditions with both constitutional and environmental components, a multifaceted, multimodal approach to treatment is recommended. The use of psychopharmacology brings dramatic results for some conditions, but ideally this will be combined with simultaneous parent guidance and possible behavioral approaches with the child. As Chess (1988, p. 6) states, "hyperactive or depressed [children] need more than a drug prescription."

Appreciation of Interprofessional Collaboration and of Parents as Partners

We have come a long way form the view that parents (especially mothers) cause or substantially contribute to their children's emotional difficulties. Our enhanced understanding of the biological components of human behavior, together with a broader awareness of the complexity of behavior, leads us to include parents as partners in helping efforts that involve their children. The Amendments to the Education of the Handicapped Act, which passed in 1986, *mandate* a family-centered approach to provision of services to infants and young children with handicaps

(Bishop, 1993; Bishop, Rounds, & Weil, 1993). That act, along with programs such as Homebuilders (Kinney, Haapala, & Booth, 1991), demonstrates belief in the importance of the parents' role in their children's lives. Studies of early intervention programs for children have shown that the most effective programs actively involve parents along with the children (LeCroy & Ashford, 1992).

In addition to the primary role of the parents in helping their own children, many other specialists are often involved in the assessment and treatment of some complicated disorders, such as ADHD. For example, special education teachers usually have an essential role in the education of a child with ADHD. In addition, the school nurse often dispenses medication to the child in the middle of the day; a pediatrician, neurologist, or psychiatrist prescribes the medication; and various other medical and educational personnel may be involved in providing support services to the child and family. Often the social worker functions as case coordinator, to insure that necessary information is transmitted among the different personnel and parents. Interprofessional collaboration and inclusion of parents as partners result in enriched information about the child, which assists the social worker/counselor while also contributing to a sense of teamwork. The ongoing challenge for the social worker is to keep the members of the "team" working together over the necessary period of time, depending on the child's needs.

Culturally Sensitive Practice

Implicit (and often explicit) throughout this book is the recognition that social workers and other practitioners with children must be prepared to work with the many different nationalities, races, and ethnic groups that contribute to diversity of the United States and the world. Children are products of the particular culture in which they grow up, and an understanding of a particular child (and his or her parents and extended family) depends to a great extent on an appreciation and respect for the uniqueness of a culture that may be very different from one's own.

Social work education requires that students examine their own cultural heritage, values, and biases, in order to sensitize them to the feelings and beliefs of others who subscribe to different points of view. As I have pointed out in Chapter 2, self-awareness about one's own cultural beliefs and an openness to the beliefs of others form the necessary foundation for the ability to interact effectively with a client from a different culture. Since no one person can realistically expect to have knowledge about *every* different culture, the essential attitude for the worker is a willingness to put aside his or her own values and to try to identify the assumptions and values of a different culture. The worker must acknowledge and believe in the concept that there is more than one valid way to raise a child.

Closer Affiliation between Child and Family Therapy

The tension between the child-centered view of assessment and treatment, and one that sees the child's problems as reflecting family dysfunction, has a long history. In their enthusiasm for a systems view, the early family therapists, according to LeVine and Sallee (1992, p. 107), believed that

> all children's problems were best dealt with by intervening in the family system. Some still subscribe to this position, but a number now agree that the difficulties of the identified child patient may be so internal ized that individual therapy is preferred. In other cases, a family member besides the identified child may be so disturbed that individual therapy with [that family member] must precede effective family intervention.

As an experienced child and family therapist and social work educator, I find that the impact of family factors on the child is uppermost in my mind. I always acknowledge the essential role of the family for the child. However, during my career I have not noted a corresponding recognition among family therapists of the influence of the *child's* problems on the family system. In my opinion, many family therapists fail to recognize that children often have their own intrinsic problems, which do not necessarily emanate from some dysfunction in the family. The essential individuality of the child, unfortunately, is thus diminished by many family systems theories and practitioners.

With this point of view as background, I urge an end to the polarization implicit in either a child-centered or a family-centered approach to helping children. It seems patently obvious that children need their families, and that families respond to their children, either by giving them a voice or by expecting them to meld into the larger family gestalt. Children who have special problems and needs cannot conform to their families' expectations. When this is the case, the best skills of both child and family therapists are required to understand each problem situation and devise an intervention that is respectful of both a child's and a family's needs. A systems view recognizes that a child's fundamental problems will affect the family, and that effective helping includes *both* child and family approaches.

Appropriate Use of Cognitive and Behavioral Approaches

Interest in cognitive-behavioral therapy has increased in recent years because of the research that attests to the effectiveness of this approach. In addition, it satisfies the desire of child practitioners to work with children in a manner that conforms to the children's developmental need for concrete, detailed information, combined with a method for tracking their progress. Cognitive-behavioral methods provide a means of contracting and of monitoring success in regard to a specific problem situation. The specificity of this approach also appeals to managed care companies, which view this method as time-limited and easy to monitor. From the child's point of view, a behavioral method that can be followed on a chart offers the empowering opportunity to identify and reward his or her own daily successes. Chapter 6 demonstrates the use of a behavioral method with a boy with ADHD, and Chapter 7 illustrates its use with a girl with a sleep disorder.

CONCLUDING COMMENTS

As a direct practitioner, I know that the various methods demonstrated through the case examples in this book can substantially help children living in stressful family and social environments. We know a great deal about how to treat and support families, school personnel, and children themselves who are in distress. However, no matter how successful the outcome of our therapeutic/helping efforts, as thoughtful practitioners we must reflect seriously about the underlying reasons for the children's difficulties, and question whether something might have been done *sooner* to forestall the predictable deterioration of the children's untreated situation.

The value of prevention as a worthwhile goal is most appealing. Almost everyone would agree with the wisdom of improving children's lives so that they will not require special remediation services. Over the years since the Community Mental Health Centers Act of 1963, there has been consistent attention to the three levels of prevention—primary, secondary, and tertiary—originally outlined by Caplan (1964).

Social workers have been especially interested in the notion of "primary prevention," which aims to "keep something unwanted from occurring" (Bowker, 1983, p. 2). This proactive approach seeks to build adaptive strengths through education, especially with groups at high risk (LeVine & Sallee, 1992). A philosophy of primary prevention implies intervening *before* a problem becomes visible; implementing a primary prevention program thus requires a leap of faith and a belief that the desired end product of improved well-being will be worth the costs of mounting such a program. Unfortunately, many politicians prefer to deal with the squeaky wheel, instead of applying some oil to prevent the squeak. Therefore, the neglect of children's well-being continues. Hewlett (1991, p. 74) points out the sad truth that although "we know what to do we don't do it." Bloom (1981, p. 214), with tongue in cheek, says: "It obviously takes a creative practitioner to prevent problems that don't exist, among persons who don't want to be bothered, with methods that haven't been fully demonstrated to be efficacious, with regard to complex situations and powerfully competing forces."

Actually not *all* children's problems lend themselves to primary intervention, valid as that concept may be for many of the social problems arising from poverty, substance abuse/dependence, violence, and lack of good schooling and nutrition. Some conditions of childhood (e.g., ADHD and other emotional, learning, and behavioral disorders with a constitutional component) may require the combined efforts of social workers and other professionals to provide ongoing necessary services to the affected children and their families. Some problems simply do not get better with the methods we have at present, no matter how skilled the worker, or how promptly help is made available.

Helping with a problem in its early phases is referred to as "secondary prevention." For example, in the case of a child with suspected ADHD, a secondary prevention approach emphasizes early screening, testing, and goal setting so that the problem situation can be managed effectively, before it reaches a dysfunctional level requiring a "tertiary prevention" approach. When disorders such as ADHD are not diagnosed and treated in an early stage, a child may become unmotivated and disruptive in class, to the point that he or she begins to engage in antisocial behavior. In later years, this may result in the need to transfer the child to a residential treatment facility. LeVine and Sallee (1992) correctly point out that tertiary prevention such as this should more appropriately be called "remediation," not "prevention."

In addition to innate conditions that require intervention in a timely manner, certain life events, transitions, and crises that may occur in the course of the child's development may create a justifiable need for services. For example, the death of a parent or sibling, parental divorce, and chronic illness in the family all generate stress that may interfere with a child's ability to carry on his or her usual activities. As demonstrated in several chapters in this book, helping interventions focused on either the individual child or the family as a unit can provide a child with the opportunity to express and receive support for his or her feelings. *Timely* interventions in circumstances like these can prevent the further escalation of the problem.

DISCUSSION QUESTIONS AND ROLE-PLAY EXERCISES

1. Indicate how you might respond to a refugee child like Alexa who refers to a "faraway place" in her drawings. Do you think that it might be too painful for the child to recall these memories, or that this would be beneficial? Give reasons for your opinion.

2. Discuss the role of the social worker as consultant to teachers. Role-play a meeting with a teacher in which the social worker tries to sensitize the teacher to a refugee child's losses as possible determinants of the child's aggressive behavior in school. How is the issue of confidentiality applicable here, and how could this be managed?

3. How can the social worker deal with his or her negative feelings about a client from a culture that puts the parents' needs ahead of those of the child, and demands the child's instant obedience to the parents' authority?

4. Identify an issue related to children that you consider as appropriate for uniting child advocates and practitioners around a specific goal or purpose. Outline a plan of action, indicating how this effort would be funded.

Appendices

Child-Related
Professional Organizations

American Association of Psychiatric
Services for Children
1200-C Scottsville Road, Suite 225
Rochester, NY 14624
Phone: 716-235-6910
Fax: 716-235-0654

American Professional Society
on the Abuse of Children
407 South Dearborn, Suite 1300
Chicago, IL 60605
Phone: 312-554-0166
Fax: 312-554-0919

Association for Play Therapy
c/o California School of Professional
Psychology–Fresno
5130 East Clinton Way
Fresno, CA 93727
Phone: 209-253-2278
Fax: 209-253-2239

Association of Pediatric Oncology
Social Workers
c/o Rod J. Herrera, M.S.W.
St. Christopher's Hospital
Department of Hematology/
Oncology
Front and Erie Streets
Philadelphia, PA 19134

Phone: 215-427-4442
Fax: 215-427-6682

Child Welfare League of America
440 First Street N.W., Suite 310
Washington, DC 20001-2085
Phone: 202-638-2952
Fax: 202-638-4004

Children's Group Therapy
Association
P.O. Box 521
Watertown, MA 02172
Phone: 617-894-4307
       617-646-7571
Fax: 617-894-1195

Council for Exceptional Children
1920 Association Drive
Reston, VA 22091
Phone: 703-620-3660
Fax: 703-264-9494

National Association of Perinatal
Social Workers
c/o Denise Knoebel
123 Cheat Canyon Park Drive
Morgantown, WV 26505
Phone: 304-594-2432
       304-598-4869
Fax: 304-598-4900

Child-Related
Professional Journals

Child Abuse and Neglect
Elsevier Science
Journals Division
660 White Plains Road
Tarrytown, NY 10591-5153
Phone: 914-524-9200
Fax: 914-333-2444

Child and Adolescent Social Work
Journal
Human Sciences Press, Inc.
233 Spring Street
New York, NY 10013-1578
Phone: 212-620-8000
Fax: 212-463-0742

Child and Family Behavior
Haworth Press, Inc.
10 Alice Street
Binghamton, NY 13904
Phone: 800-342-9678
Fax: 607-722-1424

Child: Care, Health and Development
Blackwell Science Ltd.
Osney Mead
Oxford OX2 0EL, England
Phone: 01865-206206
Fax: 01865-721205

Child Development
University of Chicago Press
Journals Division
P.O. Box 37005
Chicago, IL 60637
Phone: 312-753-3347
Fax: 312-753-0811

Child Psychiatry and Human
Development
(American Association of Psychiatric
Services for Children)
Human Sciences Press, Inc.
233 Spring Street
New York, NY 10013-1578
Phone: 212-620-8000
Fax: 212-463-0742

Child Study Journal
State University of New York College
at Buffalo
Educational Foundations Department
Bacon Hall 306
1300 Elmwood Avenue
Buffalo, NY 14222-1095
Phone: 716-878-5302
Fax: 716-873-5833

Child Welfare (formerly *Child Welfare Quarterly*)
Intercontinental Marketing Corp.
P.O. Box 5056
Tokyo 100-31, Japan
Phone: 81-3-63661-7458
Fax: 81-3-3667-9646

Children and Youth Care Forum
Human Sciences Press, Inc.
233 Spring Street
New York, NY 10013-1578
Phone: 212-620-8000
Fax: 212-463-0742

Children and Youth Services
Haworth Press, Inc.
10 Alice Street
Binghamton, NY 13904
Phone: 800-342-9678
Fax: 607-772-1424
          800-895-0582

Children's Health Care Journal
Lawrence Erlbaum Associates
10 Industrial Avenue
Mahwah, NJ 07430
Phone: 201-236-9500
Fax: 201-236-0072

Children Today
U.S. Department of Health and
Human Services
Administration for Children and
Families
Office of the Assistant Secretary
370 L'Enfant Promenade S.W.,
7th floor
Washington, DC 20447
Phone: 202-401-5180
Fax: 202-205-9688

Early Child Research Quarterly
Ablex Publishing Corp.
355 Chestnut Street
Norwood, NJ 07648
Phone: 201-767-8450
Fax: 201-767-6717

Gifted Child Quarterly
National Association for Gifted
Children
1707 L Street, N.W., Suite 550
Washington, DC 20036

Journal of Abnormal Child Psychology
Plenum Publishing Corp.
233 Spring Street
New York, NY 10013-1578
Phone: 212-620-8000
Fax: 212-460-0742

*Journal of the American Academy of
Child and Adolescent Psychiatry*
Williams & Wilkins
351 West Camden Street
Baltimore, MD 21201
Phone: 410-528-4000
Fax: 410-528-4312

*Journal of Child and Adolescent Group
Therapy*
Human Sciences Press, Inc.
233 Spring Street
New York, NY 10013-1578
Phone: 212-620-8000
Fax: 212-463-0742

Journal of Child and Youth Care
(formerly *Journal of Child Care*)
University of Calgary Press
2500 University Drive N.W.
Calgary, Alberta T2N IN4, Canada
Phone: 403-220-7578
Fax: 403-282-0085

Journal of Child Psychology and
Psychiatry and Allied Disciplines
Elsevier Science
Journals Division
660 White Plains Road
Tarrytown, NY 10591-5153
Phone: 914-524-9200
Fax: 914-333-2444

Journal of Clinical Child Psychology
(American Psychological
Association, Division of
Clinical Child Psychology)

Lawrence Erlbaum Associates
10 Industrial Avenue
Mahwah, NJ 07430
Phone: 201-236-9500
Fax: 201-236-0072

Psychoanalytic Study of the Child
Yale University Press
P.O. Box 209040
New Haven, CT 06520-9040
Phone: 203-432-0940
Fax: 800-777-9253

Forms for Assessment
of the Bereaved Child

TABLE A1. Individual Factors in Childhood Bereavement: Webb

---

1. Age _____ years _____ months   Date of birth _____
                                        Date of assessment _____

    a. Developmental stage: b. Cognitive level:
       Freud _____   Piaget _____
       Erikson _____   c. Temperamental characteristics:
                                          Thomas and Chess _____

2. Past coping/adjustment
    a. Home (as reported by parents): Good _____ Fair _____ Poor _____
    b. School (as reported by parents and teachers): Good _____ Fair _____ Poor _____
    c. Interpersonal/peers: Good _____ Fair _____ Poor _____
    d. Hobbies/interests (list) _____

3. Global Assessment of Functioning: DSM-IV, Axis V
    Current _____   Past year _____

4. Medical history (as reported by parents and pediatrician)—describe serious illnesses, operations, and injuries since birth, with dates and outcome_____
    _____
    _____
    _____

5. Past experience with death/loss—give details with dates and outcome *or* complete Wolfelt's Loss Inventory
    _____
    _____
    _____

Note. This form is one part of the three-part assessment of the bereaved child, which also includes an assessment of death-related factors (Table A2) and family/social/religious/cultural factors (Table A4). From Webb (1993, p. 31). Copyright 1993 by The Guilford Press. Reprinted by permission.

TABLE A2. Death-Related Factors in Childhood Bereavement: Webb

1. Type of death

    Anticipated: Yes _____ No _____ If yes, how long? _____ or sudden _____

    "Timeliness" of death: Age of the deceased _____

    Perception of preventability:

    Definitely preventable _____ Maybe _____ Not _____

    Degree of pain associated with death:

    None _____ Some _____ Much _____

    Presence of violence/trauma: Yes _____ No _____

    If yes, describe, indicating whether the child witnessed, heard about, or was present
    and experienced the trauma personally. _____

    _____

    _____

    Element of stigma: Yes _____ No _____

    If yes, describe, indicating nature of death, and degree of openness of family in
    discussing. _____

    _____

    _____

2. Contact with deceased

    Present at moment of death? Yes _____ No _____

    If yes, describe circumstances, including who else was present and whether the
    deceased said anything specifically to the child. _____

    _____

    _____

    Did the child view the dead body? Yes _____ No _____

    If yes, describe circumstances, including reactions of the child and others who were
    present. _____

    Did the child attend funeral/memorial service/graveside service?

    Yes _____ No _____ Which? _____

    Child's reactions _____

    _____

    Has the child visited grave/mausoleum since the death? Yes _____ No _____

    If yes, describe circumstances. _____

    _____

    _____

3. Did the child make any expression of "goodbye" to the deceased, either spontaneous
    or suggested? Yes _____ No _____

    If yes, describe. _____

    _____

    _____

Note. This form is one part of the three-part assessment of the bereaved child, which
also includes an assessment of individual factors (Table A1) and family/social/religious/
cultural factors (Table A4). From Webb (1993, p. 35). Copyright 1993 by The Guilford Press.
Reprinted by permission.

TABLE A3. Recording Form for Childhood Grief Reactions: Webb

Age of child _____ years _____ months   Date of birth _____

                                                  Date of assessment _____

See the form "Individual Factors in Childhood Bereavement" [Table A1] for recording of personal history factors.

Date of death _____
Relationship to deceased _____
   Favorite activities shared with deceased _____
   What the child will miss the most _____
   If the child could see the deceased again for 1 hour, what would he/she like to do or
   say? _____
   _____
   _____

Nature of grief reactions (describe) _____
_____

   Signs of the following feelings? Y = Yes; N = No
   Sadness _____ Anger _____ Confusion _____ Guilt _____ Relief _____
   Other _____
Source of information on which this form has been completed
_____ Parent _____ Observation _____ Other

Note. This form is an extension of "Death-Related Factors in Childhood Bereavement" (Table A2), focusing specifically on the nature of the child's grief. From Webb (1993, p. 38). Copyright 1993 by The Guilford Press. Reprinted by permission.

TABLE A4. Family/Social/Religious/Cultural Factors in Childhood Bereavement: Webb

1. Family influences
      Nuclear family: How responding to death? Describe in terms of relative degree of openness of response.
      Very expressive _____ Moderately expressive _____ Very guarded _____
      To what extend is child included in family discussions/rituals related to the deceased?
      Some _____ A great deal _____ Not at all _____
      Extended family: How responding to death? Describe, as above, in terms of relative degree of openness of response.
      Very expressive _____ Moderately expressive _____ Very guarded _____
      To what extend do the views of the extended family differ or agree with those of the nuclear family with regard to the planning of rituals and inclusion of child?
      Very different _____ Very similar _____
      If different, describe the nature of the disagreement _____
      _____

2. School/peer influences
      Child's grade in school _____
      Did any of the child's friends/peers attend the funeral/memorial services?
      Yes _____ No _____
      Was teacher informed of death? Yes _____ No _____
      Did child receive condolence messages from friends/peers? Yes _____ No _____
      Does child know anyone his/her age who has been bereaved? Yes _____ No _____
      If yes, has child spoken to this person since the death? Yes _____ No _____
      Does child express feelings about wanting or not wanting peers/friends to know about the death? Yes _____ No _____
      If yes, what has the child said? _____
3. Religious/cultural influences
      What is the child's religion? _____
      Has he/she been observant? Yes _____ No _____
      What are the beliefs of the child's religion regarding death? _____
      _____
      What about life after death? _____
      Has child expressed any thoughts/feelings about this? _____
      _____

Note. This form is one part of the three-part assessment of the bereaved child, which also includes an assessment of individual factors (Table A1) and death-related factors (Table A2). From Webb (1993, p. 39). Copyright 1993 by The Guilford Press. Reprinted by permission.

Forms for Assessment
of the Child in Crisis

TABLE A5. Crisis Situation Rating Form: Webb

---

1. Psychosocial and environmental problems: DSM-IV, Axis IV
   List problems _____

2. Anticipated _____ or sudden _____ crisis (check where appropriate)
   Amount of preparation _____
3. Single _____ or recurring _____ crisis events
   (list discrete crisis events)
   a. _____   c. _____
   b. _____   d. _____
4. Solitary _____ or shared _____ crisis experience
   Number of other individuals involved _____
5. Presence of loss factor
   a. Separation from family members (list relationship and length of separation) _____
   _____
   _____

   b. Death of family members (list relationship and cause of death) _____
   _____
   _____

   c. Loss of familiar environment (describe) _____
   _____
   _____

   d. Loss of familiar role/status (describe; temporary or permanent? _____
   _____
   _____

   e. Loss of body part or function (describe, with prognosis) _____
   _____
   _____

6. Physical injury or pain (describe, with prognosis) _____
   _____
   _____

7. Presence of violence: verbal and/or physical
   a. Witnessed _____ Verbal _____ Physical _____
   b. Experienced _____ Verbal _____ Physical _____
8. Degree of life threat
   a. Personal (describe) _____
   _____
   _____

   b. To family members (describe, identifying relationship) _____
   _____
   _____

   c. To others (describe) _____
   _____
   _____

9. Other components of the crisis situation _____
   _____
   _____

Note. This form is one part of a three-part crisis assessment, which also includes an assessment of individual and support system factors. Adapted from Webb (1991, p. 11). Copyright 1991 by The Guilford Press. Adapted by permission.

TABLE A6. Individual Factors in the Assessment of the Child in Crisis: Webb

1. Age _____ years _____ months   Date of birth_____
                                                 Date of assessment _____

   a. Developmental stage: b. Cognitive level:
       Freud _____   Piaget _____
       Erikson _____   d. Temperamental characteristics:
   c. Moral development: Thomas and Chess _____
       Kohlberg _____

2. Precrisis adjustment
   a. Home (as reported by parents): Good _____ Fair _____ Poor _____
   b. School (as reported by parents and teachers): Good _____ Fair _____ Poor _____
   c. Interpersonal/peers: Good _____ Fair _____ Poor _____
   d. Medical (as reported by parents/and pediatrician)—describe serious illnesses, operations, and injuries since birth, with dates and outcome _____
   _____
   _____
   Past or current use of medications _____
   _____

3. Coping style/ego assessment (as reported by parents and observed in interviews with child)
   a. Degree of anxiety: High _____ Moderate _____ Low _____
   b. Ability to separate from parent: High anxiety _____ Some anxiety _____
       No anxiety _____
   c. Child's ability to discuss "the problem/crisis situation": Good _____ Fair _____
       None _____
   d. Presence of symptoms (describe, including the extent to which these bind the anxiety) _____
   _____
   e. Defenses (list, indicating appropriateness) _____
   _____

4. Child's past experience with crises _____
   a. Previous losses (list, giving age) _____
   _____
   b. Major life transitions/adjustments (list, giving age) _____
   _____
   c. Past experience with violence _____
   _____
   d. Other (describe) _____
   _____

5. Global Assessment of Functioning: DSM IV, Axis V
   Current _____ Past year _____

6. Specific meaning of crisis to the child: Why is this crisis situation so difficult for *this* child at *this* time? (describe) _____
   _____

Suppliers of Play Materials

Center for Applied Psychology, Inc.
Childswork/Childsplay
P.O. Box 61586
King of Prussia, PA 19406
Phone: 800-962-1141
Fax: 610-277-4556

Creative Therapeutics
155 County Road
Cresskill, NJ 07626-0522
Phone: 201-567-7295
Fax: 201-567-3036

Kidsrights
10100 Park Cedar Drive
Charlotte, NC 28210
Phone: 800-892-KIDS
Fax: 704-541-0113

Play Therapy Associates
Toys for Psychotherapy with
Children
1750 25th Avenue, Suite 200
Greeley, CO 80631-4945
Phone: 800-542-9723
Fax: 970-351-6687

School Specialty
(Formerly New England School
Supply)
(The Book of Early Learning
Catalogue)
P.O. Box 3004
Agawam, MA 01001
Phone: 800-628-8608
Fax: 800-272-0101

Toys to Grow On
2695 East Dominguez Street
P.O. Box 17
Long Beach, CA 90801
Phone: 800-542-8338
Fax: 310-537-5403

U.S. Toy Co., Inc.
Constructive Playthings
1227 East 119th Street
Grandview, MO 64030
Phone: 816-761-5900 (Kansas City
area only)
Phone: 800-832-0572
        800-448-4115
Fax: 816-761-9295
Seven stores located nationwide

Western Psychological Services
12031 Wilshire Boulevard
Los Angeles, CA 90025
Phone: 800-648-8857
Fax: 310-478-7838

Training Programs
in Play Therapy

A comprehensive directory of play therapy training programs may be obtained for a fee from University of North Texas, Center for Play Therapy, Denton, Texas. The programs listed here represent a small selection of those available in different parts of the United States.

Boston University
School of Social Work
Postgraduate Certificate
Program in Advanced
Child and Adolescent
Psychotherapy
1 University Road
Boston, MA 02215
Phone: 617-353-3756
Fax: 617-353-7262

California School of Professional
Psychology–Fresno
Dr. Kevin O'Connor
5130 East Clinton Way
Fresno, CA 93727
Phone: 209-456-2273
Fax: 209-253-2239

Fairleigh Dickinson University
Department of Psychological Services
Dr. Charles Schaefer
139 Temple Avenue
Hackensack, NJ 07601
Phone: 201-692-2649
Fax: 201-692-2164

Fordham University
Graduate School of Social Service
Postgraduate Certificate Program in
Child and Adolescent Therapy
Dr. Nancy Boyd Webb, Director
Tarrytown, NY 10591
Phone: 914-332-6008
Fax: 914-332-7101

Pennsylvania State University
Division of Human Development and
Family Studies
Dr. Louise Guerney
University Park, PA 16802
Phone: 814-865-1447
Fax: 814-863-7963

The Theraplay Institute
1137 Central
Wilmette, IL 60091
Phone: 847-256-7334
Fax: 847-256-7370

University of North Texas
Center for Play Therapy
Dr. Gary Landreth, Director
Denton, TX 76203
Phone: 817-565-3864
Fax: 817-382-0080

References

Achenbach, T. M., & Edelbrock, C. E. (1983). *Manual for the Child Behavior Checklist and Revised Child Behavior Profile*. Burlington: University of Vermont, Department of Psychiatry.

Achenbach, T. M., & Howell, C. T. (1993). Are American children's problems getting worse? A 13-year comparison. *Journal of the American Academy of Child Psychiatry*, 32(6), 1145–1154.

Adoption Assistance and Child Welfare Reform Act, P.L. 96-272, 94 Stat. 500 (1980).

Ainsworth, M. D. S. (1979). Infant–mother attachment. *American Psychologist, 34*, 932–937.

Ainsworth, M. D. S., & Bell, S. M. (1971). Attachment, exploration, and separation: Illustrated by the behavior of one-year-olds in a strange situation. In S. Chess & A. Thomas (Eds.), *Annual progress in child psychiatry and child development* (pp. 41–60). New York: Brunner/Mazel.

Ajdukovic, M., & Ajdukovic, D. (1993). Psychological well-being of refugee children. *Child Abuse and Neglect, 17*, 843–854.

Alessi, J. J., & Hearn, K. (1984). Group treatment in shelters for battered women. In A. R. Roberts (Ed.), *Battered women and their families* (pp. 49–61). New York: Springer.

Alexander, D. W. (1992). *Something bad happened series: The world I see*. Huntington, NY: Bureau for At-Risk Youth.

Alissi, A. S., & Casper, M. (Eds.). (1985). Time as a factor in groupwork [Special issue]. *Social Work with Groups, 8*(2).

Allen-Meares, P., Washington, R., & Welsh, B. (1986). *Social work services in schools*. Englewood Cliffs, NJ: Prentice-Hall.

Amendments to the Education of the Handicapped Act, P.L. 99-457, 100 Stat. 1145–1158 (1986).

American Bar Association Working Group. (1993). *America's children at risk: A national agenda for legal action*. Chicago: American Bar Association.

American Psychiatric Association. (1994). *Diagnostic and statistical manual of mental disorders* (4th ed.). Washington, DC: Author.

Angelou, M. (1991). *All God's children need traveling shoes*. New York: Random House. (Original work published 1986)

Anthony, E. J., & Cohler, B. J. (Eds.). (1987). *The invulnerable child*. New York: Guilford Press.

Aponte, H. (1990). *Tres madres* [Videotape]. Kansas City, MO: Golden Triad.

Assistance to States for Education of Handicapped Children, 34 C.F.R. §300.13(b)(2) (1991).

Aust, P. H. (1981). Using the life story book to treat children in placement. *Child Welfare*, *60*, 535–560.

Axline, V. (1947). *Play therapy*. Boston: Houghton Mifflin.

Axline, V. (1964). *Dibs: In search of self*. New York: Ballantine.

Backhaus, K. (1984). Life books: Tool for working with children in placement. *Social Work*, *29*(6), 551–554.

Bank, S. P., & Kahn, M. (1982). *The sibling bond*. New York: Basic Books.

Barker, P. (1995). *Basic child psychiatry* (6th ed.). Oxford: Blackwell Scientific.

Barnard, C. P. (1984). Alcoholism and incest. *Focus on Family and Chemical Dependency*, *7*(1), 27–29.

Bassuk, E. L. (1993). Social and economic hardships of homeless and other poor women. *American Journal of Orthopsychiatry*, *63*(3), 340–347.

Bassuk, E. L., & Rubin, L. (1986). Homeless children: A neglected population. *American Journal of Orthopsychiatry*, *57*(2), 279–286.

Beck, A. T., Rush, A. J., Shaw, B. F., & Emery, G. (1979). *Cognitive therapy of depression*. New York: Guilford Press.

Bell, J. E. (1961). *Family group therapy* (Public Health Monograph No. 64). Washington, DC: U.S. Government Printing Office.

Belsky, J. (1993). Etiology of child maltreatment: A developmental–ecological analysis. *Psychological Bulletin*, *114*, 413–434.

Bernier, J. C., & Siegel, D. H. (1994). Attention-deficit hyperactivity disorder: A family and ecological systems perspective. *Families in Society*, *75*(3), 142–151.

Besharov, D. J. (1989). The children of crack: Will we protect them? *Public Welfare*, *46*(4), 7–11.

Bevin, T. (1991). Multiple traumas of refugees—near drowning and witnessing of maternal rape: Case of Sergio, age 9. In N. B. Webb (Ed.), *Play therapy with children in crisis: A casebook for practitioners* (pp. 92–140). New York: Guilford Press.

Bishop, E. E., & McNally, G. (1993). An in-home crisis intervention program for children and their families. *Hospital and Community Psychiatry*, *44*(2), 182–184.

Bishop, K. K. (1993). P.L. 99-457: A family-centered continuing education curriculum for social workers. *Journal of Teaching in Social Work*, *7*(2), 47–61.

Bishop, K. K., Rounds, K. A., & Weil, M. (1993). P.L. 97-457: Preparation for social work practice with infants and toddlers with disabilities and their families. *Journal of Social Work Education*, *29*(1), 36–45.

Black, R., & Mayer, J. (1980). Parents with special problems: Alcoholism and opiate addictions. In C. H. Kempe & R. Helfer (Eds.), *The battered child* (pp. 104–113). Chicago: University of Chicago Press.

Blanchard, P. (1946). Case 1: Tommy Nolan. In H. L. Witmer (Ed.), *Psychiatric interviews with children* (pp. 59–92). New York: Commonwealth Fund.

Bloch, D. A., & LaPerriere, K. (1973). Techniques of family therapy: A conceptual frame. In D. A. Bloch (Ed.), *Techniques of family psychotherapy* (pp. 1–20). New York: Grune & Stratton.

Block, J., & Margolis, J. (1986). Feelings of shame: Siblings of handicapped children. In A. Gitterman & L. Shulman (Eds.), *Mutual aid groups and the life cycle* (pp. 91–108). Itasca, IL: F. E. Peacock.

Bloom, M. (1981). *Primary prevention: The possible science.* Englewood Cliffs, NJ: Prentice-Hall.

Boulanger, M. D., & Langevin, C. (1992). Direct observation of play group therapy for social skills deficits. *Journal of Child and Adolescent Group Therapy, 2*(4), 227–236.

Bowker, J. P. (1983). Overview. In J. P. Bowker (Ed.), *Education for primary prevention in social work* (pp. 1–6). New York: Council on Social Work Education.

Bowlby, J. (1958). The nature of the child's tie to his mother. *International Journal of Psycho-Analysis, 39,* 350–373.

Bowlby, J. (1969). *Attachment and loss: Vol. 1. Attachment.* New York: Basic Books.

Bowlby, J. (1973). *Attachment and loss: Vol. 2. Separation: Anxiety and anger.* New York: Basic Books.

Bowlby, J. (1977). The making and breaking of affectional bonds. *British Journal of Psychiatry, 130,* 201–210, 421–431.

Bowlby, J. (1979). *The making and breaking of affectional bonds.* London: Tavistock.

Bowlby, J. (1980). *Attachment and loss: Vol. 3. Loss: Sadness and depression.* New York: Basic Books.

Bowlby, J. (1988). *A secure base: Parent–child attachment and healthy human development.* New York: Basis Books.

Boyd-Franklin, N., Steiner, G. L., & Boland, M. G. (Eds.). (1995). *Children, families, and HIV/AIDS: Psychosocial and therapeutic issues.* New York: Guilford Press.

Brandler, S., & Roman, C. P. (1991). *Group work skills and strategies for effective intervention.* New York: Haworth Press.

Brieland, D., Costin, L. B., & Atherton, C. R. (1985). *Contemporary social work: An introduction to social work and social welfare* (3rd ed.). New York: McGraw-Hill.

Brieland, D., Fallon, B. J., & Korr, W. (1994). Act now for children's rights. *Social Work, 39*(1), 132–134.

Bronfenbrenner, U. (1979). *The ecology of human development.* Cambridge, MA: Harvard University Press.

Browne, A. (1993). Family violence and homelessness: The relevance of trauma histories in the lives of homeless women. *American Journal of Orthopsychiatry, 63*(3), 370–384.

Bruni, F. (1995, November 24). The case of Alisa: A child dies, and the questions abound. *The New York Times,* p. B-1.

Bullrich, S. (1989). The process of immigration. In L. Combrinck-Graham (Ed.), *Children in family contexts: Perspectives on treatment* (pp. 482–501). New York: Guilford Press.

Burns, R. C., & Kaufman, S. H. (1970). *Kinetic Family Drawing (K-F-D): Research and application.* New York: Brunner/Mazel.

Burns, R. C., & Kaufman, S. H. (1972). *Actions, styles and symbols in Kinetic Family Drawings (K-F-D): An interpretive manual.* New York: Brunner/Mazel.

Caldwell, B., & Bradley, R. (1979). *Home observation for measurement of the environment*. Little Rock: University of Arkansas Center for Child Development and Education.

Call, D. A. (1990). School-based groups: A valuable support for children of cancer patients. *Journal of Psychosocial Oncology, 8*(1), 97–118.

Cambridge and Somerville Program for Alcoholism Rehabilitation (CASPAR). (1978). *Decisions about drinking* [Mimeograph]. Somerville, MA: Author.

Caplan, G. (1964). *Principles of preventive psychiatry*. New York: Basic Books.

Carlson, B. E. (1984). Children's observations of interpersonal violence. In A. R. Roberts (Ed.), *Battered women and their families* (pp. 147–167). New York: Springer.

Carrillo, D. F., Holzhalb, C. M., & Thyer, B. A. (1993). Assessing social work students' attitudes related to cultural diversity: A review of selected measures. *Journal of Social Work Education, 29*(3), 263–268.

Carter, E. A., & McGoldrick, M. (1980). *The family life cycle*. New York: Gardner Press.

Chasin, R., & White, T. B. (1989). The child in family therapy: Guidelines for active engagement across the age span. In Combrinck-Graham (Ed.), *Children in family contexts: Perspectives on treatment* (pp. 5–25). New York: Guilford Press.

Chess, S. (1988). Child and adolescent psychiatry come of age: A fifty-year perspective. *Journal of the American Academy of Child and Adolescent Psychiatry, 27*(1), 1–7.

Chess, S., & Thomas, A. (1986). *Temperament in clinical practice*. New York: Guilford Press.

Chethik, M. (1989). *Techniques of child therapy: Psychodynamic strategies*. New York: Guilford Press.

Child Abuse Prevention and Treatment Act, P.L. 93-247, 88 Stat 119 (1974).

Child Welfare League of America. (1981). *Directory of member agencies*. New York: Author.

Children's Defense Fund. (1992). *State of America's children*. Washington, DC: Author.

Chira, S. (1994, April 12). Study confirms some fears on U.S. children. *The New York Times*, pp. A-1, A-13.

Code of federal regulations. (1993, July). Parts 300–303. Washington, DC: U.S. Government Printing Office.

Combrinck-Graham, L. (Ed.). (1989). *Children in family contexts: Perspectives on treatment*. New York: Guilford Press.

Community Mental Health Centers Act, P.L. 88-164, 77 Stat. 290–294 (1963).

Congress, E. P. (1994). The use of culturagrams to assess and empower culturally diverse families. *Families in Society, 75*(9), 531–539.

Conners, C. K. (1969). A teacher rating scale for use in drug studies with children. *American Journal of Psychiatry, 126*, 884–888.

Conners, C. K. (1970). Symptom patterns in hyperkinetic, neurotic, and normal children. *Child Development, 41*, 667–682.

Copans, S. (1989). The invisible family member: Children in families with alcohol abuse. In L. Combrinck-Graham (Ed.), *Children in family contexts: Perspectives on treatment* (pp. 277–298). New York: Guilford Press.

Costin, L. B. (1969). A historical review of school social work. *Social Casework, 50*(10), 439–453.

Costin, L. B. (1987). School social work. In A. Minahan (Ed.), *Encyclopedia of social work* (18th ed., pp. 538–545). Silver Spring, MD: National Association of Social Workers.

Council on Social Work Education (CSWE). (1973). *Handbook of accreditation standards and procedures.* New York: Author.

Council on Social Work Education (CSWE). (1984). *Handbook of accreditation standards and procedures* (rev. ed.). New York: Author.

Council on Social Work Education (CSWE). (1992a). *Curriculum policy statement for baccalaureate degree programs in social work education.* Alexandria, VA: Author.

Council on Social Work Education (CSWE). (1992b). *Curriculum policy statement for master's degree programs in social work education.* Alexandria, VA: Author.

Cournoyer, B. (1991). *The social work skills workbook.* Belmont, CA: Wadsworth.

Dane, E. (1990). *Painful passages: Working with children with learning disabilities.* Silver Spring, MD: National Association of Social Workers.

Daro, D., & McCurdy, K. L. (1991). *Current trends in child abuse reporting and fatalities: The results of the 1989 annual fifty-state survey.* Chicago: National Center on Child Abuse Prevention Research, National Committee for Prevention of Child Abuse.

Davis, R. B., Johnston, P. D., DiCicco, L., & Orenstein, A. (1985). Helping elementary children of alcoholic parents: An elementary school program. *The School Counselor, 32*(5), 357–363.

Deutsch, C. (1982). *Broken bottles, broken dreams.* New York: Teachers College Press.

Deutsch, C., DiCicco, L., & Mills, D. (1979, September 24–28). Reaching children from families with alcoholism: Some innovative techniques. In *Proceedings of the 29th annual meeting of the Alcohol and Drug Problems Association of North America* (pp. 54–58), Seattle, WA.

Devore, W., & Schlesinger, E. G. (1987). *Ethnic-sensitive social work practice* (2nd ed.). Columbus, OH: Merrill.

DiCicco, L., Biron, R., Carifio, J., Deutsch, C., Mills, D. J., Orenstein, A., Re, A., Unterberger, H., & White, R. E. (1984). Evaluation of the CASPAR alcohol education curriculum. *Journal of Studies on Alcohol, 45*(2), 160–169.

DiLeo, J. H. (1973). *Children's drawings as diagnostic aids.* New York: Brunner/Mazel.

Dillard, H. K., Donenberg, B., & Glickman, H. (1986). A support system for parents with learning disabled children. In M. T. Hawkins (Ed.), *Achieving educational excellence for children at risk* (pp. 50–55). Silver Spring, MD: National Association of Social Workers.

Docker-Drysdale, B. (1993). *Therapy and consultation in child care.* London: Free Association Books.

Doka, K. (Ed.). (1989). *Disenfranchised grief.* New York: Free Press.

Dore, M. M. (1993). Family preservation and poor families: When homebuilding is not enough. *Families in Society, 74*(9), 545–556.

Doster, G., & McElroy, C. Q. (1993). Sudden death of a teacher: Multilevel intervention in an elementary school. In N. B. Webb (Ed.), *Helping bereaved children: A handbook for practitioners* (pp. 212–238). New York: Guilford Press.

Doyle, J. S., & Bauer, S. K. (1989). Post-Traumatic Stress Disorder in Children: Its identification and treatment in a residential setting for emotionally disturbed youths. *Journal of Traumatic Stress, 2*(3), 275–288.

Doyle, J. S., & Stoop, D. (1991). Witness and victim of multiple abuses: Collaborative treatment of 10-year-old Randy in a residential treatment center. In N. B. Webb (Ed.), *Play therapy with children in crisis: A casebook for practitioners* (pp. 111–140). New York: Guilford Press.

Dupper, D. R., & Halter, A. P. (1994). Barriers in educating children from homeless shelters: Perspectives of school and shelter staff. *Social Work in Education, 16*(1), 39–45.

Duvall, E. (1977). *Marriage and family development* (5th ed.). Philadelphia: J. B. Lippincott.

Education for All Handicapped Children Act, P.L. 94-142, 89 Stat. 77 (1975).

English, A. (1990). Prenatal drug exposure: Grounds for mandatory child abuse reports? *Youth Law News, 11*(1), 3–8.

Enzer, N. B. (1988). *Overview of play therapy.* Paper presented at the annual meeting of the American Academy of Child and Adolescent Psychiatry, Seattle, WA.

Erikson, E. H. (1963). *Childhood and society* (rev. ed.). New York: Norton.

Erikson, E. H. (1968). *Identity: Youth and crisis.* New York: Norton.

Eth, S., & Pynoos, R. S. (Eds.). (1985). *Post-Traumatic Stress Disorder in children.* Washington, DC: American Psychiatric Press.

Evans, M. D. (1986). *This is me and my two families: An awareness scrapbook/journal for children living in stepfamilies.* New York: Magination Press.

Ewing, C. P. (1990). *Kids who kill.* Lexington, MA: Lexington Books.

Family Educational Rights and Privacy Act, P.L. 93-380, Stat. 571, 20 (1974).

Federal Bureau of Investigation. (1991). *Uniform crime report for the United States, 1990.* Washington, DC: U.S. Government Printing Office.

Federal Emergency Management Agency. (1991a). *Children and trauma* [Videotape]. Washington, DC: Author.

Federal Emergency Management Agency. (1991b). *How to help children after a disaster: A guidebook for teachers* (FEMA 219). Washington, DC: Author.

Federal Emergency Management Agency. (1991c). *School intervention following a critical incident* (FEMA 220). Washington, DC: Author.

Feig, L. (1990). *Drug-exposed infants and children: Service needs and policy questions.* Washington, DC: U.S. Department of Health and Human Services.

Feinberg, F. (1995). Substance-abusing mothers and their children: Treatment for the family. In L. Combrinck-Graham (Ed.), *Children in families at risk: Maintaining the connections* (pp. 228–247). New York: Guilford Press.

Ford, J. M., & Youksetter, W. D. (1981). *A study of California children in group care.* Sacramento: Children's Research Institute of California.

Freud, A. (1937). *The ego and the mechanisms of defense.* London: Hogarth Press.

Freud, A. (1968). *The psychoanalytic treatment of children: Technical lectures and essays.* New York: International Universities Press. (Original work published 1946)

Freud, A. (1970). The concept of the rejecting mother. In E. J. Anthony & T. Benedek (Eds.), *Parenthood: Its psychology and psychopathology* (pp. 376–386). Boston: Little, Brown.

Furman, E. (1974). *A child's parent dies.* New Haven, CT: Yale University Press.

Garbarino, J. (1992). Developmental consequences of living in dangerous and unstable environments: The situation of refugee children. In M. McCallin (Ed.), *The psychological well-being of refugee children* (pp. 1–23). Geneva: International Catholic Child Bureau.

Garbarino, J., Stott, F. M., & Associates. (1989). *What children can tell us.* San Francisco: Jossey-Bass.

Gardner, R. A. (1983). Children's reactions to parental death. In J. E. Schowalter, P. E. Patterson, M. Tallmer, A. H. Kutscher, S. W. Gullo, & D. Peretz (Eds.), *The child and death* (pp. 104–124). New York: Columbia University Press.

Garrett, K. J. (1994). Caught in a bind: Ethical decision making in schools. *Social Work in Education, 16*(2), 97–105.

Garrity, C. B., & Baris, M. A. (1994). *Caught in the middle: Protecting children of high-conflict divorce.* New York: Free Press.

Gelles, R. J. (1979). *Family violence.* Beverly Hills, CA: Sage.

Gentry, D. B., & Beneson, W. A. (1993). School-to-home transfer of conflict management skills among school-age children. *Families in Society, 74*(2), 67–73.

George, H. (1988). Child therapy and animals. In C. E. Schaefer (Ed.), *Innovative interventions in child and adolescent therapy* (pp. 400–418). New York: Wiley.

Germain, C. B. (1968). Social study: Past and future. *Social Casework, 49*(7), 403–409.

German, C. B. (1973). An ecological perspective in casework practice. *Social Casework, 54,* 323–330.

Germain, C. B., & Gitterman, A. (1987). Ecological perspective. In A. Minahan (Ed.), *Encyclopedia of social work* (18th ed., pp. 488–499). Silver Spring, MD: National Association of Social Workers.

Gibbs, J. T., Huang, L. N., & Associates (Eds.). (1989). *Children of color: Psychological interventions with minority youth.* San Francisco: Jossey-Bass.

Gil, E. (1991). *The healing power of play.* New York: Guilford Press.

Gil, E. (1994). *Play in family therapy.* New York: Guilford Press.

Gilliland, B. E., & James, R. K. (1993). *Crisis intervention strategies* (2nd ed.). Pacific Grove, CA: Brooks/Cole.

Ginott, H. G. (1961). *Group psychotherapies with children.* New York: McGraw-Hill.

Ginsburg, E. H. (1989). *School social work: A practitioner's guidebook.* Springfield, IL: Charles C Thomas.

Gitterman, A., & Shulman, L. (Eds.). (1986). *Mutual aid groups and the life cycle.* Itasca, IL: F. E. Peacock.

Gittler, J., & McPherson, M. (1990). Prenatal substance abuse: An overview of the problem. *Children Today, 19*(4), 3–7.

Goldberg, M. E. (1995). Substance-abusing women: False stereotypes and real needs. *Social Work, 40*(6), 789–798.

Goldberg, S. B. (1973). Family tasks and reactions in the crisis of death. *Social Casework, 54,* 398–405.

Goldman, J., Stein, C. L'E., & Guerry, S. (1983). *Psychological methods of child assessment.* New York: Brunner/Mazel.

Goleman, D. (1993, December 8). New study portrays the young as more and more troubled. *The New York Times*, p. C-16.

Gonzales-Ramos, G., & Goldstein, E. (1989). Child maltreatment: An overview. In S. Ehrenkrantz, E. G. Goblstein, L. Goodman, & J. Seinfeld (Eds.), *Clinical social work with maltreated children and their families* (pp. 3–20). New York: New York University Press.

Gregory, P. (1990). *Body map of feelings*. Lethbridge, Alberta, Canada: Family and Community Development Program.

Grollman, E. (1967). *Explaining death to children*. Boston: Beacon Press.

Guerney, B. (1964). Filial therapy: Description and rationale. *Journal of Consulting Psychology, 28*, 303–310.

Guerney, L. F., & Guerney, B. (1994). Child relationship enhancement: Family therapy and parent education. In C. E. Schaefer & L. J. Carey (Eds.), *Family play therapy* (pp. 127–138). Northvale, NJ: Jason Aronson.

Guidubaldi, J. (1989). The poor achievement of children of divorce. *Children and Teens Today, 9*(5), 5–6.

Haley, J. (1973). *Uncommon therapy*. New York: Norton.

Hall, K. B. (Ed.). (1992). *Orphan train riders*. Springdale, AR: Springdale Public Library.

Hallowell, E. M., & Ratey, J. J. (1994). *Driven to distraction*. New York: Pantheon Books.

Hancock, B. L. (1982). *School social work*. Englewood Cliffs, NJ: Prentice-Hall.

Hare, J. (1994). Concerns and issues faced by families headed by a lesbian couple. *Families in Society, 75*, 125–135.

Hartman, A. (1970). To think about the unthinkable. *Social Casework, 51*, 467–474.

Hartman, A. (1978). Diagrammatic assessment of family relationships. *Social Casework, 59*, 465–476.

Hartman, A. (1991). Words create worlds. *Social Work, 36*(4), 275–276.

Harvard Mental Health Letter. (1991). Post-traumatic stress: Part II. *Harvard Mental Health Letter, 7*(9), 1–4.

Harvard Mental Health Letter. (1993). Child abuse: Part III. *Harvard Mental Health Letter, 10*(1), 1–5.

Hawkins, M. T. (Ed.). (1986). *Achieving educational excellence for children at risk*. Silver Spring, MD: National Association of Social Workers.

Hearn, G. (1958). *Theory building in social work*. Toronto: University of Toronto Press.

Heegaard, M. (1991). *When something terrible happens: Children can learn to cope with grief*. Minneapolis, MN: Woodland Press.

Hepworth, D. H., & Larsen, J. A. (1982). *Direct social work practice: Theory and skills*. Homewood, IL: Dorsey Press.

Hepworth, D. H., & Larsen, J. A. (1986). *Direct social work practice: Theory and skills* (2nd ed.). Homewood, IL: Dorsey Press.

Hepworth, D. H., & Larsen, J. A. (1993). *Direct social work practice: Theory and skills* (4th ed.). Pacific Grove, CA: Brooks/Cole.

Herman, J. L. (1992). *Trauma and recovery*. New York: Basic Books.

Hershorn, M., & Rosenbaum, A. (1985). Children of marital violence: A close look at the unintended victims. *American Journal of Orthopsychiatry, 55*(2), 260–266.

Hewlett, S. A. (1991). *When the bough breaks: The cost of neglecting our children*. New York: Basic Books.

Hickey, L. O. (1993). Death of a counselor: A bereavement group for junior high school students. In N. B. Webb (Ed.), *Helping bereaved children: A handbook for practitioners* (pp. 239–266). New York: Guilford Press.

Ho, M. K. (1992). *Minority children and adolescents in therapy.* Newbury Park, CA: Sage.

Hodges, V. G., Morgan, L. J., & Johnston, B. (1993). Educating for excellence in child welfare practice: A model for graduate training in intensive family preservation. *Journal of Teaching in Social Work, 7*(1), 31–48.

Hoffman, J., & Rogers, P. (1991). A crisis play group in a shelter following the Santa Cruz earthquake. In N. B. Webb (Ed.), *Play therapy with children in crisis: A casebook for practitioners* (pp. 379–395). New York: Guilford Press.

Homebuilders. (1990). *Homebuilders evaluation summary.* Washington, DC: Behavioral Sciences Institute.

Hooker, C. E. (1976). Learned helplessness. *Social Work, 21*(3), 194–198.

Huang, L. N. (1989). Southeast Asian refugee children and adolescents. In J. T. Gibbs, L. N. Huang, & Associates (Eds.), *Children of color: Psychological interventions with minority youth* (pp. 278–321). San Francisco: Jossey-Bass.

Hunt, K. (Director and Producer). (1992). *No place like home* [Videotape]. Berkeley: University of California Extension Center for Media and Independent Learning. (Available from 2000 Center St., Fourth Floor, Berkeley, CA 94704)

Improving America's Schools Act, P.L. 103-382, 108 Stat. 3518–4062 (1994).

Institute of Medicine. (1989). *Research on children and adolescents with mental, behavioral, and developmental disorders: Mobilizing a national initiative.* Washington, DC: Author.

James, B. (1989). *Treating traumatized children: New insights and creative interventions.* Lexington, MA: Lexington Books.

James, B. (1994). *Handbook for treatment of attachment-trauma problems in children.* New York: Free Press.

Janchill, M. P. (1969). Systems concepts in casework theory and practice. *Social Casework, 50,* 74–82.

Johnson, H. C. (1989). Behavior disorders. In F. J. Turner (Ed.), *Child psychopathology: A social work perspective* (pp. 73–140). New York: Free Press.

Johnson, H. C. (1993a). The disruptive child: Problems of definition. In J. B. Rauch (Ed.), *Assessment: A source book for social work practice* (pp. 144–157). Milwaukee, WI: Families International.

Johnson, H. C. (1993b). Family issues and interventions. In H. C. Johnson (Ed.), *Child mental health in the 1990s: Curricula for graduate and undergraduate professional education* (pp. 86–105). Rockville, MD: U.S. Department of Health and Human Services.

Johnson, H. C. (1994). [Review of *Child psychopathology: Diagnostic criteria and clinical assessment* (Vols. 1–2)]. *Families and Society, 39*(5), 613–614.

Johnson, H. C., & Friesen, B. J. (1993). Etiologies of mental and emotional disorders in children and adolescents. In H. C. Johnson (Ed.), *Child mental health in the 1990s: Curricula for graduate and undergraduate professional education* (pp. 27–46). Rockville, MD: U.S. Department of Health and Human Services.

Johnson, J. H., Rasbury, W. C., & Siegel, L. J. (1986). *Approaches to child treatment: Introduction to theory, research, and practice.* Elmsford, NY: Pergamon Press.

Johnson, M. E. (1991). Multiple losses in children of chemically dependent families: Case of RJ, age 7. In N. B. Webb (Ed.), *Play therapy with children in crisis: A casebook for practitioners* (pp. 276–292). New York: Guilford Press.

Jordan, J. V. (1991). Empathy and the mother–daughter relationship. In J. V. Jordan, A. G. Kaplan, J. B. Miller, I. P. Stiver, & J. L. Surrey, *Women's growth in connection: Writings from the Stone Center* (pp. 28–34). New York: Guilford Press.

Kadushin, A. (1987). Child welfare services. In A. Minahan (Ed.), *Encyclopedia of social work* (18th ed., pp. 265–275). Silver Spring, MD: National Association of Social Workers.

Kadushin, G. (1995). [Review of *Assessment: A sourcebook for social work practice*]. *Families in Society, 76*(1), 62–63.

Kalter, N., & Schreier, S. (1994). Developmental facilitation groups for children of divorce: The elementary school model. In C. W. LeCroy (Ed.), *Handbook of child and adolescent treatment manuals* (pp. 307–342). New York: Lexington.

Kamen, B., & Gewirtz, B. (1989). Child maltreatment and the court. In S. Ehrenkrantz, E. G. Goldstein, L. Goodman, & J. Seinfeld (Eds.), *Clinical social work with maltreated children and their families* (pp. 178–201). New York: New York University Press.

Kaplan, C. P., & Joslin, H. (1993). Accidental sibling death. In N. B. Webb (Ed.), *Helping bereaved children: A handbook for practitioners* (pp. 118–136). New York: Guilford Press.

Karls, J., & Wandrei, K. E. (1994). *Person-in-Environment: A system for describing, classifying, and coding problems of social functioning.* Silver Spring, MD: National Association of Social Workers.

Kastenbaum, R. J. (1991). *Death, society, and human experience* (4th ed.). New York: Macmillan.

Kazdin, A. E. (1988). *Child psychotherapy: Developing and identifying effective treatments.* New York: Pergamon Press.

Kinard, E. M. (1982). Experiencing child abuse: Effects on emotional adjustment. *American Journal of Orthopsychiatry, 52*(1), 82–92.

Kinard, E. M. (1987). Child abuse and neglect. In A. Minahan (Ed.), *Encyclopedia of social work* (18th ed., pp. 223–231). Silver Spring, MD: National Association of Social Workers.

Kinney, J. M., Haapala, D. A., & Booth, C. (1991). *Keeping families together: The Homebuilders model.* New York: Aldine/de Gruyter.

Kinney, J. M., Madsen, B., Flemming, T., & Haapala, D. A. (1977). Homebuilders: Keeping families together. *Journal of Consulting and Clinical Psychology, 45,* 667–678.

Klein, M. (1937). *The psychoanalysis of children* (2nd ed.). London: Hogarth Press.

Kliman, G. (1989). Facilitation of mourning during childhood. In S. C. Klagsbrun, G. W. Kliman, E. J. Clark, A. H. Kutscher, R. DeBellis, & C. A. Lambert (Eds.), *Preventive psychiatry: Early intervention and situational crisis management* (pp. 59–82). Philadelphia: Charles Press.

Knitzer, J. (1982). *Unclaimed children.* Washington, DC: Children's Defense Fund.

Kolodny, R. L., & Garland, J. A. (1984). Guest editorial. *Social Work with Groups, 7*(4), 3–5.

Koocher, C., & Keith-Spiegel, P. (1990). *Children, ethics and the law*. Lincoln: University of Nebraska Press.

Kovacs, M. (1978). *The Children's Depression Inventory: A self-rated depression scale*. Unpublished manuscript, University of Pittsburgh School of Medicine.

Krestan, J., & Bepko, C. (1989). Alcohol problems and the family life cycle. In B. Carter & M. McGoldrick (Eds.), *The changing family life cycle* (2nd ed., pp. 483–511). Boston: Allyn & Bacon.

Landreth, G. L. (1991). *Play therapy: The art of the relationship*. Muncie, IN: Accelerated Development.

LeCroy, C. W., & Ashford, J. B. (1992). Children's mental health: Current findings and research directions. In S. M. Buttrick (Ed.), *Research on children* (pp. 14–24). Washington, DC: National Association of Social Workers Press.

LeCroy, C. W., & Ryan, L. G. (1993). Children's mental health: Designing a model social work curriculum. *Journal of Social Work Education, 29*(3), 318–327.

LeVine, E. S., & Sallee, A. L. (1992). *Listen to our children: Clinical theory and practice* (2nd ed.). Dubuque, IA: Kendall/Hunt.

Levinson, B. M. (1962). The dog as "co-therapist." *Mental Hygiene, 46*, 59–65.

Levinson, B. M. (1969). *Pet-oriented child psychotherapy*. Springfield, IL: Charles C Thomas.

Levinson, B. M. (1978). Pets and personality development. *Psychological Reports, 42*, 1031–1038.

Lidz, T. (1963). *The family and human development*. New York: International Universities Press.

Lieberman, A. F. (1990). Culturally sensitive intervention with children and families. *Child and Adolescent Social Work, 7*(2), 101–120.

Lieberman, F. (1987). Mental health and illness in children. In A. Minahan (Ed.), *Encyclopedia of social work* (18th ed., pp. 111–125). Silver Spring, MD: National Association of Social Workers.

Lindy, J. (1986). An outline for the psychoanalytic psychotherapy of post-traumatic stress disorder. In C. Figley (Ed.), *Trauma and its wake: Vol. 2. Traumatic stress theory, research, and interventions* (pp. 195–212). New York: Brunner/Mazel.

Lourie, I. S., & Katz-Leavy, J. (1991). New directions for mental health services for families and children. *Families in Society, 72*(5), 277–285.

Lowenberg, F. M., & Dolgoff, R. (1992). *Ethical decisions for social work practice* (4th ed.). Itasca, IL: F. E. Peacock.

Lukas, S. (1993). *Where to start and what to ask: An assessment handbook*. New York: Norton.

Mahler, M., Pine, F., & Bergman, A. (1975). *The psychological birth of the human infant: Symbiosis and individuation*. New York: Basic Books.

Maluccio, A. N. (1985). Education and training for child welfare practice. In J. Laird & A. Hartman (Eds.), *Handbook of child welfare* (pp. 741–759). New York: Free Press.

Margolin, G. (1979). *Conjoint marital therapy to enhance anger management and reduce spouse abuse*. Los Angeles: University of Southern California Psychological Research and Service Center.

Maslow, A. (1970). *Motivation and personality* (2nd ed.). New York: Harper & Row.

McDermott, J. F., & Char, W. F. (1974). The undeclared war between child and family therapy. *Journal of the American Academy of Child Psychiatry, 13*(3), 422–426.

McFadden, E. J. (1985). Practice in foster care. In J. Laird & A. Hartman (Eds.), *Handbook of child welfare* (pp. 585–616). New York: Free Press.

McFarlane, A. C. (1990). Post-traumatic stress syndrome revisited. In H. J. Parad & L. G. Parad (Eds.), *Crisis intervention book 2* (pp. 69–92). Milwaukee, WI: Family Service America.

McGoldrick, M., & Gerson, R. (1985). *Genograms in family assessment.* New York: Norton.

McGoldrick, M., & Walsh, F. (Eds.). (1991). *Living beyond loss: Death in the family.* New York: Norton.

McGowan, B. G. (1990). Family-based services and public policy: Context and implications. In J. K. Whittaker, J. Kinney, E. M. Tracy, & C. Booth (Eds.), *Reaching high risk families: Intensive family preservation in human services* (pp. 65–88). New York: Aldine/de Gruyter.

McNamara, M. (1963). Helping children through their mothers. *Journal of Child Psychology and Psychiatry, 4,* 19–46.

Meyer, C. H. (Ed.). (1983). *Clinical social work in an eco-systems perspective.* New York: Columbia University Press.

Meyer, C. H. (1993). *Assessment in social work practice.* New York: Columbia University Press.

Michaels, D., & Levine, C, (1992). Estimates of the number of motherless youth orphaned by AIDS in the United States. *Journal of the American Medical Association, 268*(24), 3456–3460.

Millay, E. St. V. (1969). Childhood is the kingdom where nobody dies. In *Edna St. Vincent Millay collected lyrics* (p. 203). New York: Harper & Row. (Original work published 1934)

Miller, D. (1989). Family violence and the helping system. In L. Combrinck-Graham (Ed.), *Children in family contexts: Perspectives on treatment* (pp. 413–434). New York: Guilford Press.

Miller, W. M. (1994). Family play therapy: History, theory, and convergence. In C. E. Schaefer & L. J. Carey (Eds.), *Family play therapy* (pp. 3–19). Northvale, NJ: Jason Aronson.

Minuchin, P. (1995). Foster and natural families: Forming a cooperative network. In L. Combrinck-Graham (Ed.), *Children in families at risk: Maintaining the connections* (pp. 251–274). New York: Guilford Press.

Minuchin, S. (1974). *Family and family therapy.* Cambridge, MA: Harvard University Press.

Minuchin, S., & Fishman, H. C. (1981). *Family therapy techniques.* Cambridge, MA: Harvard University Press.

Mishne, J. M. (1983). *Clinical work with children.* New York: Free Press.

Moustakas, C. (1959). *Psychotherapy with children.* New York: Harper & Row.

National Association of Social Workers (NASW). (1993, July). Foster care up despite "permanency" efforts. *NASW News,* p. 9.

National Association of Social Workers (NASW). (1994, September 8). Simpson case: Confidences survive clients. *NASW News,* p. 8.

National Association of Social Workers (NASW). (1995, January). Schools act boosts social workers' role. *NASW News*, p. 1.

National Association of Social Workers (NASW). (1996, August). *NASW code of ethics* (approved ed.). Washington, DC: Author.

National Commission on Children. (1991). *Beyond rhetoric: A new American agenda for children and families*. Washington, DC: Author.

National Committee for Prevention of Child Abuse. (1990, March). *Child abuse fatalities continue to rise: The results of the 1989 annual fifty-state survey*. Chicago: Author.

National Resource Center on Family-Based Services. (1983). *Family centered social services: A model for child welfare agencies*. Iowa City: University of Iowa.

Nelsen, J. C. (1975). Social work's fields of practice, methods, and models: The choice to act. *Social Service Review, 19*, 264–270.

Newton-Logston, G., & Armstrong, M. I. (1993). School-based mental health services. *Social Work in Education, 15*(3), 187–191.

New York State Department of Education. (1992). *A parent's guide to special education for children ages 5–21*. Albany: Author.

New York State Department of Education. (1993, August). *Updated Part 200 regulations of the Commissioner of Education*. Albany: Author.

Northen, H. (1987). Assessment in direct practice. In A. Minahan (Ed.), *Encyclopedia of social work* (18th ed., pp. 171–183). Silver Spring, MD: National Association of Social Workers.

Nuñez, R. D. C. (1994). Access to success: Meeting the educational needs of homeless children and families. *Social Work in Education, 16*(1), 21–30.

Oaklander, V. (1988). *Windows to our children*. Highland, NY: Center for Gestalt Development.

O'Connor, K. J. (1991). *The play therapy primer*. New York: Wiley.

Olshansky, S. (1962). Chronic sorrow: A response to having a mentally defective child. *Social Casework, 43*, 190–193.

Oster, G. D., & Gould, P. (1987). *Using drawings in assessment and therapy: A guide for mental health professionals*. New York: Brunner/Mazel.

Palombo, J. (1985). Self-psychology and countertransference in the treatment of children. *Child and Adolescent Social Work, 2*(1), 36–48.

Papell, C. P., & Rothman, B. (1966). Social work group models: Possession and heritage. *Journal of Education for Social Work, 11*(2), 66–77.

Papell, C. P., & Rothman, B. (1984). Editorial. *Social Work with Groups, 7*(4), 1–2.

Parnell, M., & Vanderkloot, J. (1989). Ghetto children growing up in poverty. In L. Combrinck-Graham (Ed.), *Children in family contexts: Perspectives on treatment* (pp. 437–462). New York: Guilford Press.

Perlman, H. H. (1979). *Relationship: The heart of helping*. Chicago: University of Chicago Press.

Petitti, D. B., & Coleman, C. (1990). Cocaine and the risk of low birth weight. *American Journal of Public Health, 80*, 25–28.

Petyr, C. (1992). Adultcentrism to practice with children. *Families in Society, 73*(7), 408–416.

Pfeffer, C. R. (1986). *The suicidal child*. New York: Guilford Press.

Phillips, M. H., DeChillo, N., Kronenfeld, D., & Middleton-Jeter, V. (1988). Homeless families: Services make a difference. *Social Casework, 69*(1), 48–49.

Piaget, J. (1955). *The child's construction of reality.* New York: Basic Books.

Piaget, J. (1968). *Six psychological studies.* New York: Vintage Books.

Piaget, J. (1972). Intellectual evolution from childhood to adolescence. *Human Development, 115,* 1–12.

Piaget, J., & Inhelder, B. (1969). *The psychology of the child.* New York: Basic Books.

Prato, L. (1984a). *Let's talk it over.* Morristown, NJ: Jersey Battered Women's Services.

Prato, L. (1984b). *What is a shelter?* Morristown, NJ: Jersey Battered Women's Services.

Price, J. E. (1991). The effects of divorce precipitate a suicide threat: Case of Philip, age 8. In N. B. Webb (Ed.), *Play therapy with children in crisis: A casebook for practitioners* (pp. 202–218). New York: Guilford Press.

Pynoos, R. S., & Eth, S. (1985). Children traumatized by witnessing acts of personal violence: Homicide, rape, or suicidal behavior. In S. Eth & R. S. Pynoos (Eds.), *Post-Traumatic Stress Disorder in children* (pp. 19–40). Washington, DC: American Psychiatric Press.

Pynoos, R. S., & Eth, S. (1986). Witness to violence: The child interview. *Journal of the American Academy of Child Psychiatry, 25,* 306–319.

Randall-David, E. (1989). *Strategies for work with culturally diverse communities and clients.* Washington, DC: Association for the Care of Children's Health.

Rando, T. A. (1991). *How to go on living when someone you love dies.* New York: Bantam. (Original work published 1988)

Rando, T. A. (1993). *Treatment of complicated mourning.* Champaign, IL: Research Press.

Raphael, B. (1983). *The anatomy of bereavement.* New York: Basic Books.

Rapoport, J. L., & Ismond, D. R. (1990). *DSM-III-R training guide for diagnosis of childhood disorders.* New York: Brunner/Mazel.

Reamer, F. G. (1987). Values and ethics. In A. Minahan (Ed.), *Encyclopedia of social work* (18th ed., pp. 801–809). Silver Spring, MD: National Association of Social Workers.

Redl, F. (1944). Diagnostic group work. *American Journal of Orthopsychiatry, 14,* 53–67.

Remkus, J. (1991). Repeated foster placements and attachment failure: Case of Joseph, age 3. In N. B. Webb (Ed.), *Play therapy with children in crisis: A casebook for practitioners* (pp. 143–161). New York: Guilford Press.

Rhodes, J. E. (1994). Older and wiser: Mentoring relationships in childhood and adolescence. *Journal of Primary Prevention, 14*(3), 187–196.

Rice, J. K., & Rice, D. G. (1986). *Living through divorce: A developmental approach to divorce therapy.* New York: Guilford Press.

Richmond, M. (1917). *Social diagnosis.* New York: Russell Sage Foundation.

Roberts, A. R., & Roberts, B. S. (1990). A comprehensive model for crisis intervention with battered women and their children. In A. R. Roberts (Ed.), *Crisis intervention handbook: Assessment, treatment, and research* (pp. 105–123). Belmont, CA: Wadsworth.

Rogers, C. (1951). *Client-centered therapy.* Boston: Houghton Mifflin.

Rooney, R. H. (1988). Socialization strategies for involuntary clients. *Social Casework, 69*(3), 131–140.

Rose, S. D. (1967). A behavioral approach to group treatment of children. In E. J. Thomas (Ed.), *The sociobehavioral approach and applications to social work* (pp. 39–58). New York: Council on Social Work Education.

Rose, S. D. (1972). *Treating children in groups: A behavioral approach.* San Francisco: Jossey-Bass.

Rose, S. D. (1985). Time-limited groups for children. *Social Work with Groups, 8*(2), 3–16.

Rosen, H. (1986). *Unspoken grief: Coping with childhood sibling loss.* Lexington, MA: Lexington Books.

Rosen, H. (1991). Child and adolescent bereavement. *Child and Adolescent Social Work, 8*(1), 5–16.

Rosenbaum, A., & O'Leary, K. (1981). Children: The unintended victims of marital violence. *American Journal of Orthopsychiatry, 51*(4), 692–699.

Rosenberg, E. (1988). Stepsiblings in therapy. In M. D. Kahn & K. G. Lewis (Eds.), *Siblings in therapy: Life span and clinical issues* (pp. 209–227). New York: Norton.

Rothschild, M. (1986). Chronic sorrow: Plight of parents of special children. In M. T. Hawkins (Ed.), *Achieving educational excellence for children at risk* (pp. 41–49). Silver Spring, MD: National Association of Social Workers.

Rounds, K. A., Weil, M., & Bishop, K. K. (1994). Practice with culturally diverse families of young children with disabilities. *Families in Society, 75*(1), 3–14.

Rubin, J. A. (1984). *Child art therapy* (2nd ed.). New York: Van Nostrand Reinhold.

Rutter, M. (1979). Protective factors in children's responses to stress and disadvantage. In M. W. Kent & J. E. Rolf (Eds.), *Primary prevention of psychopathology: Vol. 3. Social competence in children* (pp. 49–74). Hanover, NH: University Press of New England.

Rutter, M. (1987). Psychosocial resilience and protective mechanisms. *American Journal of Orthopsychiatry, 57*, 57–72.

Rynearson, E. (1987). Psychological adjustment to unnatural dying. In S. Zisook (Ed.), *Biopsychosocial aspects of bereavement* (pp. 75–93). Washington, DC: American Psychiatric Press.

Santa Clara County Health Department. (1990). *The Loma Prieta quake: A guide to one year anniversary commemorative activities for students.* Los Gatos, CA: Author.

Sarton, M. (1973). A letter to James Stephens. In *Collected poems, 1930–1973* (pp. 42–43). New York: Norton. (Original work, Inner Landscapes, published 1936–1938)

Satir, V. (1983). *Conjoint family therapy* (3rd rev. ed.). Palo Alto, CA: Science and Behavior Books.

Saxe, L., Cross, T., & Silverman, N. (1988). Children's mental health: The gap between what we know and what we do. *American Psychologist, 43*(10), 800–807.

Schaefer, C. E., & Carey, L. J. (Eds.). (1994). *Family play therapy.* Northvale, NJ: Jason Aronson.

Schaefer, C. E., & Reid, S. E. (Eds.). (1986). *Game play.* New York: Wiley.

Schiffer, M. (1984). *Children's group therapy: Methods and case histories.* New York: Free Press.

Schlosberg, S. B., & Kagan, R. M. (1988). Practice strategies for engaging chronic, multiproblem families. *Social Casework, 69*(1), 3–9.

Schowalter, J. E., Patterson, P. E., Tallmer, M., Kutscher, A. H., Gullo, S. W., & Peretz, D. (Eds.). (1983). *The child and death.* New York: Columbia University Press.

Schwab, F. (1986). *Just tell the truth.* Charlotte, NC: Kidsrights.

Schwartz, W. (1977). Social group work: The interactionist approach. In J. B. Turner (Ed.), *Encyclopedia of social work* (17th ed., pp. 1328–1338). Washington, DC: National Association of Social Workers.

Schwartz, W., & Zalba, S. (Eds.). (1971). *The practice of group work.* New York: Columbia University Press.

Sheafor, B. W., & Landon, P. S. (1987). Generalist perspective. In A. Minahan (Ed.), *Encyclopedia of social work* (18th ed., pp. 660–669). Silver Spring, MD: National Association of Social Workers.

Shulman, L. (1984). *The skills of helping individuals and groups* (2nd ed.). Itasca, IL: Peacock.

Shulman, L. (1992). *The skills of helping individuals, families, and groups.* Itasca, IL: Peacock.

Silverman, P., & Worden, J. W. (1992). Children's reactions in the early months after the death of a parent. *American Journal of Orthopsychiatry, 62*(1), 93–104.

Slavson, S. R. (1943). *An introduction to group therapy.* New York: The Commonwealth Fund.

Slavson, S. R., & Schiffer, M. (1975). *Group psychotherapies for children.* New York: International Universities Press.

Spielberger, C. D. (1973). *Preliminary manual for the State–Trait Anxiety Inventory for Children.* Plato Alto, CA: Consulting Psychologists Press.

Sroufe, L. A. (1979a). The coherence of individual development: Early care, attachment, and subsequent developmental issues. *American Psychologist, 34,* 834–841.

Sroufe, L. A. (1979b). Socioemotional development. In J. D. Osofsky (Ed.), *Handbook of infant development* (pp. 462–516).

Sroufe, L. A., & Waters, E. (1977). Attachment as an organizational construct. *Child Development, 48,* 1184–1199.

Stark, K. D., Rafaelle, L., & Reysa, A. (1994). The treatment of depressed children: A skills training approach to working with children and families. In C. W. LeCroy (Ed.), *Handbook of child and adolescent treatment manuals* (pp. 343–397). New York: Lexington Books.

Steiner, G. L., Boyd-Franklin, N., & Boland, M. G. (1995). Rationale and overview of the book. In N. Boyd-Franklin, G. L. Steiner, & M. G. Boland (Eds.), *Children, families, and HIV/AIDS: Psychosocial and therapeutic issues* (pp. 3–16). New York: Guilford Press.

Stern, D. (1985). *The interpersonal world of the infant.* New York: Basic Books.

Strand, V. C. (1991). Victim of sexual abuse: Case of Rosa, age 6. In N. B. Webb (Ed.), *Play therapy with children in crisis: A casebook for practitioners* (pp. 69–91). New York: Guilford Press.

Straughan, J. H. (1994). Treatment with child and mother in the playroom. In C. E. Schaefer & L. J. Carey (Eds.), *Family play therapy* (pp. 99–105). Northvale, NJ: Jason Aronson. (Original work published 1964)

Straussner, S. L. A. (1989). Intervention with maltreating parents who are drug and alcohol abusers. In S. Ehrenkrantz (Eds.), *Clinical social work with maltreated children and their families* (pp. 149–177). New York: New York University Press.

Straussner, S. L. A. (Ed.). (1993). *Clinical work with substance-abusing clients.* New York: Guilford Press.

Sullivan, D. F. (1952). *Readings in group work.* New York: Association Press.

Tait, D. C., & Depta, J. L. (1993). Play therapy group for bereaved children. In N. B. Webb (Ed.), *Helping bereaved children: A handbook for practitioners* (pp. 169–185). New York: Guilford Press.

Terr, L. C. (1983). Play therapy and psychic trauma: A preliminary report. In C. E. Schaefer & K. O'Connor (Eds.), *Handbook of play therapy* (pp. 308–319). New York: Wiley.

Terr, L. C. (1988). What happens to early memories of trauma? A study of twenty children under age 5 at the time of documented traumatic events. *Journal of the American Academy of Child and Adolescent Psychiatry, 27*(1), 96–104.

Terr, L. C. (1989). Treating psychic trauma in children: A preliminary discussion. *Journal of Traumatic Stress, 2,* 3–20.

Thomas, A., Chess, S., & Birch, H. G. (1968). *Temperament and behavior disorders in children.* New York: New York University Press.

Thompson, C. L., & Rudolph, L. B. (1992). *Counseling children* (3rd ed.). Pacific Grove, CA: Brooks/Cole.

Timberlake, E. M., & Sabatino, C. A. (1994). Homeless children: Impact of school attendance on self-esteem and loneliness. *Social Work in Education, 16*(1), 9–20.

Tormes, Y. M. (1968). *Child victims of incest.* Denver, CO: American Humane Association.

Tracy, E. M. (1994). Maternal substance abuse: Protecting the child, preserving the family. *Social Work, 39*(5), 534–540.

Tracy, E. M., & Whittaker, J. K. (1993). The social network map: Assessing social support in clinical practice. In J. B. Rauch (Ed.), *Assessment: A sourcebook for social work practice* (pp. 295–308). Milwaukee, WI: Families International.

Turkel, D., & Fink, M. (1986). *Good touches/bad to touches: A child sexual abuse prevention program.* White Plains, NY: Westchester County Mental Health Association.

Turner, F. (1994). Reconsidering diagnosis. *Families in Society, 75*(3), 168–171.

Turner, F. J. (Ed.). (1989). *Child psychotherapy: A social work perspective.* New York: Free Press.

Tyson, K. (1995). *Empowering children and their caregivers: Beyond adultcentrism.* Paper presented at the annual meeting of the Council on Social Work Education, San Diego, CA.

U.N. General Assembly. (1989). *Convention on the Rights of the Child* (U.N. Document A/Res/44/23). New York: Author.

University of Kentucky College of Social Work. (1989). *Collaboration for competency: Examining social work curriculum in the perspective of current practice with children and families.* Lexington, KY: Author.

U.S. Bureau of the Census. (1989). *Current population reports* (Series P-23, No. 163). Washington, DC: U.S. Government Printing Office.

U.S. Children's Bureau. (1978). *Substance abuse and child abuse and neglect.* Washington, DC: U.S. Government Printing Office.

U.S. Department of Health and Human Services. (1993). *Eighth special report to the U.S. Congress on alcohol and health.* Rockville, MD: National Institute on Alcohol Abuse and Alcoholism.

van der Kolk, B. A. (Ed.). (1987). *Psychological trauma.* Washington, DC: American Psychiatric Press.

van der Kolk, B. A. (1989). The compulsion to repeat the trauma: Re-enactment, re-victimization, and masochism. *Psychiatric Clinics of North America, 12*(2), 389–406.

Vastola, J., Nierenberg, A., & Graham, E. H. (1986). The lost and found group: Group work with bereaved children. In A. Gitterman & L. Shulman (Eds.), *Mutual aid groups and the life cycle* (pp. 75–90). Itasca, IL: F. E. Peacock.

Vinter, R. (1959). Group work: Perspective and prospects. In *Social work with groups.* New York: National Association of Social Workers.

Visher, E. B., & Visher, J. S. (1979). *Stepfamilies: A guide to working with stepparents and stepchildren.* New York: Brunner/Mazel.

Wachtel, E. F. (1994). *Treating troubled children and their families.* New York: Guilford Press.

Wallerstein, J. (1983). Children of divorce: The psychological tasks of the child. *American Journal of Orthopsychiatry, 53,* 230–243.

Wallerstein, J., & Blakeslee, S. (1989). *Second chances.* New York: Ticknor & Fields.

Wallerstein, J., & Kelly, J. (1980). *Surviving the breakup. How children and parents cope with divorce.* New York: Basic Books.

Webb, N. B. (1983). Developing competent clinical practitioners: A model for supervisors. *The Clinical Supervisor, 1*(4), 41–51.

Webb, N. B. (1989). Supervision of child therapy: Analyzing therapeutic impasses and monitoring countertransference. *The Clinical Supervisor, 73,* 51–76.

Webb, N. B. (Ed.). (1991). *Play therapy with children in crisis: A casebook for practitioners.* New York: Guilford Press.

Webb, N. B. (Ed.). (1993). *Helping bereaved children: A handbook for practitioners.* New York: Guilford Press.

Webb, N. B. (1994a). Assessment and intervention with kindergarten children following the New York World Trade Center disaster. *Crisis Intervention and Time-Limited Treatment, 1*(1), 47–59.

Webb, N. B. (1994b). *Techniques of play therapy: A clinical demonstration* [Videotape]. New York: Guilford Press.

Webb, N. B. (1995). [Survey of Westchester County child welfare administrators.] Unpublished data.

Weick, A., & Pope, L. (1988). Knowing what's best: A new look at self-determination. *Social Casework, 69*(1), 10–16.

Werner, E. E., & Smith, R. S. (1982). *Vulnerable but invincible: A study of resilient children.* New York: McGraw-Hill.

Wertz, R. (1986, November–December). Children of alcoholics. *Chemical People Newsletter,* p. 9.

Whittaker, J. K. (1985). Group and institutional care: An overview. In J. Laird & A. Hartman (Eds.), *Handbook of child welfare* (pp. 617–637). New York: Free Press.

Whittaker, J. K. (1987). Group care for children. In A. Minahan (Ed.), *Encyclopedia of social work* (18th ed., pp. 672–682). Silver Spring, MD: National Association of Social Workers.

Whittaker, J. K. (1991). The leadership challenge in family-based services: Policy, practice and research. *Families in Society, 72*(5), 294–300.

Whittaker, J. K., Kinney, J., Tracy, E. M., & Booth, C. (Eds.). (1909). *Reaching high risk families: Intensive family preservation in human services.* New York: Aldine/de Gruyter.

Wikler, L., Wason, M., & Hatfield, E. (1981). Chronic sorrow revisited: Parent vs. professional depiction of the adjustment of parents of mentally retarded children. *American Journal of Orthopsychiatry, 51*(1), 63–70.

Wilkerson, I. (1994, May 16). Two boys, a debt, a gun, a victim: The face of violence. *The New York Times,* pp. A-1, A-14.

Williams, J. B. W., Karls, J. M., & Wandrei, K. (1989). The Person-in-Environment (PIE) system for describing problems of social functioning. *Hospital and Community Psychiatry, 40*(11), 1125–1127.

Winnicott, D. W. (1971a). *Playing and reality.* New York: Basic Books.

Winnicott, D. W. (1971b). *Therapeutic consultations in child psychiatry.* New York: Basic Books.

Wolfenstein, M. (1966). How is mourning possible? *Psychoanalytic Study of the Child, 21,* 432–460.

Woltmann, A. G. (1964). The use of puppetry as a projective method in therapy. In M. R. Haworth (Ed.), *Child psychotherapy* (pp. 395–399). New York: Basic Books. (Original work published 1951)

Yalom, I. (1985). *The theory and practice of group psychotherapy* (3rd ed.). New York: Basic Books.

Youngstrom, N. (1991, October). Drug exposure in home elicits worst behavior. *Monitor,* p. 3.

Zevon, M. (1990, September 10). Archway program group therapy. *Mount Vernon Journal,* p. 10.

Zilbach, J. J. (1989). The family life cycle: A framework for understanding children in family therapy. In L. Combrinck-Graham (Ed.), *Children in family contexts: Perspectives on treatment* (pp. 46–66). New York: Guilford Press.

Author Index

Page numbers in italics represent reference entries.

Subject Index